RUSSIA FIRST

RUSSIA FIRST

BREAKING WITH THE WEST

PETER TRUSCOTT

I. B. Tauris Publishers
LONDON · NEW YORK

Published in 1997 by
I.B.Tauris & Co Ltd
Victoria House
Bloomsbury Square
London WC1B 4DZ

175 Fifth Avenue
New York
NY 10010

In the United States of America
and Canada distributed by
St Martin's Press
175 Fifth Avenue
New York
NY 10010

A full CIP record for this book is available from the British Library

A full CIP record for this book is available from the Library of Congress

ISBN 1 86064 199 7

Library of Congress Catalog card number: available

Designed and typeset by John Saunders Design & Production
Printed and bound in Great Britain by WBC Ltd, Bridgend, Mid Glamorgan

CONTENTS

To Svetlana Truscott

ACKNOWLEDGEMENTS

My wife, Svetlana, gave me the idea of writing a book on Russia when we were staying in the Willard Hotel in Washington, in January 1996 (where Martin Luther King wrote his greatest speech, 'I have a dream'). Our project only became a reality after a hectic few months and a great deal of help and support from a number of people. Although I had spent over two years as a member of the European Parliament's Delegation for Relations with the Russian Federation, the book was effectively written between June and September 1996. However, as the book is the fruit of two years of meetings, and many more of travel and study, I am indebted to many people for their knowledge and advice on Russia, and it would be impossible to list them all here. I have met literally hundreds of politicians, business people, academics, military officers and many other people from across a broad spectrum of Russian society. But I feel obliged to record my thanks to those who have most enabled me to complete this project in the short space of time available.

As a member of the EU Delegation for Relations with the Russian Federation, I was privileged to observe both the Duma elections of December 1995, and the presidential elections of 1996. I also attended regular bilateral meetings between parliamentary delegations from the Duma, the Federation Council and the European Parliament. Having met most of the presidential candidates, I would in particular like to thank Mikhail Gorbachev, Gennady Zyuganov, Grigory Yavlinsky and Svyatoslav Fyodorov for their time. I would also like to thank Victor Chernomyrdin, Alexander Korzhakov, and Mikhail Barsukov, whom I had the opportunity to meet. Sergei Filatov, President Boris Yeltsin's campaign manager, was also kind enough to take part in a meeting, as was Nicolai Ryabov, chairman of the Central Electoral Commission. I am grateful for meeting both Duma speakers, Ivan Rybkin and Gennady Seleznyev. Vassily Lipitsky, Valentin Kuptsov, Vladimir Lukin (chairman of the Duma Foreign Affairs Committee), Dr Vyacheslav Nikonov (chairman of the Duma's Sub-Committee for International Security and Arms Control) were also generous with their time, as was Security Council member Sergei Shoigu. For assisting with arranging all these meetings, and for facilitating the task of election observation, I would like to thank the staff of the Russian Duma, and the staff of the European Parliament's EU–Russian Delegation: David Lowe, Joe Dunne, Claudia Siegismund, Frank Weiler, Ursula Bausch and Isabel Daza Moreno. I would also like to thank our hard-working Russian interpreters, who accompanied the EU Delegation at official meetings and during the long hours of the election campaign.

On the general political situation in Russia and the CIS, I have been helped by many in the diplomatic corps. Britain's ambassadors to Russia, Sir Brian Fall and Sir Andrew Wood, were friendly and most informative, as were Martin Nicholson and Eric Penton-Voak, diplomats at the British embassy in Moscow. Sir John Kerr, Britain's ambassador to the United States (formerly to the EU) will be sorely missed in Brussels, where I was also briefed by Estonian ambassador, Clyde Kull. Michael Roberts of the United Kingdom's Representation to the EU supplied me with much useful material, as did Igor Stepanov of the Brussels Russian Mission. Toivo Klaar of the Brussels Estonian embassy assisted with a visit to Tallinn, where I was honoured to meet President Lennart Meri. Alexander Trofimov, Russia's ambassador to Tallinn, filled me in on Russia's policy towards Estonia, and talks were also held with members of the Riigikogu (Estonian parliament), Sergei Ivanov and Eino Tamm. Richard Samuel, ambassador to the OSCE in Tallinn, gave me information on the status of Russian speakers in the Balts. On a later visit to the Baltic states I was also pleased to meet the prime ministers of Latvia, Lithuania and Estonia. The European Union's ambassadors from the member states (including Britain) have provided much useful information on the Baltic states. A private meeting with EU Commissioner Hans van den Broek on the newly independent states of Central Asia, provided further background material for that section of the book. Chen Ziying, vice-minister of the State Council (or Cabinet) of the People's Republic of China, gave me

Beijing's view on developing relations between China and the Russian Federation. On military and peace-keeping issues, I received extremely good briefings from Field Marshal Sir Richard Vincent DSO, of NATO headquarters in Brussels; and Lt-Col. Jean-Marie Leclerq, at the UN Department of Peace-keeping in New York. Rear-Adm. David Blackburn, head of the British Defence Staff in Washington, was kind enough to meet with me at the British Embassy, to discuss NATO and security issues. In my capacity as vice-president of the European Parliament's Security and Disarmament Sub-Committee, I also met Ismat Kitani, under-secretary-general at the United Nations, who gave me the global view.

A number of non-governmental organisations (NGOs) supplied much background briefing on human rights, the arms trade and security issues, including Human Rights Watch, the World Development Movement, the British American Security Information Council (BASIC), Saferworld, the Centre for European Security and Disarmament (CESD), the International Security Information Service (ISIS) and the Stockholm International Peace Research Institute (SIPRI).

My colleagues on the Russian delegation, MEPs Constanze Krehl, Hélène Carrère D'Encausse and Catherine Lalumière, have been distinguished and stimulating colleagues. Magdalene Hoff MEP, vice-president of the Socialist Group was very encouraging and supportive. Rob van de Water, of the Socialist Group Secretariat, was also ever co-operative and helpful.

Andrei Konoval (of Baltisky Bank, St Petersburg) and his wife Irina Timofeyeva were one of the couples who gave the business view, while Svetlana Ivanova Chernicova (my mother-in–law) monitored the national media on my behalf. Simon Osbourne, of the EU Election Unit, Moscow, was kind enough to supply me with detailed break-downs of the presidential election results, as did the OSCE. In Brussels, Thomas Grunert, Dr Norbert Gresch, David Blackman and Aneta Popescu Black (DGIV) of the Parliament's secretariat supplied me with a stream of invaluable documentation, as did Walter Massur (of the European Parliament's Delegation for Relations with Central Asia). Daniel Denruyter and Ralph Spencer from the European Parliament's Document Centre, Brussels, were very co-operative and provided access to a wide range of information sources.

Joel Martres (director of Nice Library Service) and his wife Régine were most kind to me while I was writing the bulk of the book on holiday in Nice in August 1996. Dorothy Truscott, my mother, gave me moral support, as she has done since my university days. My own staff were a pillar of strength and collectively enabled me to meet my publisher's deadline. John Blevin was a great help at the inception of the project; Emma Parkinson and Richard Ballard spent hours photocopying documents and in the library in Brussels; Paul Hetheringon my office manager and campaign organiser, provided administrative support in Welwyn Garden City; and Liz Walker did the same in Strasbourg.

Joyce Quin MP considerately supplied me with an interesting House of Commons research paper on Russia, and was kind enough to join me in two fringe meetings on the Duma and presidential elections in Birmingham and Blackpool. Jonathan Steele generously gave his time to chair the meeting on Russia at Labour's European Conference in Birmingham. I have also benefited from discussions with Robin Cook MP on Russia and related foreign policy matters in my role as a member of the European Parliament's Foreign Affairs, Security and Defence Policy Committee.

Dr Alistair Cole, Reader at Bradford University, and Professor Leonid Seleznyov of St Petersburg University both gave me the benefit of their advice on the ideas behind the book. I owe an incalculable debt to my doctoral supervisor, Dr Alastair Parker, of Queen's College, Oxford, who trained me as a historian.

The format of the book takes both a narrative and thematic analytical form, with the use of both primary and secondary sources. Generally, sources used include not only secondary material (i.e. books and articles), but also interviews, private political meetings, official documents, contemporary press and agency reports, reports from (NGOs), and Russian television and radio broadcasts. All sources are quoted extensively in the endnotes.

None of the friends listed above, however, are accountable for the final completed work, and I must take full responsibility for the ideas and errors contained therein. My publisher, Iradj Bagherzade of I.B. Tauris, gave the project an added impetus, and provided me with generous assistance and inspiration. Finally, I would like to thank my wife, Svetlana, who gave me the idea to write the book, and spent hours pouring over the manuscript, offering suggestions and encouragement. I dedicate this book to her because, as another Martin Luther said, I could do no other.

Peter Truscott
Little Chequers, Old Welwyn, Herts,
February 1997

SCHOOLS OF THOUGHT

You cannot understand Russia with logic
You cannot measure Russia by the same yardstick
Russia has a special character
You can only believe in Russia.

Fyodor Ivanovich Tyutchev, 1866 (1803–1873), career diplomat and poet

*A*CADEMICS AND COMMENTATORS have made heroic efforts to explain the political differences between different schools of thought, camps or interest groups in Russia. In the past, it has been argued that Russia, spread over two continents, was traditionally divided between a pro-Western camp (the Westernisers) and a slavophile camp (the Slavophiles). The latter represented an introvert and isolationist tendency.[1] These groups later evolved into Pan-Slavists, Romantic nationalists, Eurasianists, liberal democrats and other political permutations. The two original camps were joined by two more. One was eastward-looking, which saw Russia's future in the Pacific zone, and the other advocated a Russo-Islamic geostrategic concept, which saw Russia extending its influence towards the Indian Ocean and the Gulf (aided by the countries of Central Asia). Yet as the nineteenth century gave way to the twentieth, and the old certainties collapsed with the Soviet Union, the various schools of thought in Russia multiplied. Monarchists sought the restoration of the Tsarist Empire lost with Nicholas II, and even Communist leader Gennady Zyuganov found it amusing when he was confronted with a group of 'Monarchists for Zyuganov' during the presidential election in 1996. The paradoxes of modern Russia defy the neat labels of the past. But beneath the apparent illogicality of much of the events occurring in Russia today, there are distinct trends which are explicable and identifiable. Russian society can only be understood by delving into the country's history, geography and cultural experiences, and this is perhaps more the case with Russia than any other state with a claim to calling itself 'European'.

Studies of Russian schools of thought have identified not only the polarisation between 'Westernisers' and 'Slavophiles' but the dichotomy between the Atlanticists and the Eurasianists, the latter believing that Russia was not European, but a Eurasian entity, with interests straddling both continents. In 1992, the Speaker of the Russian parliament, Ruslan Khasbulatov, wrote that 'While [Peter the Great] imposed elements of European culture in Russia . . . the spiritual and cultural fabric of the people remained untouched. As a result, we have Russia, which is neither Europe nor Asia but a very special, very peculiar part of the world.'[2] By contrast, Hannes Adomeit stressed the 'New Thinking paradigm', while Karen Dawisha and Bruce Parrot identified four additional schools of thought.[3] Adherents of Dawisha and Parrot's first school support a democratic, multi-ethnic and pluralistic society, with a strong, perhaps authoritarian government pursuing a 'great power' foreign policy. However, this typology is undermined by including the unlikely figures of Vladimir Lukin (chair of the Duma's Foreign Affairs Committee) and former St Petersburg mayor Anatoly Sobchak in this school. Neither of the liberal reformers would support an authoritarian government.[4] The second school regards Russia as a great power, but focuses on support for Russians in the 'near abroad' (i.e. the independent former states of the Soviet Union, excluding Russia). The third school sees Russia as being at the beginning of a spiritual rebirth and revival, is essentially Slavophile and supported by figures such as Alexander Solzhenitsyn. Solzhenitsyn proposed the establishment of a Pan-Russian Union, linking the Slav republics of Russia, Belarus and Ukraine, and the 'spiritual and bodily salvation of our people'.[5] The fourth school sees the demise of the Soviet Union as a result of treachery and an international conspiracy. Apart from many in the 'red–brown' unholy alliance, including leaders of the Communist Party, the school includes Vladimir Zhirinovsky and the ultra-right.

Together with the diverse schools of thought, certain terms have become popular in describing the multifarious political groupings in modern Russia. Hence the phrase *zapadniki,* or 'Westernisers', a term dating back to the nineteenth century, and referring to those who closely associate themselves with Western values and often despise the 'backwardness' of their own Russian people. Then there are the appellations *derzhavnik* and *gosudarstvennik*, which refer to the advocates of a strong and powerful state which is able to maintain order. The *derzhavniki* or *gosudarstvenniki* are by this definition the proponents of state power, untrammelled by the niceties of the law or democratic constraints. Some commentators have seen the *gosudarstvenniki* having an influence across political blocs and in large sections of the military-industrial complex and power ministries, in effect operating as a Third Force.[6] However, there is some doubt about whether this Third Force exists at all. Asked about the so-called Third Force, Alexander Lebed said: 'The term "Third Force" is a creation of the mass media. I do not accept it.'[7] The weakness of these categorisations is that many of the leading figures appear to be both *zapadniki* and *derzhavniki* simultaneously, or have switched regularly back and forth. A prime example is Boris Yeltsin himself, who could appear to be both a Westerniser and a proponent of state power at the same time. Former Foreign Minister Andrei Kozyrev swapped sides from *zapadniki* to *derzhavniki* in 1993, and back to *zapadniki* in 1996 after entering the Duma. General Alexander Lebed, newly appointed as secretary of the Security Council in June 1996, took up what appeared to be a *derzhavniki* position in advocating state power to deal with crime and corruption, but nevertheless professed support for democracy and the market economy. Even those in the business world who appeared to support a coalition between Yeltsin and the Communist Party shortly before the presidential elections, sought political and economic stability rather than overt authoritarianism. The message is that neat labels, while convenient for commentators and historians, can be misleading, and while useful in the past, do not always suit the mercurial nature of the contemporary Russian political and economic scene – and far less the Russian character.

With the exception of the Communist Party (KPRF), well-structured and organised political parties hardly exist in modern Russia, and even the political blocs more resemble political clubs than parties with settled programmes. Individuals and interest groups change policy positions and switch support with effortless abandon, creating new political blocs and alliances in their wake. In which other political system would the Beer Lovers' Party achieve five times the votes of the Social Democrats (led by a former mayor of Moscow), as occurred in the 1995 Duma elections? However, while it is right to be cautious about simplistic categorisations, especially as applied to individuals, certain political trends can be identified in post-Gorbachev Russia. Sergei Kovalev, former Duma Human Rights Commissioner, pointed to the worrying tendency to assert *derzhavnost* (quasi-totalitarian statism), which found its external expression in the pursuit of the war in Chechnya.[8]

Kovalev argued that *derzhavnost* was being promoted as the supreme value of the new Russia, giving the unconstrained force of the state precedence over the rights and liberties of the individual. Incompatible with the rule of law, democracy and human rights, *derzhavnost* was associated with messianic, imperialist nationalism, anti-Western values and the militarist and authoritarian traditions of Russia's past. There can be no doubt that when it came to Chechnya, Kovalev's analysis rang true. Within the Kremlin, and surrounding the president, there were a core group of adherents of *derzhavnost*, often referred to as the 'war party'. The 'war party' in the Kremlin had political supporters in the Duma, notably Vladimir Zhirinovsky's Liberal Democratic Party (LDPR). However, following the first round of the presidential elections in June 1996, Yeltsin sacked the leading advocates of *derzhavnost* in the Kremlin, including his close friend and chief presidential bodyguard Alexander Korzhakov, security boss Mikhail Barsukov, Defence Minister Pavel Grachev and Deputy Prime Minister Oleg Soskovets. Yeltsin's reaction had more to do with saving his own political skin, than with any desire to defend democracy and the reform process in Russia.

Important as the appearance of *derzhavnost* was, it has been overshadowed by another political development. Evolving from traditional themes, another school of thought has arrived which has come to dominate the political agenda in Russia today. It is a more powerful force than any other, since it has influenced all the major parties and political blocs in Russia, and has been adopted by the president, the prime minister, the foreign ministry and the entire presidential administration. The new school of thought can be encapsulated in two words: 'Russia First'. Russia First does not exist independently of other schools of thought, and has for example influenced the Westerniser and Slavophile schools. However, Russia First has now become the dominant school of thought in modern Russia. Similarly, it has appealed across the political spectrum, winning support from liberal democrats, communists and nationalists, and has become a bi-partisan tenet of belief. Russia First can be defined as a school of thought in which the structural and intellectual attachment to Western political and economic values and models is being reversed, in favour of a more

balanced view encompassing Russia's traditional and historical interests. There are two closely interlinked strands to this school of thought.
First, in foreign policy terms Russia must re-prioritise its foreign policy
goals to project a more assertive image in areas of historical and traditional interest, where it calculates it can exert the most influence. These
areas include the Orthodox west (i.e. the Balkans), the southeastern
Islamic world, China, India and the Middle East, and the 'near abroad'
(i.e. the independent former Soviet republics). Second, Russia must
abandon the wholesale 'copying' of Western economic and democratic
models, in favour of a more selective 'pick and mix' policy that better
fits with the evolution of Russia's hybrid political and economic models.
These hybrid models are based more closely on Russian perceptions of
the country's needs and historic traditions. Hence the evolution of a
tsarist model of presidency and a weak Duma, with more in common
with pre-Soviet Russia than the French presidential system to which it
bears a passing resemblance. Russia First refers to more than the re-
emergence of traditional Russian nationalism or even anti-Westernism.
Instead, Russia First represents a Russian attempt to find uniquely
Russian solutions to the country's domestic and foreign policy conun-
drums. By implication, Russia First acknowledges that Russia is a
Eurasian entity, and not merely European. Boris Yeltsin's presidential
election manifesto was even more explicit on the issue of Russia's
identity, stating: 'Russia – a Eurasian state, which with its resources and
unique geo-political situation is going to become one of the largest
centres of economic development and political influence.'[9] The honeymoon with the West, and the period of close emulation dating back to
Peter the Great, is over. From now on Russia will pursue its own interests in a more assertive fashion, taking the ideas and assistance it needs
from the West, but creating its own democratic and economic models.

It has been argued here that Russia First represents a new school of
thought. This may well be controversial. It might also be advanced that
Russia First is instead a political process or reaction to an unpopular
experiment in Westernisation: the economic reforms launched by Prime
Minister Yegor Gaidar from 1992–93. To some extent it might be too
early to judge, but it is certainly true that any political movement
requires a body of thought to bring it to life, guide its principles and
explain its existence. The argument at the core of Russia First is that
the West has assumed that Russia, emerging from the Soviet period,
will develop a political and economic system based on Europe and the
United States. While this may have been tried at the beginning of

Yeltsin's era, it is not the case today. The Duma elections of 1993 and 1995, and the presidential election of 1996 show unequivocally that this will not happen. The Western model of democracy and a market economy has been decisively rejected by the Russian people. Their politicians, aware of the changing political environment, have adapted their policies to fit the changed political atmosphere. President Yeltsin dramatically changed direction to ensure re-election. The result has been the advent of Russia First and a new approach to relations with the West. Russia will adopt a more selective approach, absorbing certain Western ideas and values (including technological and commercial skills) while evolving a peculiarly Russian model of democracy and market-orientated economy. Western commentators should not be surprised that Russia is pursuing a policy of Russia First. The Americans and European states have consistently pursued their own US, Britain or France First strategies. The difference with Russia is that the country developed the Russia First school of thought in reaction to expectations that the country would ignore its own interests and copy democratic and economic models which suited the West. Russia First does represent a rejection of that strategy, and a desire to pursue national interests and policies even when these clash with the West. It is thus a normal evolution of statehood. Professor Richard Pipes of Harvard University believes that:

> Modernity and Westernization are, for all practical purposes, one and the same thing. A list of the countries enjoying the highest per-capita income today closely matches the roll of countries that have gone farthest in adopting Western ways. Conversely, the poorest countries are those which, for one reason or another, have not followed this path. Russia is no exception to the rule. Its ingrained anti-Westernism attests to an inability to adjust to the modern world, and spells poverty and regression.[10]

Richard Pipes's view that it is the Western model or nothing, shows a degree of misunderstanding of the processes at work in Russia. Nor should the Western model of democracy and capitalism be assumed to be so flawless it should be passed to less developed countries unmodified. Gennady Zyuganov, Russia's Communist leader, asserted Russia's 'equal right to follow our own path in accordance with our own traditions and conditions'. The West may not like how Russia develops, but the fact remains that Russia will develop in its own way at its own pace.

This book seeks to show the historical antecedents of Russia First, from the earliest days of the Russian Empire (Chapter 1), taking a look at the 'arch-Westerniser' Peter the Great, and his successors, including Catherine the Great, who continued his work. The historical chapter brings the book up to the Duma elections in 1995. Russia's foreign policy, its relations with the West and the near abroad are examined in detail in Chapter 2. This outlines the evolution of Russia First in the international sphere, and also considers the war in Chechnya, the arms trade, NATO enlargement and relations with China. The chapter on the military-industrial complex and the mafia (Chapter 3), outlines the economic conditions which gave rise to Russia First and the application of the strategy to domestic policy. Chapter 4 looks at the rise of the 'red–brown' alliance, and the rhetoric of Russia First, culminating in the victory of Gennady Zyuganov's Communists in the Duma elections of December 1995. The presidential elections of 1996 witness Yeltsin's wholehearted conversion to the Russia First policies of his political opponents (Chapter 5), the appointment of Alexander Lebed (Mr Russia First) as Secretary of the Security Council and the president's new cabinet. Finally, the concluding chapter brings all the different aspects of Russia First together, and takes a look at whether this school of thought will be an enduring one or just another passing fad, and what this means for relations with the West. In any event, Russia First heralds Russia's attempt to come to terms with life in the post-Soviet age, where the old certainties have melted with the snow, and the nation grapples to find a role and identity relevant for its second millennium.

NOTES

1 See Carrère d'Encausse, Hélène, MEP, *Draft report on the conclusion of the Partnership and Co-operation Agreement between the EU and Russia*, European Parliament, PE 210.337, 14 October 1994.
2 Quoted in *The Economist*, 'Russian exceptionalism: is Russia different?', 15 June 1996.
3 Adomeit, Hannes, 'Russia as a "great power" in world affairs: images and reality', *International Affairs*, 71:1 (1995), pp. 50–1; Dawisha, Karen, and Parrot, Bruce, *Russia and the New States of Eurasia*, Cambridge University Press (Cambridge, 1994), pp.199–203.
4 Author's meetings with Lukin, Strasbourg and Moscow, April and June 1996; discussions with St Petersburg politicians, December 1995.
5 Solzhenitsyn quoted in Dunlop, John, 'Russia confronting a loss of empire', in

Bremmer, Ian and Taras, Ray (eds), *Nation and Politics in the Soviet Successor States*, Cambridge University Press (Cambridge, 1993), pp. 58–9.

6 See Clark, Victoria, 'Ex-KGB man plots to cheat voters', *The Observer*, 19 May 1996.

7 Alexander Lebed quoted in *Rus Derzhavnaya*, No. 11–12, 1996, p. 5.

8 Kovalev, Sergei, 'How the West should not react to events in Russia', *Transition (Prague)*, 9 June 1995, pp. 42–3.

9 Yeltsin, Boris, *Programme of Action for 1996–2000*, 27 May 1996, p. 109.

10 Pipes, Richard, 'Russia's past, Russia's future', *Commentary*, 101:6 (1996), pp. 30–8.

CHAPTER I

'RUSSIA FIRST' AND A RETURN TO HISTORY

ANY UNDERSTANDING of modern Russia must begin with an understanding of how Russia's history has shaped the present. This chapter identifies and explains some of the historical antecedents of the central theme of the book, 'Russia First'. It argues that Russia's 'Westernising' course during 1991–93, and the subsequent shift away from the West, should be seen as part of a recurring pattern in Russian history, beginning with the reign of the 'arch-Westerniser', Peter the Great (1682–1725).[1] The chapter therefore considers some of the causes of Russia's troublesome and complex relationship with the West (understood for most of the period to mean Western Europe), and shows how the country's domestic and international orientation is inextricably intertwined. Professor Richard Pipes captures the essence of Russia's troubled relationship with the West:

> We thus confront a conundrum: a country which borders on Europe, which is inhabited by people who physically resemble Europeans, which for the past three centuries has insisted on being regarded as part of Europe, and which has shown both in political and in its cultural life the ability to be European, nevertheless has found it next to impossible to build a social and political regime that is based on a European model.[2]

RUSSIA'S 'GEOPOLITICAL PREDICAMENT'

Russia's geopolitical setting, as the bridge between the two continents of Europe and Asia, and its physical environment are the two essential conditioning factors in the country's socio-political development (including foreign policy), the development of state–society relations, and the formation of its political and cultural identity. What has been termed Russia's 'geopolitical predicament' has had important consequences for the development of the Russian state. First, whatever the configuration of its historical borders, the Russian landmass has not afforded Russia natural barriers against outside invasions which have repeatedly threatened Russia's internal stability and external security. Russian suffered incursions by the Mongols, Ottoman Turks, Poles, Swedes, French and Germans. This partly explains why militarism has been closely linked to the principle of autocracy in Russian history. Frontier zones have played a vital role in determining Russia's ability to resist invasion and in maintaining the internal stability of the state. Hence, looking at present-day Russia, it becomes apparent why the Russian Federation feels the need to develop a security structure based upon the Commonwealth of Independent States (CIS), designed to secure the frontiers of its 'near abroad'. Similarly, the end of the *cordon sanitaire* which Eastern Europe provided during the Soviet period has re-cast the traditional problems of frontier security zones in a new light. From this historical standpoint, it is easy to understand why the proposed enlargement of NATO to Russia's doorstep provokes such bitter domestic opposition.

Second, Russia's physical setting, distancing the country from the sources of dynamic Western civilisation, has retarded Russia's socio-economic development, historically placing it at both an economic and military disadvantage relative to Western Europe, and later both the United States and Japan.[3] As Alfred Rieber has noted:

> Through its long history Russia, whether Muscovite, Imperial or Soviet, has often, though not always, lagged behind other major powers in certain key demographic, economic, and technological indices that have been generally accepted as the measures of power, status, and influence in international politics.[4]

The very vastness of Russia encouraged a unique Russian psychology. Even today the Russian Federation comprises 126 nationalities composed of distinct racial and linguistic groups, including followers of Islam, Judaism and Buddhism. Whilst Russia therefore may be said to have lagged behind Western cultural and artistic movements, it enriched its own experience through its imperial contact with an extensive range of different cultures, religions and peoples. The Russian Empire expanded by absorbing contiguous territories and their inhabitants, unlike the European empires which developed by conquering overseas territories. A fundamental difference was that while the European countries built their nation-states first, and then expanded their empires, with Russia nation-building and imperial development went hand-in-hand.[5] Russia *was* the Empire, as the territories controlled by the tsar incorporated increasing number of nationalities and cultures. The Russian state's identity was a multi-cultural one, intertwined with the concept of the Russian Empire. This is also why the break-up of the Soviet Union (USSR) has been so traumatic for Russian people. Apart from the loss of status, the dismemberment of the old Russian Empire (called the Soviet Union under the Communists) created a crisis of identity. The diminution of Empire diminished the sense of 'Russianness', and raised the question of what being Russian meant. This in turn helps explain the attraction of the nationalist and Communist pledge to restore the Empire, and hence the historical Russian identity. The Bolshevik attempt to create a 'Soviet' nationality was a passing fad; what really counted for Russians was the reassurance of their own imperial identity. Sergei Razgonov summed up the sense of loss and the identity crisis: 'We [Russians] are no longer one-sixth of the earth's surface . . . But we continue to carry within ourselves one-sixth of the globe – from Riga to Shikotan. It is a scale we have become accustomed to. Ah, how difficult it is to part with it . . . From that former Homeland, we will be required to emigrate, all of us, to the last man.'[6]

One of the dominant themes of modern Russian history has been its persistent attempts to 'catch up' with the West through periods of modernisation along Western lines, hence the term 'Westernisation'. These phases have had the dual aim of buttressing and legitimising the internal and external power of the Russian state. Hugh Seton-Watson captured the essence of Russia's reliance on modernisation and Peter the Great's place in Russian and world history when he stated:

Modernization in the West happened: in Russia it was willed by the ruler. Peter the Great is not only a great figure in the history of

Russia: he is the first, and perhaps still the outstanding example, of a type which subsequently appeared in many countries of Asia and Africa . . . For the great majority of the human race modernization has been a deliberate, not a spontaneous process: Western experience is not typical but exceptional.[7]

Successive tsars and Soviet leaders have pursued autocracy and militarism, as mutually supportive aims in themselves and to stave off attacks which have threatened the existence of the state. Periodically, they have accelerated the development of key sectors of commerce and later industry, in order to enhance military power.[8] This process reached its apogee during the reigns of Peter the Great and Catherine the Great (1762–96). Though Tsar Peter is seen as the great Westerniser, the pattern was established progressively in the preceding two centuries. Nevertheless, it is no historical accident that both Mikhail Gorbachev and Boris Yeltsin have compared themselves to Peter the Great, to embellish their credentials as great reformers from above. Gorbachev, tried unsuccessfully under *perestroika* to close the technological gap with the West by importing Western technology and know-how, and by encouraging an influx of Western capital and investment. President Yeltsin's initial reform programme aimed at developing a full-blooded Western-style democracy and market economy. Both Gorbachev and Yeltsin could be described as 'Westernisers' at different periods in their careers, although with varying degrees of commitment and application.

The import of Western technology and expertise, and the presence of Western experts in privileged positions in Russian government and administration, has raised what Reiber has called 'the double dilemma for Russian governments . . . the spectre of dependence on foreign powers and . . . [the questioning] of the fundamental worth of Russian culture in comparison with that of the economically more developed countries'.[9] Historically, attempts have sometimes been made by Western rulers to exploit Russia's economic backwardness and reliance on Western technological expertise and capital for political ends. Political concessions could be extracted that gave the West a lever on both Russia's internal politics and its foreign policy. Russian leaders have also had to contend with domestic reaction to the appearance of foreign dependency, particularly from those who stood to lose from a foreign presence. Opposition to borrowing from the West was often couched in terms of an affront to traditional values, inciting anti-

Western campaigns which culminated in tsarist cultural pogroms or show-trials for those with Western contacts or training in the Soviet period.

Parallels can again be drawn with the contemporary period in Russia's history. The anti-Western backlash from the perceived dependency on Western technical and economic assistance has focused on international organisations like the International Monetary Fund (IMF) and World Bank. Former Prime Minister Yegor Gaidar became a potent symbol of dependency on the West, following his close association with Western economic schools of thought and his government's 'shock therapy'. The nationalist-patriotic tendency have also pointed up the link between economic dependency and foreign policy, portraying Western economic assistance as a deliberate tool to keep Russia weak while NATO advances up to its Western borders.

For both Peter the Great and Catherine the Great, Westernisation combined technological advancement along Western lines with the importation of Western (i.e. European) cultural values and modes of behaviour. In Tsar Peter's case, this went as far as trying to induce Russians into thinking with a Western mindset. However, these attempts to introduce a 'cultural revolution from above' were only partially successful, as they went against the grain of Russia's own historical and cultural development. According to Alfred Rieber's analysis, the Russian state has historically 'been located physically or viewed culturally on the margin of three great culture areas: the Byzantine empire to the southwest, the Latin West, and the Islamic world to the southeast. (More recently, given the shift from religious to secular cultural identities, Europe may be substituted for the two Christian cultures).'[10]

Rieber further noted:

In Moscow's earliest struggles to acquire wealth and security in the frontier zones that surrounded it, its rulers sought to legitimize their state power by claiming a share of the political and cultural legacies of the three culture areas. The Russian tsars desired Moscow to be recognized as part of Europe, as heir to Byzantium, and as successor to the Golden Horde. In conducting their foreign policy, they appeared in different guises as Renaissance prince, Basileus, and Khan. The three roles did not always harmonize well in international politics, and at home the tsars were something more than the sum of the three roles. But to have ignored or repudiated as utterly alien any one of these cultural areas would have incurred serious political consequences.[11]

The centuries-old dilemma about Russia's European or Eurasian vocation is rooted precisely in Russia's identity crisis. Deliberate policies of Westernisation designed to close the cultural gap between Europe and Russia have failed to resolve the Russia–Europe dichotomy. Periods of Westernisation have nourished the arguments of domestic opponents, strengthening the hands of those who claim that the process is a betrayal of Russia's cultural heritage. Instead, they have advocated a specifically Russian path of development, putting 'Russia First'. Russia may once again find it is obliged to pursue some policies which enable it to 'catch up' with the West, as Neumann has suggested: '*any* regime, no matter how bent it may be initially on following a specifically Russian path of development, is likely to discover that maintaining the position of Russia in its international setting may demand a certain copying of European models'.[12]

While the cycle of *rapprochement*–detachment from the West and more especially with Europe has been a salient feature of Russian history, the development of Russia First has encouraged a new approach to Western relations. For the foreseeable future, rather than merely emulating the West, Russia will adopt a more selective approach which absorbs certain Western ideas and values (including technological and commercial skills), whilst evolving a peculiarly Russian model of democracy and a market-orientated economy. In short, Russia will attempt to catch up, but will at the same time seek to assert its own traditional values, aims and objectives, embodied in a 'Russia First' strategy.

THE HISTORICAL ANTECEDENTS OF RUSSIA FIRST: RUSSIA, THE WEST AND WESTERNISATION

Historically, Russia has been profoundly influenced by a sense of chronic insecurity, determined by its experiences of foreign invasion and subjugation, dating back to the 'Mongol Yoke'. The Asiatic influence has been counterbalanced by Russia's economic, political, religious and cultural links with the West. Chronic insecurity, influences from both the East and West, have led to the evolution of today's Russia as a heterogeneous, Eurasian entity, straddling two continents and many different cultures. Pyotr Chaadayev, one of the early nineteenth-century Westernisers, said, 'We do not belong to any of the great families of mankind, neither to the East nor to the West.'[13] The search for a 'Russian identity' is not a simple one, and to a certain extent futile, as there is no single concept which encapsulates modern Russia. Rather Russia is a product of its history and experiences, which have led to it developing neither a Western nor an Eastern society, but something between the two. But Russia's historical experiences help explain how modern Russia has evolved into the society it is today, and how it has come to reject Western values and embrace Russia First.

Kievan Rus (the precursor to modern-day Kiev) provided modern Russia with the legacy of Russian Orthodoxy. Prince Vladimir I's choice of the Byzantine variant of Christianity in 988 had important consequences for the later development of Russia, since it both bound Russians to the continent but also marginalised the country culturally. Orthodoxy helped reinforce and perpetuate Russian traditions of deference to authority and the patriarchal nature of society.[14] Some of the most important influences of the formative periods in West European history, such as the Renaissance and the Reformation, simply passed Russia by. 'There was no Renaissance among us,' lamented Nikolai Berdyaev, the early twentieth-century philosopher. Meanwhile, Russia's Orthodoxy stranded the country in a medieval mindset as Europe moved on. The poet and writer Alexander Pushkin wrote in the early nineteenth century:

There is no doubt that the Schism [within the Church] has separated us from the rest of Europe and that we have not taken part in any of the great developments which have been shaking it, but we have had our special mission. It was Russia with its endless expanses that absorbed the Mongol conquest and thus Christian civilization was saved. To achieve this goal we had to exist in a unique manner: we remained Christians, but at the same time we became alienated from the Christian world. This is how, as a result of our martyrdom, Catholic Europe could make energetic progress without any hindrance.[15]

Seeing itself as the ideological leader and defender of the Orthodox world, Russia found itself faced with appeals for slavic solidarity which conflicted with its obligations as a member of the European states system.[16] Russia's unique religious and cultural isolation from Europe laid the seeds of the nation's identity crisis and sense of alienation. The

Russians stood on the fringes of the great historical events influencing the European continent during the Renaissance and Reformation, and were not at their heart. Apprehension at being side-lined and surpassed by developments in Western Europe persisted through to the twentieth century .

The decline of Kievan Rus and the submission to the Mongol Yoke in 1240 has led some to overstate the Asiatic influence on Russia, epitomised by the Marquis de Custine's epigram in 1839: 'Scratch a Russian and you will find a tartar.' Despite the Eurasian school of the 1920s arguing that the Mongol invasion 'was the decisive event in Russian history', the Asiatic influence on Russian society can be exaggerated. Russia in effect became a vassal state, administering itself.[17] As Edward Acton noted, 'the impact of the Mongols on Russia's social and political development was limited by the countervailing influences and by the form that their rule took'.[18] The importance of the Mongol invasion was more psychological than anything else, later rulers invoking the Mongol 'bogeyman' to justify territorial expansion and authoritarian excess. As the centre of political gravity shifted northwards to Muscovy, Russia's security concerns encompassed the west (Lithuania) as well as the vulnerable southern and eastern flanks.

Novgorod is sometimes mentioned as an example of the fact that Russia is not completely devoid of democratic traditions. A prosperous city-state that belonged to the Hanseatic League through which it traded with northern Europe, Novgorod remains an example of what might have been if the city had been allowed to flourish. Novgorod participated 'in the process of sea-borne trade which trained the burgher class of medieval Europe in capitalist enterprise'.[19] But when Ivan III (the Great, 1462–1505) conquered the city in 1478, he obliterated all vestiges of the 'semi-democratic' representative bodies that had embodied its freedom and prosperity. Novgorod and, by extension, Muscovy were therefore denied the opportunity of developing along the lines of the city-states, whose traditions of liberty and the rule of law were to form the foundation of the West European nation-state.[20]

Expansion continued under both Ivan III and his successor Vasily III (1505–33), taking in the principalities surrounding Muscovy and seizing the Ukraine. Lithuania, and later Lithuania–Poland, posed a persistent threat to Muscovy and Russia over the coming centuries, both in military and cultural terms. Ivan and Vasily were acutely aware of the vulnerability of the south and eastern flanks to attacks from the Mongols. It was in response to these security threats that Ivan III had established the foundations of Russian absolutism and militarism, by centralising power in his own hands and subordinating the warrior class to his service through a system of land tenure. Ivan III's power was unchecked by legal and institutional limitations and he claimed the power of appointment and all executive, legislative and judicial authority.[21] While Ivan centralised power and imposed bondage, Western Europe was experiencing the Renaissance, decentralisation and the unravelling of feudal society. Once again, Russia was out of step with Western 'civilisation'.

Ivan III also embarked upon a limited phase of Westernisation, employing Western ballistics experts to help him modernise his army and Western architects to work on his building projects. Ivan's efforts were the first major attempt at 'Westernisation', to improve Russia's performance by borrowing ideas to 'catch up' with the West. Ivan III's reign saw the roots of the tsarist absolutism and militarism that stifled Russia up to the Bolshevik Revolution in 1917, and persisted in its Soviet form until Gorbachev's *perestroika*. Hugh Ragsdale concludes of Ivan III's reign that 'the revolution that Ivan accomplished was the great watershed of Russian political tradition. Ivan's statecraft was the great prototype, a classic Russian system of absolutism and militarism under cautious and scrupulous control.'[22]

Ivan IV (1533–84), better known as Ivan the Terrible, succeeded Vasily III. His first official act was to crown himself tsar (the word is derived from 'Caesar') in a grand ceremony modelled on the coronation of the Byzantine emperors. This symbolised not only Ivan's unfettered and semi-divine power but also the continuity between Muscovy and Byzantium, which had been propagated in the doctrine of Muscovy as the 'Third Rome'.[23] The doctrine was employed by successive rulers to nourish the tsarist ideology, extolling the purity of the Russian faith and the internal cohesion of the state. It also implied moral superiority to the West (given the fall of the first Rome), which was a useful argument for opponents of 'Westernisation' at various junctures in Russian history.[24] Ivan IV's early reign continued the reforms of Ivan III before it degenerated into the bloodletting that earned him his unsavoury epithet. Ivan the Terrible continued the work of his predecessor in modernising the army partly through the import of Western technologies. He showed 'a strong desire for more contact with the West, an area in which he anticipated Peter the Great'.[25] Ivan IV sent his German agent, Hans Schlitte, to the Hanseatic cities in 1547 to hire skilled technicians to transfer Western technology to Muscovy.

Schlitte's mission ended in failure following his arrest in Lübeck. Later, in 1553, Ivan welcomed a party of English sailors led by Richard Chancellor which led to the founding of the Muscovy company in 1555, establishing regular trade between England and Muscovy. Ivan's successful wars against the khanates of Kazan and Astrakhan were followed by the disastrous Livonian War (1558–83) and led to the invasion by the Crimean Tartars in 1571 and occupation by the Poles in the 'Time of Troubles' (1598–1613).

During this period the question of Russia's relations with the West became a fully-fledged debate. On the one hand, the Polish–Lithuanian invaders were seen as a Western variant of the Mongol invaders, who should be repelled with a minimum of contact, so preserving Orthodoxy inviolate. On the other hand, early Russian 'Westernisers' viewed the occupation as an opportunity to learn from and 'catch up' with the more politically and economically advanced Poles. To this end the 'Westernisers' supported Poland's unsuccessful dynastic ambitions to have Wladyslaw of Poland crowned tsar of all the Russians. Ivan Timofeev, a contemporary observer, wrote that the effect on Russian people was that they were 'turning their backs to each other. Some look to the East and others to the West'.[26] The debate over whether Russia should look primarily to the West or the East can thus be dated back to the late sixteenth century, and indicates that Russia's search for an identity has a long history. The embryonic Westernisers faded into the background in the seventeenth century, resurfacing with renewed vigour during Peter the Great's reign.

Ivan IV's enduring legacy was to encourage the enserfment of the majority of the population just as this system was being undermined in the West. This perpetuated Russia's economic and social backwardness, particularly vis-à-vis the West. Ivan the Terrible's infamous oprichnina amounted to a purge of perceived enemies (especially the boyars), plunging the country into a state of virtual civil war. The second half of Ivan's reign also eliminated the development of a 'proto-bourgeoisie', which had been evident in the convocation of the first Zemsky sobor.[27] Elsewhere in Europe, the growing power of an evolving bourgeoisie provided a counterweight to absolutism, as witnessed in the English Civil War (1642–45).

Commercial, diplomatic, military and cultural links between Russia and Europe steadily intensified during the sixteenth and especially the seventeenth centuries. As Edward Acton noted: 'the more closely historians examine the seventeenth century, the more precedents they find for the innovations associated with Peter the Great'.[28] Peter the Great (1682–1725) may have been guilty of exaggerating the extent of Russia's isolation from Europe to justify his policy of Westernisation. Nevertheless, his reign marked a decisive break with Russia's past. War and Westernisation were the two mutually dependent and self-reinforcing preoccupations of Tsar Peter's reign. Peter succeeded in elevating Russia to the status of a major European power and established the basis for a century-long expansion of the Russian Empire that ushered in the Imperial age. Peter embarked upon a systematic process of Westernisation, inspired by the rational thought of the European Enlightenment. This course of reform aimed at the complete transformation of Russia into the mirror-image of the nation-states of Western Europe. Peter's cultural revolution from above endeavoured not only to remove the visible signs of Russian culture but to transform the Russian mentality, so promoting Western modes of thought and behaviour.

Peter the Great's own early years were influenced by his childhood in the foreign suburb of Moscow, where he was freed from the constraint of a traditional Orthodox upbringing and exposed to Western influences.[29] Peter's 'Grand Embassy' to Western Europe in 1697–98, enabled the young tsar to learn about the West, picking up technical expertise and skills. At this time he visited Deptford and Amsterdam, famously spending time as a carpenter in a Dutch shipyard. He also encouraged experts to bring their skills back to Russia, a policy he pursued throughout his reign. Peter also studied many of the aspects of Western culture, including dress, manners and customs, introducing tobacco and the potato to Russia. Potato planting today is one of Russia's great traditions, practised in every village and on most dachas across the vast country.

According to legend, Peter was so impatient to transform Russia that he summoned his boyars and cut off their beards, ordering all noblemen to do likewise. He had a coin minted that read 'The beard is a useless burden,' and later imposed taxes on beards and even blue eyes. The beard embodied Orthodox manhood, and its removal was a deeply symbolic act, as well as an affront to traditional culture. The courtiers were also ordered either to replace their traditional clothes with German or English-style dress or to face fines, whilst French became the language of the Court and the upper classes. Peter also obliged his boyars to refine their manners and forbade them to act in any way which might be construed as vulgar in the West. However, most of Peter's cultural revolution only affected the upper classes of

Russian society. The vast majority of the population (mainly the peasantry) remained oblivious to Peter's cultural reforms, and their traditional customs and religion continued unabated.[30]

The Grand Embassy had furnished Peter with a number of ideas which were to become the motors for his 'Westernisation' programme: the modernisation of Russia's military (including the creation of a navy) and the structures of state. Peter set up a standing army, borrowing the idea from the West, and established a revenue base capable of paying for his military campaigns. Tsar Peter's reforms took the form of enlightened despotism, similar to the *Polizeistaat* of Austria and Prussia. Absolutism was the instrument for Russia's bid to catch up with the West in political, economic and cultural terms.[31] Peter reformed central government, and doubled the number of civil servants (to around 4,000), who remained ill-trained and corrupt. Adapting ideas from the West, Peter founded a number of institutions of higher learning, including an Academy of Sciences, a school for mathematical sciences and navigation, and military and naval schools. Most of Peter's educational reforms were geared to technical teaching, to serve the interests of the state, and only nobles were given a rudimentary education. The intelligentsia remained a limited breed in Russia society, and lagged behind the West in terms of size and development.

One of the striking features of Peter's reign was that he trebled the state revenue in real terms, despite a relatively unchanged level of population.[32] This was achieved partly through administrative reform, the use of the army to collect taxes, and the introduction of new taxes, such as a poll-tax (levied annually on tax-paying males). Peter's tax-collection record was enviable by modern Russian standards. The Church was also required to pay higher taxes, and was effectively converted into a department of state in 1722 with a secular bureaucracy. Notwithstanding this development, the Church's influence on the Russian people remained undiminished. According to Hugh Seton-Watson, 'politically, this influence normally operated in favour of autocracy, nationalism, and intolerance towards non-Russians'.[33] Russian Orthodoxy thus reinforced Peter's power base, but also insulated the population at large from many of the cultural and psychological influences of Westernisation.

Peter the Great encouraged the development of mercantilism, the predominant form of trade in Western Europe and another imported idea. His over-riding objective was to make Russia self-sufficient in the 'war-industries', such as armaments, textiles and metallurgy. Peter introduced tariffs to protect native industry, which also benefited from tax breaks, serf labour and subsidies. This was the seventeenth- and early eighteenth-century version of a 'Russia First' economic policy. The tsar sought to subordinate trade and economic interests to the needs of the state, creating an early version of a nascent military-industrial complex. Military power and self-sufficiency was rated more highly than growing trade and economic prosperity. With access to the Baltic and Black Seas secured by military campaigns, sea-borne trade expanded. The resultant economic growth (which was a by-product of military success) led to urban development, but not the evolution of a bourgeoisie. Merchants, industrialists and nobles did not interact in any institutional sense, and Peter failed to summon the Boyars' Duma or *Zemsky sobor*, preferring to concentrate power in his own hands. Russia's autocratic tendencies were strengthened during the Petrine era.

The Russian tsarist historian, Vasily Osipovich Klyuchevsky, calculated that Peter was engaged in wars for all but thirteen months of his thirty-six year reign. Driven to establish an empire, Peter formally assumed the title Emperor of All Russia in 1721, following the Treaty of Nystadt. Henceforth Muscovy came to be known as the Russian Empire. When Peter became tsar in 1694, 'the coveted access to the Baltic and Black Seas was still lacking, the area under Moscow's rule was approaching that of today's Russian Federation. A vast Empire was taking shape.'[34] Tsar Peter's crowning foreign policy success was to establish Russia as the new dominant power of the Baltic region. He acquired the territories of what is now Estonia and parts of Latvia, and access to the Baltic Sea in the Great Northern War against Sweden (1700–21). Peter founded the new capital of his Russian Empire in St Petersburg, on the Gulf of Finland, securing his 'Window on the West' that heralded Russia's arrival as a great European power. St Petersburg symbolised the whole ethos of Peter's reforms, and the 'Venice of the North' became one of the great cities of contemporary Europe, replete with elegant Western architecture. Peter's campaigns in the south were less successful, returning the Black Sea fortress of Azov (captured in 1696) to the Ottomans, following a failed campaign in Turkish Moldova. Nor was he successful in subjugating the Crimean Tartars or in a campaign launched late in his reign against Persia, although he did manage to assert control over parts of the Ukraine. Peter had yet to unite all 'the Russian land' under tsarist control; this task was left to his successors, particularly Catherine the Great.[35]

Peter's reforms had been subordinated to his two over-riding aims of establishing a Russian Empire and elevating Russia to the status of a major power in Europe. He achieved this by exposing Russia to its first period of concerted Westernisation, without turning Russia into a mirror image of the European states his reforms had emulated. While his military-industrial and economic reforms touched the whole population, his cultural revolution only affected society's elite. Peter reinforced a system whereby the majority of the population were enserfed under a slaveholding nobility, who were in turn locked into state service under the tsar. The pace of the reforms, the burden of taxation and the brutality of the tsar's authority increased popular resentment against the process of Westernisation. Tsar Peter's assault on the traditional aspects of life, particularly Orthodoxy, sowed the seeds of persistent grassroots antagonism to the imposition of Western values which remains to this day. Traditional xenophobic and anti-Western attitudes found expression in opposition movements, such as the Don Cossack revolution of 1707–8, but were easily suppressed by the state. Opposition was more overt in the traditional elements of the upper classes, but was also swiftly subdued by an over-bearing tsar. Peter himself crushed opposition ruthlessly and cruelly, participating in the torture and execution of his opponents. The reaction against Westernisation left enduring scars on the popular Russian psyche. As Hugh Ragsdale noted:

> Russians saw themselves persecuted and scorned by Europeans for generations, and so the choice of cultural model that Peter forced them to make was totally graceless. In fact, Russia developed from that time a painfully ambivalent attitude to Europe. The xenophobia was old, and the xenomenia was new, but henceforth they would always be simultaneous.[36]

Russian society was divided between the Court and a large section of the aristocracy which embraced Westernisation, and the vast majority of the population and elements of the nobility which thoroughly rejected it. For Russian society as a whole, cultural Westernisation was only skin-deep and confined to the elite. Resentment towards Westernisation was the dominant mood in Russia, if the population thought about the subject at all. Most Russians, living in their villages hundreds or thousands of kilometres from Moscow and St Petersburg, were left unmoved, ignorant and uninterested. The failure of Westernisation to take root in Russian society had profound effects on future relations with the West. Russia First was nourished by the historical failure of Russia to wholeheartedly embrace Western values. The population's traditional and long-standing hostility to Westernisation ensured popular support for the concept of Russia First, as it emerged towards the end of the twentieth century.

None of Peter the Great's five successors up to the reign of Catherine the Great (1762–96) maintained his zeal for reforms or imperial conquest. They did, however, toy with Westernisation to varying degrees. Anna (1730–40) germanicised her Court under the influence of Ernst Biron, which gave rise to the term *Bironshchina* – 'the bad rule of Biron', coined by those who resented Biron's German influence. Germanic influence at Court further infuriated those who felt Russia's identity was being undermined by foreigners. Anna reinforced this sense of cultural alienation by introducing Italian opera to Russia. Her successor, Elizabeth (1741–61), had a penchant for Western luxuries and expensive tastes, which she promoted ardently. Peter III (1761–62) offended Russian traditionalists with his affinity with all things Prussian, and entered an alliance with Frederick of Prussia, whom Elizabeth had fought in the Seven Years War (1756–63).

Catherine the Great followed in the footsteps of Peter the Great as Russia's second great Westerniser. Catherine ruled as an enlightened despot, drawing on the pre-eminent political concepts of the age to carry out a number of important domestic reforms while consolidating the existing social order. In her foreign policy, she raised Russia's power and prestige to greater levels than under Peter the Great. Her approach was more programmatic than Peter's, but grounded in the same rational, pragmatic and progressive ethos that sought to close the gap between the powers of Western Europe by maximising the country's wealth and power. The closing years of her reign, however, marked a retreat from Westernisation as Catherine began to fear the penetration of ideas that led to the French Revolution.

Born and raised in Germany, but educated in France, Catherine was naturally receptive to the most influential political ideas of the day that emanated from France and Germany. Her political philosophy was an eclectic mix of many of these ideas, and was contained in her *Instruction*, which combined the ideas of enlightened despotism, a body of laws that checked the power of the monarchy, and the organisation of Russian society along the lines of West European estates (distinctive social classes with defined rights, including those to property). In practice her social reforms considerably improved the position of the aristocracy while worsening the life of the peasantry. Catherine consolidated her own power by conferring privilege on the nobility, effectively turning them into a separate state within the state. The 1785 Charter of the Nobility abolished universal service to the state and, together with the Law on Administration of the Provinces, in practice denied the serfs any rights and left them at the mercy of the aristocrats.

Catherine sought to introduce two socio-political reforms influenced by Western thinking. First, she intended a degree of emancipation in the political classes below the nobility in order to enhance their productive capacity in the cause of modernising Russia.[37] Her Charter of the Towns in 1785 was heavily influenced by contemporary French thought. Catherine consulted Diderot and her ambassador in Paris, D.M. Golitsyn. However, the institution of an elective form of self-government, designed to promote a flourishing merchant class as the backbone of a new Russian middle class, did not survive the outbreak of the French Revolution four years later. Having drawn much of her inspiration for her political programmes from the France of the seventeenth and eighteenth centuries, Catherine abruptly halted Westernisation in a bid to stem the flow of ideas associated with the French Revolution. The abandonment of social and political reform, repeated later in Russia history, had profound consequences for the future of the monarchy and the development of democratic institutions in Russia.

Catherine's socio-political reform was also short lived. This involved Catherine's earlier experiment with an elective legislative commission, set up in 1767. It embodied Catherine's attempt to give some expression to her attachment to contemporary European political thinking, especially the idea of establishing a society of orders (*Ständestaat*). This would bestow civil, but not political, equality on all citizens, and therefore grant rights to the peasantry. The commission therefore represented a broad cross-section of Russian society. However, opposition from the nobility and the Pugachev peasant rebellion of 1773–74 scuppered the reform, as Catherine abandoned any notion of reforming serfdom in the face of the threat to her own position.

Catherine pursued her educational reforms with greater success, after consulting Emperor Joseph II of Austria and basing her reforms on those of his mother, Maria Theresa. Building on the secular education system initiated by Peter the Great, Catherine established a three-tier schooling system in St Petersburg, as a pilot scheme for her reforms. This was extended under a general plan of national education to the Russian provinces in 1786, by which time she had also founded the

Russian Academy to promote literary and linguistic study. By the end of her reign, Catherine the Great had greatly extended the structure of Russian education in terms of the number of schools and training facilities. Formal education was still only available to a very small proportion of the Russian population.

Under Tsaritsa Catherine, Russia's intellectual elite began to flower, profiting from her regime of intellectual openness and cultural attachment to Europe. Catherine frequently corresponded with some of the great figures of the Enlightenment, including Voltaire, Grimm and Diderot. The French-speaking aristocracy increasingly participated in this process of cultural development and, unlike in Tsar Peter's time, enthusiastically embraced Western ideas, customs and values. A leisured and educated class became established in Russia which indicated that the 'scientific, moral and political ideas of the Age of the Enlightenment were beginning to reach at least a stratum of the Russian people, to bring out their great latent abilities'.[38] For Catherine, like Peter the Great before her, the primary objective of exposing her Court and diplomatic corps to contemporary European thinking was an attempt to imbue them with learning that would improve their administrative, military and technical skills for the pursuit of war. This in turn would raise Russia's international standing and bring 'her Court, diplomatic corps and the cultural life of her elite abreast of her more refined rivals'.[39] Westernisation was not undertaken for its own sake, but as a means to an end. The ultimate goal was to strengthen the state and bring it up to a level whereby it could compete with its European neighbours.

Catherine expanded the Russian Empire more than at any time since the sixteenth century. Her first campaign against Turkey (1768–74) broke the Ottoman vassalage of the Crimean Tartars, strengthened Russia's southern border, and established control over the northern coast of the Black Sea. She annexed the Crimea in 1783, and began construction of the Black Sea Fleet, which afforded Russia access to the Mediterranean and boosted its commercial prospects. Catherine's destruction of the Polish state, through the three partitions of 1772, 1793 and 1795, absorbed Lithuania and the rest of the territories which today constitute Latvia, Belarus and western Ukraine. Catherine's westward expansion extended Russia's frontier zones and preceded future entanglement in continental affairs in the nineteenth and twentieth centuries. Russia proved herself a match for the pre-eminent naval power of the day, Britain, and repelled Sweden's attempt to regain control of the Baltic Sea in 1787–88.

The military successes of Catherine's reign took Russia to new heights of international prestige and power in the European states system. Russia's Empire now stretched from the Baltic to the Black Sea and across the Caucasus, according it great influence over the Baltic and Central Europe. Over the half-century that followed Catherine's rule, her successors continued to expand the Empire and the country's influence as a 'Great Power'. Paul I (1796–1801) annexed Georgia, while Alexander I conquered most of eastern Transcaucasia. Alexander's reign was dominated by the wars with Napoleon, which culminated in the bitter battle of Borodino outside Moscow and the defeat of the French Emperor in 1812, graphically portrayed in Lev Tolstoy's epic *War and Peace*. Napoleon briefly occupied Moscow, but was frustrated by the Russians' desertion of the city, which they stripped of provisions and set on fire. The loss of his *grande armée* on the winter retreat from Moscow hastened the demise of the Napoleonic Empire. Only one thousand fit French troops of the 100,000 who invaded Russia made it home. Despite exhibiting signs of instability and schizophrenia, Tsar Alexander extended Russia's western borders to their farthest point. Subject to periods of religious mania, he died mysteriously at Taganrog in 1825. There were persistent reports that the tsar had not died but had fled to Siberia to become a hermit. To allay these rumours the authorities opened Alexander's coffin in 1865; it was found to be empty. His successor, Nicholas I (1825–55), won the epithet the '*gendarme* of Europe', as, in a bid to preserve the order of the *ancien régime,* Russia resolved a series of conflicts throughout a Europe beset with political upheavals. At the same time, Nicholas extended Russia's borders into the southern Caucasus and Central Asia. By the time of the Crimean War (1853–56) the Russian Empire covered the territory that would later constitute the Soviet Union, with the exception of the four Central Asian republics of Turkmenistan, Uzbekistan, Tajikistan and Kyrgyzstan.[40]

The 'Decembrist' uprising of 1825 in St Petersburg was the first important manifestation of the conflict between the Westernisers and what can be loosely described as the conservative nationalists. The Decembrists advocated a constitution that would enable the country to pursue political and economic development along European lines. Russia would take its rightful place among European nations, since it formed part of the 'cultural entity of nations' which constituted Europe.[41] The Decembrists called for the abolition of serfdom, reform of the courts, a free press, the establishment of a constitutional monarchy with an elective legislature and the creation of a federal system based on thirteen states.[42] Constitutionalism implied checks on the executive power of the state which the tsar was not willing to countenance, and the uprising was easily crushed. One of the supporters of the Decembrists was Alexander Sergeyevich Pushkin (1799–1837), the famous poet and writer, who had already been exiled to Moldova for his links with opposition groups amongst the young aristocracy of St Petersburg. Pushkin exemplified those members of the Russian intellectual elite who supported the 'Western' values of constitutionalism and social reform, but were intense Russian patriots. For Pushkin, there was no conflict between being both a Westerniser and a patriot who loved his country and its unique Russian soul. While the Decembrists were Westernisers, they believed passionately in adapting Western practices to make Russia a greater country. Russia would maintain its unique character, whilst reforming its institutions, legal structures and social conditions. Although the Decembrist uprising ultimately failed, it provided the impetus for the so-called Great Reforms of 1855–65. Serfdom in Russia was finally abolished in 1861, earlier than in Poland and Romania or Abraham Lincoln's abolition of slavery in the United States.

Opposition and reaction crystallised around various tendencies. Russian 'Messianism' questioned Russia's place in Europe and its European identity. The official response was the 'Doctrine of Official Nationality'. Propagated by education minister S.S. Uvarov in 1833, the latter sought to legitimise the tsar by references to a glorious historical, military and cultural past, founded on three distinctly Russian principles: autocracy, orthodoxy and nationalism (or nation-mindedness). The Doctrine of Official Nationality remained the state's official response to Westernising tendencies until it was pushed into the margins and co-existed with the romantic nationalists, who came to be known as the Slavophiles. During Russia's 'marvellous' or 'glorious' decade (1838–48), so-called because of the flowering of the intelligentsia, the Slavophiles developed a position defined and inspired by contemporary German romanticism. This defined the Russian nation in terms of its unique Russian Slavic (especially linguistic) roots, the ancient peasant commune and the country's Orthodox religion. The Slavophiles therefore espoused a return to these specifically Russian virtues, reversing the path taken by the arch-Westerniser, Peter the Great. The Westernisers stressed how Russia had already developed along European lines, but continued to lag behind its continental counterparts. Some Westernisers argued that in order to catch up with the West, Russia had to emulate all aspects of West European development, while others argued for a more selective approach. The arguments of the nineteenth century seem familiar, and they are. The debate between Slavophiles and Westernisers continued into the twentieth century, following the peaks and troughs in Russia's relations with the West.

The Crimean War served to highlight the limits of Russia's military capability in the face of superior West European forces and technology. As Russia's influence waned in Europe it turned to expansion in Central Asia to underpin its 'Great Power' status. As Dietrich Geyer put it: 'Central Asia therefore played a subsidiary role in Russian policy-making: its importance was derived not from the intrinsic value of the conquered territories but from the role it played in European affairs.'[43] Russia could now only compete against the European powers (especially England) in theatres outside Europe itself. Fyodor Dostoyevsky summed up Russia's paradox: 'In Europe we were hangers-on and Slaves, whereas we shall go to Asia as masters. In Europe we were Asiatics, whereas in Asia we, too, are European. Our civilising mission in Asia will bribe our spirit and drive us thither.'[44] Dostoyesky failed to share Pushkin's Westernising zeal, and looked to the East to achieve Russia's Great Power ambitions.

During the tsarist era Russia remained thoroughly Western in its attitude towards Asia and its conquered territories. Westernisers and Slavophiles, in spite of their differences, agreed that Russia was a Christian country with more in common with Europe than Asia.[45] In Turgenev's words, Russia was no different from her older European sisters 'only a little broader in the beam'. The conflict with the West was strictly fraternal. Orthodoxy, the Byzantine legacy, and Slavism necessitated close links with Christian Europe and the classical inheritance. Militarily speaking, Russia lagged behind the West as the latter was transformed by the Industrial Revolution and its concomitant social changes. This realisation heralded a new phase in Russia's debate about its relations with Europe and its internal development compared to the West, eventually giving rise to a form of aggressive pan-Slavism. Russia thus retreated from its role as the '*gendarme* of Europe', slipping into conflict over the Balkans with the other European powers.

Russia's international prestige and status as one of the pre-eminent powers of Europe could be said to have reached its apogee by the time of the Crimean War. This was achieved in the first half of the nineteenth century under the leadership of staid political regimes. The passing of Catherine the Great's reign marked the end of any attempt at systematic Westernisation, and the demise of the monarch's role as an agent of political and social progress. Catherine's programme of Westernisation, built on the reforms of Peter the Great, closed the political, military and cultural gap with Europe to its narrowest point in Russian history. The French Revolution ended the process, and isolated the absolutist tsarist system from mainstream European politics. It was natural that the emerging Russian intellectual elite should be exposed to the ideas that guided Western Europe's political, economic and social development that gave birth to the industrialised liberal democracies of the nineteenth century. The result was a recurrent tension between those advocates of Russian development along Western lines, and the conservative forces of the state and intelligentsia who espoused a Russian path that preserved the country's existing political and social order. Increasingly, the latter found expression through a developing form of Russian 'romantic nationalism'. Russia's debate on Europe raised fundamental questions about Russia's self-identity and the nature of its political, economic and social development. This discourse became an almost permanent feature of Russia's political life, eventually becoming the most divisive issue of the day in the nineteenth and early twentieth centuries.[46]

The state sharply curtailed public debate in response to the revolutions that swept across Europe in 1848. The Westernisers only reappeared with Russia's defeat in the Crimean War. Alexander II responded with limited Westernising reforms of the state apparatus and the introduction of elected local councils (zemstva). This failed to satisfy the Westernisers, who split into three groups: the liberal constitutionalists, the Russian socialists (who became populist and no longer Western orientated) and the Marxists. Conterminously, the Crimean War acted as a catalyst for the progressive transformation of romantic nationalism from its 'Slavist' guise into an aggressive, revanchist pan–Slavism which emerged in the 1880s. Pan-Slavism found expression in the foreign policies of Alexander III and later, Nicholas II, who evolved its most extreme form of Russification.

Russia's 'marvellous decade' witnessed the emergence of the political forces that competed for power and popular support in the run-up to the October Revolution of 1917. The position of each was linked to how it believed Russia should develop with reference to Europe as a political, economic and social model. For the sake of brevity and to avoid rehearsing a familiar period of Russian history, suffice it to say that the Bolshevik concept of Marxism was eventually triumphant. This was not before the liberals had enjoyed a period of pseudo-parliamentarism (1905–14), when, in a bid to appease rising opposition, the tsar allowed the convocation of a number of elected Dumas with nominal legislative powers. In the meantime, Russian self-confidence and the institution of the monarchy was shaken by humiliating defeat in the Russo-Japanese War of 1904–5, and the subsequent revolution of 1905. Russia was shown as unable to compete on a global scale, and the defeat was the more mortifying since it was administered by a supposedly inferior Asiatic power. An upsurge of nationalism nevertheless encouraged Nicholas II to take Russia into the First World War. Catastrophically unprepared for modern warfare, the Russian army was totally outclassed by the German armed forces, and suffered horrendous casualties. Russia's inability to match Western Europe was cruelly exposed, and the country slid into civil war and revolution.

The advent of Lenin's Bolshevik regime and the development of a new state ideology forced all the other positions out of the debate, with the exception of romantic nationalism, which was used by the state to assert the Soviet Union's moral superiority over Europe.[47] Soviet state ideology and hence Russian self-identity was defined in contradistinction to European values. Europe as a political and economic model was thus no longer to be emulated, but served as the antithesis of the Soviet model. Western Europe also acted as a reference point against which the Soviet Union's political, economic and military 'superiority' could be measured. The Second World War itself reinforced Russia's security fears, following the German invasion and the loss of 26 million Russian citizens in the conflict. The Great Patriotic War, as it was known in Russia, implanted further in the Russian psyche the need to protect the country's frontiers from foreign invaders, whether the threat came from the south, east or west. Stalin's propaganda, in seeking to mobilise Russian defence of the motherland, played on Russia's glorious past, and appealed to innate Russian nationalism, rather than attempting to galvanise support for socialism. Russia's relations with the West changed with the emergence of the United States as the dominant force in post-war international relations. After the Second World War, the 'West' came to refer to both Western Europe and the United States, which was seen as the leading power in the Western camp (arguably this had been the case since the First World War).

Former Soviet President Mikhail Gorbachev opened up the debate on the course of internal reform. Gorbachev's own statements contained repeated references to a 'common European home', stressing that Europe was a cultural whole of which Russia was a rightful member, based on the country's political, commercial and cultural links with European nations. Gorbachev said in 1988:

> Some in the West are trying to 'exclude' the Soviet Union from Europe. Now and then, as if advertently, they equate 'Europe' with 'Western Europe'. Such ploys, however, cannot change the geographic and historical realities. Russia's trade, cultural and political links with other European nations and states have deep roots in history. We are Europeans. Old Russia was united with Europe by Christianity . . . The history of Russia is an organic part of the great European history.[48]

Russia's identity and its relationship with Europe returned to the forefront of political debate. The liberal Westernisers and the romantic nationalist positions were reconstituted in a form not greatly dissimilar to their pre-Soviet guises. The former tried to push *perestroika* in a more Westernising direction, the latter reacted against this and the anti-Russian character of *perestroika*. In this sense, Russia was beginning to return to its pre-Soviet history.

When the Soviet Union collapsed, the nascent Russian Federation rushed headlong into the reform course advocated by the liberal Westernisers. The task was to 'rejoin Europe' by integrating Russia as hastily and thoroughly as possible by emulating Western political and economic models. In short, a new course of Westernisation was plotted, surpassing the ambitious programmes of Peter the Great and Catherine. However, this strategy fell apart with the impact of Prime Minister Gaidar's reforms of 1992–93, which ushered in widespread disillusionment with the West and all it stood for. Instead, Russia saw the growth of a virulent form of nationalism, epitomised by Vladimir Zhirinovsky's extreme Liberal Democratic Party and its success in the 1993 Duma elections. It would be perverse to describe Zhirinovsky's nationalists as 'romantics', but they had inherited aspects of the romantic nationalist movement, the Slavophiles and pan-Slavism. The liberal-Westernisers themselves found it politically expedient to distance themselves from the unpopular West. This can be seen in the shift of Foreign Minister Andrei Kozyrev from apparent 'Westerniser' to proto-nationalist, and the development of a 'Eurasian' economic and political strategy amongst liberal parties like Grigory Yavlinsky's Yabloko.

By the time of the 1995 Duma elections, any concept of 'Westernisation' was dead. Instead, there was a broad political consensus that when it came to foreign and domestic policy, Russia would pursue a policy of 'Russia First'. Instead of emulating the West, Russia would develop its own unique political and economic model, drawing on its long troubled history and unique experiences as a Eurasian entity. 'Westernisation', begun in earnest by Peter the Great three hundred years before, had run its course and expired. Given the political, economic and social forces at work in Russia today, there seems no prospect of its early revival. The process of Westernisation had always been a top-down phenomenon and had never penetrated the roots of Russian society, which had remained insulated from mainstream Western values (including non-Orthodox religion). Without support from Russia's political elite, Westernisation is destined to fade away into historical oblivion. The ascendency of Russia First will ensure that Russia pursues its own path of development, which, although similar in some respects to Western models, is distinct from them. More significantly, Russia's pursuit of its own strategic goals and the assertion of its Eurasian identity will lead to increasing divergence between the interests of the Russian Federation and the West.

NOTES

1 'Westernisation' should be understood as having four aspects: economic, military, administrative and cultural. Thus understood this definition can be applied to both the pre- and post-Soviet period. See Rieber, Alfred, 'Persistent factors in Russian foreign policy: an interpretive essay', in Ragsdale, Hugh (ed.), *Imperial Russian Foreign Policy*, Cambridge University Press (Cambridge, 1993), p. 324.

2 Pipes, Richard, 'Russia's past, Russia's future', *Commentary*, 101:6 (1996), p. 31.

3 As suggested by William McNeil, there are three periods of history as defined by cultural dominance. The third period from 1500 to the present is that of Western cultural dominance. Cited in Ragsdale, Hugh, *The Russian Tragedy: The Burden of History*, M.E. Sharpe (New York and London, 1996), p.15.

4 Rieber, 'Persistent factors in Russian foreign policy, pp. 322–33.

5 Dawisha, Karen, and Parrott, Bruce, *Russia and the New States of Eurasia: The Politics of Upheaval*, Cambridge University Press (Cambridge, 1994), p. 26.

6 Cited in John Dunlop's article, 'Russia: confronting a loss of empire', in Bremmer, Ian, and Tara, Ray (eds), *Nation and Politics in the Soviet Successor*

States, Cambridge University Press (Cambridge, 1993), pp.68–9. Dunlop makes the point that the Russian public prefers 'nation-building' to 'empire-saving' and the loss of life associated with the latter.

7 Seton-Watson, Hugh, *The Russian Empire, 1801–1917*, The Clarendon Press (Oxford, 1967), p. 728.

8 Dawisha and Parrott, *Russia and the New States of Eurasia*, p.5.

9 Rieber, 'Persistent factors in Russian foreign policy', p. 327.

10 Rieber, 'Persistent factors in Russian foreign policy', pp. 344–5.

11 Rieber, 'Persistent factors in Russian foreign policy', p. 345.

12 Neumann, Iver, *Russia and the Idea of Europe: A Study in Identity and International Relations*, Routledge (London and New York, 1996), p. 203. (Italics in the original.)

13 See 'Russian exceptionalism: is Russia different?', *The Economist*, 15 June 1996, pp.19–21.

14 Acton, Edward, *Russia: The Tsarist and Soviet Legacy*, Longman (London and New York, 1995), p. 4.

15 From Alexander Pushkin's *A Letter to P. Ya. Chaadayev*, quoted in Starovoitova, Galina, 'The ghost of Weimar Germany', in Isham, Heyward, *Remaking Russia: Voices from Within*, M.E. Sharpe (New York and London, 1995), p.131.

16 Rieber, 'Persistent factors in Russian foreign policy', p. 352.

17 Acton, *Russia: The Tsarist and Soviet Legacy*, p. 9.

18 Acton, *Russia: The Tsarist and Soviet Legacy*, p. 9.

19 Seton-Watson, *The Russian Empire*, p. 74.

20 See Ligachev, Dimitrii, 'I object: what constitutes the tragedy of Russian history', in Isham, Heyward (ed.), *Remaking Russia: Voices from Within*, p. 57; Pipes, 'Russia's past, Russia's future', p.31; and Seton-Watson, *The Russian Empire*, p.10.

21 Acton, *Russia: The Tsarist and Soviet Legacy*, p.17.

22 Ragsdale, *The Russian Tragedy*, p.20. On Ivan III, see the same source, pp.18–20.

23 The doctrine was contained in a letter written by the monk, Filofey, to Vasily III in 1520.

24 Rieber, 'Persistent factors in Russian foreign policy', p. 350.

25 Brown, Archie, Kaser, Michael and Smith, Gerald (eds), *The Cambridge Encyclopedia of Russia and the Former Soviet Union*, Cambridge University Press (Cambridge, 1993), p.79.

26 Neumann, Iver, *Russia and the Idea of Europe*, p.10. See this page also for the period of the Polish occupation.

27 Acton, *Russia: The Tsarist and Soviet Legacy*, p.23. The *Zemsky sobor* ('assembly of the land') was a consultative body to advise the Tsar on the course of reform and his foreign ventures. It was not elected but consisted of nobility, clergy and leading merchants appointed by the tsar. Acton notes that it ' represented at least a first step towards and institutional framework for dialogue between state and commoners. The dialogue was not destined to prosper. The 1560's marked the beginning of a period of economic dislocation and social upheaval which stunted the development of Muscovy's fragile "proto bourgeoisie." '

28 Acton, *Russia: The Tsarist and Soviet Legacy*, p. 37.

29 Brown, Kaser, and Smith, (eds), *The Cambridge Encyclopedia of Russia and the Former Soviet Union*, p. 83.The suburb was actually established by Alexis in 1652 under pressure from traditionalists who wanted to protect the Orthodox Muscovites from the Western influences that the growing number of immigrant soldiers, merchants, architects, craftsmen, shipwrights and doctors (whom they deemed to be foreign heretics) brought with them (Acton, *Russia: The Tsarist and Soviet Legacy*, pp. 36–7).

30 Brown, Kaser, and Smith (eds), *The Cambridge Encyclopedia of Russia and the Former Soviet Union*, p. 85.

31 Ragsdale, *The Russian Tragedy*, p. 50.

32 Acton, *Russia: The Tsarist and Soviet Legacy*, p. 37.

33 Seton-Watson, *The Russian Empire*, p. 35.

34 Acton, *Russia: The Tsarist and Soviet Legacy*, p. 16.

35 Seton-Watson, *The Russian Empire*, p. 10.

36 Ragsdale, *The Russian Tragedy*, p. 61.

37 Brown, Kaser, and Smith (eds), *The Cambridge Encyclopedia of Russia and the Former Soviet Union*, p. 87.

38 Seton-Watson, *The Russian Empire*, p. 40.

39 Acton, *Russia: The Tsarist and Soviet Legacy*, p. 60.

40 Acton, *Russia: The Tsarist and Soviet Legacy*, p. 42.

41 Neumann, *Russia and the Idea of Europe*, p. 19.

42 See Starr, S. Frederick, 'A usable past', in Dillon, Alexander and Lapidus, Gail (eds), *The Soviet System: From Crisis to Collapse*, (Boulder, Colorado, p. 12.

43 Geyer, Dietrich, *Russian Imperialism: The Interaction of Domestic and Foreign Policy 1860–1914*, trans. by Bruce Little, Berg (Hamburg, Leamington Spa and New York, 1987), pp. 94–5.

44 Dostoyevsky, Fyodor, *The Diary of a Writer*, George Braziller (New York, [1881], 1954), p. 1048.

45 Dawisha and Parrott, *Russia and the New States of Eurasia: The Politics of Upheaval*, p. 30.

46 Neumann, *Russia and the Idea of Europe*, p .21.

47 Neumann, *Russia and the Idea of Europe*, p. 129.

48 Neumann, *Russia and the Idea of Europe*, p. 162.

CHAPTER 2

RUSSIA, RELATIONS WITH THE WEST AND THE NEAR ABROAD

RELATIONS BETWEEN Russia and the West have often blown hot and cold. This is especially the case if one takes a longer historical view of the relationship over the last three hundred years, since the days of Peter the Great. Relations undoubtedly warmed under Gorbachev (a man Margaret Thatcher could do business with), and entered their most optimistic phase between 1992 and 1994.[1] But from 1994, and particularly after the Duma elections in December 1995, it was apparent that the long honeymoon with the West was over. No longer would Russia subordinate its interests to the West. Romantic ideas of Russia joining NATO, and being accepted as an equal member of the Western club, were dead. True, Russia still wanted to join the World Trade Organisation, receive support from the International Monetary Fund and be part of a new G8, but Russia would not allow herself to be dictated to by the West. There were certain national interests Russia would pursue in the face of bitter Western opposition, whether they were supplying nuclear technology to Iran or developing arms trade. Similarly, Russia would protect its interests in its own backyard, not only in Chechnya (part of the Federation), but in its 'near abroad', including Transcaucasia, the Baltic states and Central Asia.

The evolution of Russia's foreign policy under Boris Yeltsin epitomised the drift towards Russia First, whereby the government consciously re-prioritised its goals to project a more assertive stance in areas of traditional and historical interest. For Russia, the aim was to assert its 'great power' status, even if this led to a clash of interest with the West. Indeed, convincing the West that Russia was still a global power to be reckoned with, which could not be ignored, became a primary aim of Russian policy. This desire to challenge and compete with the West was in stark contrast to the latter days of the Gorbachev era, or the first year of the Yeltsin administration. Increasingly, Russia demanded acceptance of its role as a great power, whether it was in former Yugoslavia, NATO, the Middle East, the 'near abroad' or the Far East. The raw assertion of Russian power and influence, at once both undermined and apparent in the conflict in Chechnya, symbolised the shift to a Russia First strategy.

Russia First became the dominant political school of thought in Russia which, in turn, came to determine foreign policy formulation. This chapter looks at how this process evolved, and how Russia First came to influence all aspects of foreign policy, especially relations with the West and the near abroad.

THE HONEYMOON: YELTSIN AND KOZYREV

Mikhail Gorbachev set the scene for relations with the West in the mid-1980s, beginning with the on-site inspection of military facilities (agreed at the Stockholm Conference on Security and Cooperation in Europe (CSCE) – in 1986); scrapping intermediate-range nuclear missiles under the 1987 Washington Treaty; reducing conventional forces under the 1990 Conventional Forces in Europe (CFE) Treaty; withdrawing forces from Afghanistan in 1989; and consenting to German unification and NATO membership (1990). Russia even supported UN sanctions against its old ally Iraq in 1990 and 1991.

This process of working closely with the West, and shedding the old antagonisms of the past, continued under Russian President Boris Yeltsin and his foreign secretary, Andrei Kozyrev. Yeltsin had been popularly elected president of the Russian Federation in June 1991, then the Russian Soviet Federal Socialist Republic (RSFSR), one of the fifteen republics of the Soviet Union. Kozyrev had been appointed Russian foreign minister in October 1990, while Yeltsin was still chairman of the RSFSR Supreme Soviet. Between 1990 and 1991, the Yeltsin–Kozyrev position was deemed even more pro-Western than

Gorbachev's, with its emphasis on a free market economy, devolution to the republics, Europeanism and Atlanticism. The coup attempt of August 1991 was followed by the collapse of the Soviet Union in December the same year. Yeltsin was ruthless in destroying what was left of Gorbachev's power base: the old Soviet Union. The dismemberment of the Soviet Union was the price Yeltsin was eager to pay to eliminate Gorbachev and establish himself as the undisputed leader of the Russian Federation.

Touring the world between 1991 and 1992, Yeltsin embarked upon a courtship of the Western club's institutions, including the General Agreement on Tariffs and Trade (GATT), the IMF, the G7 and the North Atlantic Treaty Organisation (NATO). Membership of the Atlantic Alliance was touted, and Kozyrev warned of the dangers of Russia becoming a third-rank state if it failed to integrate into the democratic community of nations and the world economy. Yet storm clouds were already gathering on the horizon. In a seemingly bizarre speech to the CSCE in Stockholm in December 1992, Kozyrev shocked his audience by denouncing Western interference in the Baltic states, told them to keep their noses out of the states of the former Soviet Union, demanded an end to Serbian sanctions, and promised full military support to Bosnia. He also told his listeners that the territory of the former Soviet Union could not be considered a zone in which CSCE norms were wholly applicable. He went on to say that it was essentially a post-imperial area in which Russia had to protect its own interests by all available means, including military and economic ones. Kosyrev's explanation that his speech was a parody, and a warning of what could happen were Yeltsin to be defeated by his domestic opposition, failed to reassure the international community. Later, during the course of 1993 and 1994, Kozyrev repeated such statements in earnest.

Yeltsin himself had set the tone for Kozyrev's apparently uncharacteristic lurch away from Western-inspired liberalism. President Yeltsin had told the Congress of People's Deputies back in April 1992, eight months before Kozyrev's speech in Stockholm, that 'Russia is rightfully a great power by virtue of its history, of its place in the world, and of its material and spiritual potential'. In October, two months before Kozyrev's speech, Yeltsin had told Russian foreign ministry officials that Russia was 'a great world power', which should not 'shy away from defending' its own interests, even at the risk of being condemned as imperialistic. He had torn into the foreign ministry officials, complaining that the ministry lacked consistency and suffered from too much 'ad hocism'. Policy towards CIS countries should have priority. Yeltsin had said he was disappointed with the attitude of the West, particularly the United States, which often saw Russia as a state that always said 'yes', forgetting that Russia was a great power, albeit with temporary difficulties. The only ideology the foreign ministry should follow was to defend Russia's interests and security, Yeltsin had added. Thus Kozyrev's Stockholm speech had reflected a tentative policy position previously outlined by Yeltsin himself. Although at this stage the policy consisted largely of rhetoric, the concept of Russia First had already been aired by late 1992. However, it was only the growing political momentum of the nationalists and communists, and the reversal of fortunes for the Western-leaning democrats, which saw Russia First dominate the domestic and international agenda.

Two other issues had weakened Kozyrev's pro-Western position. The first was the foreign minister's support for sanctions against Serbia, voted through the UN Security Council in May 1992. Kozyrev was attacked by opponents in the Supreme Soviet for abandoning Russia's traditional allies, the Serbs. Russia's foreign policy over the Bosnian crisis was constantly criticised. Two of Kozyrev's most outspoken critics were Yevgeny Ambartsumov, then head of the Supreme Soviet's Committee on International affairs and External Economic Relations, and Oleg Rumyantsev, the head of the Constitutional Committee.[2] The second issue which briefly reared its head was the question of the return of the disputed Northern Territories and Southern Kurile Islands to Japan. Yeltsin had supported a proposal, agreed in 1956 but never carried out, which suggested exchanging the two smaller islands of the Kurile chain in return for a peace treaty and a normalisation of relations with Japan. However, following growing domestic opposition, a planned visit by Yeltsin to Tokyo in September 1992 was called off four days before it was due to take place. Opposition was particularly strong in the military, the Supreme Soviet and the Security Council of the Russian Federation.

Both these foreign policy issues had the effect of weakening Kozyrev's position, and hence the foreign ministry's pro-Western strategy. Calls for Kozyrev's resignation had come as far back as 1991. Initially protected by Vice-Premier Gennady Burbulis, and then the president, Kozyrev's position became even more difficult following the December 1993 Duma elections. With the ultra-nationalist Liberal Democrats in first place, with 23 per cent and sixty-four seats, and the communists third with forty-eight seats, the Duma was distinctly hostile to a Western-orientated foreign policy. Finally the West's decision to expand NATO and the growing crisis in Chechnya spelt the end of Kozyrev's attempts to present an unabashed pro-Western strategy. Boris Yeltsin, too, realised it was finally time to distance himself from an overtly pro-Western policy.

The writing had been on the wall by the end of 1992. By early 1994, the 'Western' camp was in retreat, with Russia First in the ascendant. Emerging from a meeting in Geneva in April 1995 with Warren Christopher of the United States, Andrei Kozyrev said: 'The honeymoon has come to an end', the United States and Russia had entered a 'sobering period', and their post cold-war honeymoon had ended 'not in divorce, but in a growing inability to resolve the problems' that they faced.[3] The meeting came after concerns over Chechnya, the planned sale of Russian reactors to Iran, NATO enlargement and the peace process in former Yugoslavia. Tensions over Russia's pro-Serbian stance had threatened the work of the five-nation contact group, comprising the United States, Russia, Britain, France and Germany. Following the Duma elections in December 1995, Russia's love affair with the West was finally over. Russia First had come to dominate political thinking and guide government policy.

CHECHNYA AND STRAINED RELATIONS WITH THE WEST

The conflict in Chechnya had a profound effect on both domestic and foreign policy issues in Russia. Its effect on the psychology of the Russian people and their political leaders should not be underestimated. The crisis in Chechnya originated in the disintegration of the Soviet Union. Elections for the presidency of the Chechen–Ingush Autonomous Republic were held on 27 October 1991, and won by former Soviet Air Force General Dzhokhar Dudayev. Initially, Yeltsin considered cancelling the elections, but instead declared a state of emergency in the republic on 8 November, after Dudayev declared independence. Yeltsin sent interior ministry troops to Chechnya to enforce the decree, but backed down after opposition groups such as 'Democratic Russia' opposed the use of force.

There were a number of reasons why Russia could not accept Chechen independence. The most important factor was the need to maintain Russia's territorial integrity, and the importance of avoiding self-determination for the myriad of minority groups (over a hundred) in the Russian Federation. Failure to check any move towards self-determination for ethnic groups in Russia could reduce the Federation to its sixteenth-century borders, before Ivan IV conquered the khanate of Kazan. A federation treaty had been signed by all but three of the twenty-one republics and autonomous regions of the Russian Federation on 31 March 1992. The three exceptions were Tartarstan, Bashkiria and Chechnya. Tartarstan later signed a bilateral treaty with Moscow on 3 February 1994 which allowed it to collect its own taxes and have responsibility for its own foreign economic relations. Tartarstan put a broad gloss on the agreement and even suggested opening its own consulates in the European Union to conduct separate bilateral relations. The agreement could also be interpreted differently in Moscow and Kazan, especially in defining who controlled developments in foreign relations, economic and monetary policy. In effect, the agreement allowed Tartarstan to declare its own sovereignty as a republic within the Russian Federation.[4] Similar negotiations resulted in agreements concluded with Bashkiria on 25 May 1994. Chechnya, however, refused to negotiate a treaty similar to the Tartarstan Treaty, and held out for full independence from the Russian Federation.

It must be said at this point that there were considerable historical and demographic differences between Tartarstan and Chechnya. Tartarstan comprised an island of Tartars at the heart of the Russian Federation (ethnically 48.5 per cent of the population are Tartars, 43.2 per cent Russians). Mixed marriages between Russians and Tartars are common, and the republic is heavily dependent upon the Russian military-industrial complex, which has massive plants in the area. Finally, Tartarstan has been part of the Russian Empire since the sixteenth century. Chechnya, by contrast, was only absorbed into the Russian Empire in the late nineteenth century, after a long and bitter struggle. There is relatively little ethnic integration, and Chechnya by its very geographical position is on the fringes of the Russian Federation, bordering the Caucasus. Economically, apart from oil, Chechnya has never been an important part of Russia's integrated economy. Chechens still have bitter memories of the Stalinist deportations of 1944, when the population was forcibly deported to Kazakhstan, only being allowed to drift back in the late 1950s.

Second, Chechen independence was a threat to the Russian state as it could have led to instability on Russia's Caucasian frontier. Traditionally an unstable region, the Caucasus had historically seen conflicts between Russia and her neighbours in Turkey and Iran. Muslim unrest in the region could lead to direct conflicts with Russia's ancient adversaries, the Turks and Iranians.

Third, there was the whole vexed question of the potential threat to the Russian Federation from the spread of Islam, particularly its fundamentalist movement. This could not only have produced an Islamic Chechen republic on Russia's borders, but also encouraged the Federation's Muslim minorities to declare self-determination. This could have had a fatally destabilising effect on the Russian Federation, ultimately resulting in the disintegration of the country and its eighty-nine component parts (or Subjects of the Federation).

Finally, there were economic reasons for wishing to keep Chechnya in the Russian Federation. Apart from the general principle of territorial integrity, this was the most important factor leading to the armed conflict, and it certainly influenced its timing. Chechnya is an oil-producing republic, strategically situated in an area through which an oil pipeline had been planned. It also contained a number of important oil refineries, centred on its capital, Grozny. However, the pipeline was what really mattered to Russia. The planned pipeline would link the huge oil fields in Kazakhstan with the Russian port of Novorossisk on the Black Sea. Chechen independence would deprive Moscow of its oilfields and refineries as well as its planned pipeline, which instead would have to be re-routed north through safer Russian territory.[5]

For three years after Dudayev's unilateral declaration of independence, the Russian authorities procrastinated, offering desultory talks. From May 1994, Moscow offered talks based on the 'Tartarstan model'. Dzhokhar Dudayev again refused to compromise, and the Russians moved towards supporting the Chechen opposition in what was developing into a civil war. Dudayev responded by declaring martial law on 12 August. Two opposition attempts to storm Grozny, supported by Russian troops, were launched in October and November 1994. Dudayev's threat to execute Russian prisoners galvanised Yeltsin and the Security Council into action. Last minute talks between Defence Minister Pavel Grachev and Dudayev failed, and the Security Council meeting of 7 December decided to send Russian troops into Chechnya in force. It is clear that support for military action came from Grachev, and General Alexander Korzhakov, Yeltsin's personal bodyguard and confidant. The military was ill-prepared for the subsequent assault on Grozny, using ill-trained young conscripts. The initial Russian attempt to seize the capital was a costly failure.

A factor in the timing of the Russian assault was undoubtedly the question of oil. The massive Caspian Sea oil development was worth billions of dollars to the Russian economy. General Dudayev's control of Chechnya's oil refineries and pipelines gave him and his cohorts control over hundreds of millions of dollars of oil. In September 1994, a consortium of mostly Western companies signed a $7.4 billion agreement to exploit three oilfields off the coast of Azerbaijan. There was only one problem, the oil pipelines from Baku ran through Chechnya. Grozny was also a centre for oil refining. LUKoil, the Russian oil concern, was keen to use the Grozny route, taking oil from Baku on the Caspian Sea to the Russian Black Sea port of Novorossisk. Initial oil production would be around 4 to 5 million tonnes a year, rising to 30–40 million tonnes. Action became essential, as Georgia and Iran were offered as alternative routes for the oil. Furthermore, there was the future routing of the massive Tengiz oilfield in Kazakhstan which Chevron had agreed to develop under a $20 billion agreement. The latter development, led by the Caspian Pipeline Consortium, a Russian–Omani–Kazakh venture, has since decided to bypass Chechnya by running from Tikhoretsk to Komsomolskaya. Ironically, this route runs just north of the Russian town of Budennovsk, the scene of a bloody attack and hostage crisis initiated by Chechen rebels in June 1995.

The oil pipelines in Chechnya thus had to be secured, if Dudayev and his cronies were not to bleed the Russians dry by diverting the oil and the associated oil revenues. Dudayev's regime was widely held to be corrupt, with close links to mafia gangs dealing in oil, drugs and arms. In February 1996, the Azerbaijan International Operating Company (AIOC, a twelve-member multinational consortium) finally agreed to ship crude oil from Baku via Russia's pipeline network passing through Chechnya to Novorossisk on the Black Sea (from mid 1997). Hedging its bets because of the conflict in Chechnya, the AIOC also agreed to proceed with the additional route through Georgia, running from Baku on the Caspian Sea to Poti in Georgia and Midyat in Turkey. From here the pipeline network would join an existing pipeline to the Turkish port of Ceyhan.[6]

Western condemnation of the growing civilian and military casualties of the Chechen conflict were a source of irritation and embarrassment for the Russian authorities. With 40,000 civilian and military deaths in the first eighteen months of the conflict (many were ethnic Russian civilians unable to escape from Grozny), Yeltsin realised that the war would have to end, or peace talks progress, if he was to be re-elected president in June/July 1996. Domestically, there was a great deal of opposition to the war in Chechnya, both from families sending conscript sons to the conflict, and from the Duma. A movement of Russian 'mothers against the war' sprang up, and gained international support.[7] Only Vladimir Zhirinovsky's Liberal Democrats consistently supported the military response to the Chechen crisis. Democrats within the Duma feared that the military operations in Chechnya would reinforce Yeltsin's authoritarian tendencies, strengthen the hardline 'war party' in the Security Council, and encourage the president increasingly to by-pass the Duma and rule by decree. Chechnya also reinforced the Security Council as a latter-day Politburo, which increasingly took the key economic, military and foreign policy decisions, overruling the authority of the foreign ministry. The Security Council included the heads of Russia's security apparatus, and formulated policy in areas such as defence, foreign policy, economics, finance and health. As a concession to the Federal Assembly, Yeltsin co-opted both speakers of the Duma and Federation Council on to the Security Council (Ivan Rybkin and Vladimir Shumeiko, respectively). Nevertheless, the Duma continued to feel constitutionally side-lined when it came to issues of national security.

Perhaps the most important effect of the crisis in Chechnya in foreign policy terms was to give the first practical example of the 'Russia First' policy at work. Russian policy towards Chechnya was not mere rhetoric, as previously enunciated by both Yeltsin and Kozyrev; it was an example of Russia putting its own interests before the sensibilities of the West. The practical outcome was a bloody, brutal war with scant regard being paid to human rights or the lives of young conscripts or civilians. Grozny and Chechen villages were bombarded without mercy, and often without military logic (some pro-Moscow villages were attacked by Russian forces). Reports of Russian massacres and looting, for example in the village of Samashki, were widespread.[8] Chechen counter-attacks were hardly less brutal.

Russia had indicated that its territorial integrity and national security were not a matter for international negotiation. However, Russia's willingness to resort to large-scale military force, even in the name of territorial integrity, sent shivers down the spines of some of its neighbours in the 'near abroad', including the Baltic states, Caucasus, Central Asia and Ukraine. The worrying implication was that Russia might resort to military intervention in the near abroad should its security interests be threatened in its own backyard. The West's attitude to the Chechen crisis was ambivalent. On the one hand, the West did not like to be seen condoning human rights abuses and the shelling of innocent pensioners in Grozny. On the other hand, there were important strategic and geopolitical reasons for keeping Russia 'on-side', and propping-up President Yeltsin as the best ruler Russia was likely to have. Although patchy, there was more likelihood of political and economic reform continuing under Boris Yeltsin than some of his hardline colleagues in the Kremlin or Duma. The fall of Yeltsin could result in an unstable Russia, with a pronounced anti-Western bias. Alternatively, Yeltsin himself could have been pushed further into the arms of the hardline nationalists' so-called 'war party', developing a vocal anti-Western position.

There were many other reasons to prevent the isolation of Russia and its mercurial president. Russia was still a nuclear power, with large stockpiles of nuclear warheads, which could become an international nuisance should its strategic capability fall into the hands of a hardline, expansionist regime. At the very least, the smuggling of nuclear material, already a problem, could become an epidemic, with the threat of fissile material ending up in the hands of terrorists. An isolated Russia would create further problems for Europe in combating the growth of organised crime, drugs and arms smuggling. Internal strife in Russia could spill over into Central Asia and the Caucasus, where after a fashion, Russia was maintaining a degree of stability (for example, in Georgia and Tajikistan). The role of Russia as a potential counterbalance to growing Chinese power in the Far East could also be forfeited.

So, the balance of interests lay in the West supporting President Yeltsin and his government, despite personal misgivings. Hence, in March 1995, the IMF agreed to unfreeze the $6.25 billion stand-by loan, suspended because of the war in Chechnya. Yeltsin thanked both President Clinton and Chancellor Helmut Kohl for their understanding attitude towards Russia, safe in the knowledge that the IMF money could help underwrite the cost of the war in Chechnya. But Western leaders had initially been divided in their response to the conflict in Chechnya. In January 1995, François Léotard (French defence minister) and Danish Prime Minister Poul Rasmussen demanded economic sanctions in response to Russian human rights abuses in Chechnya. The Republican-dominated US Congress urged President Clinton to boycott the fiftieth anniversary celebrations of the end of the Second World War, held in Moscow in May 1995. Austria, Sweden, Denmark and Norway called for sanctions, but were resisted by the

United Kingdom, France, Germany and the United States. Germany's Klaus Kinkel and Britain's Douglas Hurd argued that sanctions would strengthen the position of Russia's nationalists. US Secretary of State Warren Christopher felt Yeltsin was the only person able to maintain political stability and control in Russia. The United States made a distinction between Russia's right to maintain its territorial integrity and sovereignty in Chechnya, and condemnation for its unacceptable human rights abuses in the conflict.

The European Union played its role in the unfolding Chechen drama. In March 1995, European Union foreign ministers decided to freeze an interim trade agreement with Russia, as a response to human rights abuses in Chechnya. The interim agreement was itself the first planned step of the Partnership and Co-operation Agreement (PAC) between the EU and Russia, largely a trade agreement, leading to negotiations to establish a free trade area after 1998. The EU eventually approved the interim accord, on condition that its humanitarian aid shipments had uninterrupted access to Chechnya. Incidentally, this condition was never met, and the human rights clause in the PAC signed with Russia was completely ignored by Yeltsin's government. Lamely, EU officials claimed that Russian negotiators had been promised the human rights suspension clause would only be used in drastic circumstances. 'They were concerned,' an EU official was reported as saying, 'but we said we needed it in case another coup attempt like the one which occurred in August (1991) were to succeed.' Resolutions from the European Parliament condemning human rights abuses in Chechnya were met with angry responses from the Duma and Federation Council. Russian parliamentarians insisted the question of Chechnya was an internal matter, which affected Russia's territorial integrity.[9] The Europeans were told to keep their noses out of Russia's internal affairs. In Chechnya, the Russians were determined to put the perceived interests of Russia above any moral qualms experienced in the West. The Chechen conflict was a clear case of the Russians pursuing a Russia First strategy, despite diplomatic and moral condemnation from Europe and the United States.

RUSSIAN OPPOSITION TO NATO ENLARGEMENT

Although the West managed to avoid a serious deterioration in relations with Russia over Chechnya, NATO enlargement was a much more difficult question to handle. Many in Russian government and security circles had hoped the pro-Western stance of Kozyrev would lead to the disappearance of NATO, and its replacement by a pan-European security structure. An analysis by the Russian Foreign Intelligence Service characterised NATO as a defence alliance with enormous offensive capabilities, wedded to a bloc mentality.[10] For a long time the Russians hoped the Organisation for Security and Co-operation in Europe (OSCE, formerly the CSCE) would take over the role, and fill the vacuum vacated by NATO. Duma Speaker Ivan Rybkin was still hoping this would be the case as late as March 1995. Rybkin said he wanted to see a 'peace belt', stretching from the Atlantic to the Urals, and expressed his preference for the OSCE to undertake this role.[11] The Russians were genuinely surprised and shocked that the West failed to take this idea seriously.

From a Russian point of view, NATO was a military alliance established to counter the Soviet Union and its Eastern European satellites. Having lost 26 million people in the Great Patriotic War of 1941–45, Russia is almost paranoid about the potential security threat to its borders. This feeling of insecurity is especially true in military and security establishment circles. NATO enlargement in Eastern Europe and the Baltic states would bring the Atlantic Alliance to its Kaliningrad frontier, and to within 150 kilometres of St Petersburg on its north-west border. Any Westerner who believes Russians could accept such an expansion of a military alliance to Russia's borders with equanimity is forgetting history. The Russians have not forgotten, either the siege of Leningrad and the half a million lost in the city in the Second World War, or the earlier invasions by Napoleon, Charles XII of Sweden, or the Tartar hordes. Russian perceptions of security are therefore a sensitive political issue amongst the political elite, the military and the population at large.

As early as 1993, it was clear that the Russians were to be disabused of their naïvety regarding the dissolution of NATO. The Partnership for Peace Programme (PfP) was devised in October 1993, largely as a sop to the Russians to prepare them for NATO enlargement. NATO formally invited other European countries to become allies at the summit in Brussels in January 1994, as foreseen in Article 10 of the Washington Treaty.[12] The PfP programme was also endorsed at the Brussels summit, and by the end of 1994 twenty-three countries (including ten CIS members and Russia) agreed to participate. NATO saw PfP as not only a means to calm Russian fears about NATO expansion, but also as a way to slow-down demands from the Central and East European Countries (CEEC) for early membership of the Alliance. Militarily, PfP also gave NATO the opportunity to begin the process of harmonising and integrating the forces and command structures of the applicant states.

Initially, the Russian response to PfP was less than enthusiastic, with Kozyrev declining to sign the PfP framework agreement on behalf of the Russian Federation. A month after Kozyrev refused to sign the PfP framework agreement, Russia launched its assault on Chechnya. Kozyrev eventually signed the PfP framework document on 31 May 1995, almost a year after Russia agreed to participate in the programme.[13] On 25 May 1994, Russian Defence Minister Grachev proposed to NATO a 'consultation mechanism' and 'broader dialogue', above and beyond what was offered to Russia under PfP. Russia was already seeking a special relationship, appropriate to her 'great power' status, and certainly objected to being treated on the same level as her East European neighbours. The proposed consultation would take place at every level, from experts to Head of State. General Grachev said: 'We are suggesting creating . . . an active mechanism for mutual consultations on all kinds of problems of European and global security.'[14] Russia also demanded that a legally binding protocol or statement be attached to the framework document to acknowledge Russia's special position as a European 'great power'. Faced with opposition from other PfP states and NATO, Russia dropped the idea, but still pursued its demand for a special relationship with the Atlantic Alliance.

Unlike the other PfP countries of Central and Eastern Europe, Russia's ultimate aim was not membership of NATO. Nevertheless, from the Russian point of view it was generally better to be in the PfP, with some influence over NATO, than outside with none. As Vitaly Churkin, deputy foreign minister said, 'As long as it is not a member of this programme, we may fear NATO accepting decisions contrary to Russia's interests.'[15] There was also a sense that, as a great power, Russia should be jointly deciding the major issues of the day with NATO. The concept of the PfP itself was straightforward. The PfP is a framework for detailed, operational military co-operation, involving multinational European security based around NATO. Partner states can join NATO forces in peace-keeping, disaster relief, and search and rescue missions. The idea is to prepare most participating states for membership of NATO. For some countries, notably the Czech, Slovak and Polish republics, PfP merely recognises existing co-operation, taking place under NATO command in former Yugoslavia. PfP emphasises civilian control of the military, and transparent defence budgets and policies. According to General George Joulwan, the Supreme Allied Commander Europe, 'Allies and non-NATO partners will share military doctrine, training, and joint military exercises with the goal of bringing our former adversaries to the east more in line with common standards, procedures and doctrine.'[16] To join PfP, the partner nation had to submit to NATO a work programme outlining the forces and military assets it was willing to contribute to the PfP, along with a description of which activities and exercises it would like to participate in.

In August 1993, in Warsaw, President Yeltsin stated Russia would have no objections if Poland joined NATO. Yeltsin's words were soon repudiated as the Russian security and political establishment combined to oppose NATO enlargement. In November 1993, Yevgeny Primakov, head of external intelligence and future foreign minister, publicly opposed NATO expansion. Speaking at the Foreign Ministry Press Centre in Moscow, Primakov said that he was speaking with the full support of the defence department and the Armed Forces General Staff. He stated that he opposed the expansion and raised concerns about Germany's role in the Atlantic Alliance. NATO enlargement would create a 'siege mentality' in Russia, pushing it behind a Western *cordon sanitaire*.[17] For the Russian security establishment, the enlargement of NATO would rekindle the Cold War, and bring the Alliance's forces closer to the heart of the Russian Federation.

Russia's opposition to NATO enlargement has not always been entirely consistent. Surprisingly, Russia's position showed some flexibility even after the resignation of Andrei Kozyrev as foreign minister following the December 1995 Duma elections (and harsh criticism from President Yeltsin). Kozyrev, a victim of the success of the growing strength of the nationalists and communists, was replaced by the pragmatic but avowedly hardline Yevgeny Primakov, the 67-year-old former head of the intelligence service. Primakov, an expert on the Middle East, could not be accused of Western liberalism. But even Primakov suggested in March 1996 that Moscow would not object to Central European countries joining NATO, as long as integrated military units did not move closer to Russia's borders.[18] He also suggested limiting NATO's expansion to Poland, Hungary, and the Czech and Slovak republics.[19] This idea was swiftly dropped by

Moscow. Later the same month, President Boris Yeltsin, visiting Oslo, made another suggestion which again seemed to contemplate Russian acceptance of the principle of NATO expansion. The previous September, Yeltsin had said: 'Those who insist on an expansion of NATO are making a major political mistake. The flames of war could burst out across the whole of Europe.'[20] Back in March 1995, at the signing of the Stability Pact in Paris, Andrei Kozyrev had urged the West not to rush to expand NATO, and called for NATO to be replaced by a new comprehensive security structure (i.e. the OSCE).[21]

Yet in Oslo, Yeltsin suggested that former Warsaw pact countries could join the Alliance's political committee without being integrated into its military structures. This seemed to imply that Yeltsin and Primakov were aware that Russia's total opposition to NATO enlargement was not working. There was a need to change tack and tactics. However, Yeltsin made it clear he was still not happy with the prospect of NATO enlargement. Speaking on 30 April 1996, a month after his Oslo proposal, Yeltsin said:

> The preservation, much less the expansion, of NATO is not merely an attempt to preserve Cold War-era foreign policy mechanisms and thinking, but also follows the path of least resistance in everything relating to the elaboration and development of a modern security system in Europe that meets the new realities . . .
> The existing security system in Europe cannot be considered effective if it is capable only of reacting – albeit effectively – to various conflicts.[22]

The West repeatedly told the Russians they could not have a veto over NATO enlargement. Warren Christopher, US Secretary of State, told Yeltsin in Moscow in March 1996 that NATO would proceed with its plans to widen its membership to include Central and East European countries, such as Poland, Hungary and the Czech Republic, despite Russian objections.[23] Nevertheless, the West was aware that the PfP programme alone would not be enough to satisfy the Russians, and allay their fears about NATO enlargement. Meeting in Carcassonne, in south-west France in March 1995, EU foreign ministers agreed on the idea of a non-aggression pact with Russia.[24] However, the Russians regarded such a proposal in isolation as inadequate.

Of more substance was the package considered by NATO, designed to offer Russia a closer security relationship with the Atlantic Alliance.

The framework for this initiative was agreed by the North Atlantic Council on 22 June 1994, when NATO ministers agreed a document entitled 'Areas for Pursuance of a Broad, Enhanced NATO/Russia Dialogue and Co-operation'. This document laid out proposals to achieve a political framework for NATO–Russia relations, elaborating basic principles for security co-operation, as well as the development of mechanisms for political consultations.[25] It also outlined how a 'special relationship' could be developed with Russia. First, NATO proposed sharing information with Russia on European security, military doctrines, preventative diplomacy, conversion of defence industries and defence budgets. Second, NATO proposed this would be done through *ad hoc* '16 + 1' discussions, involving Russia in the North Atlantic Council and Political Committee 'as appropriate', informal consultations and high-level visits. Exchange of military information between NATO and Moscow would be stepped up. Third, NATO would consult Russia on the proliferation of weapons of mass destruction (including nuclear, chemical and biological weapons), nuclear safety issues (including smuggling and pollution) and specific crises in Europe. Finally, NATO and Russia would co-operate in the fields of peace-keeping, security, ecological clean-up, science, technology and in the humanitarian field. Andrei Kozyrev approved the document, at a meeting of the North Atlantic Council in Noordwijk Aan Zee, The Netherlands, on 31 May 1995.[26]

So although the Russians were unable to stop the process of NATO enlargement in its tracks, they were successful in their secondary aim of developing a special relationship with NATO. It has to be said that this was necessarily an evolutionary relationship, based largely on an *ad hoc* approach to consultation on European security issues. Javier Solana, Secretary General of NATO, spelled out the deal on offer to Russia in a speech at Warsaw University on 18 April 1996. On the question of NATO enlargement, Solana did not mince his words to his Polish audience:

My first and foremost point is this: NATO enlargement will happen. The free choice of alignment must be the very basis on which any post-Yalta Europe must be built. It is also in our fundamental security interest to ensure that the new democracies continue to develop in a positive direction and participate in all aspects of the construction of Europe. For over four decades political and military cooperation in NATO has resulted in a degree of transparency and trust that has created a historically unique zone of stability among its members. It should be our goal to extend this zone of stability by giving our neighbours an opportunity to become part of this unique security culture.[27]

NATO enlargement was thus not negotiable in principle. Solana also rejected the idea of partial NATO membership floated by Yeltsin and Primakov. Solana stated that all those who joined NATO would be full members, with all the benefits and obligations that implied. 'NATO,' he said, 'is not interested in semi-detached members, and we are certainly not interested in ideas for political but not military membership of NATO.' All those who joined NATO would be covered by Article 5, guaranteeing collective defence under the Washington Treaty, and would have to be capable of fulfilling their obligations. Solana stated it was in NATO's interests to see a strong and democratic Russia, as a stable and reliable partner for the Alliance. A strong bond between NATO and Russia would be a key element of the 'new security order'. The NATO Secretary General pointed to Russian co-operation in IFOR in peace-keeping in the former Yugoslavia, as an example of existing practical co-operation. Russia, he pointed out, had been offered a relationship that would allow the partners to 'prevent and end regional crises and conflicts; to prevent nuclear proliferation; to devise common strategies for dealing with new security challenges; and to develop together a cooperative approach to European security'. Solana concluded by promising to pursue a NATO–Russia relationship which allowed both sides to tackle the problems they faced together: 'It would be a historical mistake to create new dividing lines in Europe or otherwise isolate Russia. We want to work closely with Russia because a healthy and co-operative partnership between NATO and Russia can and must be a key foundation of security in post-Cold War Europe.'

Thus in return for accepting NATO enlargement, Solana made it clear that Russia would obtain a formal and permanent 'special relationship' with NATO. However, the Russians still hesitated. A special relationship, with regular consultation and information exchange was all very well, but not if it meant Russia had to acquiesce in the face of the accession of all the Central and Eastern European Countries (CEECs) to full NATO membership. Yeltsin, Primakov and the Duma still had some cards up their sleeves, notably the Conventional Forces in Europe (CFE) Treaty and the START II ratification. The CFE Treaty had been signed between the Warsaw Pact countries and NATO on 19

November 1990. It set limits on the weapons that could be deployed in designated regions of Europe and the then Soviet Union. The Russians have continually pressed for the revision of the treaty since the end of the Cold War, on the grounds that the situation has changed markedly since it was ratified. The Russian military high command has campaigned against the treaty being applied to the north Caucasian district, which has become increasingly volatile since the collapse of the Soviet Union.

There was also the matter of the Russian forces returning from central and eastern Europe, which were repositioned along Russia's northern and southern flanks, including in the Leningrad military district adjacent to the Baltic states.[28] The West has argued that under the Tashkent Agreement of May 1992 and the Oslo final document of June 1992, the Russians accepted the limits imposed by the CFE, even under the current circumstances. Under the Tashkent agreement, the CIS could decide their overall deployment within the CFE ceiling. The Russians continued to argue for revised CFE limits, saying that the current treaty threatened its security in the Caucasus, and warned that they might take unilateral action. Defence Minister Pavel Grachev and the military establishment established a clear link between the CFE and NATO enlargement, arguing that expansion of the Atlantic Alliance would invalidate the CFE Treaty. Grachev's position had wide political support in the Duma.[29]

President Yeltsin said in May 1996 that 'Russia has been, is and will continue to be a great world power and will maintain reliable, strong and combat-ready armed forces.'[30] The reality was already somewhat different. Russia signed the START (Strategic Arms Limitation Treaty) II in January 1993, after Yeltsin agreed to the complete elimination of Russia's heavy land-based missile force. These concessions were opposed domestically, and in November 1993, Russia's military doctrine stressed greater reliance on nuclear weapons to counterbalance the decline of conventional military forces. After the collapse of the Soviet Union, Russia had declared herself responsible for her nuclear inheritance. By July 1992, Russia completed the transfer of all nuclear weapons without incidence. In January 1994, it was a signatory to the Trilateral Agreement, providing for the transfer of Ukrainian strategic warheads to Russia. President Kuchma of Ukraine told the Parliamentary Assembly of the Western European Union that this task had been completed in June 1996.[31] By 2003, if the START II proposed cuts are carried out, Russia's nuclear arsenal will be reduced to 3,000 warheads and that of the United States to 3,500. This would be to reduce their levels to around the number of warheads in the 1960s.

Yet the ratification of START II was becalmed in the Duma for over three years. There were several reasons why the Duma failed to ratify START II with any degree of haste. First, Russia used nuclear weapons as a bargaining chip to develop its 'special relationship' with NATO. Yeltsin and the Duma calculated that the Atlantic Alliance would be more motivated to offer Russia special consideration if START II had not yet been ratified. Second, the communist and nationalist-dominated Duma used the non-ratification of START II to indicate their displeasure with NATO expansion. Again, reluctance to ratify could wring concessions from NATO. Finally, it was Russia's strategic nuclear arsenal which gave the country any credible claim to being a 'great power'. The weakened state of the armed forces as a whole had been painfully confirmed to the world in Chechnya. If the Russians could not stop NATO enlargement, as was increasingly becoming apparent, then they had to obtain the best possible terms to guarantee Russia's security and establish the country's 'special relationship' with NATO. However, this had to be on the basis of equality, not the inferiority of Russia *vis-à-vis* the Alliance, with due regard paid to Russia's need to be accepted as a 'great power'. This was more for domestic political reasons than out of any sense of objective reality, although many in the Duma and military establishment ardently hoped Russia could once more become a great power.

NATO's agreement to start detailed negotiations with Russia in December 1996, leading to the possible conclusion of a charter or treaty governing relations between the Atlantic Alliance and the Russian Federation, can be seen as a limited foreign policy success for Yeltsin's government. While NATO prepared to announce which Central and East European states would start negotiations to join the Alliance at its summit in Madrid in July 1997, it had also recognised the importance of developing a 'special relationship' with Russia. A separate agreement with Russia would enhance co-operation with Moscow, associating the Russian Federation with the expansion of NATO. At the same time the negotiations, due to begin in January 1997, would discuss the revision of the Conventional Forces in Europe (CFE) treaty. Proposals from NATO included the formation of an Atlantic Partnership Council, linking twenty-seven countries (including neutrals, countries from Eastern Europe and the former Soviet Union) and giving Russia a direct say in the political discussions of the Atlantic Alliance. This would give Russia effective political membership of NATO, but would exclude it from decisions on collective territorial defence. Futhermore, NATO announced it would not deploy tactical nuclear forces on the territory of new NATO members in Central and Eastern Europe for the 'forseeable future'. Prime Minister Chernomyrdin's statement opposing NATO enlargement at the Lisbon Summit of the Organisation for Security and Co-operation in Europe (OSCE) on 2 December 1996 was seen as ritualistic by the West. Russia's Defence Minister Igor Rodionov acknowledged later the same month that a treaty between NATO and Russia could 'possibly' compensate Moscow for the enlargement of the Atlantic Alliance. NATO planned to admit its first new members by July 1999, the fiftieth anniversary of the formation of the Atlantic Alliance. From Russia's point of view, NATO's stance had at least acknowledged Russia's international importance, and the essential role it played in maintaining security and stability in Europe. Russia's acceptance as a 'great power' (at least in its own eyes) was seen as a vindication of Moscow's tough negotiating stance on NATO expansion. To that extent, NATO's careful wooing of Russia was seen as a success for the Russia First strategy. However, many inside Russia remained implacably opposed to NATO's eastward expansion. Visiting Strasbourg in December 1996, an all-party inter-parliamentary delegation from the Duma and the Federation Council expressed unanimous opposition to NATO enlargement. Nevertheless, Russia's parliamentarians found themselves marginalised as the NATO roller-coaster speeded up. President Yeltsin and Foreign Minister Primakov were already at the stage of negotiating Russia's new relationship with the enlarged Atlantic Alliance.[32]

NUCLEAR SALES TO IRAN, ARMS EXPORTS AND CHINA

Despite the humiliation over failing to halt NATO expansion, there were three areas where Russia was successful in setting the foreign policy agenda in the face of opposition from the West. These three areas epitomised Russia's determination to pursue a Russia First strategy in the foreign policy sphere, despite engendering a conflict with Western interests. The first area was the sale of nuclear technology to Iran. Following a contract signed on 8 January 1995, Russia agreed to sell two light-water reactors to Iran. The United States has consistently opposed the $800 million contract, on the grounds that it could help Iran develop nuclear weapons. However, Russians see American pressure as an attempt to undermine its nuclear technology exports to a profitable market. Politically, the Russians see the contract as giving leverage in discussions over the expansion of NATO and CFE limits. President Yeltsin can also portray the contract as an example of Russia putting its own commercial and political interests above those of the West. The sale of the reactors to Iran can thus be seen as a clear example of Russia First in practice. Yeltsin refused to bow to American pressure to cancel the deal, so underlining the point that Russia would not kowtow to the West when its vital interests were at stake.

Defense Secretary William Perry raised the contract with Russian Prime Minister Victor Chernomyrdin in Moscow in April 1995, and the item was again on the agenda in the US–Russian summit a month later. The United States raised the issue of nuclear proliferation, while the Russians countered that Iran complied with all the necessary inspection and supervision provisions of the Nuclear Non-Proliferation Treaty (NPT) and the International Atomic Energy Agency (IAEA). The Russians pointed out that the United States was willing to supply similar reactors to North Korea. The Pentagon supplied the Russians with intelligence that suggested the Iranians were 5–10 years away from developing their own nuclear capability, which would be assisted by the Russian nuclear contract. There were some divisions within the Russian foreign ministry and Duma about the wisdom of the contract, given the possibility of proliferation and the potential threat to Russia's own security. Nevertheless, Russia's commercial and tactical interests won the day, a dubious victory for Russia First.[33]

The second area where Russia vigorously pursued its foreign policy agenda in the face of opposition from the West was over the issue of arms sales. Soviet and Russian arms sales had continued to decline during both the late Gorbachev and early Yeltsin periods. Sales had fallen from around $12 billion a year in the early 1980s to $7.8 billion in 1991, $3 billion in 1992 and $2.5 billion in 1993.[34] Whereas the Soviet Union had vied with the United States for the title of the globe's largest arms exporter, by 1993 it had fallen to sixth place in the world's rankings. It is estimated that sanctions against Iraq, Libya and former Yugoslavia cost the country up to $30 billion in lost contracts. Following Western-led policy towards 'rogue states' thus cost Russia dear in terms of lost exports, hard currency earnings and job security for millions employed in the arms producing sector. At stake was the very viability of the military-industrial complex, and scores of Russian cities dependent on the defence sector for their main employment.

It was not lost on Russian leaders that this was one area where Russia could compete with the West, especially in terms of the high quality of the new technology employed, and the skills of its workforce and scientists. To abandon arms exports would not only generate massive unemployment but would also ensure Russia lost its own technological and skill base in the arms manufacturing sector. This research, design and production capacity was of great strategic importance to Russia. It was no wonder, therefore, that this was one area where Yeltsin and the security establishment firmly put Russian interests first. In practice, Russia First in this policy area resulted in arms exports to potential Western adversaries, such as China, Iran and Syria. Hence, Russia supplied China with missile guidance systems, S-300 surface-to-air missiles and SU-27 fighters. It sold submarines, SU-24 and MIG-29 aircraft to Iran, and T-27 tanks to Syria. Yeltsin embarked upon a strategy of increasing arms sales to underpin the military-industrial complex, signing arms deals with Beijing and New Delhi in December 1992 and early 1993 respectively. This also dovetailed nicely with the Russia First policy of closer co-operation with the East, to counterbalance the influence of the West. Arms export deals were also signed in the Middle East (including the United Arab Emirates), and the Russian government encouraged arms sales further by agreeing to establish an export–import bank and provide export credits. The aim was to increase arms exports to $9 billion a year, below the peak of the 1980s, but a significant increase on the early 1990s.[35]

Finally, there was the strategy of developing closer ties with China, often referred to as playing the 'China card' (as used by Nixon against the Soviet Union in 1971). President Yeltsin's visit to Beijing in April 1995 consolidated a marked improvement in Sino-Russian relations. Yeltsin's visit had one political aim and a number of practical objectives. Politically, it was important to show Russia and China could work together in a range of areas to further their mutual strategic interests. A close Sino-Russian working relationship could be a counterbalance to the influence of the West. This would also be in tune with the desire of the majority of the Duma (including the Communists) to build up a close partnership in both the Far East and the West, so not putting all Russia's eggs in the Western basket. Gennady Zyuganov's presidential election programme called for relations with China to be a top priority, while Vladimir Lukin, Yabloko's chairman of the Duma's Foreign

Affairs Committee, also supported closer ties with China. Lukin felt it made sense to develop commercial and political links in both the East and West, while Zyuganov particularly admired China's economic model.[36] In practical terms, Yeltsin could see a number of benefits for Russia in building better relations with China.

Economically, bilateral trade between Russia and China amounted to $5.4 billion in 1995, about one-tenth of Sino-US trade. Russia had a healthy $2.13 trade surplus with China in 1995, up from $1.9 billion in 1994. Yeltsin hoped to improve further Russia's commercial links and trade, and the summit included a memorandum of understanding for the joint development of a pipeline to transport Siberian gas to Chinese consumers and industry. Russian industry was also bidding to take part in the $30 billion 'Three Gorges' dam project, and to provide conventional and nuclear power stations to China. Accompanied by a large group of Russian businessmen, Yeltsin's entourage was particularly interested in increasing arms sales to China. In 1995 China had ordered an additional squadron of twenty-four SU-27 fighters from Russia, at an estimated cost of $2.5 billion, in addition to the twenty-six SU-27 fighters which China had contracted to buy in 1992. China was also buying Russian submarines and the C-300 solid fuel anti-aircraft missile. Russia was in a relatively strong position to boost its arms exports, given the West's reluctance to sell China its latest military equipment.

Yeltsin's government also saw agreement with China as a counter to NATO's plans for Eastern enlargement. General Pavel Grachev, then Russia's defence minister, said in November 1995 that 'if NATO looks east, then we will also look east and find allies with whom we can solve security problems'. Boris Yeltsin thus initialled a five-way agreement in Beijing, providing for border security consultations with China and the three former Soviet Central Asian republics of Kazakhstan, Kyrgyzstan and Tajikistan. The question of border demarcation in the far east was still of concern to Russian nationalists, and on the eve of Yeltsin's visit the governor of the far eastern Primorsk region, Yevgeny Nazdratenko, denounced the 1991 treaty dealing with the border issue as 'unjust'. The issue had led to armed clashes between border guards in the 1960s, and some Russian nationalists warned that the Chinese intended to annex Siberia. The fears of Russians in the far east account for the good electoral performance of Zhirinovsky in 1993, Zyuganov in the Duma elections of 1995, and Zyuganov and General Lebed in the first round of the presidential elections in June 1996. However, the Chinese were more interested in economic matters at the Beijing summit than any security threat to the 4,300-km Sino-Russian border. With Russia's preoccupation with NATO enlargement and the crisis in Chechnya, it was of greater importance to the Russians to ensure that the border issue was defused. Yeltsin's dismissed Governor Nazdratenko's fears as a 'minority view' and focused on more pressing matters in his talks with the Chinese.[37]

The People's Republic of China was pleased to do business with Yeltsin. Russia supported China over its position opposing Taiwanese independence, and Yeltsin's call for a 'socially orientated market economy' neatly matched China's desire for a 'socialist market economy'. Ironically, but not surprisingly given the ideological conflicts of the past, the Chinese showed every sign of welcoming Yeltsin's victory over their fellow Communist, Gennady Zyuganov. Chinese television reported that President Jiang Zemin and Prime Minister Li Peng both welcomed Yeltsin's presidential victory. Mr Jiang sent a telegram of congratulations to President Yeltsin, and was reported as saying that 'In recent years, Sino-Russian relations have flourished and thrived, bounding forward each day.' Jiang Zemin was trained in Moscow at the Stalin car works, and is a Russian-speaker. Yeltsin's visit to Beijing was hailed as the start of a 'new age' in Sino-Russian relations, and a foreign ministry statement crooned that the 'Sino-Russian strategic partnership orientated toward the twenty-first century on the basis of equality and mutual trust will be further enhanced'.[38] The Chinese leadership was suspicious of the national-patriotic alliance led by Zyuganov, and feared that its strident nationalism could be a recipe for conflict in Russia's Far East. For China, Yeltsin was a far more stable and reliable partner. Yeltsin was thus in the enviable position of having the blessing of both the leaders of the G7 and Beijing. He also hoped he might be able to play one off against the other. Playing the 'China card', and the re-orientation away from exclusively close relations with the West, was a necessary part of Moscow's Russia First strategy. In future, Russia would seek closer relations with China to counterbalance the power and influence of the West.

THE NEAR ABROAD

Russia continued to regard the former states of the Soviet Union (i.e. her 'near abroad') as being within the Russian Federation's legitimate 'sphere of influence'. After the break-up of the Soviet Union, Russia followed a dual-track policy towards the former Soviet republics in her near abroad. On the one hand, Russia pursued a policy of integration, largely through the mechanism of the Commonwealth of Independent States (CIS), founded at Minsk in December 1991. On the other, Russia continued to dominate its former Soviet neighbours through flexing her economic, political and military muscle. This was particularly the case in the Baltic states, which, anxious to maintain their unqualified sovereignty, remained aloof from the CIS. Russia's growing desire to develop the CIS (along similiar lines to the European Union in some respects) and her attempts to dominate the Baltic states mirrored the mounting ascendency of Russia First as the foundation of government policy. In the early days of the break-up of the Soviet Union, Russia showed little inclination to develop her relations with the near abroad, relying on her blosoming relationship with the West. As the relationship with the West cooled, and Russia First came to dominate political thinking, Russia once again turned her attention to re-establishing her hegemony in her near abroad. This was to be achieved through a Russian-led CIS, giving Moscow extensive political, military and economic leverage over her neighbours in the former Soviet republics. With the Baltic states, Russia had to rely on implicit threats and her economic might to bring the recalcitrant Balts into line. In this context Russia First was indicative of a re-prioritization of foreign policy objectives, placing greater emphasis on re-creating Russian supremacy in the near abroad.

In September 1995, President Yeltsin signed a decree declaring Russia's vital interest in integration within the CIS. Since its inception, the CIS has provided a useful discussion forum for its member states, of which there are now twelve. Frequent ministerial meetings and regular bi-annual summits have led to the signature of a large number of agreements, few of which have been implemented. CIS meetings have dealt with a broad agenda of economic, political and security ties. Russia offered CIS members military and economic co-operation to draw them towards integration.[39] In November 1995 and January 1996, CIS leaders agreed to a joint air-defence system, creating air defences in Tajikistan, Kyrgyzstan and Georgia, and up-grading those of Kazakhstan, Uzbekistan and Armenia. Russia promised to cover the costs of the necessary improvements, and was given effective control of the air defence system.[40] A payments and customs union agreement was signed by Russia, Belarus and Kazakhstan in January 1996, shortly followed by Tajikistan and Kyrgyzstan (with Uzbekistan moving closer to joining).

The CIS Summit of Heads of State, held in Moscow on 19 January 1996, apart from looking at the customs union, adopted documents on various security problems including the protection of airspace, social and legal guarantees for ex-servicemen, obligations of CIS members to resolve the conflict in Abkhazia, extension of the peace-keeping mandate in Tajikistan, and conflict prevention within the CIS. The summit also established a Council of Interior Ministers, designed to improve co-operation against organised crime, appointed a new commander of the peace-keeping force in Tajikistan, and agreed a cultural programme for the next year. On 27 March 1996, the CIS Council of Defence Ministers agreed that a new body be set up, the Joint Chiefs of Staff of the CIS. This body was established under the chairmanship of General Mikhail Kolesnikov, chief of the Russian general staff. Two days later, the presidents of Belarus, Kazakhstan, Kyrgyzstan and Russia signed an 'Integration Agreement' in Moscow. The agreement, which other states of the CIS may join, was aimed at creating 'a community of integrated states'. It provided for the deepening of integration in the economic and humanitarian spheres (especially in the fields of science, education, culture and social affairs), whilst respecting each country's sovereignty and principles, with a commitment to non-interference in each other's internal affairs.[41] On 2 April 1996, President Yeltsin and President Lukashenko of Belarus took the process of integration further, and signed a 'Union Agreement' in Moscow. This accord established a Commonwealth of Sovereign Republics, envisaging a common foreign policy, joint efforts to ensure the security of both countries and a common economic market. Each country was to retain its sovereignty, independence, territorial integrity and other national symbols.[42]

BELARUS

The 'Union Agreement' between Belarus and Russia caused immediate concern in Belarus itself, as opposition groups saw the agreement as the first step to full assimilation and absorption by the Russian Federation. Thousands of protestors marched through the Belarus capital of Minsk, a few days before the agreement was due to be signed, fearing the end of the country's independence. Protestors recalled the short-lived Belarussian People's Republic of 1918, which lasted nine months before being divided between Poland and the Soviet Union. The demonstration was ruthlessly broken-up by the crack OMON militia, warrants were issued for the arrest of opposition leaders of the Popular Front of Belarus (Zyanon Paznyak and Syarkei Naumchyk) and about two hundred people, including leading opposition politicians and journalists, were arrested during the clashes.

The Belarussian president, Alexander Lukashenko, had made no secret of his desire for integration with Russia since his election in 1994, and had received public support for his policy in a referendum held in May 1995. Lukashenko proceeded to clamp down on the Belarussian press, ban trade unions and ignored his own constitutional court. In mid-March 1996, Lukashenko dismissed the editor-in-chief of the leading daily paper, *Narodnaya Gazeta*, following a debate on the freedom of the media in Belarus. The Belarussian president had shown a distinct lack of enthusiasm for the parliamentary elections in December 1995, and even put the Russian language back on an equal footing with Belarussian.[43] Lukashenko, a former collective farm boss, also replaced the country's red-and-white national flag with a Soviet-style version. Despite denials from Yeltsin and the Kremlin that Belarussian sovereignty would be affected, the move caused concern in Ukraine and amongst other CIS members.[44] Belarus was perhaps the likeliest candidate for full integration with Russia, given its weak sense of national identity and poor economic shape. The measure was also a populist move by Yeltsin, given the nostalgia for the re-creation of the Soviet Union, epitomised by the vote of the Duma on 15 March 1996 to denounce the agreement dissolving the Soviet Union and establishing the CIS five years before.

There is no doubt that the Belarussian opposition, and the other CIS countries had cause for concern. Yeltsin himself had said that the CIS was a 'kind of springboard for strengthening the ties between the former USSR republics in the future'.[45] The 'Union Agreement' looks far more significant that a simple customs union, as presented by Yeltsin. Apart from eliminating trade barriers (under Article 4), the agreement also provided for a single currency (Article 7) and a Supreme Council, consisting of the Heads of Government, and Speakers of the two parliaments (Article 9), together with a joint parliamentary assembly with the power to adopt model legislative acts (Article 10). The Supreme Council would also establish an executive committee as a permanent executive body. The two countries would also co-ordinate their foreign policy, and co-operate on security, border protection and crime. Clearly, this was no mere customs agreement, but was the precursor to political, military and economic integration in all but name. The agreement was also open for accession by other states, a obvious invitation to other CIS members to join Russia's overpowering embrace.[46] However, all the indications are that Russia itself would stop short at full absorption of Belarus, given the heavy economic and financial burden this would represent. Instead, Russia aimed to turn the CIS into its own type of European Union, creating a zone of close political, economic and military integration, with Russia taking the major decisions. This would in fact be re-establishing the former Soviet Union, without having the economic burden of maintaining an empire. A CIS dominated by the Russian Federation is a classic example of putting Russia First.

Lukashenko's increasingly authoritarian style of government, following the referendum of 24 November 1996 (widely regarded as rigged), which increased presidential powers at the expense of the parliament and Constitutional Court, proved to be somewhat embarrassing even for Yeltsin's government. Under the terms of the referendum, Lukashenko could appoint the upper house of the parliament and select members of the electoral commission and half the Constitutional Court. The proposed new constitution would also extend the president's term in office by two years. The European Union reacted by suspending aid programmes (with the exception of those covering democratisation) and the ratification of a partnership agreement with Belarus. The European Union's Council of Ministers issued a statement reiterating its 'deep concern about the democratic legitimacy and constitutionality of the Belarus referendum and the new constitution'.[47]

UKRAINE

The only slight dampener on the whole Russian-led CIS concept was that it was not working very well. Unlike the rest of the former republics belonging to the Soviet Union, the Baltic states would not join the CIS, let alone embark upon closer integration. Participation from the twelve CIS members was fitful and uncertain. The CIS Inter-Parliamentary Assembly struggled for a role and lacked any sense of purpose or direction.[48] Integration might have been possible with a core group of the CIS, such as Belarus, Kazakhstan, Kyrgyzstan and possibly Tajikistan, but it was deeply unpopular with states like Ukraine. The CIS thus developed its own form of variable geometry, with members opting into and out of particular accords. Russia and Ukraine reached some agreement in bilateral talks during 1995, although Kiev was still suspicious of Russia's integrationist policies. March 1995 saw agreement on Ukraine's debt between the two countries, initiated by the IMF. Presidents Yeltsin and Kuchma also announced settlement of the Black Sea Fleet question in June 1995, although the details still remained unresolved. A month later Kiev signed a treaty of co-operation and friendship with Belarus, but resisted further moves towards closer integration with its CIS neighbours.

With a high proportion of ethnic Russians in the east of the country, and a majority in the Crimea, Ukraine acted swiftly to exert its control over the separatists in the peninsula by suspending the constitution and ejecting the pro-Russian Crimean president. Yeltsin's government pointedly failed to support calls by ethnic Russians for Crimean independence from Ukraine. The Russian Federation's stance over the Crimea was seen as a quid pro quo for Ukraine's support for Russia's response to the crisis in Chechnya, in defence of its territorial integrity. Russia could hardly fight a war defending its own territorial integrity against secessionists in Chechnya, while supporting Russian secessionists in the Crimea against Ukraine.[49]

One area where Russo-Ukrainian co-operation was successful was over the question of the transfer of Ukrainian tactical and strategic nuclear weapons to Russia. President Kuchma announced the completion of this process in April 1996, when addressing the parliamentary Assembly of the Western European Union. Kuchma told the assembled parliamentarians that the last strategic nuclear weapons based on Ukrainian soil had been transferred to Russia. However, he also indicated that final agreement had not been reached on the division of the Black Sea Fleet, and said that although Ukraine did not wish to apply for NATO membership, it wanted to join the European Union. It was clear that President Kuchma wanted to align Ukraine with the West, but not at the cost of wholly alienating Russia by seeking NATO membership. Nevertheless, EU membership would clearly detach Ukraine from Russia's sphere of influence, and avoid Kiev being dominated by Moscow. Western commentators expressed fears that Ukraine may find itself in a no-man's land between East and West, acting as a 'buffer zone' between Russia and NATO, with the danger that Ukraine would fall under Russian domination. Kuchma was in a vulnerable position, especially given Ukraine's dependence on Russia for debt relief and energy supplies. Ukraine was struggling to repay a £1 billion loan from Russia for energy supplied since independence.[50]

The West's response was to encourage Ukraine to maintain its arm's length relationship with Russia. In Berlin in June 1996, NATO's defence ministers stated: 'We remain convinced that an independent, democratic and stable Ukraine is one of the key factors of stability and security in Europe'. Western leaders sought to support Ukraine's independence through its participation in NATO's 'Partnership for Peace' programme, attendance at the Western European Union, membership of the Council of Europe and financial aid (the IMF provided a £1 billion credit). The EU also signed a partnership and co-operation agreement with Ukraine.[51] With a population of 52 million and its strategic geopolitical position, both Russia and the West sought to attract Ukraine to their own spheres of influence.

THE BALTIC STATES

There is no doubt that Russia had special interests and responsibilities in what has become known as its 'near abroad'. Even with its shorn empire, Russia remained both a European and Asian power, ranging over eleven time zones and over 4,000 miles from St Petersburg in the west to Vladivostock in the far east. Its links to the republics of the former Soviet Union were strong, whether in the Baltic states, Transcaucasus, Black Sea, central Asia or the far eastern region. Ethnically, politically, economically and militarily, Russia had vital interests and connections in all fourteen former Soviet republics. Regional co-operation amongst the states of the former Soviet Union was to be welcomed; reintegration dictated by Moscow would be resisted by the majority. This was nowhere more true than in the Baltic states. It was in the Baltic states that the plight of the ethnic Russians, Russian-speakers cast adrift by the collapse of the Soviet Empire, was most pronounced. Twenty-five million Russians lived beyond the borders of the Russian Federation in the 'near abroad', but it was those living in the Baltic states who caused most anguish to the motherland.

The Baltic states of Latvia, Lithuania and Estonia were fiercely independent, and wary of the embrace of the Russian bear. All three states looked to the West for security guarantees and membership of the European Union. Fifty years of Soviet occupation, dating from the

Stalin–Ribbentrop Pact, were a painful but recent memory. In November 1995, all three prime ministers of the Baltic states reiterated that they saw the need for security as the primary reason for joining the European Union.[52] Membership of NATO, it was hoped, would follow membership of the EU. Of course, there were other reasons for wanting to join, including the desire to become members of the European family once again and to raise living standards to Western levels. But fear of the Russian Federation and domination by Moscow were top of the agenda in the capitals of Tallinn, Riga and Vilnius.

Although Russia indicated it was relaxed about the Baltic states joining the European club, membership of NATO was another matter. Estonia, Latvia and Lithuania had already signed up to the Partnership for Peace (PfP) programme, which encourages co-operation and consultation on making Baltic military structures more compatible and transparent. Although Russia was itself participating in the PfP, there was a general consensus amongst Russia's political blocs that NATO enlargement should not include the Baltic states, or the deployment of nuclear weapons on the Federation's borders. From Russia's point of view, NATO was formed to counter the former Soviet Union, and remains an anti-Russian bloc. To extend this military alliance up to say, Estonia, would put NATO to within 150 kilometres' striking distance of St Petersburg. No military strategist in Russia would accept such a military deployment. Russia's ambassador to Finland, Yury Deryabin, said in an interview with a Finnish newspaper: 'No matter what [the Baltic countries] say, can you imagine a situation where Russia would have an organization like NATO on its border? Obviously, protecting Russia's security interests would then come into play. Some kind of corresponding measures would have to be taken.'[53] The Atlantic Alliance, fully aware of such sensibilities, made no firm guarantees on membership to the Baltic states. Many Western politicians and commentators also made the point that the Baltic states would be militarily impossible to defend against a conventional military attack from Russia, making any NATO guarantee worthless and incredible.[54] Such a guarantee could also undermine the whole basis of NATO, which is predicated on the assumption that NATO will fulfil its military guarantees and prevent the rout of its allies.

Security was only one of the problems facing the Baltic states as they sought to assert their independence from Russia. All three countries were plagued by political instability, and even Lithuania, which was run by former Communists and considered the most politically stable of the

trio, was riddled with internal problems. Lithuania's President Algirdas
Brazauskas sacked Prime Minister Adolfus Slezevicius in the wake of
the January 1996 banking scandal which also saw the resignation of the
chairman of the central bank. Prime Minister Slezevicius had thought-
fully withdrawn his own substantial personal savings from Lithuania's
Innovation Bank (LAIB), two days before ordering its closure.[55] In
Latvia, over thirty banks crashed in 1995, affecting half the nation's
personal assets. Estonia's government was brought down by a bugging
scandal involving Interior Minister Edgar Savisaar of the Centrist Party.
Inflation in 1996 continued to be rampant, at around 27 per cent in
Latvia, 30 per cent in Estonia and 40 per cent in Lithuania. Each
country suffered from budget deficits over the same period, with
unemployment almost double the official average of 8 per cent in all
three countries. Economically, the bulk of Estonia and Latvia's trade
had switched from the East (mainly Russia) to the West, while
Lithuania's trade was still largely with Russia. Estonia was felt to have
made the most progress economically, achieving economic growth and
performing better than any of the other republics absorbed into the
Soviet empire. Right-wing governments dominated the post-Soviet
coalitions in Latvia and Estonia. The three countries also had to face
the cost of clearing-up the nuclear and environmental legacy which had
blighted the Baltic Sea region.[56]

Politically, the main bone of contention between Russia and the
Baltic states remained the issue of Russian speakers. There was also
the question of a border dispute between Estonia and Russia, which
could have proved an obstacle to improved relations. The dispute
largely revolved around Estonian recognition of *de facto* boundaries
(demarcated under the Soviet Union), in return for Russian acceptance of Estonian sovereignty and independence under the 1920
Tartu Treaty.[57] The Russian minority issue only related to Estonia
and Latvia, since the Russian minority in Lithuania was less than 10
per cent of the population, and there was no history of friction.
However, in Latvia and Estonia the Russian-speaking population is
over 30 per cent and native Latvians make up just over half the
population. Both the Estonian and Latvian governments resented the
'Russification' policy of the former Soviet regime, whereby Russians
were sent to the Baltic states to live and work, and regarded many of
the Russian speakers as part of the Soviet strategy to erase their
cultural identity.

Citizenship laws, residency and travel permits remained a problem for many Russian speakers in the two countries and a cause of political tension with the Russian Federation. In both countries, citizenship and employment in certain spheres required the holder to pass language tests, assuming a knowledge of the law and constitution. It has to be said this caused difficulties for Russian speakers, particularly the elderly, and in some areas where there was a lack of Estonian and Latvian language courses. There were also complaints that the courses were expensive and the language examinations subjective, with no criteria for achieving a pass laid down. There was feared that the Soviet suppression of the Latvian and Estonian language would be followed by intolerance towards the Russian language, with the phasing out of Russian in schools in areas where Russian speakers were in the majority. Together, in Latvia and Estonia, there were around 1,390,000 ethnic Russians, out of a total population of 4,260,000. A plebiscite held in Latvia in February 1996 which sought to restrict citizenship to those who had lived in the country prior to 1940, failed by a 4,500 votes.[58]

Russia was determined to keep the pressure on Estonia and Latvia to give equality of treatment to Russian speakers. For their part, Estonia and Latvia feared Russian speakers could become a 'fifth column' in the event of a hostile government taking power in Moscow. The irony was that the more Latvia and Estonia resisted the full integration of the Russian minority, the more they were likely to encounter alienation and possible political instability. Most Russian speakers wished to remain living in Estonia and Latvia because of the prospects of a better standard of living and quality of life than that available in the Russian Federation. Russia itself would prefer ethnic Russians to remain in the Baltic states, thus avoiding the cost of mass relocation, including housing and employment. Dual nationality was suggested as a compromise, but was not well received in Latvia and Estonia, which feared divided loyalties, especially since many in the Russian minority had relatives in the Federation.[59] A better prospect would have been to offer Russian speakers citizenship provided they swore an oath of loyalty to their new countries, so avoiding the danger of increasing alienation and isolation. Yet in spite of these political tensions, Russia completed its troop withdrawals from Lithuania in September 1993, and Latvia and Estonia by August 1994. Earlier, in 1993, Yeltsin had told Chancellor Kohl that the withdrawal of troops from the Baltics would only 'take place according to plan if the problems of the Russian speaking population were solved in a just manner and if there were no discrimination in these states against the Russian population'.[60]

Andrei Kozyrev had also played the 'Baltic card', in his transition from liberal 'Westerniser' to avowed nationalist, following the successes of the nationalists in the Duma elections of late 1993. Speaking to Russian diplomatic representatives in the CIS and Baltic states in January 1994, Foreign Minister Kozyrev told his listeners that the defence of Russian minority rights in the near abroad was a vital strategic issue for Russian diplomacy. He advocated dual nationality for Russian speakers, and called for a retention of a Russian military presence in the area. Visiting the Russian Cultural Centre in Tallinn, Kozyrev told his audience that Russia would never forget them, and that the withdrawal of Russian forces from Estonia would free Russia's hands and enable it to defend them by any means at its disposal. Some commentators have since put a gloss on Kozyrev's remarks promising to use military force if necessary to protect the rights of Russians in the near abroad. However, senior Russian diplomatic sources have confirmed that is exactly what Kozyrev meant.[61] On 23 April 1996, Russian foreign ministry spokesman Grigory Karasin accused Estonia of deliberately pursuing an anti-Russian policy. Russian-Estonian relations continued to deteriorate as Russian speakers in Estonia complained of a law passed by the parliament in April 1996 which would effectively bar them from standing in local elections. The draft legislation would have required non-Estonian candidates to pass examinations in the Estonian language.[62]

On the whole, Russia's policy towards the Baltic states was confined to rhetoric rather than action, or even concrete policy initiatives. The suspicion remained that the difficulties of Russian speakers in the Baltic states were merely exploited for Russian domestic political consumption. The fate of Russian speakers in Latvia and Estonia was seen as a form of political virility amongst Russian politicians, particularly nationalists or those who wished to associate themselves with patriotism. Generally, the more extreme the politician, the more extreme the rhetoric, and the less the likelihood of the rhetoric being transformed into policy. Vladimir Zhirinovsky, the ultra-nationalist, talked of re-creating the Soviet Union and absorbing the Baltic states by force. The Communists under Gennady Zyuganov spoke of a 'voluntary' reformation of the Soviet Union, but admitted this would not apply to the Balts. Crocodile tears were shed for Russia's lost citizens (who in any event preferred staying where they were), but there was no sign of real concern amongst Russia's political elite. The issue of Russian speakers in the near abroad was a useful drum to bang at election time, and to put pressure on the Baltic states when it suited Russia's interests.[63]

The plight of Russian speakers in the Balts struck a chord with the electorate back home in the Russian Federation, and reinforced the population's sense of nostalgia and loss of Empire. Such emotions were combined with sympathy for fellow Russians stranded in the near abroad by the dissolution of the Soviet Union. The fact that most Russian speakers would prefer to remain living in the Baltic states, where conditions were generally better than could be offered by an over-stretched Russia, was often overlooked. Whatever the facts, Moscow's Russia First strategy ensured that the plight of Russian speakers living in the near abroad remained near the top of the political agenda, at election time at any rate. In asserting its foreign policy priorities in the political atmosphere of the late 1990s, Russian politicans could not afford to overlook those Russian citizens who lived beyond its frontiers in the near abroad. Given the sometimes tense relations with Latvia and Estonia over the rights of Russian speakers, Moscow was certain to seek to impose its will on the Baltic states, if only to impress voters at home. From a geo-strategic point of view, and bearing in mind the desire of the Baltic states to join NATO, Russia would also try to ensure that the Balts did not slip from its sphere of influence into the camp of the Atlantic Alliance. The wish of Latvia, Estonia and Lithuania to join the European Union was regarded with benign disinterest in Moscow. However, Russia could be expected to fight NATO membership for the Baltic trio until the bitter end. Russia's strident and determined opposition to the Baltic states joining NATO was yet another indication of the policy of putting Russia First. While the Kremlin's leadership hinted that it may accept NATO enlargement to Central and East European countries (such as Poland, Hungary and the Czech Republic), this indulgence had never extended to the Baltic states. Recognising the strength of Russia's views, and the problems this would entail for NATO, the West put the question of membership for the Balts on the back-burner. This, too, could be seen as a victory of sorts for Russia First.

TAJIKISTAN

In February 1993, President Boris Yeltsin said that Russia 'continues to have a vital interest in the cessation of all armed conflicts on the territory of the former Soviet Union', adding that the 'moment has come when responsible organizations, including the United Nations, should grant Russia special powers as a guarantor of peace and stability in the region of the former Union. Russia has a heartfelt interest in stopping all armed conflicts on the territory of the former Soviet Union.'[64] However, the fact was that Russia deliberately manipulated the armed conflicts in its near abroad to promote its own political and strategic interests, often with tragic consequences for the civilian populations concerned. In the Central Asian republic of Tajikistan, Russian forces assisted the pro-Russian government from late 1992 onwards, intervening to close the border with Afghanistan to prevent incursions from Islamist rebels seeking to overthrow the Tajik administration. Russia took upon itself the responsibility of leading the CIS peace-keeping forces in Tajikistan, to counter the Tajik and Afghan *mujaheddin* fighters who regularly crossed the border to mount hit-and-run attacks on Russian border guards and other targets. In April 1995, Russian retaliation for attacks by the Afghan *mujaheddin* included the bombardment of a bazaar in the northern Afghan town of Taloqan which was said to have killed 125 civilians.

Russia had 8,500 troops based in Tajikistan in 1994, and by early 1996 other CIS countries such as Kazakhstan and Uzbekistan were showing signs of growing weary of the CIS peace-keeping operation.[65] CIS leaders put increasing pressure on the Tajik leader and former member of the Soviet Communist Politburo, Imamali Rakhmonov, to come to an agreement with his rebels. With more pressing worries in Chechnya and budgetary constraints in the run-up to the presidential elections, Moscow also became exasperated by the conflict, with Yeltsin saying that Russia 'can't hold Tajikistan by the hand'. Nevertheless, the Russian operation had succeeded in Tajikistan on a number of levels. First, it had secured the near abroad against incursions by the Islamists in Afghanistan, so preventing Muslim fundamentalism from reaching the Russian Federation itself. Second, it had bound the Tajik government closer to Russia, and made it more dependent upon Moscow for its security and very survival. Third, Russia has strengthened its hand in encouraging Tajikistan to move closer to the CIS and further integration with Russia; hence the Tajiks' assent to joint security arrangements with the Russian Federation and other CIS members. In pursuing closer relations with Tajikistan, including a programme of military and economic co-operation, and by securing the borders of its near abroad, Russia was determinedly drawing Tajikistan back into its geopolitical sphere of interest. Tajikistan, initially unwillingly, was part of Moscow's game plan of putting Russia First. Increasingly, Russia's foreign policy priorities were shifting from the West to the east and south, to its own near abroad.[66]

TRANSCAUCASIA

While Russian action in Tajikistan could almost be regarded as laudable, in view of the threat from the Afghan *mujaheddin*, the same could not be said of Russia's role in Transcaucasia (Georgia, Armenia and Azerbaijan). Despite the demise of the Soviet Union, by 1994 Moscow had recovered much of its influence in the Transcaucasian region. Since gaining independence, Armenia opted for a close alliance with the Russian Federation. By exploiting the difficulties of Azerbaijan and Georgia with the secessionist regions of Nagorny Karabakh and Abkhazia respectively, Moscow obtained the leverage to pressurise the two recalcitrant former Soviet states to join the CIS along with Armenia. At the beginning of 1995, Russia's hand was further strengthened when Georgia signed a treaty granting Moscow four military bases on its territory for twenty-five years.[67] Russia's strategy in Transcaucasia was designed to re-assert the hegemony of the Russian Federation in the region, following the demise of the Soviet Union. In Transcausia, putting Russia First translated into a ruthless policy of divide and rule, including fomenting civil conflict to increase the region's dependence on Moscow. Russia's vital strategic interests in the region were pursued at a massive human and economic cost to the people of Transcaucasia.

Later, Russia's influence was somewhat eroded for two reasons. The first reason related to the Chechen conflict. The war in Chechnya strengthened the relative position of Georgia and Azerbaijan in their relations with Moscow. Russia needed the co-operation of both countries that lie adjacent to the rebel republic of Chechnya to deny Chechen rebels a base from which they could harry Russian forces. Second, there was the question of economic trends. Since 1994, the three Transcaucasian countries had embarked upon implementing economic reform programmes. Additionally, Russia's blockade of its southern borders as a result of the Chechen conflict led the three states to strengthen their economic ties with other countries. For the second half of 1995, figures showed that Russia was displaced by Turkey as Georgia's largest trading partner. Azerbaijan and Georgia also began to develop a close trading and political relationship. In March 1996, President Shevardnadze of Georgia and Azerbaijan's President Aliyev signed a 'declaration for a peaceful Caucasus', which they suggested could form the basis for a settlement of the region's conflicts.

Armenia was severely weakened by Azerbaijan's seven-year blockade in response to the dispute over Nagorny Karabakh which had been supported by Turkey since 1995. Armenia thus turned to forging new links with Iran, in spite of religious differences (Armenia is mainly Christian, Iran Shiite Muslim). Trade between the two countries expanded rapidly, and Iran was set to overtake Russia as Armenia's largest trading partner. President Ter-Petrosian of Armenia visited Tehran in May 1996, and the two countries planned the completion of a new cross-border rail link. At the end of 1994, the Azerbaijani government signed an agreement with a mainly Western international consortium for the exploitation of offshore oil fields in the Caspian Sea. Russia was unhappy with the fact that the Azerbaijani oil would pass through Georgia, by-passing Russian territory, pipelines and port facilities. Under agreements signed with Russia, in February 1996, after months of speculation, it was finally agreed that Azerbaijani oil would also be transhipped through Russia's existing pipeline network to the Black Sea port of Novorossisk.[68]

Georgia was an early victim of Russian *realpolitik* and the Russia First strategy. In 1992–93 conditions of near anarchy broke out in Georgia, as a civil war ensued between President Gamsakhourdia, who had to flee the capital Tbilisi after ruling in an increasingly autocratic manner, and supporters of former Soviet Foreign Minister Eduard Shevardnadze. Meanwhile, Russia supported the secession of Abkhazia and South Ossetia from Georgia, as a way of pressurising the Georgian republic to join the CIS. One hundred thousand Abkhaz took on four million Georgians and won, while Russian intervention also brought about the collapse of Gamsakhourdia's attempt to re-instate himself by force (he committed suicide in December 1994). More than 200,000 Georgians fled Abkhazia during the height of the conflict. Again, Russian aims were achieved, although at the cost of terrible civilian suffering as thousands died in the civil war. Georgia's very survival as a state had been in question and, although dismembered, Shevardnadze realised that it was better to work with the Russians than try to keep them at arm's length. Georgia joined the CIS on 9 October 1993 and, as noted above, granted Russia four military bases on its soil. The CIS Summit of Heads of State of 15 April 1994 agreed on the role of Russia in protecting the borders of Georgia and Armenia, and reported on CIS peace-keeping in the Georgian/Abkhaz conflict zone. Russia had succeeded in bringing a reluctant Georgia into the CIS, and its political orbit. Moscow also gained a military foothold in the Caucasus, both in terms of stationing 5,000 peace-keeping troops in the republic and establishing military bases on Georgian territory. Times were as good for Russia as under the old Soviet Union, without the cost of running Georgia and subduing Transcaucasia. Georgia had been brought firmly under Russian influence, joined the Russia-led CIS, and had to accept the presence of Russian troops on its soil. Moscow had succeeded in bringing Tbilisi to heel, a lesson Shevardnadze would not forget. Once again, Russia had extended its access to the Black Sea, and Tbilisi was looking to Moscow.

The failed assassination attempt on Shevardnadze on 29 August 1995 strengthened the former foreign minister's hand, as he disbanded the militias and gained economic support from the IMF. Shevardnadze easily won the presidential election of 5 November 1995 with 74 per cent of the vote. But Georgia's problems were momentarily complicated by political developments in Moscow. At the beginning of February 1996, Abkhazian separatist forces carried out a series of punitive operations against Georgian refugees which led to a new exodus to Georgia. The rise in tension was linked to the imminent June presidential elections in Russia. A month before, on 19 January, President Shevardnadze scored a political victory when he persuaded CIS leaders to impose a full blockade on Abkhazia. At the beginning of February, the Georgian government declared all trade with Abkhazia would be banned, with only limited humanitarian supplies permitted. Shevardnadze had thus come to acknowledge the CIS as a useful tool in his struggle against the Abkhazian separatists.

Abkhazian President Ardzinba stepped up his lobbying of Yeltsin's communist opponents in Moscow in response to Shevardnadze's measures. At the beginning of February 1996, Ardzinba was received by the chairman of the Duma's committee for CIS affairs, a meeting which led to strong protests by the Georgian government. In April 1996, a delegation from the Duma visited Abkhazia without informing the Georgian authorities. Moscow's communists (KPRF) took a strongly pro-Abkhazian line, in contrast to Yeltsin's increasingly close ties with Tbilisi and Shevardnadze. Communist support for Abkhazia was politically expedient for a number of reasons. First, it contrasted with Yeltsin's pro-Georgian position, and his 'abandonment' of the separatists, who were close to Moscow (and initially encouraged by the Kremlin). Second, it fitted in with the Communist Party's idea of re-creating the Soviet Union, by destabilising Georgia and effectively detaching part of its territory and putting it under the control of Moscow's surrogates. Third, it gave concrete expression to the commu-nists' support for kith and kin living beyond the borders of the Russian Federation, even though the Abkhazians were not ethnic Russians. The mutual support provided to each other by separatists in Chechnya and Abkhazia made this position somewhat inconsistent, as the communist members of the Duma supported separatists in Abkhazia but condemned the threat to Russian territorial integrity posed by Chechen rebels in Chechnya.[69]

Yeltsin's Russia First strategy was slightly more sophisticated. The conflicts in Abkhazia and South Ossetia were useful tools for bringing Georgia into the CIS and under Moscow's thumb. With Yeltsin's strategy, it was not necessary to control Georgian territory physically, or to re-absorb Georgia into a greater Russian Federation. The mere threat of instability, the stationing of Russian troops, and Moscow's influence through the CIS, was enough to ensure Georgian compliance with Russia's political and strategic leadership in Transcaucasia. Moscow's Russia First strategy had, on the basis its own criteria, succeeded in Georgia.

Armenia inherited the crisis in Nagorny Karabakh from the Soviet Union. The Nagorny Karabakh Soviet, an Armenian-populated enclave in Azerbaijan, had demanded unification with Armenia on 20 February 1988. Anti-Armenian pogroms followed in Sumgait, Kirovabad and Baku. In February 1990, the Azerbaijan-Armenian war began in earnest with an Azeri assault on the Shaumian region. Moscow had made itself directly responsible for Nagorny Karabakh in 1989, and played both sides off against each other in the conflict. Initially, the Soviet regime in the Kremlin appears to have supported Azerbaijan in its attempt to maintain the territorial integrity of the borders established by Stalin in 1921. On 10 December 1991, following the collapse of the Soviet Union, Nagorny Karabakh became independent by referendum. The war continued to escalate, with the Nagorny Karabakh defence forces taking the Shushi and Latchin corridor in the spring of 1992 which provided a link between the region and Armenia. With the support of Russia, which had now switched sides in the war, the Armenians of Nagorny Karabakh widened the Latchin corridor. The Nagorny Armenians went on to take control of the Kelbadjar region, and the region between Fizouli, the Iranian frontier and Latchin.

Again, Russia provided clear moral and materiel support to Armenia. For its part, Armenia and the authorities in Yerevan replied by lending support to Russia by engaging wholeheartedly in the CIS. Moscow was laying down two markers for Azerbaijan. First, it should participate fully in the CIS. Azerbaijan had 'opted-out' of CIS agreements on security measures and joining the Inter-Parliamentary Assembly. By 1993 Azerbaijan had got Moscow's message, and on 24 September President Geidar Aliyev signed CIS accession documents, and agreed to sign the CIS Charter and Treaty on Collective Security (CST). Azerbaijan had succumbed to Russia's ambitions to influence the region through the mechanism of the CIS. In February 1996, the two countries reached preliminary agreement on joint policing of their common border. Second, Russia was warning Azerbaijan not to ignore Moscow's interests when it came to the question of Caspian oil. Russia was particularly fearful that Turkey and Iran, its historical rivals in the region, would gain control of Caspian oil supplies. Baku duly noted the latter, and agreed to route at least one major pipeline through Russian territory. LUKoil, the Russian State oil company, also obtained a 10 per cent stake in the Azerbaijan International Operating Company (AIOC).[70] Russia's vital interests in Azerbaijan were secured politically, militarily and economically. Azerbaijan had been compelled to fall into line with Moscow, or find itself literally out-gunned in the conflict with Armenia, which had received military backing from Russia.

The Nagorny Karabakh region remained calm between 1994 and 1996, following a ceasefire agreed in May 1994. Russian troops, through the CIS, also maintained a peace-keeping presence, with around 5,000 troops based in Armenia. President Yeltsin's statement in February 1996 that the Nagorny Karabakh enclave had little hope of independence from Azerbaijan caused dismay in Yerevan.[71] Adding to Armenia's woes, the energy shortage caused by the blockade forced Armenian President Levon Ter-Petrosian to put the Medzamor nuclear plant back in service. The Medzamor nuclear station is probably the world's most dangerous nuclear plant, sited as it is in a highly unstable earthquake zone. President Ter-Petrosian of Armenia was re-elected president on 23 September 1996, after allegations from both the opposition and international observers of widespread fraud at the polls.[72]

Meanwhile, parliamentary elections in Azerbaijan in November 1995 confirmed Azerbaijan's reputation for also being less than democratic, and strengthened President Aliyev's hold on the country. President Aliyev, a former Politburo member and head of the KGB, moved closer to Moscow in 1996, as relations with Iran deteriorated. Although a secularized country, Azerbaijan has ethnic, religious, political and cultural links with Iran. Azerbaijan has, like Iran, a Shiite majority. Notwithstanding, relations between Iran and Azerbaijan soured after Baku rejected a bid by Iran's oil company to participate in the AIOC oil consortium. Iran had effectively been squeezed out by Moscow. Relations continued to be tense, and in a press conference in Baku on 1 March 1996, Azeri Foreign Minister Hasan Hasanov accused his Iranian counterpart, Ali Akhbar Velayati, of supporting Armenia over the Nagorny Karabakh conflict.[73] In the event, the only winner in the struggle over Nagorny Karabakh was Moscow's Russia First policy.

MOLDOVA

Russia's tried and tested strategy of divide and rule (as applied in Georgia, Armenia and Azerbaijan) also worked in Moldova. Russia used the same tactics of piling on the pressure by fomenting civil conflict, so bringing Moldova under Moscow's thumb. Russia First necessitated Moldova's incorporation within Russia's sphere of influence, and submission to the Kremlin's will. Here, Moscow once again became involved in a regional dispute, with slightly more justification as it was supporting ethnic Russians who feared Moldovan and Romanian domination. It was here in Moldova that General Alexander Lebed, as commander of the 14th Army, established his national reputation before the 1995 Duma elections. Lebed gained national fame for protecting the ethnic Russians of the Trans-Dniestr region, enforcing a ceasefire and clamping down on corruption in the army and beyond. Adored by his troops and ethnic Russians and Ukrainians living in the near abroad, Lebed was less beloved by the Russian military high command, whom he came increasingly to criticise over rife corruption and incompetence during the war in Chechnya. Nevertheless, General Lebed helped Moscow's cause by bringing Moldova to heel, and ensuring the Moldovans played their full part in the CIS, as desired by the Kremlin. After dealing with Lebed, Moldova meekly agreed to Russian, Moldovan and Trans-Dniestrian troops being deployed in Moldova under a trilateral agreement.[74] On 8 April 1994 Moldova ratified her accession to the CIS Almaty Declaration, the Minsk

Agreement and the Treaty on Economic Union, with the Moldovan president signing the CIS charter a week later. By February 1995, despite its constitution declaring its neutrality, Moldova agreed to participate in CIS military zones proposed by Russia, so enhancing CIS security, on an 'ad hoc basis'.[75]

Moldova, a small republic of just over 4,360,000 people, was almost totally dependent on Russia and other CIS members for supplies of fuel and raw materials at intra-CIS contractual prices, and as outlets for Moldovan agricultural exports. Sandwiched between Romania and south-eastern Ukraine, Moldova was ethnically diverse. Around 63 per cent of the republic's population was Moldovan/Romanian. This was the largest group (about 40 per cent of the population of Trans-Dniestria), although not all spoke Romanian, many preferring Russian, and many more having learnt Russian at school rather than their mother tongue. Ethnic Russians constituted 14 per cent of the total population of Moldova. The city of Tiraspol on the left bank of the Dniester is the main Russian city, but has a mixed population of Russians, Moldovans and Ukrainians as well as a large Russian Army presence. Ethnic Ukrainians constituted around 12 per cent of the national population, and there were also Bulgarian and Gagauz minorities. Russia's 14th Army, part of the Odessa Military District, formerly commanded by General Lebed, had 18,000 men across Moldova, and was the largest military unit in the country.

The conflict began in Moldova with fears that the Moldovan Republic would unite with Romania. These fears were increased by laws passed in 1989 establishing Romanian as the official language. A large part of the present territory of Moldova, historically known as Bessarabia, had at some point in history been part of Romania. The majority of the population in Trans-Dniestria is of Russian or Ukrainian descent and, following a referendum, the Declaration of an Autonomous Trans-Dniester region was promulgated on 2 September 1990. An ethnic Russian, Igor Smirnov, was declared president of an 'independent' Trans-Dniestria, although the territory is not internationally recognised. Violence in November 1990 escalated into fighting in the autumn of 1991, intensifying in the spring of 1992. Poorly organised Moldovan police forces were confronted by the 'Dniester Guards', with resulting high casualties, and damage to property and infrastructure. The Dniester Guards were openly backed by the Russian 14th Army, a multi-ethnic force still drawn from all parts of the former Soviet Union. A ceasefire was declared in July 1992 and peace-keeping arrangements were established under the auspices of Russia and Moldova, with Trans-Dniestrian participation. Some 3,300 Russian troops were brought to Moldova to act as peace-keepers alongside the 14th Army.[76] The rebels sought complete control over their own destiny in a confederal arrangement and the right to self-determination in the event that Moldova merged with Romania. The Moldovan authorities in Caisson instead offered the rebels control over local services, control over aspects of the region's economy, a bicameral regional parliament and the right to self-determination in the event of unification with Romania. The separatists continued to hold out for full independence. In August 1994, as a symbol of defiance, the Trans-Dniestrian rebels introduced their own currency, the Dniester rouble.

The February 1994 national parliamentary elections in Moldova saw an improvement in relations between Moldova and Russia. The winners of the election were the pro-statehood Agrarian Democratic party (with 43 per cent) and the pro-Russian Socialist party (22 per cent). The chairman of the Agrarian Democratic party, Petru Lucinschi, outlined his party's programme as full independence from Romania and Russia; rejection of Russia's demand for military bases; withdrawal of Russian troops; demilitarisation Moldova; and participation in the economic (but not politico-military) agreements in the CIS and other international organisations. Greater Moldovan involvement in the CIS was particularly significant. On 28 July the Moldovan parliament approved a new constitution. The new constitution proclaimed Moldova a sovereign, united and indivisible state, with provisions allowing for the creation of autonomous regions. The constitution also declared 'Moldovan' the state language, as opposed to Romanian, which had been proclaimed the official language in 1989. The parliament also voted to give up the country's national anthem, which was identical to the Romanian one. Both initiatives were seen as pro-Russian and pro-CIS policies promoted by the new ruling parties. The constitution also pledged to protect the use and development of other languages used by the local population, including Russian. Incidentally, the new constitution declared Moldova's 'permanent neutrality', a status which came under increasing Russian pressure as Moldova was sucked into the joint security arrangements agreed by the CIS.

The Trans-Dniester Region did not participate in a plebiscite initiated by Moldovan President Snegur on 6 March 1994 which sought to assert popular support for the country's independence. The separatist authorities in Tiraspol took this as an indication of the region's determination to achieve its own statehood. Moldova's newly elected prime minister, Andrei Sangheli, pursued a policy of integration with the CIS and strengthening closer ties with other CIS countries, as a counterweight to the instability threatened by the secessionists. Although Moldova argued for the complete withdrawal of the 14th Army, Moscow wanted it to stay, using the threat of secession by the 'Trans-Dniester Republic' to maintain its military presence. Estimates suggested there were around 345,000 tonnes of Russian weapons and equipment based on Moldovan soil. Moscow deliberately frustrated Moldovan plans to set up an army fully independent of the CIS joint command. While Mr Popov, the Moldovan foreign minister, stated that Romania was Moldova's foreign policy priority, he also acknowledged that Russia was still the country's main trading partner (with Romania in second place).[77]

Russia's grip on Moldova, politically, militarily and economically, was unyielding. Like Azerbaijan and Georgia, Moldova discovered its attempts to turn away from the Russian bear were both dangerous and futile. Moscow's Russia First policy meant that Moldova remained firmly within Russia's immediate sphere of influence. Riding to power on a wave of pan-Romanianism, President Snegur and the Agrarian Democrats turned their backs on the concept of a united Greater Romania. This retreat from pan-Romanianism caused intense disappointment in Romania itself, and the cooling of relations between Caisson and Bucharest. For Moldova, the trick is to assuage relations with both Moscow and Bucharest, to avoid being swallowed by either or both, as occurred in the nineteenth century. Territorial insecurity in Russia's near abroad is a historical fact of life.

CENTRAL ASIA

Central Asia was also an area of crucial strategic importance for Moscow. Consisting of Kazakhstan, Kyrgyzstan, Tajikistan, Turkmenistan and Uzbekistan, Central Asia has immense oil and gas reserves in the Eastern Caspian and Northern Kazakhstan regions, and is a major supplier of uranium and other minerals. From the Kremlin's point of view, it was essential to restore influence in the region following the dissolution of the Soviet Union and years of political neglect. Under President Yeltsin's administration, Russia First entailed a reappraisal of the importance of the region, which had been virtually ignored during the honeymoon period with the West. The result was a strategy which not only sought to regain Moscow's regional hegemony, but also to impose an economic stranglehold on Central Asia (routing trade through Russia), to encourage participation in the Russian-led CIS, and to assert Russia's military role as guardian of the region's territorial integrity.

The first presidents of the three energy-rich republics (Kazakhstan, Turkmenistan and Uzbekistan) were all former Soviet Communist Politburo members, and their governments have been characterised by authoritarian forms of leadership. The newly independent states of Central Asia were amongst the poorest of the republics of the former Soviet Union, despite some extremely valuable natural resources. Given their relative poverty (Tajikistan had an estimated gross domestic product per head of $815), Moscow had lost little of net value with the disintegration of the Soviet Union.[78] Indeed, it had been argued that there was no benefit which would accrue to Russia if the Central Asian states were re-integrated into a 'Greater Russia' either directly or via integration through the CIS.[79]

President Yeltsin's administration had long advocated policies which put the health of the Russian economy above support for other former Soviet republics. Begun in the Soviet era, this early Russia First strategy had been antipathetic to Central Asia, regarding it as an undeveloped burden on Russian resources. Gennady Zyuganov's Communist and nationalist supporters also treated Central Asia as of secondary importance, compared to the Baltic states and Moldova, arguing that Russia should reclaim its debts from its impoverished neighbours.[80] Political instability, particularly in Tajikistan, insecure borders and inter-regional rivalry made Central Asia a potential political and economic liability to any partner state or overlord. The Russian Federation also had other relationships and policy areas arguably of greater importance, for example relations with the West, Ukraine, Baltic states, Caucasus, China, Iran and the Indian sub-continent.

Nevertheless, Central Asia was of significant importance to Moscow for a number of reasons. First, there was the potential threat to Russia's security if the Kremlin did not assist with maintaining the region's territorial integrity. There was the possible spread of Islamic fundamentalism to contend with, whether it be on the Tajik-Afghan border or elsewhere. The spread of fundamentalism into Russia's Muslim territories is a traditional fear of Moscow. Second, it made sense to ensure that the region's oil and gas products were exported to and via Russia, especially when it came to the question of building pipelines. Third, it was better to have Central Asia in Russia's sphere of influence than to let it fall under the sway of Turkey or Iran, historical Russian enemies, and competitors for control of oil and gas supplies. Hence the importance of integrating Central Asia with the CIS, whilst not shouldering any of the region's economic problems. Fourth, Russia had to support Central Asia against any Chinese expansionist tendencies. In any event, it is true to say that Russia's relations with the states of Central Asia varied considerably, as did relations among the five states. From the point of view of the Central Asian states, co-operation with Moscow meant preferential terms of trade, cheap Russian credits, and easy access to Russian raw materials, energy and markets.

Half the size of the United States, Kazakhstan is a land of treeless steppes and barren deserts. Abused by the Soviet regime for seventy years, Kazakhstan was both the Soviet Union's dumping ground and experimental heart: for nuclear tests at Semipalatinsk and space exploration at Baikonur. In this land of the gulag and the cosmonaut, independence came as quite a shock. The country was a mixture of Turkic-speaking Kazakhs, ethnic Russians and a variety of other nationalities. Kazakhstan emerged from the Soviet Union a poor, environmentally devastated land, but with a good energy and transport infrastructure, and an educated workforce. Early indications that Russia was reluctant to allow Kazakhstan to join the CIS were overcome by Kazakh President Nursultan Nazarbayev, who pressed for early membership. Nazarbayev's pro-CIS and pro-Moscow position was heavily influenced by the fact that Russia imported 90 per cent of Kazakhstan's output and supplied most of its oil and other requirements. From Russia's point of view, the relationship with Kazakhstan was as much commercial as strategic.

On 27 April 1996 Moscow approved the construction of a 750-km oil export pipeline from Tengiz in Kazakhstan on the Caspian Sea through southern Russia to the Black Sea port of Novorossisk. The pipeline would open up the Caspian Sea region as an important energy source for Europe and Asia in the twenty-first century. Russia accepted Kazakhstan's sovereignty over the gas and oil deposits discovered by Soviet geologists in return for an equity stake in the pipeline consortium for the Russian state and Russian oil companies. The $1.5 billion pipeline would be built by the Caspian Pipeline Consortium (CPC) by the end of the century, giving the Russian government and two Russian oil companies, LUKoil and Rosneft, a combined 44 per cent share in the pipeline. Construction would be mostly financed by Western oil companies, including Chevron, Mobil, BP and Agip, which accepted that the Russians would have to be given a generous equity stake in order to guarantee transport and access to Western markets. Such projects would enable Russia to become a major player in the supply of energy to Western markets in the twenty-first century, despite the fact that many of the richest deposits lay outside the territory of the Russian Federation.[81]

With neighbours like Russia and China, President Nazarbayev had to chart a careful political course. Russia remained Kazakhstan's major trading partner, and controlled access to export routes for oil and gas. Militarily, Russia was a bulwark against any attempts by China to encroach upon eastern Kazakhstan (the capital, Almaty, is 300 km from the Chinese border). To pacify the Chinese, Nazarbayev kept silent about Chinese nuclear tests, held just across the border, and clamped down on the Uighur minority, which supported an Uighur independence movement in northern China. With a large Russian minority (35 per cent in 1995) out of a total population of 17 million, President Nazarbayev offered concessions to keep ethnic Russians from deserting Kazakhstan. There were 458,000 fewer Russians in Kazakhstan in 1995 than in 1989, and over 1 million more Kazakhs. In 1994, Muslims outnumbered non-Muslims in the country for the first time since the 1920s. A further 480,000 ethnic Germans left Kazakhstan for Germany after the break-up of the Soviet Union.[82] The haemorrhage of Russians was particularly damaging for the Kazakh economy, as the ethnic Russians tended to be the most highly skilled members of the workforce and dominated the state bureaucracy. Nazarbayev was careful to avoid the overt discrimination the Russians in the near abroad have suffered in the Baltic states, for example maintaining Russian and German schools, although the teaching of Kazakh as a second language was introduced. Nazarbayev himself more often addressed his people in Russian rather than Kazakh. Both the head of the president's administration and leading ministers were ethnic Russians. These tactics reduced the flow of emigration, as only 25,000 people emigrated from Kazakhstan in the first quarter of 1996, compared with half a million in 1994.[83]

Part of Nazarbayev's success was to encourage both foreign investment and optimism in his country's future. However, it was not all a fairy tale success story. Since 1994, Nazarbayev, like his Central Asian colleagues, developed authoritarian tendencies. President Nazarbayev dissolved the previous parliament or Majilis on a legal technicality in March 1995, when the parliamentary elections were declared 'illegitimate' following a ruling by the Constitutional Court. There had been allegations of voting irregularities and electoral manipulation. Nazarbayev used the court ruling to exert his presidential authority and rule by decree. Having dismissed the parliament, Nazarbayev promptly held a referendum extending his term of office until the year 2000. A new constitution followed, based on the French presidential system, further strengthening Nazarbayev's position.[84] When the Russian Duma voted to ignore the 1991 dissolution of the Soviet Union, Nazarbayev acted swiftly to ban local branches of Lad (Harmony), a Russian minority party. The Russian newspaper, *Komsomolskaya Pravda* was banned in May 1996 after it printed a statement by Alexander Solzhenitsyn, calling for the partition of Kazakhstan between Russians and Kazakhs.[85]

Facing a docile Majilis, elected in December 1995 from mainly government supporters in an election widely seen as manipulated by the president, Nazarbayev in effect ruled Kazakhstan with no substantial constitutional constraints. Meanwhile, Kazakhstan continued to develop its close relationship with Russia. Joining the customs union with Russia, which included Belarus and Kyrgyzstan, Nazarbayev saw the agreement as purely in Kazakhstan's economic interests, saying 'Why should we let the Russian market pass us by? It's profitable for us to send our goods there. When we signed the quadrilateral agreement, we made sure this agreement would not clip our wings and that it would leave no room for imperial ambitions.'[86] With such a practical approach to Russo-Kazakh relations, Nazarbayev could expect his warm and close relations with Moscow to continue indefinitely. Yet, although Nazarbayev may not have liked to admit it, Kazakhstan was also being drawn into Russia's security orbit through joint military co-operation agreed under the auspices of the CIS. This included participation in a joint military command and peace-keeping operations in Tajikistan.[87] In Kazakhstan's favour, it was perhaps in both countries' interests to remain separate entities, even if moving closer towards each other in terms of political, economic and military co-operation.

Of the remaining Central Asian states, Tajikistan, Kyrgyzstan and Turkmenistan were dependent upon Moscow, with only Uzbekistan asserting a more independent position. In 1993, US Vice-President Al Gore called the republic of Kyrgyzstan a 'bulwark of democracy in the region'. For many years the country had been referred to as an 'island of democracy' in Central Asia. With China on its eastern border, Uzbekistan to the west (neither known for their democratic norms), increasingly autocratic Kazakhstan to the north, and strife-torn Tajikistan to the south, Kyrgyzstan sounded like a positive paragon of democratic values in comparison. Kyrgyzstan acquired three times more investment and aid per capita than any other former republic of the Soviet Union.[88] The country's reputation for constitutional probity collapsed when Kyrgyz President Askar Akayev decided to hold the presidential election one year ahead of schedule in December 1995. Akayev thus joined the presidents of Turkmenistan, Uzbekistan and Kazakhstan, who avoided elections and extended their terms in office in 1994 and 1995. Akayev's move was preceded by the sacking of the parliament's speaker, and the dissolution of the whole parliament in September 1994. Akayev easily won the presidential election, after three of the six presidential candidates were disqualified from standing, due to alleged registration irregularities. President Akayev followed up his electoral coup by holding a referendum in February 1996, which amended the constitution and increased his own powers. Sadly, even after such obvious electoral manipulation, Kyrgyzstan passed for a relatively democratic country in Central Asia.

President Askar Akayev's greatest threat came not from internal political opposition, but from social unrest and conflict between the country's ethnic Kyrgyz and Uzbek populations. Social unrest flowed from the weakness of the economy, poverty and the inability to pay wages regularly. In 1995, gross domestic product per head of the population was estimated at just $302, while the economy remained dominated by an inefficient agricultural sector.[89] Although the government banned the minority Uighur society, this was, as in the case of Kazakhstan, more a sop to China than an indication of widespread political repression. Nor had there been the sweeping use of imprisonment and use of violence as witnessed in Turkmenistan and Uzbekistan. Mainstream groups faced harassment in Kyrgyzstan, rather than outright bans. In addition to social unrest and inter-ethnic conflict, Akayev feared the regional ambitions of Uzbekistan, seen as the strongest power in Central Asia. Kyrgyzstan, with 4.75 million inhabitants, had less than a quarter of Uzbekistan's total population. To counter the threat from Uzbekistan, President Akayev sought closer integration with the CIS, relying on the Russian bear to hold the Uzbeks in check. Returning the favour of Yeltsin's support during his presidential election campaign, Akayev backed Yeltsin's presidential bid, declaring that 'every leader makes mistakes and Mr Yeltsin has also made them'.

President Akayev's support for the CIS especially endeared him to Moscow, with Yeltsin declaring enthusiastically, 'The energy with which Akayev is carrying out reforms calls for admiration. A country that has such a leader has a big future.'[90] On 29 March 1995 the Kyrgyz Republic joined the customs union between Russia, Belarus and Kazakhstan. The customs union envisaged the creation, within five years, of a community of integrated states, including inter-parliamentary and inter-governmental bodies. While Russia remained reluctant to bankroll Kyrgyzstan or the other Central Asian states, the CIS strategy did ensure that the Russian Federation had in effect projected its forward defences beyond its formal frontier. This also tied in with Moscow's overall Russia First policy, and the re-assertion of Russia's leadership in Central Asia. From the point of view of Kyrgyzstan, Russia was a guarantee against the spread of conflict from Tajikistan, or potential aggression from Uzbekistan. A few days before signing the customs accord, to placate the Russian minority and smooth relations with Moscow, the Russian language was placed on a equal footing with Kyrgyz. President Akayev also hoped this would halt the exodus of ethnic Russians, who had declined from 22 per cent of the population in 1989 to 17 per cent in 1996. As in much of Central Asia, ethnic Russians tended to predominate in managerial and skilled roles, and the Kyrgyz economy would find it difficult to replace them in the medium to short term. In a move beneficial to Russia, ITAR-TASS reported on 15 April 1996 that $132 million of Kyrgyzstan's debt to the Russian Federation would be paid off in equity stakes in thirty-nine industrial firms.[91]

Tajikistan's President Imamali Rakhmonov continued to face a disastrous political situation in the spring and summer of 1996, with a war raging between government and opposition forces, backed by Afghan *mujaheddin*. In the wake of the 1992 civil war, parties associated with the anti-communist regime of September–November 1992 were banned. Internal clashes between factions from the Kulyab and Leninabad regions, and a rebellion in early 1996 from previously loyal military commanders, added to President Rakhmonov's woes. With the country facing deteriorating political conditions, Tajikistan became increasingly dependent upon Western aid, with the World Food Programme estimating that around 85 per cent of the population were living below the poverty line in 1996. Aid donors included the US

Department of Agriculture and the European Union, with the latter providing 5,500 tons of flour in May 1996.[92]

Meanwhile, Russia maintained its support for Tajikistan's territorial integrity, stationing a motor-rifle division in the country. Russia was joined in its peace-keeping task by Kazakhstan, Kyrgyzstan and Uzbekistan, which agreed to contribute troops to secure the Tajik-Afghan border at a CIS summit in January 1993. On 24 August these forces were then placed under one single (Russian) command.[93] Tajikistan's dependence on Russia's military support, and its adherence to Moscow's leadership in the CIS, earned President Rakhmonov the ire of President Karimov of Uzbekistan. In the Uzbek capital of Tashkent, President Rakhmonov became known as 'Russia's man'.[94] Russia showed signs of growing increasingly wary about being drawn deeper into the Tajikistan conflict, especially against the background of its experiences in Afghanistan and Chechnya. Notwithstanding Russia's caution, the war on the Tajik-Afghan border gave Moscow the excuse for a military presence in the region, increased its influence in Central Asia, and fulfilled its aim of containing the spread of militant Islamism.[95]

Gas and oil-rich Turkmenistan was one of the most repressive of the Central Asian republics. President Saparmurad Niyazov, a former first secretary of the Turkmen Communist Party, ruled the country with an absolute iron grip. In December 1991, the governing Turkmen Communist Party changed its name to the Democratic Party of Turkmenistan. The last presidential elections were held in June 1992, where Niyazov was the sole candidate, and the next presidential election was scheduled for January 2002. With the exception of the Peasant Justice Party, a government-sponsored opposition party, all other political parties are banned. Initially, Niyazov pursued an anti-Russian card, discriminating against the 400,000 ethnic Russians, out of a total population of 4.5 million. However, in response, Moscow stopped providing food supplies, and clamped down on bilateral trade. Turkmenistan also relied on Russia for access to Western markets to sell its gas. Gas production accounted for about 60 per cent of Turkmenistan's GDP and 75 per cent of all exports.[96] President Niyazov swiftly realized that the policy would lead to large-scale emigration of the skilled ethnic Russian workforce and professional elite, and promptly switched his policy to one of bowing to Moscow's preponderant influence. Avdy Kuliev, former Turkmen foreign minister, complained:

In the end, Niyazov realized that he couldn't survive without Russia, and now he's prepared to sign any treaty, any agreement, and he doesn't stop to consider how it might affect Turkmenistan in the future. There is a secret treaty on military affairs that is not in Turkmenistan's interests, but he signed it all the same. I don't know the specific details, but I know that Russia has military facilities on the territory of Turkmenistan that it is keen to maintain.[97]

President Niyazov's pro-Russian stance had more to do with survival than moral or political conviction. For Niyazov the main security threat came not from Russia or Iran, but Uzbekistan. President Islam Karimov of Uzbekistan had publicly expressed his contempt for President Niyazov. Turkmenistan had avoided joining the Central Asian Economic Union (which included Uzbekistan, Kazakhstan and Kyrgyzstan), and unlike Tajikistan, is not politically or economically dependent upon Uzbekistan's goodwill. President Niyazov had also prevented his officials from attending any meetings to discuss President Karimov's dream of a political union of the Central Asian states, which he called Turkestan.[98] Niyazov preferred to develop bilateral relations with Russia and its neighbours in preference to closer integration through the CIS, which was relatively poor in implementing its decisions. Turkmenistan, had, however, warily sheltered under Moscow's protective wing in order to resist the regional ambitions of Uzbekistan. This suited the Russian Federation, as it increased Turkmenistan's dependency on its overbearing Russian neighbour. Creating dependency was an effective tool in implementing Moscow's Russia First strategy in Central Asia.

One bone of contention was the status of the Caspian Sea, which abuts Turkmenistan. Turkmenistan believed the Caspian was a sea in judicial terms, but did not denounce the 1921 and 1940 Soviet-Iranian treaties which defined the Caspian Sea as a lake. The legal definition is an important one, determining access to the oil and gas deposits in the Caspian. If the Caspian were to be defined as a sea, this would imply economic exclusion zones and the physical division of the sea amongst the adjoining states, whereas a lake would mean the joint sharing of its natural resources amongst those who lived along its shores.[99] It was clearly in Russia's interests to see that the Caspian remained a lake in legal terms, since this gave it rights over the whole of the Caspian Sea, and its vast resources. Had the Caspian been defined as a sea, this would have left Russia with control only over a part of the area, and it would have had no claim on those larger sections of the Caspian Sea ceded to other countries. Economically, and strategically, Russia benefited from maintaining the status quo, which gave Moscow greater access to resources, and effective control of future developments and seaborne trade. Russia First would ensure that there was no change in Russia's position in the Caspian, as the Kremlin sought to maintain its political and economic stranglehold on the huge inland sea.

Despite pleas for pan-Turkic solidarity, Turkmenistan upset Turkic-speaking Azerbaijan by supplying gas and electricity to Armenia, breaching Baku's blockade in the dispute over Nagorny Karabakh. Relations with Iran also cooled following the abandonment of the Turkmenistan–Iran–Turkey pipeline (opposed by the United States), and a decision to involve an Israeli firm in a joint refinery venture with the National Iranian Oil Company. Tehran maintained a boycott of all links with Israel. On February 1996, Turkmenistan and Turkey signed a memorandum of agreement of understanding in Ankara on future gas supplies. The two countries agreed that Turkmen gas would be supplied to Turkey via Kazakhstan, Russia and Georgia, with a new pipeline being required in 2010, as capacity needs increase. Economically, Turkmenistan's GDP of $1,610 per capita reflected an economy largely dependent upon gas, with an inefficient agricultural sector, exacerbated by large-scale conversion from cotton to grain production. One of the major outstanding problems was the poor payment record of CIS states for Turkmenistan's gas, especially in Transcaucasia.[100]

Turkmenistan was thus almost as reliant upon Moscow as in the days of the Soviet Union. In terms of trade, Russia had the Ashkhabad authorities in an armlock. Turkmenistan's gas, its most important export by far, had to be exported via Russia. With Moscow blocking access to world markets, much of Ashkhabad's gas was sold to the unreliable and uncreditworthy CIS, while Russia kept the profitable markets for itself. Gazprom, the massive Russian gas monopoly, not only squeezed Turkmenistan out of Western markets, but gained control of the sale of Turkmen gas to the CIS. Gazprom further demanded participation in an Afghan–Pakistan pipeline project, should it come off the ground. In terms of security, Turkmenistan relied on Russia, both to protect its borders with Iran and Afghanistan, and shield it from an overweening Uzbekistan. In spite of Turkmenistan's resistance to multilateral agreements through the CIS, Moscow continued to press for Ashkhabad's participation in further CIS integration.[101]

At the CIS Summit in Ashkhabad, held on 22–23 December 1993, the twelve CIS heads of state established the Council of CIS Foreign Ministers, and agreed the role of Russian troops in protecting Turkmenistan's borders with Iran and Afghanistan. As a result, some 8,500 Russian troops were sent to secure Turkmenistan's borders which became, like Tajikistan, the front line of Russia's defences against radical Islamism.[102] Turkmenistan also agreed to join the CIS Economic Union as a full member. Together with other CIS defence ministers, Turkmenistan went further and agreed to inaugurate the CIS's Collective Security Council. It is true to say that Turkmenistan did often stay aloof from a number of CIS summits, and refused to go along with some CIS proposals, for example customs union legislation, CIS border protection, and the formation of CIS military regions.[103] However, this was also the case with other CIS members, and in Moscow's eyes the CIS was merely one mechanism to influence and put pressure on its neighbours in its near abroad. Overall, Russia achieved almost all its foreign policy aims in Turkmenistan, economically, politically and militarily. In all these spheres, in spite of Turkmenistan's protestations of independence from Moscow, President Niyazov found his country's interests subordinate to those of Russia. Russia First had triumphed in Turkmenistan.

As seen from the Kremlin, Uzbekistan was the most independent-minded of the Central Asian states, whilst it sought to establish its sovereignty and regional supremacy. Uzbekistan has the largest population of any of the Central Asian states, and with 22.8 million inhabitants, outnumbers the combined populations of Turkmenistan, Kyrgyzstan and Tajikistan. Its president, Islam Abdughanievich Karimov, was a former first secretary of the Uzbekistan Communist Party. Karimov transformed the Communist Party into the People's Democratic Party, and was elected president of an independent Uzbekistan with 86 per cent of the vote on 29 December 1991. Opposition parties had been forced out of the Ali Majilis (parliament), which was controlled by the People's Democratic Party. The presidential election due to take place in 1996 was cancelled following a referendum on 27 March 1995 which extended President Karimov's mandate until the year 2000. Political repression and harassment of opponents was endemic in Uzbekistan.[104]

Both the United States and the European Union (EU) sought to improve their relations with Uzbekistan, despite its poor human rights record. This could be seen as part of a Western strategy to pursue constructive engagement, rather than coercion, to encourage Tashkent to improve its human rights record. A landlocked country surrounded by landlocked countries, Uzbekistan lies in a geostrategic location between Russia, China and the Islamic world. Uzbekistan was thus perceived as being a potential bulwark both against a resurgent Russia and an ambitious Iran. Tashkent could therefore help in preventing the recreation of the Soviet Union by the front or back door, and assist in containing the spread of Iranian-backed Islamic fundamentalism in Central Asia. Finally, there was the matter of trade. EU member states already had three times more bilateral trade with Uzbekistan than with all the Transcaucasian republics combined.[105]

Burgeoning trade and the opportunities for Western companies created the preconditions for a cosy relationship. Uzbekistan did have its economic problems, nonetheless, particularly its dependence on the cotton harvest, and its attempts to become self-sufficient in food and fuel. The IMF was critical of the fact that Tashkent was not only uninterested in economic reform, but also failed to understand the rationale behind it. The IMF forecast a decline in real gross domestic product of 1.5 per cent in 1996, fuelled by the drop in cotton prices and the disastrous grain harvest. A year before, with inflation running at an estimated 270 per cent, Uzbekistan's gross domestic product per head had been $1,989, the second highest in Central Asia after Kazakhstan's $2,271.[106]

For the West, however, the lack of democracy and free speech in Uzbekistan was embarrassing, quite apart from the country's inability to address economic reform. During a visit by Uzbek President Karimov to Paris in April 1996, President Jacques Chirac gave his blessing to a Partnership and Co-operation Agreement (PCA) between the EU and Uzbekistan. The EU–Uzbekistan PCA was initialled in Tashkent on 29 April 1996, replacing the 1989 Trade and Co-operation Agreement with the Soviet Union. Two years before in Tashkent, President François Mitterrand had criticised Uzbekistan's human rights record and called for free elections. EU Commissioner Hans van den Broek, responsible for relations between the EU and the newly independent former Soviet states, declared on 9 April 1996 that Uzbekistan had made 'serious progress in ensuring that human rights were defended and economic reforms carried out'.[107]

No doubt the view is very different from Brussels than from a cell in Tashkent, but the Commissioner's statement underlined how the EU had already undermined its stand on human rights by signing a

Customs Union agreement with Turkey and an EU agreement (PCA) with Russia while the war raged in Chechnya.[108] Predictably, the argument also ran that PCAs had already been signed with Kyrgyzstan, Kazakhstan and Belarus, where there were also breaches of fundamental democratic and human rights.[109] This argument, however, undermines the whole point of including human rights clauses in EU (and US) bilateral agreements, since if they are to be widely ignored, it merely makes the West look weak and hypocritical. Seized with a bout of conscience, the European Parliament stalled on ratifying a number of PCAs on human rights grounds (for example with Russia, Kazakhstan, Belarus and Uzbekistan), but has so far given way after pressure from the Council of Ministers and the European Commission.

Like all the former Soviet republics (with the exception of Belarus), Uzbekistan reacted angrily to the Duma's declaration on 15 March 1996, condemning the dissolution of the Soviet Union. In response, President Karimov orchestrated a virulent anti-Russian media campaign, and published a book entitled 'Our people's path is the path of independence, freedom and thorough-going reform'. The Ali Majilis voted to change names of towns and regions from Russian to Uzbek, and attacked proposals by Kazakh President Nazarbayev for a Eurasian Union of former Soviet republics. In a television interview on 23 March, President Karimov also ridiculed 'Comrade Lukashenko', President of Belarus, for supporting the reintegration of former Soviet states. Already critical of the CIS, Karimov became even more outspoken in his opposition of its integrationist tendencies after the March Duma vote. He had previously pointedly stated that Uzbekistan would protect its own frontiers, implicitly condemning Kazakhstan and Kyrgyzstan for accepting Russian border guards. Later, in a speech published on 13 April 1996, President Karimov lambasted the CIS, Kazakhstan and Kyrgyzstan, claiming the CIS risked becoming a 'Community of Dependent States'. CIS integration was 'a policy of condemning oneself to vegetate in the backyard of the world economy, for the sake of ideological stereotypes from the past'.

The reaction from Uzbekistan's neighbours was perhaps predictable. Resistance to President Karimov's dream of creating a Central Asian entity called Turkestan, with Uzbekistan playing a role as the dominant regional power, has been pronounced. Kazakhstan and Kyrgyzstan have been less than enthusiastic participants in the Central Asian Economic Union (CAEU), set up after an initiative from Tashkent. The lack of diplomatic progress was not enhanced by President

Karimov's recurrent proclivity to abuse and show contempt for the other Central Asian presidents, particularly Presidents Akayev of Kyrgyzstan and Niyazov of Turkmenistan (the latter declining to join the CAEU). Nevertheless, the three CAEU countries have agreed to establish a joint peace-keeping battalion for UN duties which would include Russian troops.

Bearing in mind Uzbekistan's regional ambitions, its armed forces were modest, amounting to around 35,000 troops, which, although the largest in Central Asia, were only just bigger than the 20–25,000 Russian peace-keepers based in Tajikistan. The Uzbek military relied heavily on ethnic Russian officers following independence, which was underlined by the appointment of a Russian, Colonel Vladimir Pilyugin, as chief of staff. By 1996, the officer corps was still only around 60 per cent Uzbek. Uzbek military doctrine stressed that the army is defensive in nature and would promote a policy of neutrality. However, intervention in the internal affairs of neighbouring states might be justified for the sake of regional stability, as laid out in the Uzbek document 'A Collective Security Programme in Central Asia', which was approved in 1995. Uzbekistan's qualified policy of neutrality had already been tested in Tajikistan, where Uzbek units participated in the civil war, and to which the country sent a battalion of peace-keeping troops back in 1992. President Karimov repeatedly asserted that Uzbekistan would not take sides in the conflict, while establishing forty military posts on the Tajik-Uzbek border and announcing that Tashkent would protect Tajikistan's airspace. President Rakhmonov of Tajikistan welcomed Uzbekistan's support, declaring that the Uzbeks and Tajiks are 'blood brothers. When things are hard we turn to our blood brothers.'[110]

Relations between Uzbekistan and Turkmenistan continued to be strained. President Karimov waited five years after Turkmenistan's independence to travel to Ashkhabad to meet President Niyazov. Water-resource management, and oil and gas deposits on the countries' mutual borders were of significant interest to both Tashkent and Ashkhabad. A secure border with Turkmenistan was essential for Uzbekistan, given the instability in Tajikistan. At a summit in January 1996, the presidents agreed a border protection agreement. Uzbekistan also had an interest in the conflict in Afghanistan and was accused by Afghan officials of supplying arms to rebel forces under the command of General Abdul Rashid Dostum, an ethnic Uzbek, based in northern Afghanistan. Without direct intervention in the war, Uzbekistan maintained an embargo (particularly on oil) against those parts of Afghanistan controlled by Dostum's rival, Ahmed Shah Massoud. Protecting Uzbekistan's 156-kilometre border with Afghanistan is an obvious priority for Tashkent, although relations between President Karimov and the Rabbani government were cool to non-existent.[111]

Uzbek-Russian relations grew stronger as a result of the conflicts in Tajikistan and Afghanistan, as both countries had a vested interest in regional stability. Condemning the March 1996 Duma resolution declaring the dissolution of the Soviet Union unconstitutional, Karimov also told Yeltsin in a telegram that he supported Russia's democratic reforms and its co-operation with Uzbekistan. He added that there was no alternative to the CIS, and accepted Russia's right to a 'leading role' amongst the newly independent states, including to a certain extent Central Asia. Karimov was careful to back Yeltsin in his presidential bid for re-election, although without any great enthusiasm. Uzbekistan's main concerns with the CIS were the pace of integration and the need to protect the sovereignty of individual states. Russia had assisted Uzbekistan's military development by transferring Russian military bases and units to Tashkent's control from 1992 (including the 15th Air Defence Division of the Russian Air Force). Russia agreed to train Uzbek troops, and supply Russian arms and equipment. These agreements provided for the stationing of Russian personnel on Uzbek territory. The two countries also co-operated over peace-keeping in Tajikistan, joint military manoeuvres and signed agreements on border service co-operation, southern border security, joint provision of armed forces and monitoring of the Tajik-Afghan border. Both Uzbekistan's Defence Minister Akhmedov and Foreign Minister Komilov stated that while the Uzbeks were happy to co-operate with Russia, the Uzbeks would not be pushed into any agreement the country did not like, nor give up its position as sole guarantor of its border with Afghanistan. Uzbekistan's desire to make its point accounted for its periodic absences from CIS meetings, including the CIS Interparliamentary Assembly in February 1996, which discussed border protection in Tajikistan, amongst other issues.

Russia's new foreign minister, Yevgeny Primakov, visited Uzbekistan twice in February 1996. President Karimov declared after the visits that 'Russia has been and will remain Uzbekistan's strategic partner. This hinges on the communality of approaches to the assessment of the danger of fundamentalism's onslaught from the south.' Karimov added: 'If Russia always remembers that [Uzbekistan is an equal partner], we are prepared to co-operate.' Tashkent, however, put limits to this co-operation, including failing to support Moscow's opposition to NATO's enlargement, and putting Uzbek border guards under Russian command. Although Uzbekistan was not the most malleable of the former Soviet republics, Moscow remained well pleased with its relationship with Tashkent. For all President Karimov's posturing on independence and sovereignty, Moscow had a tremendous degree of influence over Tashkent's defence apparatus, border security and economy. Russia trained and supplied Uzbek forces, and engaged in joint peace-keeping operations. Uzbekistan participated in most CIS initiatives designed to improve collective security, and closer economic co-operation, involving the evolution of a customs union. Gradually, Uzbekistan was sucked into greater CIS integration, even if grudgingly so. Militarily, the relationship was mutually beneficial. Russia used Uzbek forces to carry some of the burden of protecting the Tajik and Afghan borders. Uzbekistan had the comfort of knowing that if the situation deteriorated, it could call on Russian support.[112]

Economically, Uzbekistan was still dependent upon its CIS neighbours, with 43 per cent of its trade with the former Soviet Union in 1995 (down from 58 per cent in 1994). Russia remained an essential, but declining market for Uzbekistan's vital cotton crop. Diversify as it might, Moscow's presence was ubiquitous in Tashkent's affairs. On 15 April 1996 President Karimov stated that he wanted better relations with Moscow. In an effort to appease the West and Russia, Karimov stated, 'Iran's way is unacceptable to us', but later the same month, in February 1996, he welcomed the Iranian foreign minister on an official visit to Uzbekistan. Incidentally, Uzbekistan also imposed the American-inspired oil embargo against Iran in May 1995, chilling relations with Tehran, but improving Tashkent's standing in Washington. Uzbekistan continued to walk its diplomatic tightrope, at one time curtsying to Russia, at other times Iran or the United States. Occasionally, it would even make a bow in the direction of the European Union. But the dominant relationship was with Moscow. As for the Kremlin, Tashkent's ducks and dives were watched with benign tolerance, while Moscow continued to put Russia First in Central Asia.[113]

CONCLUSION

For Russia, relations with the West were not as important as they once were. Initially, Russia's relationship with the West dominated foreign and domestic policy. By the end of 1992, questions were already being raised about the wisdom of Russia's overtly pro-Western foreign policy, first by Yeltsin, then by Kosyrev. By early 1994, the pro-Western camp was in retreat, and following the Duma elections in December 1995, Russia's love affair with the West and all it stood for was over. The honeymoon following the collapse of the Soviet Union in 1991 had been brief. Of more concern, Russia, which had an on-off love affair with the West since the times of Peter the Great, was once again looking to develop its own unique identity. In foreign policy terms, this could be seen in the distinct development of a Russia First strategy, both in terms of Russian relations with the West and its near abroad. Increasingly, Russia was putting its own national interests before its desire to curry favour with the West. This was brutally displayed in the case of Chechnya, where Russia pursued its policy of Russia First in the face of relatively mild disapprobrium from the West. It was difficult for the West to portray Russia as a paradigm of democracy and the market economy when it was blithely bombing thousands of its own citizens. While the West had some understanding of Russia's position in Chechnya, in terms of the need to defend its territorial integrity, the West (particularly the United States) was less understanding about Moscow's dealings with Iran, China and international arms sales. Here were examples where Russia was determined to pursue its own agenda, even in the face of Western opposition.

On NATO enlargement, Russia had to face up to the reality that it would not stop the Atlantic Alliance's eastern expansion. General Alexander Lebed, after his appointment as Secretary of the Security Council following the 1996 presidential elections, said that he was not opposed to NATO's enlargement, but believed it would merely be a costly and futile exercise on the part of the West. However, General Lebed's views were not widely shared in the Kremlin. Russia remained wary of NATO expansion, which it saw as a potential security threat to Russia. Prime Minister Victor Chernomyrdin, Foreign Minister Yevgeny Primakov, Defence Minister Igor Rodionov and President Boris Yeltsin continued to express disquiet about NATO enlargement. Moscow's strategy was to impose conditions on NATO's enlargement, demanding a 'special relationship' for Russia, and was determined to continue opposing NATO membership for the Baltic states. Nor would it view the placing of NATO forces (especially with a nuclear capability) on its borders with equanimity.

Russia First produced a shift in Moscow's priorities from the West to the south and east. In the early part of Yeltsin's presidency, Moscow tended to neglect its near abroad. The near abroad became increasingly important to Russia, as its overtly pro-Western phase under Yeltsin faded. Moscow used the mechanism of the CIS to exert pressure on its neighbours in the near abroad, in an attempt to create a type of 'European Union', establishing a zone of close political, economic and military integration, with Russia taking the lead. In practice, the CIS did not function entirely effectively, with many decisions not being fully implemented. But the CIS was merely one of the mechanisms Russia used to reassert its influence over the newly independent states of the former Soviet Union. Moscow intervened in internal conflicts, such as in Moldova, Georgia, Armenia, Azerbaijan and Tajikistan to re-establish its influence in parts of the former Soviet Empire. Elsewhere, it used the fear of instability to regain its foothold in a country (for example Turkmenistan, Kyrgyzstan and Uzbekistan), or flexed its economic muscle. Countries like Ukraine and Kazakhstan realised the strength of Russia's economic stranglehold on their respective economies, and so did the oil-producing countries of the Caspian Sea. In the case of the Baltic states, Russia resorted to threats, while in Belarus, President Lukashenko's desire for integration was almost embarrassing.

The West remains important for Russia. However, it was a fact of political life in the Russian Federation that there were greater priorities for the Kremlin than approval from Washington or Bonn. In the current political climate in Russia, and with the general disenchantment with the values espoused by the West, Moscow is seeking to re-build the Russian Empire. At the end of the twentieth century, that no longer meant Russia would have to invade its neighbouring states to regain its lost authority. As the United States discovered many years ago, there are other, more subtle, ways to build and hold an empire. Russia, as it looked at the wreckage of what was the Soviet Union, decided it would put Russia First in the brave new post-communist world, both in its dealings with the West and its near abroad.

NOTES

1 Author's meeting with Mikhail Gorbachev, June 1996.
2 Buszynski, Leszek, 'Russia and the West: towards renewed political rivalry?', *Survival*, 37:3 (1995), p.106. On the Bosnian crisis in August–September 1996, which also weakened Kozyrev's position, see Chapter 4, pp. 157–60.
3 Sheridan, Michael, 'Russia and the US remain cordial but poles apart despite talks', *Independent*, 24 March 1995.
4 Author's visit to Kazan and meeting with Vice-President Vassily Likachev in March 1995. See also *White Book of Tartarstan: The Way to Sovereignty: 1990–93*, Official Collection of Documents (Kazan, 1993).
5 On all this, see Buszynski, 'Russia and the West', pp. 114–18.
6 European Parliament, *Background Note on the Political Situation in the Three Transcaucasian Republics*, PE 218.355, 11 June 1996; Carrère d'Encausse, Hélène, MEP, *Draft Report on Developing Relations Between the European Union and the Transcaucasian States*, European Parliament, PE 217.251, 1 April 1996.
7 Visit of the 'Soldiers' Mothers of Russia and St Petersburg' to the European Parliament, 28 May 1996, and see also *Statement of Appeal of the Union of North Caucasian Women, the Soldiers' Mothers of Russia and St Petersburg and the Centre for Peacemaking (Moscow)*, May 1996.
8 Kovalev, Sergei, 'How the West should *not* react to events in Russia', *in Transition* (Prague), 9 June 1995, pp. 42–3.
9 Cited in Wise, Elizabeth, 'Winding road to a new entente', *European Voice*, 11–17 April 1996. See also Carrère d'Encausse, Hélène, *Report on the Conclusion of an Agreement on Partnership and Cooperation Between the European Communities and the Russian Federation*, European Parliament, PE 210.337, 22 November 1995. (The author was shadow rapporteur for this report.) The PCA was finally ratified by the European Parliament on 29 November 1995. The PCA and the Interim Trade Agreement (also delayed) entered into force on 1 February 1996. See also Chapter 3, pp. 110, 112–13, for Russia–EU economic relations. On relations with the Duma and Federation Council over Chechnya: author's meetings with Russian parliamentary delegations to the European Parliament, March 1995 and December 1995.
10 Adomeit, Hannes, 'Russia as a great power in world affairs: images and reality', *International Affairs*, 71:1 (1995), p. 49.
11 This point was raised during discussion between the author and Ivan Rybkin during a meeting with the European Parliament's delegation for relations with Russia, March 1995.
12 NATO, *Study on Enlargement*, September 1995, official document of the European Parliament, PE 214.609.
13 NATO, *Areas for Pursuance of a Broad, Enhanced NATO–Russia Dialogue and Cooperation*, document issued at Noordwijk Aan Zee, The Netherlands, 31 May 1995. Meeting between ministers of the North Atlantic Council and the foreign minister of the Russian Federation.
14 Morgan, Jenna and Butcher, Martin, 'NATO and military security in Europe: the Partnership for Peace, *NATO Alerts Network*, June 1994, pp. 3–5.
15 Quoted from in *Atlantic News*, no. 2610, p.1, cited in Morgan and Butcher,

'NATO and Military Security in Europe, p. 3.

16 Joulwan, George, *Statement before the House Armed Services Committee*, 23/04/94, p.9, quoted from *Atlantic News*, no. 2610, p.1, cited in Morgan and Butcher, 'NATO and Military Security in Europe, pp. 6–7.

17 Buszynski, 'Russia and the West, p. 110.

18 Thornhill, John, 'Yeltsin suggests compromise on NATO expansion', *Financial Times*, 26 March 1996.

19 Wise, Elizabeth, 'Winding road to a new entente', *European Voice*, 11–17 April 1996.

20 Thornhill, John, 'Yeltsin's bear has two faces', *Financial Times*, 12 June 1996.

21 Sheridan, Michael, 'Russia warns against NATO growth', *Independent*, 21 March 1995.

22 Yeltsin, Boris, in *Rossiyskiye Vesti*, 30 April 1996.

23 Thornhill, 'Yeltsin suggests compromise on NATO expansion'.

24 Barber, Lionel, 'EU supports non-aggression pact to ease Russian fears over NATO', *Financial Times*, 20 March 1996.

25 See NATO, *Ministerial Meeting of the North Atlantic Council in Berlin, 3 June 1996, Final Communiqué*.

26 NATO, *Areas for Pursuance of a Broad, Enhanced NATO–Russia Dialogue and Co-operation*, document issued at Noordwijk Aan Zee, The Netherlands, 31 May 1995. Meeting between ministers of the North Atlantic Council and the foreign minister of the Russian Federation.

27 Address by Javier Solana, secretary general of NATO, at the University of Warsaw, 18 April 1996.

28 Adomeit, 'Russia as a 'great power' in world affairs', pp. 48, 60–1.

29 Buszynski, 'Russia and the West', p. 119. This point was also stressed during a meeting between the author and a delegation from the Duma, held in Brussels, September 1995.

30 Interfax news agency, 23 May 1996.

31 7 June 1996, WEU Assembly, Paris (the author was present).

32 On NATO's proposals and Russia's reaction see: Clark, Bruce, 'Russia to take a tough line as Europe weighs security system', *Financial Times*, 2 December 1996; Black, Ian, 'Moscow wins nuclear pledge', *Guardian*, 3 December 1996; Clark, Bruce and Wise, Peter, 'NATO to start talks with Russia', *Financial Times*, 3 December 1996; Palmer, John, 'Moscow's softer stance takes NATO by surprise', *Guardian*, 12 December 1996; Clark, Bruce, 'Moscow attacks NATO expansion', *Financial Times*, 19 December 1996; author's meeting with Russian parliamentarians from the Duma and Federation Council, fifth European Parliament/Russia Interparliamentary Meeting, Strasbourg, 11 December 1996; author's discussions with NATO officials, Brussels, December 1996.

33 Buszynski, 'Russia and the West', p. 120.

34 Interfax (Moscow), 18 November 1992; Lloyd, John, 'Russia boosts arms trade', *Financial Times*, 1 December 1993, cited in Adomeit, 'Russia as a 'great power' in world affairs', p. 58.

35 Adomeit, 'Russia as a 'great power' in world affairs', pp. 48–9, 57–8.

36 Meetings between the author, Vladimir Lukin and Valentin Kuptsov (separately) in Strasbourg, April 1996; and between the author, Lukin and

Zyuganov (separately), Moscow, June 1996.

37 Thornhill, John, 'Beijing finds an old ally in Moscow', *Financial Times*, 16 March 1996; Clark, Bruce, 'Yeltsin looks to Asia as G7 keeps him out of the club', *Financial Times*, 23 April 1996; Higgins, Andrew, 'China plays a "Russia card" ', *Guardian*, 23 April 1996; Meek, James, 'Yeltsin's forgotten compatriots curse their lot', *Guardian*, 30 April 1996; author's discussions with Zyuganov, Kuptsov and Lukin.

38 *Guardian*, 6 July 1996.

39 Foreign and Commonwealth Office, 'The Commonwealth of Independent States (CIS): A Chronology, December 1991–April 1996', *Background Brief*, May 1996.

40 See International Institute for Strategic Studies, 'Troubled Times for Russia', *Strategic Survey 1995/96* (Oxford, 1996), pp. 123–6.

41 European Parliament, *Text of the Quadrilateral Treaty between Russia, Belarus, Kazakhstan and Kyrgyzstan*, EP Official Document, PE 217.285, 6 May 1996.

42 See European Parliament, *Union Treaty between Russia and Belarus*, Official EP document, PE 217.284, 6 May 1996.

43 See Schroedter, Elisabeth, MEP, *Draft Opinion on the Interim trade Agreement between the EU and Belarus*, Official EP document, PE 217.546, 28 May 1996.

44 Reeves, Phil, 'Belarus patriots assail union with Russia', *Independent*, 25 March 1996.

45 Yeltsin, Boris, in *Rossiyskiye Vesti*, 30 April 1996.

46 See European Parliament, *Union Treaty between Russia and Belarus*.

47 On the referendum in Belarus and the EU's reaction, see: Kaminski, Matthew, 'Belarus president claims manadate', *Financial Times*, 26 November 1996; 'EP/Belarus', *Agence Europe*, No. 6876, 16–17 December 1996, p. 6; author's discussions with Russian parliamentarians on relations with Belarus, and the European Parliament's *ad hoc* delegation to monitor the referendum in Belarus, fifth EP/Russia Interparliamentary Meeting, Strasbourg, 11 December 1996; European Parliament, *Council Statement of 6 December 1996 Concerning Relations with Russia*, Delegation for Relations with Russia, EUR/DL/cs, 10 December 1996; European Parliament, *Background Note on the Political Situation in the Russian Federation*, PE 219.134, 27 November 1996, p. 7.

48 Meeting between the author and CIS Inter-Parliamentary Assembly Delegation, Brussels, 7 March 1996.

49 Although Russia has a good claim on the Crimea in the sense that it was historically a Russian territory, ceded by the Ukrainian president of the Soviet Union, Nikita Khrushchev, from Russia to the Ukraine. The overwhelming majority of the population (67 per cent) are ethnic Russians, with the rest composed of ethnic Ukrainians (26 per cent) and Tartars (7 per cent).

50 On energy issues see Kaminski, Matthew, 'Ukraine exploits its energy pipeline monopoly', *Financial Times*, 15 March 1996, and *Guardian*, 12 July 1996.

51 On Kuchma and the West: see the author's report for the European Parliament on the WEU Assembly, Paris, 3–6 June 1996, *Forty-First Ordinary Session of the Assembly*, PE 218. 376, 13 June 1996, pp. 3–4; the author was present during President Kuchma's address and his question and answer session at the WEU Assembly on 5 June 1996; NATO, *Ministerial Meeting of the North Atlantic Council in Berlin, 3 June 1996, Final Communiqué*. Also based on the author's

confidential talks with Western diplomats and NATO personnel.

52 Author's visit to the Baltic states in November 1995, as part of the European Parliament's delegation for relations with Latvia, Lithuania and Estonia. This point was confirmed by the author's earlier meeting with President Lennart Meri, in June 1995.

53 Cited in Carnegy, Hugh and Kaminski, Matthew, 'Prosperity without security', *Financial Times*, 3 May 1996.

54 A view shared by Robin Cook MP, Labour's shadow foreign secretary, at meeting held to discuss foreign affairs in London on 9 July 1996.

55 Girnius, Saulius, 'Caretaker government faces financial crisis', *Transition* (Prague), 17 May 1996, p. 39.

56 See the author's article on the Baltic states, 'Baltics face up to life without "Big Brother" ', *European Voice*, 21–27 March 1996; Helgadottir, Birna, 'Russians bridle at being called aliens on the Baltic', *The European*, 8–14 February 1996.

57 On this and Russian-Estonian relations, see the author's report on the Europe agreement with Estonia, European Parliament official document, PE 214.603/fin. 25 October 1995.

58 See Truscott, 'Baltics face up to life without "big brother"'; author's meetings with EU ambassadors in Latvia, Lithuania and Estonia, November 1995; Kuchina, Galina, 'Bid to bar non-Lett from citizenship fails in Latvia', ITAR-TASS, 23 February 1996. See also Helgadottir, 'Russians bridle at being called aliens on the Baltic'; Rehn, Elisabeth, MEP, *Report on the Europe Agreement with Latvia*, Official European Parliament document, PE 214.601/fin, 25 October 1995, and Poettering, Hans-Gert, MEP, *Draft Report on the Europe Agreement with Lithuania*, European Parliament, official document, PE 212.602/fin. 25 October 1995. Also based on author's meeting with Russian community leaders from Narva, November 1995, and author's meetings with Russian-speaking members of the Estonian parliament, June 1995.

59 Author's meeting with the Russian ambassador to Estonia, inTallinn, June 1996.

60 ITAR-TASS, 11 July 1993.

61 *Pravda*, 27 May 1994; Rehn, *Report on the Europe Agreement with Latvia*; meetings held by the author with senior diplomats, including the Russian ambassador to Estonia, June 1995.

62 Girnius, Saulius, 'Relations with Russia turn bitter', *Transition* (Prague), 31 May 1996, pp .42–5.

63 This conclusion follows the author's many meetings with politicians of all political blocs from the Russian State Duma and Federation Council between 1994 and 1996.

64 ITAR-TASS, 1 March 1993.

65 Ware, Richard, 'Developments in Russia', *House of Commons Research Paper*, 94/72, 20 May 1994, House of Commons Library, p. 31.

66 See International Institute for Strategic Studies, 'Troubled times for Russia', *Strategic Survey 1995/96*, pp. 124–5; *L'Etat du Monde: Annuaire économique et géopolitique mondial, 1996*, La Découverte (Paris, 1995), pp. 644–9; European Commission, *Towards a European Union Strategy for Relations with the Independent States of Central Asia*, official EU document, COM(95)206 final, 10 October 1995, pp. 2–41. See also, pp. 58–60 for the CIS agreements and

institutional arrangements.

67 On Transcaucasia, see European Parliament, *Background Note on the Political Situation in the Three Transcaucasian Republics*, official document, PE 218.355, 11 June 1996, pp.1–10; Foreign and Commonwealth Office, 'The Commonwealth of Independent States (CIS)'; Adomeit, 'Russia as a 'great power' in world affairs', pp. 46–48; International Institute for Strategic Studies, 'Troubled times for Russia', *Strategic Survey 1995/96*, pp. 124–5; Carrère d'Encausse, Hélène, MEP, *Draft Report on Developing Relations between the European Union and the Transcaucasian States*, European Parliament official document, PE 217.251, 1 April 1996, pp. 5–13.

68 See also above p. 42 and below, p. 76.

69 Meetings by the author with members of the KPRF bloc in the Duma, April 1996; meeting with delegation from CIS Inter-Parliamentary Assembly, Brussels, March 1996; meeting, with Vladimir Lukin, chairman of the Duma Foreign Affairs Committee, Strasbourg and Moscow, April and June 1996, respectively.

70 Carrère d'Encausse, *Draft Report on Developing Relations between the European Union and the Transcaucasian States*, pp. 5–11.

71 European Parliament, *Background Note on the Political Situation in the Three Transcaucasian Republics*, p. 9.

72 See Thoenes, Sander, 'Gulf grows wider between Armenia and its president', *Financial Times*, Weekend, 5–6 October 1996; also Williams, Selina, 'Ter-Petrossian keeps power amid vote-rigging claims', *The European*, 26 September– 2 October 1996.

73 European Parliament, *Background Note on the Political Situation in the Three Transcaucasian Republics*, pp. 7–8.

74 Lebed assumed command of the 14th Army in Moldova in June 1992. For Lebed's role in Moldova, see European Parliament, *First EP–Moldova Interparliamentary Meeting (with Lebed and others), 19 April 1995*, European Parliament official document, PE 211.578 fin., 27 July 1995.

75 European Parliament, *Background Note on the Political and Economic Situation in Moldova*, European Parliament official document, PE 210.445, 21 November 1994, pp.2–16; Foreign and Commonwealth Office, 'The Commonwealth of Independent States (CIS)', pp. 7–9.

76 Ware, 'Developments in Russia', p. 31.

77 European Parliament, *Background Note on the Political and Economic Situation in Moldova*, pp. 9–10.

78 Economist Intelligence Unit, *EIU Country Report, 2nd quarter 1996: Kazakhstan*, Economist Group (London, 1996), p. 42.

79 See Kortunov, Andrei, 'Russia, the "Near Abroad," and the West', in Lapidus, Gail (ed.), *The New Russia: Troubled Transformation*, Westview Press (Boulder, San Francisco and Oxford, 1995), p. 168.

80 Economist Intelligence Unit, *EIU Country Report, 2nd quarter 1996: Kazakhstan*, p. 5; author's meetings with Gennady Zyuganov, December 1995, June and July 1996.

81 Robinson, Anthony and Thoenes, Sander, 'Kazakhstan: glow of prosperity amid the ashes', *Financial Times Survey*, 11 July 1996.

82 Economist Intelligence Unit, *EIU Country Report, 2nd quarter 1996:*

Kazakhstan, pp. 10–11.

83 Robinson and Thoenes, 'Kazakhstan'.

84 Dave, Bhavna, 'A new parliament consolidates presidential authority', *Transition* (Prague), 22 March 1996, pp. 33–7.

85 Economist Intelligence Unit, *EIU Country Report, 2nd quarter 1996: Kazakhstan*, pp. 9–10.

86 Quoted in *Financial Times*, 23 July 1996.

87 See above pp. 58–60, on CIS military co-operation and institutional arrangements.

88 See Pannier, Bruce, 'Kyrgyzstan: the shrinking shores of Central Asia's "island of democracy"', *Transition* (Prague), 5 April 1996, pp. 56–60.

89 Economist Intelligence Unit, *EIU Country Report, 2nd quarter 1996: Kyrgyz Republic*, Economist Group (London, 1996), p. 14.

90 Pannier, Bruce, 'Kyrgyzstan', p. 60.

91 Economist Intelligence Unit, *EIU Country Report, 2nd quarter 1996: Kyrgyz Republic*, p. 16.

92 Economist Intelligence Unit, *EIU Country Report, 2nd quarter 1996: Tajikistan*, Economist Group (London, 1996), pp. 17–26.

93 Foreign and Commonwealth Office, 'The Commonwealth of Independent States (CIS)', p. 4.

94 See *L'Etat du Monde: Annuaire économique et géopolitique mondial, 1996*, pp. 644–9; Economist Intelligence Unit, *Country Report, 2nd Quarter 1996: Uzbekistan*, Economist Group (London, 1996); and European Parliament, *Economic and political situation in Uzbekistan*, Background note, 19 June 1996, pp. 1–14.

95 See also above pp.69–71.

96 Economist Intelligence Unit, *EIU Country report, 2nd quarter 1996: Turkmenistan*, Economist Group (London, 1996), p. 30.

97 Kuliev was foreign minister in 1990–92. Quoted in Bezanis, Lowell and Fuller, Elizabeth, 'There is only one way out – by getting rid of this leader and this government', *Transition* (Prague), 17 May 1996, p. 37; see also pp.34–8.

98 Economist Intelligence Unit, *EIU Country Report 2nd Quarter 1996: Turkmenistan*, p. 33.

99 Carrère d'Encausse, *Draft Report on Developing Relations Between the European Union and the Transcaucasian States*, p. 11.

100 Economist Intelligence Unit, *EIU Country report, 2nd quarter 1996: Turkmenistan*, pp. 35–40, 41–2.

101 Economist Intelligence Unit, *EIU Country report, 2nd quarter 1996: Turkmenistan*, pp. 35–40, 41–42 and *L'Etat du Monde: Annuaire économique et géopolitique mondial, 1996*, p. 644.

102 Ware, 'Developments in Russia', p. 31.

103 See Foreign and Commonwealth Office, 'The Commonwealth of Independent States (CIS)', pp. 1–12; author's meeting with CIS parliamentary delegation, Brussels, March 1996.

104 See *L'Etat du Monde: Annuaire économique et géopolitique mondial, 1996*, pp. 644–8.

105 'EU/Uzbekistan', *Agence Europe*, No. 6645, 16 January 1996, p. 7.

106 European Parliament, *Economic and Political Situation in Uzbekistan*,

Directorate General for Research, 19 June 1996: cotton accounted for 57.8 per cent of the value of Uzbekistan's exports in 1995; see also Economist Intelligence Unit, *EIU Country Report, 2nd Quarter: Uzbekistan*, Economist Group (London, 1996), pp. 55–6, 64–5.

107 Economist Intelligence Unit, *EIU Country Report, 2nd Quarter: Uzbekistan*, pp. 47–8. Despite the human rights abuses in Uzbekistan, EU Foreign Affairs Commissioner Van den Broek confirmed the Commission was in favour of ratifying the PCA with Uzbekistan. Private meeting with the author, Strasbourg, 17 September 1996.

108 Neither of which the author voted to ratify in the European Parliament.

109 Wood, Michael, *Ouzbekistan*, Foreign Affairs Secretariat of the European Parliament, 18 July 1996; European Commission, *Towards a European Union Strategy for Relations with the Independent States of Central Asia*, COM(95)206 final, Brussels, 10 October 1995. [Note: the author is the European Parliament's rapporteur on 'Towards a European Union Strategy for Relations with the Independent States of Central Asia', due for completion in 1997.]

110 See Kangas, Roger, 'Uzbekistan: taking the lead in Central Asia', *Transition* (Prague), 3 May 1996, pp. 52–4.

111 *L'Etat du Monde: Annuaire économique et géopolitique mondial, 1996*, pp. 648; Kangas, 'Uzbekistan, pp. 54–5.

112 Kangas, 'Uzbekistan', pp. 54–5; European Parliament, *Economic and Political Situation in Uzbekistan*; Foreign and Commonwealth Office, 'The Commonwealth of Independent States (CIS)', pp. 1–12.

113 Economist Intelligence Unit, *EIU Country Report, 2nd Quarter: Uzbekistan*, pp. 50–7; *L'Etat du Monde: Annuaire économique et géopolitique mondial, 1996*, p. 648.

CHAPTER 3

RUSSIA'S ECONOMY, THE MILITARY-INDUSTRIAL COMPLEX AND THE MAFIA

THE RUSSIAN FEDERATION inherited an economic system in total disarray following the collapse of the Soviet Union. Yeltsin, listening to a host of advisers from the West, adopted a policy of economic 'shock therapy' in 1992 which was to be implemented by a young team under Prime Minister Yegor Gaidar. Gaidar sought to reverse the economic decline of the 1980s and bring about a Western-style market economy. By 1996, it was clear that the reform process he initiated had failed to bring the country to the promised land. Production had continued to slump, while the majority of the Russian people saw their living standards plummet. The population expressed their dissatisfaction at the polls in the Duma elections of 1993 and 1995, bringing about a remarkable volte-face in government policy. Russia's earlier 'shock therapy' and large-scale privatisation strategy was replaced by a domestic version of Russia First. Protectionism became the order of the day, with the Russian government giving privileges and advantages to domestic companies and entrepreneurs, often against the background of complaints from the West. Strategic industries remained under state control, and foreign investment in the most sensitive or profitable sectors of the Russian economy was restricted for foreign investors. Russia boosted its arms sales, in the face of Western hostility, to support the crumbling military-industrial complex and secure defence sector jobs.

This Russia First strategy was directed from above and deliberately designed to exclude foreign investors from having a significant stake in Russia's most important industries, particularly the energy and raw material sectors (dominated by oil and gas). Elsewhere, including in the financial sector, Western companies found themselves at a disadvantage compared to Russian companies and entrepreneurs. Legal protection for foreign investors was either poor or non-existent. The Russia First strategy was also unique since there was a political and ideological hostility to foreign investors having influence over the Russian economy. Russia First not only meant economic privileges for Kremlin insiders, but deliberate discrimination against foreign investors, as a matter of policy. Russia's economy, and the profitable and viable sectors that remained, were to be reserved for Russians. The outcome was that the early drive for privatisation and liberalisation of the economy was abandoned, in favour of a hybrid form of a market economy where the rules were made by Russians, for the benefit of Russians.

With the arrival of famous brand names like McDonald's, Pepsi Cola and Benetton on the streets of Moscow and other major Russian cities, it might appear that Russia had joined the world's select club of Western-style capitalist countries. However, looks can be deceiving, the old Soviet command economy is gone, but not buried. Instead, Russia has witnessed the development of a pseudo-market economy, characteristically different from a fully-functioning Western market system. The Russian model is characterised by the operation of market forces in a criminal environment, with weak legal and contractual parameters, and dominated by a government-favoured elite. It can also be classified as a 'robber-baron' form of capitalism, more reminiscent of nineteenth-century America or the Chicago of the 1920s than the second millennium. Russian society has been divided into 'winners' and 'losers', with the former defending their entrenched position, often in collusion with elements of the political elite, up to and including President Yeltsin's 'inner circle'. The ten million Russian small-traders are at the bottom of the entrepreneurial ladder, but also have a stake in the current system which they did not have under the Soviet regime that stifled entrepreneurship.[1] But for the vast majority of the Russian people market reforms have meant declining living standards, deteriorating health and rising poverty. Economic reform has increasingly been associated in the Russian popular mind with growing crime and corruption.

The course of economic reform has been one of the main fault lines in Russia's post-Soviet society. The political conflict that raged over the constitutional distribution of power that culminated in the October 1993 coup attempt was exacerbated by the dispute between advocates of Gaidar's 'shock therapy', and their opponents. The latter group preferred a slower, more socially-orientated approach, and included influential members of the *nomenklatura* and old-style industrial managers.[2] The conflict between the two groups was sometimes presented as a clash between those who slavishly followed the West, and others who defended Russia's national and social interests, putting 'Russia First'. Yegor Gaidar in particular was associated with the West and the International Monetary Fund (IMF), which backed the prime minister's memorandum outlining his reform strategy in February 1992. Gaidar also had the backing of US government officials, the World Bank and the European Bank for Reconstruction and Development. The link between economic reform and Western influences was made by the opponents of 'shock therapy' (including communists and nationalists) with some effect, and helped bring about Gaidar's political demise. By tapping into the well of public disaffection with the economic reform process, a connection was established between Western-inspired reforms and declining living standards in the minds of many Russians. The Russian Communist Party (KPRF) exploited this linkage to the full, rebuilding their political support in the process. The communists' message was mainly to the country's economic losers, especially the poor and elderly. It was a rich political seam, which was also mined by the nationalists (with great success in 1993). By contrast, Yegor Gaidar never recovered from his image as a 'shock therapist' in 1992–93 and a lapdog of the West.[3]

Despite the political opposition ranged against him, Victor Chernomrydin (Gaidar's successor) sought to maintain the basic policy tenets of the 'IMF course', albeit at a slower pace. While successive Chernomyrdin governments pursued the stabilisation programme agreed with the IMF and other international organisations, the Yeltsin administration also introduced some populist measures. Such doses of 'populism' were particularly marked in the run-up to the presidential election, and were designed to mitigate the worst social effects of the economic reforms. Yeltsin's spending pledges were so extensive that they were unlikely to be fully implemented, but they did recognise the real pain inflicted by the aftermath of Gaidar's 'shock therapy'. The president's economic populism extended to preferential treatment for some of the monopolistic flagship enterprises of the Soviet era, such as

Gazprom and Zil, which the government justified by citing the 'national interest'. Often, the national interest happened to coincide with the business interests of Yeltsin's 'inner circle'.

Russia's desire to meet the requirements of the Western-inspired stabilisation programme had much to do with the country's need for Western loans, credits, favourable debt rescheduling and technical support. It was not in Russia's financial and economic interests to disengage totally from the West, especially when Western institutions had shown a willingness to relax conditions in response to political expediency. Any Russian tendency to disengage from the West was also diminished by the requirements of the global economy. Autarky is no longer an option for an economy seeking growth and dynamism. The collapse of the Soviet Union necessitated a reorientation of Russian trade Westwards, away from the captive markets of the former Soviet republics and Eastern Europe. However, there remained a certain duality in Russian economic policy, which on the one hand encouraged trade with the West and inward investment, and on the other sought to protect domestic industries and maintain Russian ownership. Thus Russia wished to attract foreign investment, but declined to significantly revise legislation prejudicial to overseas investors. Russia First in the domestic sphere therefore manifested itself in protective measures designed to protect inefficient industries from foreign competition, and safeguarded the interests and profits of those sectors of the economy which were relatively competitive (such as the energy sector). From a populist point of view, this could be presented as protecting Russia's national interests, and more importantly, jobs. In practice, some of the greatest beneficiaries were the new business elite, and the president's 'inner circle'. The message to the international audience was somewhat different. Here, the emphasis of the government was placed on economic reform, and streamlining Russia's nascent market economy.

The overall direction of Russia's economic policy was therefore closely aligned with the country's general shift towards Russia First. The strategy of integration into the world's economy (and membership of leading international financial institutions) had been balanced by the pursuit of closer economic ties with traditional partners and emerging markets. This trend had been accompanied by a growing interest in opening up markets in the Asia–Pacific region. Russia, in another example of Russia First applied to the economic sphere, had been more willing to defy the West by trading with so-called pariah states, notably Iran and Iraq. Russia's tendency to pursue its own economic interests in the face of Western opposition, and its desire to use its economic muscle to re-establish spheres of influence, were part and parcel of a Russia First strategy.

THE LEGACY OF THE SOVIET ERA

Seventy years of communism left an indelible mark on the structure of the Russian economy. The command structure was inefficient, slow to adapt, and dependent on all parts of the Soviet Union to produce the goods and services required to keep the economy going (helped by subsidised imports from the Eastern bloc). With the disintegration of the Soviet Union, this system fell apart. The independence of the former Soviet republics, and the detachment of Eastern Europe, led to economic dislocation as the Soviet Union dissolved. The interdependency of the old system, with its dispersed specialised production centres, ceased to operate in a market system determined by inter-state payments. The reality of the market meant that it was no longer economically viable for former Soviet states to supply each other at a loss. Regions such as Russia's far east were particularly badly hit, as under the Soviet system transport costs were effectively borne by the state. Unlike the countries of Central and Eastern Europe, Russia had no real experience of modern capitalism to draw on in its struggle to transform the economy. In the past, Russia had briefly flirted with elements of Western-inspired mercantilism to underpin Peter the Great's drive for Westernisation. Once serfdom had been abolished in 1861, Russia embarked on a period of rapid industrialisation, peaking in the 1890s, which witnessed a limited indigenous capitalist culture. But the vast majority of the Russian people were untouched by the experience, and their centuries-old mode of behaviour continued virtually unchanged. Much of the impetus for Russia's nineteenth-century industrialisation programme came from West European companies, skills and capital.[4] The emergence of this primitive form of capitalism was a by-product of the political and military needs of the state, rather than an effort at early economic transformation.

The economic inheritance after the years of Soviet rule left Russia with a dysfunctional economic system which had started to atrophy in the mid to late 1980s. The economic reform process began against the backdrop of dismantling the Eastern trade bloc COMECON, the dissolution of the Soviet Union (disrupting trade and payments systems), the absence of a market economy, obsolete capital stocks and technology, a poor infrastructure (especially in telecommunications), and limited integration into the global economy.[5] Geopolitical and military considerations had largely determined the structure of the Soviet Union's economy. Sustaining the huge military-industrial complex led to a disproportionate development of heavy industry at the expense of light industry and services. Moreover, high military expenditure ensured the Russian Federation inherited a huge fiscal burden.[6]

Set against this grim background, Russia nevertheless enjoys certain advantages which could generate considerable wealth in the future. The Russian Federation accounts for 11 per cent of the world's oil output, and 10 per cent of the world's proven oil resources are located on Russian soil. Russia is also amongst the world's premier producers of raw materials and energy, producing 30 per cent of the world's gas, 10 per cent of its hard coal, 14 per cent of its iron ore, and 10–15 per cent of the earth's non-ferrous metal ores.[7] These resources give Russia enormous potential as an exporter, as raw material and energy prices are steadily raised to world market levels. The raw material, energy and agricultural sectors provide enormous scope for improved efficiency, as technological innovations increase production, cut waste and lower unit costs. Russia further benefits from a massive internal market, with significant opportunities for growth in the Commonwealth of Independent States (CIS) and the Baltic states. Most of the former Soviet republics were dependent on Russia's energy supplies, including Armenia, Ukraine, Moldova, Georgia, Belarus and the Baltic states. In 1992, Russia was effectively subsidising these countries with its energy supplies to the tune of $15 billion.[8] Russia accounted for 90 per cent of oil and 60 per cent of total CIS production in 1995.[9] Moscow is increasingly focusing its efforts on the transformation of the CIS into a closer-knit trading bloc, which it hopes may come to resemble a Eurasian variant of the European Union.

The Russian Federation has a well-educated and trained workforce, which has shown remarkable flexibility and adaptability in the face of severe economic upheaval. However, in the medium to long term, action will have to been taken to preserve Russia's skill-base, under immense pressure due to the significant deterioration in the educational, technical and military training systems over recent years.

Both the direction and composition of Russia's trade has undergone a fundamental change since liberalisation of the economy began in 1992. The collapse of COMECON led to a re-orientation of trade away from

Russia's former trading partners. Trade with advanced industrial countries grew by 22 per cent in 1994 and 20 per cent in 1993, while with former COMECON countries it fell by 20 and 17 per cent respectively over the same period. The collapse of the rouble zone reinforced the trend as trade with former Soviet Union (FSU) countries declined, while trade with non-FSU countries continued to expand. In 1993, trade with FSU countries decreased by 30 per cent over 1992, but increased with non-FSU countries by 11 per cent (by value).[10] By 1994, the Russian share of world trade had fallen to less than 1 per cent. Russia thus sought to replace its lost captive markets by developing trade with the rest of Europe (particularly the European Union), its 'near abroad' (including the CIS), Asia and the Pacific Rim. By 1995 the European Union (Russia's largest trading partner) accounted for an estimated 45 per cent of Russia's total trade, while the CIS still accounted for 30 per cent of Russian trade.[11]

THE STRUGGLE FOR ECONOMIC STABILISATION

Prime Minister Victor Chernomyrdin heralded 1995 as a 'turning point', when Russia's third attempt to bring about stabilisation through an austerity programme would finally bring inflation and government spending under control. This was to be achieved through tough monetary and fiscal policies, whilst stabilising the rouble. Towards the end of 1995, the government claimed to see the first 'green shoots of recovery'. Yet by early 1997 Yevgeny Yasin, Russian economics minister, conceded that Russia had failed to turn its economy around in 1996, as earlier predicted by the government. Yasin acknowledged that the government's only significant economic success had been the fall in inflation, from 230 per cent in 1995 to 22 per cent in 1996. However, for the vast majority of the Russian population any improvements in their living standards were imperceptible, as real incomes continued to fall.[12]

The monthly rate of inflation fell from 17.8 per cent in January 1995 to 1.6 per cent in May 1996, the lowest monthly rate on record since price liberalisation began in January 1992. The budget deficit was cut from 10.4 per cent of gross domestic product in 1994 to 2.9 per cent in 1995, financed in part by the expansion of the government debt market, external credits (for the first time) and IMF loans. All these improvements were put at risk by the free spending pledges and Yeltsin's largesse in the run-up to the presidential elections.[13] The collapse in industrial production, which had accelerated from 1990 onwards, gave some signs of bottoming out by the end of 1995 as real GDP 'only' fell by 4 per cent over the year. The value of the rouble had been stabilised and successfully defended within the government's established corridor (r. 4,300–r. 4,900 : $1), leading to a 70 per cent appreciation in real terms in 1995. This trend continued into 1996, although on 1 July that year the government replaced the rouble corridor with a crawling peg system, which allowed the rouble to depreciate slowly. Thereafter the government would only defend the rouble if it depreciated by more than 1.5 per cent a month, thereby reinforcing its commitment to a monthly inflation rate of 1.9 per cent.[14]

Russia's output position, whilst not as dire as in the early 1990s, still showed a 6 per cent decline in the first four months of 1996. Russian gross domestic product fell by 6 per cent in 1996 as a whole, as the country experienced its fifth consecutive year of economic contraction. From 1990 to 1995 output declined by a staggering 39 per cent. Industrial output (which had halved since 1992) fell by 5 per cent in 1996, making Russia's recession one of the worst in modern history.[15] The government's success in combating inflation had been more marked. By mid-1995, retail prices had risen to levels 3,000-4,000 times greater than in 1990. This hyper-inflation caused widespread misery by wiping out savings, pushing up real costs, and discouraging domestic and foreign investment. In 1995, the government curtailed credits to struggling enterprises. Traditionally, government financing patterns followed a strong seasonal cycle. The government tended to maintain strict fiscal and monetary discipline in the first half of the year, only to succumb to pressure from the powerful agricultural, energy and military-industrial lobbies in the second half. The result would be a flood of cheap state credits, pushing up inflation rates as the money supply was increased. Yeltsin's administration avoided following this pattern in 1995, in the run-up to the Duma elections. Notwithstanding, in the politically far more important presidential elections, the government let rip with its spending pledges, leading to the temporary suspension of the $10.2 billion IMF loan facility after the presidential elections. This was underlined when the Central Bank was ordered to release $1 billion to pay for defence plants, teachers' wages and benefits, and vacation allowances for inhabitants in the far north. In spite of resistance from the Central Bank, which viewed the government edict as 'unlawful', the bank was forced to transfer the money to the federal budget. Legislation passed in 1995 removed the Central Bank's legal capacity to unilaterally increase the money supply by extending credits, which were then used to pay off inter-enterprise arrears on a non-market basis. This did not, however, prevent the government from circumventing its own financial regulations when it wanted to. The slippage in financial and monetary discipline during the presidential elections led to Russia's growth forecasts for 1996 and 1997 being revised downwards. In 1996, Russia was facing a federal budget deficit of 9.6 per cent of gross national product, or 11.8 per cent if local budget deficits were included. As Yevgeny Yasin, Russia's economics minister said in 1996: 'We would have just about squeezed through this year, if it had not been for the elections.'[16] Even with Russia's poor economic performance, the country still registered a healthy $15 billion balance of trade, or the equivalent of 4 per cent of gross domestic product in 1995. The problems with Russia's growing budget deficit partly reflected the lack of an efficient and workable tax and revenue system. Tax revenues in 1996 were projected to be 40 per cent short of government targets.[17] The general lack of effective economic reform meant that much of the Russian economy remained outdated, monopolistic and relatively unproductive.

The European Union developed a range of measures to assist the transition of Russia's economy and nascent democracy. Measures covering co-operation in defence conversion, mining and raw materials, the agricultural and energy sectors, science and technology, together with the fostering of business links have been in place since the inception of the EU's Tacis programme in 1991.[18] The EU's grant aid technical assistance programme has the threefold aim of supporting the transition to a market-orientated democracy, the development of partnerships and networks at all levels, and the integration of Russia into the world economy. It offers Russia the benefit of Western know-how through consultancy based projects, covering structural, institutional and legal reforms, and is targeted to strategically important regions. From 1991 to 1994 ECU 630m (US $846m, and about 60 per cent of the CIS total) was committed to 420 projects, with a budget of ECU 506m set for 1995.[19] However, there were complaints that Tacis mainly benefited Western consultants, who were paid large fees to identify how Russian markets could be exploited by Western companies. The European Commission promised their Russian partners that future projects would focus more on achieving practical benefits for the recipient country and its population.[20] The EU's image was not enhanced by the resignation in February 1996 of its ambassador in Moscow, Michael Emerson, who was discovered to be involved in a project to set up a private consultancy in Russia at the end of his period in office. The affair generally increased Russian scepticism about the motives behind Western aid for the country.[21]

THE LEGACY OF THE MILITARY-INDUSTRIAL COMPLEX

The overall structure of the Russian economy has, despite its weakness, changed dramatically since the beginning of the reform process. This change can be attributed to the collapse of the centrally-planned system, and the effect this has had on the vitally important military-industrial complex. The defence industry absorbed a disproportionate share of national resources, with Soviet defence spending accounting for anything from 20 to 35 per cent of gross domestic product.[22] This helps explain the dramatic fall in Russian output following the collapse of the Soviet Union. Some 80 per cent of the Soviet Union's defence industry was concentrated in the Russian Federation. A World Bank report in 1992 estimated that 5.4 million people (7.5 per cent of the total workforce) were employed in Russia's military-industrial complex.[23] Defence production was also highly concentrated on a regional basis, with for example 50 per cent of the workforce in the Volga *oblast* (region) and 43.5 per cent in Novosibirsk *oblast* working in defence-related industries. With the decline in defence orders and government financial support for the military-industrial complex, the potential for heavy job losses and social dislocation was enormous. As Julian Cooper stated, the military-industrial complex presented Russia with a real challenge:

> The important issue for Russia . . . and the world at large is whether the Soviet defence industry legacy can be reduced in size and restructured to make it compatible with the country's true economic strength and new security requirements without provoking social unrest with a potential to check or reverse the broader transformation policy.[24]

Under Prime Minister Gaidar, the Russia government immediately began the task of reforming the defence industry. One of the main problems the government faced was the fact that the defence sector was highly dependent upon state credits to keep it afloat. In 1992 the government introduced its 'shock therapy', reducing defence spending to 4.3 per cent of gross domestic product (GDP), and defence procurement orders by 68 per cent. Defence spending remained at much the same level over subsequent years. Following a protracted wrangle over the size of the defence budget in 1993–94 (led by Defence Minister Pavel Grachev), the military-industrial lobby failed to wring substantial concessions from the government, with defence spending eventually accounting for 4.4 per cent of GDP in 1994. This was comparable to defence expenditure in the West, where in the same period US defence spending amounted to 4 per cent of GDP, with British and French defence budgets standing at around 3 per cent of GDP. In the 1995 budget the government prioritised defence spending in crucial areas, such as the nuclear strategic forces, and cut back elsewhere. Successive Russian governments thus signalled their intention to radically downsize and restructure the defence sector, whose influence gradually waned.

The defence industry thus experienced a dramatic fall in output, exacerbated by falling demand and arms reduction agreements with the West. Total output in the defence industry in 1993 was barely half its 1990 level (55 per cent), with military and civilian production falling to 30 per cent and 75 per cent of their respective 1990 levels. This trend continued throughout 1994, with civilian production declining at an accelerating rate. Although the civilian share of output rose from 50 per cent in 1990 to nearly 80 per cent in 1993, this trend had more to do with the contraction of the defence sector than the success of Russia's conversion from defence to civilian production.[25] Russia attempted to slow the rate of decline of defence production by actively encouraging arms exports, especially from 1995 onwards. It was hoped this would provide a limited 'engine' for the recovery of the defence sector and the economy as a whole. Russia targeted its arms sales on areas where it was deemed competitive in world markets, including such defence products as combat aircraft, tanks and missile systems. The Russian Federation also sought to export defence-related equipment and arms to the developing world. Figures released in August 1996 by the US Congressional Research Service suggest that Russia had become the world's largest arms exporter to the developing world, with China its biggest customer. Russia's arms sales to the developing world increased by 62 per cent in 1995, and were worth $6 billion. By comparison, US sales were $3.8 billion.[26] Russia's policy of actively pursuing increased arms sales to the Third World and countries viewed as hostile to the West brought Russia into direct conflict with Western interests. The Russian Federation pursued an assertive Russia First strategy to underpin its defence sector, despite the tensions this undoubtedly created in its relationship with the West. This was explicitly recognised in the foreign ministry's concept paper of March 1993 which acknowledged 'the possibility of friction on specific questions in areas where Russian enterprises prove competitive (space, arms exports and others)'.[27] Nevertheless, Russia subsequently stepped up its exports to the Third World and the 'pariah' states, underlining the ascendency of Russia First.

Conversion and diversification from military to civilian production was not a great success in Russia. This was partly due to chaotic government administration, poor defence sector reorganisation, and the lack of any coherent conversion strategy. State funding was also cut in 1993, partly in response to the low level of uptake of federal funds for conversion projects. Projects were poorly selected and supervised, while some funding was clearly diverted for maintaining employment, for social facilities, and for paying-off debts. There were also technical, quality and distribution problems with conversion projects.[28] In 1994, more emphasis was placed on regional projects, and specialised areas such as the space and aviation sectors, where Russia remained competitive on a global scale. Even so, regional enterprises continued to press Russia's regional authorities to mitigate the social aspects of restructuring, rather than adopt wholesale conversion . Russia's conversion strategy was thus a relative failure, having only a marginal effect on Russian companies.[29]

Privatisation of the defence sector achieved mixed results, encountering a number of problems during the privatisation process itself. The privatisation process was the subject of considerable political controversy, not least at governmental level. Andrei Kokoshin, the civilian first deputy defence minister in 1992, set out a strategy in his National Industrial Policy. This envisaged creating a number of financial-industrial groups (FIGs) to drive the privatisation process in the defence industry. This essentially amounted to a corporatisation of the defence industry by encouraging the alliance of defence enterprises, commercial and insurance companies to underpin productive capacity. The move was opposed by Anatoly Chubais, then head of the State Committee for the Management of State Property, who favoured the break-up of enterprises rather than the creation of new conglomerates.[30]

Nevertheless, a presidential decree promoting the development of FIGs was signed at the end of 1993, although it contained a number of legal constraints. In practice, only fifty-five FIGs had been set up by the end of 1994, with ten more established in 1996. Many enterprises were reluctant to give up their status as independent joint-stock companies, whilst financial-commercial concerns regarded the defence sector as high-risk.

Privatisation in the defence industry thus generally proceeded along the lines set out in the 1992 privatisation programme. The first stage involved the drawing-up of a list of companies to be privatised. Some 25 per cent of the defence sector, or 449 enterprises, were identified for privatisation. The state retained different levels of ownership depending on the importance of the enterprise for national security, varying from the complete ownership of enterprises deemed vital for national security, to partial ownership (in the form of a 'golden share') for those of lesser importance. In the latter case, the board of directors would represent the rights and interests of the state. Seventy-eight companies were privatised in 1992, with the pace accelerating in 1993. By the end of 1993, 500 companies had been privatised or were in the course of being privatised. This was part of Prime Minister Yegor Gaidar's 'shock therapy.' A second phase of privatisation was launched in 1994, which followed a three-option model determining the relative weights of worker, management and state control. The state was still to maintain complete control over key strategic entities, which were not destined for privatisation. This phase of the process accelerated the overall rate of privatisation, so that by mid-1994 more than a thousand enterprises had been privatised (with 454 remaining under state control). The process was due to be completed by the end of 1996, with 50 per cent of enterprises privatised under the general procedure, 35 per cent subject to the government's golden share, and 15 per cent under varying degrees of state control.[31] These figures only covered those enterprises remaining in the defence sector. Overall, it was intended that around 60 per cent of former defence enterprises would become independent private companies.[32]

By the end of 1994 an estimated 2 million personnel had left the Russian defence industry.[33] Many employees transferred to other economic sectors, but the full scale of the shake-out was disguised by massive under-employment and support for practically bankrupt enterprises with cheap state credits. The defence sector operated well below its productive capacity, with management showing a marked reluctance to shed employees and close under-utilised plant. The result in many cases had been that employees remained on the books of enterprises which had no orders, and therefore could not afford to pay their workers' wages. Increasingly, in order to protect jobs and strategic sectors of Russia's military-industrial complex, Moscow came to rely on a combination of state support and an arms export drive, with the emphasis on the latter. The Kremlin, in its desire to preserve what was left of the military-industrial complex, pursued a Russia First strategy that led to political disagreements with the West over the supply of arms to pariah states and unstable regions, and economic competition to seize lucrative new defence markets. With the loss of captive markets in Eastern Europe, Moscow developed ever closer links with China, which rapidly became its largest arms market and an eager purchaser of Russia's high-tech military hardware.

STRUCTURAL CHANGE IN THE RUSSIAN ECONOMY

The transmogrification of the military-industrial complex has helped precipitate a dramatic structural shift in the Russian economy. Previously, the economy laid greater emphasis on developing heavy industry at the expense of light industry, services and a consumer goods sector. While the heavy and light industrial sectors have contracted, the service sector has grown considerably in the early 1990s. The service sector accounted for around 50 per cent of gross domestic product in 1994, compared to 33 per cent in 1990.[34] Retail and banking services grew most rapidly in this sector. It has been argued by Vincent Koen and Michael Marrese that Russia has witnessed the development of the 'survivalist' versus the 'subsidised' enterprise. The former have restructured or emerged in response to price liberalisation, cuts in subsidies, real interest rates and privatisation. They have actively sought out new markets, clients and products. The latter, however, have undertaken little or no restructuring, either because they have been excluded from the privatisation process, lack investment or can avoid closure by lobbying federal and regional authorities for subsidies or favours.[35]

Thus economic policy-making and enterprise behaviour is based on a mutually beneficial and corrupt relationship between government and some sectors of Russian industry. This has led Russia towards the development of a monopolistic, oligarchic economy, instead of Western-style capitalism. The banking sector perhaps best exemplifies this trend, with its dynamic entrepreneurship contrasting with a primitive and under-regulated system in which crime and corruption are endemic. Banking also exemplifies the emergence of a 'get rich quick' class of entrepreneurs, while the system itself verges on the abyss of collapse. By 1996, there were over 2,500 private banks in Russia, many of which made relatively easy money during periods of high inflation. The value of subsidised credits to industrial enterprises amounted to around 30 per cent of gross domestic product in 1992. These credits were issued at an interest rate of 10 or 20 per cent per annum, while at the time in 1992 inflation was running at 2,500 per cent a year. Although the aim was to boost falling agricultural and industrial production, the main beneficiaries were bankers with good contacts who held on to the money. In the process, some bankers made a fortune by simply borrowing cheaply from the government, and either re-investing the money in high-yield bonds, or recycling the money in expensive short-term loans. Bankers enriched themselves while production levels in Russian industry were collapsing .[36]

The banking sector failed to develop along Western lines, with very few offering a personal customer service, cheque books or more than short-term loans. The stabilisation of the rouble led to a lack of liquidity in the banking sector which threatened the viability of a number of banking institutions, many of which had to rely on central bank funding to preserve their liquidity. The emergence of the banking sector as a centre of financial power led to bankers entering the political arena to seek favours from the ruling elite. Oleg Boyko, head of Olbi (one of Russia's 'big eight' banks), consciously courted President Yeltsin in order to protect his business interests. Boyko initially gave financial backing to Russia's Choice (then linked to the president), later switching to Stabilnost, a new bloc loyal to Yeltsin, when Gaidar's party withdrew its support. Vladimir Gusinsky, head of the Most banking and media empire, found himself harassed and forced into exile when he backed the president's opponents.[37] The banking sector was indicative of the failure of the Russian reform process to tackle the economy's structural problems. Russia still lacked a comprehensive legal and institutional framework, necessary to underpin a fully functioning market economy. The absence of such a legal-institutional framework was not conducive to the development of a favourable commercial environment, corporate governance or significant inward investment.

Price liberalisation freed most, but not all prices, with the ministry of economy calculating that controlled prices covered 30 per cent of gross domestic product (GDP) at the beginning of 1995.[38] Partly this was due to price controls at regional and local level, which continued to regulate some transport, rent and food prices, combined with export quotas to prevent local food shortages. It was also the result of the State Committee for 'anti-monopoly policy and the support of new economic structures' imposing price controls to protect selected monopolies. The energy sector resisted price liberalisation, and by 1995 oil prices had only reached 50 per cent of world levels. Russian energy exports brought windfall profits to producers without fully supporting the exchange rate, while under-pricing and the reluctance of the government to increase taxation reduced the sector's revenue potential. This in turn worsened the government's budgetary position and exacerbated its revenue shortfall. In 1995 the energy sector accounted for about 15 per cent of total GDP, while tax revenues from the sector were projected to net only around 2 per cent of GDP.[39]

Prime Minister Victor Chernomyrdin, as former head of the huge natural gas monopoly Gazprom, was pivotal in ensuring the energy sector received privileged government treatment. Gazprom itself accounted for between 7 and 8 per cent of Russia's GDP, held a third of the world's proven gas reserves, and supplied more than a fifth of Western Europe's gas. Potentially, Gazprom was worth more than the combined value of all the companies listed on the London Stock Exchange. A Gazprom international share launch in October 1996 priced the company's shares at four times the cost of its shares on the domestic market. The international offering represented just 1 per cent of Gazprom's shares, and indicated the flagship company's determination to restrict foreign share ownership and influence. Moscow's Russia First strategy meant that Gazprom, as a vitally important national economic asset, must remain under Russian management and control. An injection of foreign capital would be welcome, but any attempt to obtain foreign leverage over the company would be resisted. Because of Gazprom's close relationship with the Kremlin, there was also a widespread belief that the company was not paying its fair share of domestic taxation.[40]

After a unified exchange rate was introduced in 1992, the Russian government allowed the rate to float, within the limits of a currency corridor introduced in July 1995. In nominal terms the rouble declined enormously from 1991 to 1993, but appreciated thereafter in real terms, except during two brief but acute exchange rate crises. The first crisis occurred in September 1993, following President Yeltsin's dissolution of the Supreme Soviet and the storming of the White House. The second took place in October 1994 and was known as 'Black Tuesday'. The rouble steadily recovered though it experienced upward inflationary 'blips'. It continued to appreciate throughout 1995 and the first half of 1996. The Russians' lack of confidence in their own currency could be seen in the massive outflow of dollars to overseas havens. In 1991–92 this peaked at $10–15 billion, and by 1995 the figure was about $5–6 billion, falling to an estimated $1–4 billion in 1996. Ivan Rybkin, the former speaker of the Duma, estimated in 1995 that the 'new Russians' kept $100 billion abroad.[41] The downward trend indicated a cautious but growing confidence in the country's financial and political stability. The rouble was finally made convertible on the current account from May 1996, making it easier for importers to obtain foreign currency and for exporters to retain their earnings.[42] In economic terms, Russia First was designed to improve trading conditions and financial stability within the country for the benefit of Russian entrepreneurs (especially those with government contacts). Political and financial stability would also boost inward foreign investment, while Russian corporate and legal structures ensured that the most profitable companies remained under Russian ownership and control.

PRIVATISATION

The overall privatisation process itself brought mixed results. On the face of it, the number of enterprises privatised appeared impressive. By December 1995, 122,000 firms had been privatised, accounting for more than 80 per cent of the industrial workforce. Over 75 per cent of small-scale businesses had been privatised, with the process fully completed in the *oblasts* of Nizhnii Novgorod, Kurgan, Ryazan, Irkutsk and Khabarovsk.[43] However, many of the newly privatised enterprises remained dependent on soft credits from the Central Bank for their survival. The widespread phenomenon of 'insider domination' meant that many enterprises were run according to the interests of individual managers or employers which often bore little relation to market demand. Some Russian ministries maintained control over certain strategic sectors of the economy which covered one-third of the enterprises working in the fields of mineral resources, military facilities, nuclear reactors, rail and water transport.

Employees and managers affected by privatisation were granted concessions giving them 'pre-emptive' rights on substantial parts of their enterprises.[44] Shares or blocks of shares could be purchased under preferential terms. Managers and workers were given the option of three privatisation models, and some three-quarters chose the model which guaranteed them overall control of their enterprise through a 51 per cent stake. Managers and employees thus often colluded in an attempt to protect their enterprises from external pressures. Managers were reluctant to relinquish control, while workers feared the effects of restructuring and the accompanying job losses. It has been estimated that enterprise insiders (managers and workers) emerged as majority stakeholders in nearly 70 per cent of all Russian enterprises.

Voucher privatisation, giving each Russian citizen the right to acquire assets in enterprises, was designed to counterbalance the 'privileged' position of managers and employees, and to embody the principle of fairness. When it was launched at the end of 1992, however, 'voucherisation', covered only a third of the total amount of property to be privatised. Initial public interest in voucher auctions, where vouchers could be used to buy shares in enterprises, was low. Moreover, enterprises resisted 'voucherisation' fearing outside intrusion, and saw little advantage in receiving vouchers instead of cash investment. By the completion of voucher privatisation in July 1994, of those enterprises subject to voucher privatisation, 24,00 had been 'corporatised' and 15,000 privatised, accounting for 83 per cent of total employment and 60 per cent of all industrial assets.[45]

Voucher privatisation accounted for 31 per cent of total sales in the privatisation process. However, the whole process (led by Anatoly Chubais) was widely criticised for entrenching the position of enterprise 'insiders', who rapidly snapped up the virtually worthless vouchers from a disillusioned public.[46] With the end of voucher privatisation, the government decided the remaining shares would be sold for cash (an option accounting for 15 per cent of privatisation). This involved selling off the remaining 7,000 state-owned companies, as well as residual state-owned shares in privatised companies. This stage of 'cash privatisation' also covered the disposal of some of Russia's oil and gas enterprises, considered to be the country's most internationally competitive and attractive companies. Of particular interest to foreign investors, the sales were planned to boost the federal coffers as the government stood to receive 49 per cent of sale proceeds, with the remainder benefiting regional authorities.[47] In contrast to the first stage of privatisation, the second stage was much slower. The government was led by political pressure to keep around 3,000 enterprises, classified as 'important to the national interest', under public control. Powerful political lobbying by firms like Gazprom successfully persuaded the administration to delay sales of further packets of shares.

By adopting a broad definition of enterprises which had to be protected as 'important to the national interest' the Kremlin ensured that foreign influence was constrained, while at the same time Russian 'insiders' were rewarded. Privatisation and the policy of retaining control of 3,000 'national interest' enterprises thus benefited political and financial 'insiders' with close links to the Kremlin, who profited from cheap purchases of government stock, and those 'insiders' who retained control of the strategic state enterprises. In any event, the privatisation process became a form of *nomenklatura* privatisation', with effective control staying in the hands of Soviet era factory directors. Within the 3,000 'national interest' enterprises, the existing members of the *nomenklatura* remained in control. In private or public enterprises, the *nomenklatura* were the winners. However, a number of the privatised enterprises did fall under the control of the cash rich 'New Russians', who had in many cases amassed their fortunes in dubious (and criminal) circumstances. Thus even the privatisation process was influenced by a Russia First policy, which was designed primarily to secure Russia's strategic interests against foreign encroachment, and to enrich those close to the government. The whole privatisation process had been characterised by a distinct lack of transparency, and allegations of unfair asset evaluation and availability.

The investment climate in Russia was generally unfavourable for both the domestic and foreign investor, particularly the latter. Foreign investment accounted for only 1 per cent of share ownership in the country by 1994.[48] The legal and institutional framework in Russia provided an insufficient degree of protection and clarification of foreign investors' ownership rights. The share registration process was extremely underdeveloped, with a real risk that an outsider's shareholding could be inaccurately recorded, or even wiped off a company's books. As no central share registration system was established, companies kept their own register of shareholders, leaving obvious scope for inaccuracies or manipulation. Foreign investors had great difficulty in establishing control over recalcitrant Russian managers, with some disputes over whether overseas owners legally won control after purchasing a dominant shareholding.[49] It was a problem that Anatoly Chubais, the architect of the privatisation programme, freely admitted was one of the main failings associated with the privatisation process.

Russia's Central Bank also discriminated against foreign investors buying government bonds. The Central Bank's deputy governor, Andrei Kozlov, informed foreign investors in July 1996 that the bank would 'clamp down' on overseas investors who sought the same lucrative terms as locals. Foreign investors' returns were capped at around 20 per cent annually (and guaranteed in dollars), but this was less than half the yield available to local buyers. Western investors had circumvented these restrictions, mainly by lending money to local agents who would then buy bonds on terms offered to local buyers. It was estimated that 10 per cent of government debt was held by foreigners in this form. Announcing the clamp-down, Kozlov said he hoped there would be a 'peaceful withdrawal' from such schemes. One Western banker remarked: 'If they want foreign capital they have to offer parity with local investors.' However, the whole incident indicated that there appeared to be one set of rules for Russians, and another for foreigners. In protecting the position of Russian investors at the expense of foreign investors, the Central Bank was exposing a crude Russia First attitude. Russian interests and profits would come first, whatever the cries of 'foul' from the West.[50]

Many enterprises also attached less than favourable conditions to sales of shares. Gazprom again provides a ready example of this form of Russian protectionism. Shareholders buying shares in Gazprom were obliged to offer their shares back to the company before they could be sold to outsiders. Under this scheme Gazprom was able to buy shares back at 'book value', the price being dictated by Gazprom, since it had no public books.[51] This had nothing to do with developing an open market system, and everything to do with ensuring Gazprom's directors maintained control of the company at all costs. It is another example of the country's Russia First strategy as applied to the economy, putting Russian economic interests before those of foreign investors. It also conveniently suited the interests of Russia's economic elite, who were closely linked to the Kremlin's 'inner circle'. Even those Russian entrepreneurs outside the favoured 'inner circle' accepted the logic of keeping the profitable parts of the Russian economy protected from foreign control.

Russia's economic transformation following the collapse of the Soviet Union was stunted by weak inward investment. The cumulative total of foreign direct investment (FDI) remained low, amounting to US$4.4 billion at the end of 1995, according to the UN Economic Commission for Europe (ECE). At the beginning of 1995, Russia accounted for 13.4 per cent of the total $24.9 billion stock in the Central and East European states, coming third behind Hungary and Poland. Per capita FDI in Russia at the beginning of 1995 was only US$29.65, compared with US$962 in Hungary (the leading recipient of foreign investment in Central and Eastern Europe). In 1995, China attracted twelve times more foreign investment than Russia. Arkady Volsky, chairman of Russia's Union of Industrialists and Entrepreneurs, estimated that the Russian economy had the potential to receive $10–12 billion in foreign capital annually.[52] The Russian government took some steps to foster Russia's image as a more investor-friendly country, with the aim of boosting foreign confidence. Russia signed twelve investor protection agreements with EU and EFTA member states, while the Duma passed a law on production-sharing agreements in December 1995. But in July 1996, after pressure from Communists in the Duma, the government was forced to reduce the number of oil fields and other natural resource sites it was proposing to open up to foreign investment. The number of proposed production-sharing sites was cut from 200 to sixty, following Communists' claims that the government was selling out Russia's national interests to foreigners.[53] This concern to protect the country's economic assets against foreign ownership and influence is an indication of how Russia First impinged upon domestic policy and political attitudes.

Foreign investment and the privatisation process were an integral part of the Russia First strategy, and impacted directly upon domestic economic policy. The privatisation process was designed and implemented to favour Russian 'insiders', with little opportunity for significant foreign involvement. Similarly, foreign investment opportunities in Russia's premier enterprises were structured in such a way that external investment rarely led to external control. This commercial environment was assisted by a legal framework that favoured domestically owned companies and obfuscated foreign share-owning rights. In other words, while Russia encouraged both privatisation and foreign investment, it ensured that the most viable enterprises remained under Russian control. Foreign investment was welcomed, but only in so far as it boosted Russian profitability and did not lead to foreign ownership. Russia had therefore embarked upon large-scale privatisation, and provided opportunities for foreign investment, but baulked at creating an open, market economy. The Russian market was neither open, nor a true market economy. In this sense, the Kremlin created a hybrid market economy, ensuring Russian dominance by creating conditions of unfair competition and blatant protectionism. These domestic conditions in turn restricted foreign investment in the Russian market. As the vote in the Duma over opening up production sites to foreign investment showed, there was an ideological hostility to large-scale foreign ownership and investment which implied foreign control of Russian resources. To this extent, Russia First meant not only giving preference to Russian-owned and controlled enterprises, but downright hostility to foreign influence over the economy. This aspect of the Russia First strategy symbolised the country's bloody-minded and nationalistic approach to foreign investors which was at its most strident amongst communist and nationalist deputies of the Russian Duma.

Despite this resistance to foreign ownership, some of the country's premier energy companies were eager to tap foreign sources of finance, whilst maintaining Russian control. To this end, LUKoil auctioned a 9.2 per cent stake in the company in September 1995, attracting a $250m bid from an American company, Atlantic Richfield. Similarly, in September 1996, Gazprom finally announced it would be selling 9 per cent of its shares to foreign investors. The first step was to launch itself on the international global markets by selling a 1.5 per cent stake in the form of global and depository receipts. Gazprom's move marked a small but significant opening up of Russia's flagship company, without risking foreign interference in the running of the enterprise. Although Gazprom was Russia's richest company, with generous legal and tax breaks provided by its friends in government, the company was still anxious to amass adequate investment capital to fund its ambitious and expensive projects.

Attempts by the government to quicken the pace of the privatisation process and swell federal coffers in conjunction with the banking sector, swiftly ran into difficulties. In autumn 1995, the government borrowed 9 trillion roubles from a consortium of eight banks, in return for collateral in the form of state shareholdings. Vladimir Potanin, Chairman of Oneximbank, was instrumental in drawing up the 'shares-for-loans' scheme. Potanin was appointed deputy prime minister with responsibility for the economy in August 1996.[54] However, the operation was later thwarted by a ruling from the ministry of justice, which declared the shares-for-loans scheme invalid. A parliamentary committee was established in February 1996 to rule on the legality of the privatisation process as a whole. The shares-for-loans scheme was abandoned in

April 1996, primarily to defuse political controversy in the run-up to the presidential elections. Prime Minister Chernomyrdin ordered the Committee for the Privatisation of State Property to repay the loans made to the government by the banking consortium. The government instead decided to opt for a more selective and targeted approach to privatisation. The incident indicated the often incestuous relationship between Russian banks and the government over the privatisation process. Apart from the lucrative business of trading in government securities and loans, Russian banks often acted as 'front' companies, channelling government credit to favoured ailing industries.

The slow pace and limited interest shown in the second stage of privatisation stands in contrast to the first phase. The government developed a 'mix and match' approach, comprising cash auctions for specific share packets (with only some open to foreign bidders), and the direct purchase of stakes by strategic investors.[55] Since the 1995 Duma elections, criticism of the privatisation process has grown, with Moscow Mayor Yury Luzhkov one of its most vocal critics. The cases of Norilsk Nickel and Zil are examples of a growing trend towards limited de-privatisation. Yury Luzhkov orchestrated the effective re-nationalisation of Russia's famous car-manufacturer, when Moscow city authority bought out Microdin, a private Zil shareholder. Microdin's 30 per cent stake in Zil had been insufficient to force through a restructuring of the industrial giant. Luzhkov preferred to attribute Zil's financial crisis to 'ill-conceived privatisation', rather than to any problems in the company itself.[56]

Political opposition to privatisation was reflected amongst the Russian public. An estimated 20–25 per cent of Russia's labour force worked in enterprises untouched by privatisation, and therefore did not receive any shares. There were a number of reported cases where managers exploited legal loopholes (such as forming separate companies under their control), so that they gained far more shares than they were entitled to. Estimates suggested that top management acquired 9 per cent of shares through the initial privatisation process, while workers secured 56 per cent. The Trade Union Research Centre subsequently estimated that managers and employees held 20 and 30 per cent of voting shares respectively.[57] The concentration of share ownership in managers' hands illustrated the extent of 'secondary' share purchases, which reinforced managerial control. Ironically, the privatisation process strengthened the position of many *nomenklatura* managers, who had been appointed in the Soviet era. It was not surprising that these managers were thus often slow to adapt to the demands of the evolving market.

This whole trend broadly describes the phenomenon of 'nomenklatura privatisation', which reinforced the general perception that privatisation only benefited a relatively small circle of insiders. The first appearance of the phenomenon was during the era of perestroika, when 'spontaneous privatisation' developed as the laws on enterprise control were relaxed. A number of the old nomenklatura made handsome gains during this period through asset stripping, and former party apparatchiks became the mainstay of the new 'capitalist' class. A Moscow survey of Russia's top one hundred business people found that 61 were former members of the nomenklatura. High profile examples include Nikolai Ryzhkov, Gorbachev's former prime minister, who became chairman of Tveruniversal Bank, and Sergei Yegorov, former head of the Russian Republic office of the State Bank, who became president of the Association of Russian Banks.[58]

Gazprom provides the most significant example of 'nomenklatura privatisation'. Although excluded from the official privatisation programme, 60 per cent of the stakes in the company ended up in the hands of a few company insiders, favoured politicians, and banks owned by former members of the nomenklatura. Privatisation 'scandals' are not limited to the old nomenklatura. Connections with up-and-coming financial institutions have also led to dubious business deals. Oneximbank, led by the 35-year-old Vladimir Potanin, developed close links with Alexander Korzhakov, at that time Yeltsin's security chief. In an auction to control 38 per cent of Norilsk Nickel (already part-owned by the bank), Oneximbank was named as the government's auctioneer and duly announced its own offer of $170m was the winning bid, despite the fact that it was only $100,000 above the minimum, and that a rival had offered twice the amount.

Moscow's plans to privatise the Russian telecoms market, announced in December 1996, were also criticised for detering Western investors and favouring Russian banks. Under the plans, which upset the World Bank, the government confirmed a merger of the state's telecoms holdings in Rostelekom and Svyazinvest, its long-distance operators. A 25 per cent stake in the combined companies was offered to a single buyer for $1.2 billion, 40 per cent below some valuations. The terms were said to favour banks which helped finance Yeltsin's re-election campaign, such as Most Bank and Alfa Bank. A $400m cash bond was required in advance of the sale, and foreign companies were given inadequate time to prepare a thorough bid. The winning consortium was also to be asked to speed up payment of telephone bills, a stipulation that favoured Russian banks with their extensive branch networks. The World Bank feared the proposals would stifle competition in the Russian telecoms market. Citing national security, the Russian government sacked the Western banks advising on the telecoms privatisation, including NM Rothschild. The whole incident was another example of Russia First at work in the domestic sphere, with the blatant economic protectionism (and favours to the charmed 'inner circle') gaining ascendency over market reform and the operation of a free market.[59]

The Russian economy faces a number of structural defects, arising from its limited experience of a true market economy system. Russia's securities markets are under-developed and under-regulated, and the country has a fragile small and medium-sized company sector. Markets are also often highly segmented and concentrated along regional or sub-regional lines, with many single-industry towns. It is here that the legacy of the Soviet command economy is most apparent, with the lack of a good infrastructure, information and communication networks. Concentration risks social dislocation as specialised or monopoly firms become insolvent in the new economic climate. The spectre of mass unemployment hangs like a threat over the whole economy, as the government struggles to rebuild Russian industry. Only time will tell if the attempted economic transformation turns the economy around, or the country continues to stagger from crisis to crisis.

THE IMPACT OF ECONOMIC REFORM ON THE RUSSIAN POPULATION

The Russian Federation's economic reforms had a devastating effect on the majority of the Russian people. Yet it was not until the autumn of 1994 that an opinion poll showed a majority of the population wanting an end to the economic reform process. For many people, the economic reforms promised opportunity and Western-style wealth. Legendary as Russian patience may be, by 1994 most Russians had had enough of impoverishment and falling living standards. The growing distance between rich and poor, and the appearance of a poverty gap, became the country's most burning political issue. The sight of ostentatious *nouveaux riches* or so-called 'New Russians', replete with Mercedes,

BMWs and designer clothes, provided a daily reminder of the 'winners' and 'losers' in post-Soviet Russian society.

The emergence of a new 'capitalist consumer' culture has been hailed by some as a sign that Russia's experience of economic reform has not been all bad. It is indisputable that consumer goods became widely available, banishing the queues and shortages of the Soviet and early transition periods. In 1994 50 per cent of Russia's imports were consumer goods, primarily coming from the West. A flourishing retail sector sprang up, with chains of medium-sized stores, and thousands of small street kiosks spread throughout Russian towns and cities. Imported Western goods were put on sale with a mark-up of up to 30 per cent, making a healthy profit for their Russian distributors. Whilst many Western imports were beyond the price range of the average Russian, their very exclusivity made them more attractive to the 'New Russians'. The consumer revolution thus exacerbated the outward signs of the poverty gap evident in Russian society.

The Western-influenced 'consumer revolution' was not to everyone's liking. Moscow's mayor, Yury Luzhkov, took steps to ban non-cyrillic public advertising hoardings bearing Western brand names across the city. The Russian language has been invaded by some 10,000 English words, a fact that was resented by advocates of linguistic purity, particularly the Russian Communist Party. Foreign words such as *blu dzhins* (blue jeans), *kompiuternye aksesuary* (computer accessories), *diler* (dealer) and *ofshor* (offshore) had 'invaded' the Russian language. The government responded by establishing the Russian Language Council, similar to the Académie Française, grouping together academics, writers and prominent politicians. The Language Council was charged with drafting a Russian equivalent of the French Tourbon laws, to defend the native language against foreign influences. If adopted, these would have the effect of regulating the use of non-Russian language in the media and advertising. To some extent the proposed laws can be seen as the manifestation of Russia First on a cultural level, designed to limit the West's linguistic and psychological influence on Russian society. Anti-Western attitudes had also been displayed by the Duma over the issue of Acquired Immune Deficiency Syndrome (AIDS), when deputies had voted in favour of compulsory tests for foreign visitors, to prove they were not HIV-positive. President Yeltsin's compromise that this should only apply to visitors staying in Russia for more than three months was still regarded as a sign of hostility to 'foreign' influences.[60]

The gap between rich and poor in Russia widened rapidly between 1992 and 1994, but slowed during 1995. Even so, the poverty gap remained large, with the richest tenth of the population earning 13.5 times more than the poorest tenth in 1995 (the figure was 14.2 in 1994). So-called 'New Russians', representing between 3–5 per cent of the population (about 4.4 to 7.2 million people) had an average monthly income of between $500 and $100,000 in 1995, with the rich concentrated in the Moscow area. The most prosperous 20 per cent of the population received 50 per cent of household incomes. It has been estimated that 50 per cent of the emerging entrepreneurial class is made up of former professionals, such as engineers and teachers.[61] Medium income earners probably constituted around 25–30 per cent (37m–44.4m) of the population, although given the unknown size of the second economy, this figure is a broad estimate.

Low-income earners (based on 1994 figures) accounted for 30–35 per cent (44.4m–51.8m) of the population. Essentially, the people in this category had sufficient income to purchase basic necessities such as food, lodgings, medicaments and clothing. However, low-earners could easily slip into the category of people defined as 'destitute', which accounted for 15–20 per cent (22.2m–29.6m) of the population. Destitute people had enough to meet their basic living requirements such as food and basic lodgings, but had nothing extra to buy new clothes or medicines. Some 5–10 per cent (7.4m–14.8m) of the population could be defined as people in a position of 'extreme material distress', suffering from extreme poverty, including food shortages. Various estimates place the number of Russians living below the poverty line in April 1996 at around 22 per cent, or 32.5 million people. This is a considerable improvement on the figures for April 1995, which estimated those living in poverty at 29 per cent, or 42.9 million people. Nevertheless, the position in 1996 remained fairly dire, and estimates put the number of people experiencing impoverishment since the beginning of the economic reforms at 45 million.[62]

Victor Ilyushin, appointed by Yeltsin as a first deputy prime minister with resposibility for social policy after the presidential election in 1996, said: 'We have to admit that poverty is widespread. The number of citizens on incomes below the subsistence level is about one-quarter of the Russian population.' At the time the official subsistence level stood at around $60 a month. Ilyushin further admitted that real incomes had fallen by 40 per cent since 1991, while income differentials had increased dramatically. In 1992, one-third of Russia's population lived below the poverty line. While the proportion of the population living on subsistence levels had declined somewhat over the intervening years, Ilyushin was aware of the inability of the government to provide a social welfare safety net. By October 1996, due to poor tax revenues, the public health authorities had only received 60 per cent of their budget, education 65 per cent and culture 30 per cent. 'We can only pay wages, and even here problems are arising,' Ilyushin concluded.[63]

The broadly defined socio-economic categories disguised a certain social fluidity, with frequent movement between the various groups. Obtaining a second job or extending a share of cultivatable land may be enough to ensure a relatively secure living. However, redundancy, wage arrears or illness can push individuals quickly into poverty. In Russia's socio-economic climate, many people have lived in relative insecurity and are susceptible to rapid and dramatic changes in their personal well-being. Rising poverty has also had a differential impact, with the most vulnerable social groups including single-parent families with young children, elderly people (especially living alone on low pensions), disabled people and minorities inhabiting the distant reaches of the Russian Federation.[64]

There are other socio-economic indicators that show that social conditions have deteriorated in Russia since 1991. Life expectancy for men and women fell from 63.5 and 74.3 years respectively in 1991 to 57.3 and 71.1 years (respectively) in 1994. Mortality and infant mortality rates have shown a marked increase during the same period, from 11.4 and 17.8 (deaths per 1,000 inhabitants) respectively to 15.7 and 18.6 respectively. The number of medical personnel per head of the population in Russia matches Western countries such as the United Kingdom and the United States. However, acute under-funding has led to a crisis of health care in the country, unknown in the Soviet period. The state's health-care service for all but the new rich has deteriorated sharply since the demise of the Soviet Union. Medical staff are poorly paid and motivated, with health funding declining from 3.4 per cent of total expenditure in the Soviet era to 1.8 per cent in 1994. Payment is necessary to obtain treatment, with authorised charges for operations, blood products and certain medication.[65] With an average monthly wage in March 1996 of 740,000 roubles ($153), the price quoted for a heart-bypass operation in a state hospital the same year was 28–35m roubles, far beyond the reach of the average Russian.[66] The incidence of serious infections and disease has increased sharply in recent years, as a result of the deteriorating provision of health care. There have been increasing numbers of cases of tuberculosis, diphtheria, cholera, dysentery, salmonella and hepatitis. About 40,000 cases of diphtheria were recorded in 1994, compared with only 800 in 1991.[67] Whilst under communism there were special health facilities for the elite, Russian private health care remains in its infancy.

Other statistics offer further evidence of the side-effects of the economic reform process. The homicide rate jumped by 50 per cent in 1992 and 34 per cent in 1993.[68] The suicide rate increased by 17 and 23 per cent respectively for the same period. These statistics provided a background of poverty, deteriorating health, rising crime and social alienation for the majority of the Russian people. While a minority benefited from the economic reforms, the majority faced an uncertain future. Almost two-thirds of the population saw their standard of living drop after 1991, while only around one in ten saw their living standards improve.[69] The average monthly wage of $153 in March 1996 had fallen by 10 per cent in real terms since January 1992. In the year to March 1995, real pay decreased over the year by 33 per cent.[70] The average monthly wage stood at 654,000 roubles in January 1996, while the salary required for basic subsistence stood at 620,333 roubles per month.[71] At the same time, wages have been shrinking as a proportion of household income in Russia, from two-thirds in 1992 to 40 per cent in 1995.[72] The non-wage income has come from secondary activities, including small-scale trading and the produce from country plots and dachas. Some 60 per cent of Russians work on private plots, producing potatoes, vegetables and other food to put on their tables.[73]

Even with the dramatic shrinkage of Russia's economy following the economic reforms, the country did not experience the mass unemployment which might be expected from such upheavals. Part of the reason why this did not materialise lies in the different bases and criteria used to define unemployment. By April 1996 the unemployment rate calculated by Goskomstat according to international definitions (including officially registered unemployed and those available and able to work) reached 8.8 per cent of the workforce or 6.4 million people. The figure was expected to reach 9.5 per cent, or 7 million people, by the end of the year. In addition, in 1994 4.8 million people worked part-time, with a staggering 20–30 per cent of those who had jobs on forced leave for months.[74] However, it is also recognised that the secondary economy absorbs a number of people who either have several jobs or are 'unemployed', with up to 33 per cent of those classified as unemployed working in secondary or informal activity. The apparently low rate of

unemployment is also partly due to the slow pace of enterprise restructuring, and the reluctance of factory managers to initiate large lay-offs.
Nevertheless, there has been a marked increase in the separation rate
(i.e. the leaving ratio in proportion to total employment) in industry
from 14 per cent in 1990 to 29 per cent in 1993. Dismissals for
economic reasons accounted for 18 per cent, while more than 50 per
cent were voluntary 'quits', half of whom found new jobs within four
months.[75]

Rising wage arrears have been an indication of the slow pace of
restructuring within Russian industry. Arrears rose steeply when the
phasing out of directed credits began in early 1994. By October 1994
wage arrears totalled 22.5 trillion roubles, falling back to 6.4 trillion
roubles in June 1995. In the presidential pre-election period, the gap
between owed and paid wages in the budget-financed economy fell to
2.8 trillion roubles (in the private sector the gap remained 21.1 trillion
roubles). This was the result of President Yeltsin's effort to pay wage
arrears before polling day, as he diverted $1 billion from the Central
Bank to boost his re-election hopes. Following the presidential election
in July, wage arrears rose steeply, reaching an estimated $9 billion by
the end of 1996. One of the surprising statistics has been the lack of
concerted national strike action to protest against wage arrears. In
OECD countries around 5 per cent of the workforce on average strike
in any year. In Russia, during 1995 less than 0.7 per cent of the
workforce went on strike. There are several explanations for the lack of
strike action in Russia before 1996. First, strike action is usually taken to
improve conditions, wages or protect jobs. In the Russian context,
strike action is unlikely to have any of these effects, and may simply
hasten the demise of unviable enterprises. Second, the trade union
movement was fragmented and leaderless, as many former activists had
themselves moved into business or politics. Many of the Soviet trade
unions fell apart with the demise of the Soviet Union, or became more
regionally or locally based. The changing role of the state has meant
that national unions have been deprived of state support, with a
consquent decline in financial backing and organisational strength.
Third, many employees prefer to switch jobs rather than suffer low or
irregular wages, or pursue a strike without strike pay. However, even
given these weaknesses, there were some signs of trade-union militancy
in 1996, with the teachers', miners' and nuclear power workers' unions
taking strike action over wage arrears. In December 1996, Mr Vitaly
Budko, chairman of the main coalminers' union, claimed 80 per cent of

Russia's 500,000 miners were taking strike action to obtain payment of wage arrears (some miners had not been paid since June), while demanding the resignation of the government.[76]

Thus the Duma and presidential elections took place in an atmosphere of disenchantment with the Western-inspired economic reform process. Whilst the Russian public had eagerly desired rising living standards and new economic and personal opportunities, these benefits had only been secured by a minority: the old *nomenklatura*, enterprising professionals and the 'New Russians'. The poor peasant and the poor unskilled worker were either untouched by the economic reforms, or made worse off. The average Russians, Mr and Mrs Ivan Ivanovich, saw their living standards drop. The political consequences were witnessed in the 1995 Duma elections, and reinforced by the 1996 presidential contest. In the aftermath of the Duma elections, President Boris Yeltsin began to distance himself from his government's economic reform programme. In his address to the Federal Assembly on 23 February 1996, Yeltsin promised to make amends. He said he would pay public sector workers regularly, compensate people for savings wiped out by inflation in 1991–92, encourage the private sector (reducing unemployment) and provide access to accommodation for all. In an election year, Yeltsin was listening hard to the electorate's economic concerns. Economic transformation and falling living standards had become the most prominent issue in political debate, and the state of the economy dominated the presidential campaign. Meanwhile, support for the economic reform process itself dwindled, while the credibility of Western-style reformers reached their nadir.

The rejection by the electorate of Western-inspired economic reforms created the political conditions whereby Russia First could flourish. If the West and all its works were to be rejected due to the perceived failure of the economic reform process, something would have to be put in its place. Russian politicians swiftly adapted to the new political climate and responded to the widespread feelings of disenchantment. The reponse, Russia First, called for uniquely Russian solutions to the country's problems, with less reliance on the West and the assertion of Russia's 'great power' status. Russia First filled the vacuum left by the failure of the pro-Western political and economic lobby.

CRIME AND THE MAFIA

Russia is said to be experiencing the 'Great Criminal Revolution' analogous to Chicago in the 1920s. In 1995 2.75 million crimes were registered, of which 1.6 million were classified as serious. This compares with a total of 1.3 million crimes reported during 1986, under President Gorbachev.[77] Economic transformation has created enormous opportunities for the growth of criminal activity and criminal networks, largely because the economy is un-regulated or operates in a legal void. The collapse of the Soviet regime removed a crucial societal control mechanism, with the residual state apparatus incapable of halting the rising tide of crime. Criminal activity occurs throughout the economic system, ranging from petty crime, the widespread phenomenon of rent-seeking, to highly organised 'mafia' networks. Since 1992, it is estimated that the crime wave has cost the Russian economy over 60 trillion roubles (over £9 billion), causing severe damage to the economic reform process as a whole.

Underground economic activity boomed when private enterprise was first liberalised under Gorbachev in 1987. Statistics provided by the Russian Union of Producers and Entrepreneurs showed that 49 per cent of business people admitted to having been active in the Soviet underground economy, which supported a thriving black market. Under the Soviet system, these early 'entrepreneurs' were regarded as criminals. Gangs also operated in cities controlling rackets, involving the growing fringe of small enterprises, and including city markets selling agricultural and consumer goods. These activities multiplied during the last years of the Soviet regime and further expanded after the dissolution of the Soviet Union. Experts have estimated that between 30 and 50 per cent of criminal profits are spent on bribing state officials in order to obtain credit at favourable rates, export licences, privileged information about the most profitable enterprises prior to privatisation, or simply to avoid arrest and conviction. Anders Aslund has argued that the opportunity for crime in the state apparatus has spawned 'an extreme aggressive, risk-taking culture', which is rooted in the tradition of 'an uncommonly aggressive imperial elite, which accepts no inhibitions or limitations whatsoever'.[78]

The fact that early entrepreneurs were in effect outlaws under the Soviet system has linked business with criminality in the minds of the Russian public. Many of these early 'criminals' went on to become the vanguard of the new business elite, especially since they tended to be one of the few groups of people with access to significant savings and supplies of hard currency. This gave the early entrepreneurs a head start in Russia's rush to capitalism, and enabled them to use funds accrued in the Soviet period to build up (and purchase) businesses in the era of economic reform. Some of these early entrepreneurs were downright criminals with mafia connections, while others paid protection money to the mafia to survive, financially and literally. For the average Russian, it was difficult to tell the difference between legitimate business and criminality, a distinction blurred in any event by the pervasive influence of the mafia. However, the idea of business as a form of criminal activity is not new in Russian history. In fact, it is deeply ingrained in the Russian psyche, where business and business-men have more often been associated with theft than honest trade. Alexei Tolstoy wrote in his book *Peter the Great*:

> A country where the population derives its sustenance from knavery is a bad country . . . Russian merchants pray to God that he help them swindle more skilfully; this they call shrewdness. O, I know this damned country only too well . . . One should only come here with a gun under one's coat . . . Even for one who has the misfortune to be born here, it is hard to become accustomed to the rudeness and dishonesty of the Russians. As if they were all possessed by demons!'[79]

Those who have done business with some of the 'New Russians' will know exactly what Tolstoy was getting at. For many in Russian business today, the real point is not to get rich by trade, let alone manufacturing anything which someone may wish to buy, but to get rich at any cost. Whether fraud, or any actual exchange of goods and services is involved, is almost immaterial. It is the Russian people's perception of business people as crooks and private trade as a form of fraud which is deeply imbedded in the Russian psyche. Doing business in Moscow today can be rather like doing business in the Chicago of the 1920s, the main difference being that rival American gangs did not use rocket launchers to settle disputes.

The opportunities for 'rent-seeking' (defined by Anders Aslund as any activity which exploits a monopoly position or attempts to gain access to state subsidies, as opposed to profit-seeking) through privi-leged access and criminality have grown dramatically since 1991. The level of organised criminality in Russia has been far worse than that experienced elsewhere in the former Soviet bloc, where countries are also undergoing radical economic transformation. Arbitrage (particularly in the raw materials, gas, oil and metal sectors), import subsidies, subsidised credits and *nomenklatura* privatisation have been identified as the four main methods of rent-seeking prevalent in Russia.[80] Around 30,000 crimes have been linked to the privatisation process alone. Rent-seeking has tended to be concentrated in the energy, agriculture, trade and banking sectors, allowing massive fortunes to be accumulated in a very short space of time. These fortunes, in several cases believed to have made the individual concerned dollar billionaires, are often the result of collusion between the political elite and the so-called 'red barons' (members of the old Soviet *nomenklatura*, who are often directors of Russian enterprises). One of the most notorious cases of well-connected rent-seeking involved the National Sports Fund, controlled by Yeltsin's tennis coach and sports minister, Shamil Tarpischev. Tarpischev was also close to Alexander Korzhakov, Yeltsin's bodyguard.[81] The stated official purpose of the fund was to promote Russian athletics, providing funding through a presidential decree which created a tax loophole, so that the Sports Fund paid no duty on massive imports of cigarettes and alcohol. The fund (through a front company) became the largest importer of these commodities in the country, depriving the treasury of billions of dollars of much-needed revenue.

There were other ways Russians enriched themselves. The export of commodities could be extremely lucrative, particularly oil, natural gas and other raw materials. At one point, because price liberalisation was not applied across the board, domestic oil prices were only 1 per cent of the world market level. Well-connected individuals simply obtained export quotas and licences, bought the commodities at domestic prices and sold them on the world market, pocketing the difference. Company directors, traders and corrupt officials made massive personal fortunes as a result. The total value of such export profits has been estimated at 30 per cent of gross domestic product (GDP) in 1992. The mafia became closely involved with the profitable metals sector, whilst oil executives selflessly opposed domestic oil price rises as late as 1995. Import subsidies were another scam beloved by the mafia and the New Russians. Import subsidies were retained for essential imports in 1992, with importers paying only 1 per cent of the official exchange rate when buying hard currency from the government. The government subsidised food and other essential imports with Western commodity credits.

However, the food was sold at market prices in Russia, with traders siphoning off the subsidies. These import subsidies accounted for 15 per cent of GDP in 1992. Fortunes were made, government spending tapped, and the Russian public was worse off than before. Subsidised credits and import subsidies were scrapped in 1993, but by then Russia's new breed of entrepreneurs had moved on to pastures new.[82]

Mafia-type crime has become pervasive throughout the Russian economy. There are thought to be around 150 mafia groups with 100,000 members, many from Caucasian backgrounds. The Caucasus has Sicily's reputation for being the mafia's heartland. The Russian ministry of internal affairs has estimated that mafia groups control about 35,000 to 40,000 enterprises, plus 400 banks. A large proportion of the companies are in the import–export business, generating large sums of money. According to the British National Criminal Intelligence Service (NCIS), the mafia groups' income is equivalent to 40 per cent of Russia's GDP. Some $3 billion of this money is invested overseas, with Cyprus and the Bahamas the favourite destinations. The Russian mafia reportedly had good links with the Italian Mafia, who were providing the Russian gangs with capital and an international money-laundering service. In May 1995, British police cracked a money-laundering operation involving $50m (£32m) of Russian mafia cash.[83] Up to 40 per cent of new business people (overwhelmingly businessmen rather than women) are thought to have drawn their starting capital from these mafia-controlled companies. Crime is also widespread at the lower levels of the economy. Ministry of internal affairs figures suggest that in large towns and cities about three-quarters of privatised firms and commercial banks are hit by racketeering, costing them between 10 and 20 per cent of their total turnover. Total revenues from racketeering in the retail trade alone are estimated at 3 per cent of GDP.[84]

Russia's prosecutor-general has identified eight regions of an 'extreme political complexion' which are Moscow, St Petersburg, Krasnoyarsk, Irkutsk, Kemerovo, Perm, Sverdlovsk and Chelyabinsk. These regions account for one-quarter of all crimes committed in Russia, and perhaps one-third of all those crimes associated with organised criminal activity. According to the regional directorate for fighting organised crime, there were around a thousand organised criminal groupings in the Ural/Siberian area alone at the beginning of 1995. Amongst their leaders were some twenty-six *vory v zakone* ('thieves-in-law' or the Russian criminal elite), who controlled over 12,000 state and commercial enterprises. In the city of Yekaterinburg (Yeltsin's home town) in the Sverdlovsk region for example, organised crime syndicates are well entrenched. The region has the country's highest rates of crime in general and violent crime in particular. Gang wars periodically break out, such as between the giant 'Uralmarsh' and 'Tsentralnaya' syndicates, or between Caucasian groups and the so-called 'blue gangs' (made up of former prisoners from the region's labour camps).[85]

Mafia crime has also spawned a significant increase in serious and violent crime. There were 30,000 reported murders in Russia in 1994, three times the per capita rate of the United States. Kidnapping and armed assault increased by 100 per cent and 600 per cent respectively in the first six months of 1995, compared to the same period in 1994. Contract killing has also risen rapidly, with over 500 reported killings in 1994. Commercial bankers have been the targets of repeated attacks. Since the beginning of 1992 eighty-five bankers have been attacked, and of these forty-seven have been killed.[86] These contract killings have claimed some high profile victims, including the popular head of Russian Public Television, Vladislav Listyev; the well-known banker Ivan Kiveldi; and Dmitri Kholodov, a journalist who was investigating alleged corruption in the Russian army.

It was hoped that Kiveldi's murder might have been the catalyst for the government to take effective measures to tackle such crimes, especially given the presence of some leading political figures at his funeral. Earlier attempts to crack down on the killings, such as the Duma's law on 'Organised Crime' passed in July 1995, merely provoked a new round of murders, including seventeen gangland assassinations. Political measures have been more successful in tackling petty rather than serious crime. Partly this failure to deal with organised crime can be explained by major *lacunae* in Russian law. The deputy prosecutor general and the Moscow criminal investigation department have claimed there are no provisions in the country's criminal code to bring prosecutions in high-profile cases. Certainly, there has been no attempt to bring leading criminal figures to justice, reflecting both the difficulty of winning a conviction and the lack of political will to face down extremely powerful people. Corruption has permeated the Russian state. In 1993–94 the general prosecutor's office reported that investigatory bodies dealt with criminal cases against 344 Russian members of parliament. Only 13 per cent were convicted, the low figure being accounted for by the fact that parliamentarians were protected by legal immunity. Parliament thus became an attractive option for the seriously criminally inclined.[87]

Russian law has been inherited from Soviet law adopted in the 1960s, in which some crimes did not officially exist, or were only applicable to state officials.[88] Russia has lagged behind in developing laws to deal with organised crime and corruption, and laws on firearm possession and financial crimes remained weak. Both the upper and lower houses of parliament adopted a new criminal code in December 1995 which was rejected by President Yeltsin following opposition to some clauses by the ministry of internal affairs. Where the police and security forces have been granted new powers of investigation, this has drawn criticism from human rights groups, who feared civil liberties could be infringed. This took place against the background of heightened security measures as the Chechen crisis escalated, with bombs exploding on Moscow's streets.

Even where the law permits effective action, conviction rates are low because of under-resourcing and demoralisation within the police force. Police officers frequently complain they are poorly equipped and trained, and are unable to counter increasingly sophisticated and better armed criminals. In the period January–September 1995, 164 law enforcement officers were killed and 340 injured. Low pay and poor conditions have prompted many high-ranking officers to quit the forces for more lucrative jobs elsewhere, especially in the private security sector where wages can be over ten times higher. The flourishing private security sector has been quoted as employing up to 800,000 bodyguards, many former serving officers in the police, armed forces or the KGB.[89] Low pay is also the root cause of widespread corruption, notorious amongst the traffic police with their 'spot fines', which has helped to undermine public confidence in the police force as a whole. In some cases, such as that of Yevgeny Roitman, head of the Tver Regional Organised Crime Administration, high-ranking police officers have been directly involved in organised crime. Co-ordination between the different branches of the security forces is limited, hampering the fight against organised crime, and has been known to degenerate into open rivalry.

CONCLUSION

The Russian people's experience of economic reform had therefore not been an entirely happy one. Although there was by 1995 some closing of the 'poverty gap' that had opened up in 1992, the yawning chasm between rich and poor was still immense. For most Russians, economic reform had meant a decline in their material standard of living, with 32 million people living below the breadline. Massive reductions in defence expenditure exacerbated the problem of falling production and GDP. The entire military-industrial complex was in intensive care. Millions of Russians also experienced significant wage arrears, short-time working or long periods of involuntary (and unpaid) leave. Life expectancy declined while infant mortality and the incidence of disease rose as the former Soviet welfare state disintegrated. The only compensating factors were a boom in the consumer sector (although many goods were unaffordable), and increasing opportunities for foreign travel. Against this largely miserable background, the Russian population watched as crime figures went through the roof, and the mafia spread like a virus through society.

These economic conditions caused a political reaction. Western-style economic reform was largely discredited in the public's eyes, along with its political adherents. The Duma election results in 1993 had seen the first public reaction to Russia's unfolding economic reforms, combined with general political dissatisfaction with Yeltsin's leadership. The outcome was a victory for Vladimir Zhirinovsky's ultra-nationalist Liberal Democratic Party. The Duma elections of December 1995 confirmed this trend, although by this time the main beneficiary of discontent was the Russian Communist Party (KPRF) under Gennady Zyuganov. With the changing political environment, government policy changed too. Russia First became the dominant theme of both foreign and domestic policy. In the domestic sphere Yeltsin's administration developed a whole series of protective measures to insulate Russian enterprises and favoured 'insiders' from Western control and competition. This could be seen in the government's determination to keep strategic sectors of the Russian economy under direct state control, and to limit and restrict Western investment in its most profitable companies (such as Gazprom and LUKoil). In order to restore falling levels of production and lost export markets, the Russian government launched a drive to expand arms exports, against the will of the West. Ignoring Western protests, Russia stepped up exports of arms and sensitive technology to the Third World, China and the 'pariah' states of Iran and Iraq. This was an unequivocal example of Russia First in action. Russia pressed ahead because it regarded arms exports as essential for its domestic economy and to restore influence abroad. Even on the cultural level, there was a reaction against Westernisation, as Moscow sought to limit the spread of the English language.[90]

However, all these developments did not mean that Russia completely turned its back on the West. Russia still needed the West's financial credits (notably from the IMF and World Bank), and sought membership of the world's main industrial clubs, including G7, the World Trade Organisation (WTO) and the Paris Club. But the political and domestic atmosphere had changed. The West's chance to whole-heartedly convert Russia to a Western-style market economy and democracy had passed. Russians were not impressed with the system being foisted on them, with so much pain and social cost. Instead, Russians would move towards a market economy at their own pace, protecting Russian interests and jobs, and largely ignoring complaints from the West about protectionism and the preferential treatment given to Russian investors. Russians would make money from the market, but the money would mainly stay in Russian hands. This suited most Russians nicely, from the market traders, the rich New Russians, the financial and commercial elite, the mafia and the government. Some individuals seemed to manage to belong to all these categories simultaneously. In any event, Russia First meant the economy would be less than wholly open to the West, as the Russian people tried to rebuild its shattered fabric.

NOTES

1 Freeland, Chrystia, 'Kremlin demands its cut of Russia's suitcase-trade', *Financial Times*, 2 August 1996.
2 Steele, Jonathan, *Eternal Russia: Yeltsin, Gorbachev and the Mirage of Democracy*, Faber and Faber (London and Boston, 1994), p. 291.
3 See Chapter 4, pp. 164–6 for the impact of Gaidar's association with shock therapy on the electoral performance of Russia's Choice in the Duma elections, December 1995.
4 See Chapter 1, p. 12.
5 Economist Intelligence Unit, EIU Country Profile 1995–96: *The Russian Federation*, Economist Group (London, 1996), p.12 and Koen, Vincent and Marrese, Michael, 'Stabilisation and structural change in Russia, 1992–94', in Banerjee, Biswajit; Koen, Vincent; Krueger, Thomas; Lutz, Mark; Marrese, Michael, and Saavalainen, *Road Maps of the Transition; The Baltics, the Czech Republic, Hungary and Russia*, International Monetary Fund (Washington, 1995), pp. 53– 5.
6 See below, pp. 113–14.
7 Economist Intelligence Unit, *EIU Country Profile 1995–96: The Russian*

Federation, p. 12.

8 Dawisha, Karen and Parrott, Bruce, *Russia and the New States of Eurasia: The Politics of Upheaval*, Cambridge University Press (Cambridge, 1994), p. 174.

9 Figures from 'Ekonomika stran SNG...', p. 2, cited in Rutland, Peter, 'Russia's energy empire under strain', in *Transition* (Prague), 3 May 1996. See also Chapter 2, for a more in depth look at the issue of Russian energy supplies to CIS countries, and its use as a political lever.

10 OECD, *OECD Economic Surveys: The Russian Federation*, pp. 15–16.

11 European Parliament, *Background Note on the Economic Situation of Russia and Relations with the EU*, PE 219.133, 27 November 1996, pp. 4, 7.

12 Thornhill, John, 'Russian output falls again', *Financial Times*, 22 January 1997.

13 See Chapter 5, pp. 213–14 for details of Yeltsin's electoral spending pledges.

14 Economist Intelligence Unit, *EIU Country Report, 2nd Quarter 1996: The Russian Federation*, p. 24.

15 Both total output figures expressed in terms of gross domestic product (GDP) and industrial production figures are thought to be exaggerated for a number of reasons: GDP figures are inaccurately adjusted to take account of the activities of new enterprises, whereas the phenomenon of deliberately under-recording output for tax-evasion purposes may be particularly pronounced among Russian firms. This is illustrated by the discrepancy between Russian electricity consumption, which has fallen by half as much as estimated GDP fell in the period 1990–95, and that in Eastern Europe where electricity use fell roughly at the same rate. See Russian Centre for Economic Policy, *Russian Economic Trends, Monthly Update, 13 June 96*, published jointly by the Russian European Centre for Economic Policy and the Centre for Economic Performance, London School of Economics (London, Moscow, 1996), p. 4.; on the 1996 figures and Yevgeny Yasin, see Thornhill, John, 'Russian output falls again', *Financial Times*, 22 January 1997.

16 Economist Intelligence Unit, *EIU Country Report, 2nd Quarter 1996: The Russian Federation*, p. 18; on the Central Bank and the IMF loan, see Chapter 5, pp. 201–2 and p. 213 respectively.

17 'Russia's fear-worse factor', *The Economist*, 1 June 1996, p. 26.

18 The original acronym TACIS stood for 'Technical Assistance to the Commonwealth of Independent States'. Since 1993 it has been written in small letters to indicate the fact that not all programme recipients have been members of the CIS at all times or at all (Mongolia). Tacis is therefore now a generic name for the programme, which functions on a bilateral rather than CIS co-ordinated basis.

19 Russia also received emergency aid targeted at vulnerable groups of the population amounting to ECU354m (US$475m) from 1990 and was also granted ECU1 billion (US$1.34 billion) in loans for the import of food and medical supplies over the same period. Source: Tacis, *Russia: The European Union's Tacis Programme*, Tacis Information Office (Brussels, 1996).

20 Author's discussions with Russian business men, 1995–96; author's meetings at the European Commission Moscow's office, March 1995.

21 Author's meeting with Michael Emerson (as part of the EU–Russian Delegation, December 1995; European Parliament, *Fraud Allegations*, Delegation for Relations with Russia, 4 March 1996 (Brussels, 1996); Helm,

Sarah, 'EU man in Moscow behaved "deplorably"', *Independent*, 29 February 1996; Bremmer, Charles, 'Briton in EU graft inquiry resigns', *The Times*, 19 February 1996.

22 OECD, *OECD Economic Surveys: The Russian Federation, 1995*, Centre for Co-operation with the Economies in Transition (Paris, 1995), p. 3.

23 Kapstein, Ethan and Mills, Catherine Marshall, 'Conversion militaire dans les régions russes', *L'Observateur de l'OCDE* (Paris, 1995), p. 39.

24 Cooper, Julian, 'Defence industries in Russia and other post-Soviet states', in Parrott, Bruce (ed.), *State Building and Military Power in Russia and the New States of Eurasia*, M.E. Sharpe, (New York and London, 1995), p. 65.

25 All figures taken from Cooper, Julian, 'Defence industries in Russia and other post-Soviet states', pp. 66–67.

26 Parish, Scott, 'Russia Leads U.S. in Arms Sales to the Developing World', *Daily Digest*, Vol. 2, No. 161, 20 August 1996, OMRI (Prague, 1996), p. 3.

27 Cited in Dawisha and Parrott, *Russia and the New States of Eurasia*, p. 170.

28 Sanchez-Andres, Antonio, 'The transformation of the Russian defence industry', *Europe–Asia Studies*, Vol. 47, No.8 (1995), pp. 1285–6.

29 Sanchez-Andres, Antonio, 'The transformation of the Russian defence industry', p. 1283. For an illustration of a successful case of conversion we may cite the example of Nizhnii-Novgorod Nitel contained in Cooper, 'Defence industries in Russia and other post-Soviet states', pp. 78–9. In the period 1989–93, this leading producer of radar systems and televisions reduced the military share of its total output from 80 per cent to 20 per cent, yet managed to sustain its overall level of output before achieving a 25 per cent growth rate in 1993.

30 Cooper, 'Defence industries in Russia and other post-Soviet states', p. 71.

31 All figures are taken from Sanchez-Andres, 'The transformation of the Russian defence industry', pp. 1271–2.

32 Cooper, 'Defence industries in Russia and other post-Soviet states', p. 79.

33 Cooper, 'Defence industries in Russia and other post-Soviet states', p. 68.

34 Figures according to the State Statistics Committee (*Goskomstat*), cited in OECD, *OECD Economic Surveys: The Russian Federation, 1995*, p. 5.

35 Koen and Marrese, 'Stabilisation and structural change in Russia, 1992–94', pp. 62–3.

36 Aslund, Anders, 'How some Russians got rich', *Financial Times*, 31 May 1996.

37 For more on Gusinsky and his clash with the president, see Chapter 5, pp. 217, 240.

38 OECD, *OECD Economic Surveys: The Russian Federation, 1995*, p. 27.

39 Flanders, Stephanie, 'Reformists aim to be third time lucky', *Financial Times Survey: Russia*, 10 April 1995, p. 6.

40 Corzine, Robert, and Thornhill, John, 'Foreign premium on Gazprom offer', *Financial Times*, 7 October 1996; author's private information.

41 Birman, Igor, 'Gloomy prospects for the Russian economy', *Europe–Asia Studies*, Vol. 48, No. 5 (1996), p.739.

42 Economist Intelligence Unit, *EIU Country Report, 2nd Quarter 1996: The Russian Federation*, p. 23.

43 OECD, *OECD Economic Surveys: The Russian Federation, 1995*, p. 77.

44 OECD, *OECD Economic Surveys: The Russian Federation, 1995*, pp. 67–8.

45 Russian Privatisation Agency, cited in OECD, *OECD Economic Surveys: The*

Russian Federation, 1995, p. 77.

46 See Chapter 4, pp. 184–5 for Chubais's role as the architect of the privatisation programme and his overall role performance prior to his 'sacking' in January 1996.

47 Figures in Rutland, Peter, 'Privatisation in Russia: Two Steps Forward, One Step Back?', *Europe–Asia Studies*, Vol. 46, No.7, (1994), p. 1120.

48 Figures from survey data in a paper by Blasi, J.R. 'Corporate governance in Russia', cited in OECD, *OECD Economic Surveys: The Russian Federation, 1995*, p. 80.

49 Author's discussion with European business men and women operating in Russia, Moscow, summer 1996.

50 Freeland, Chrystia, 'Russia to shut "backdoor" access to government bonds', *Financial Times*, 23 July 1996.

51 OECD, *OECD Economic Surveys: The Russian Federation, 1995*, p. 99.

52 *Finansovye izvestiya*, 6 October 1995, cited in Gurushina, Natalia and Szilagyi, Zsofia, 'Seeking foreign investment in Hungary and Russia', *Transition* (Prague), 26 January 1996, p. 24.; European Parliament, *Background Note on the Economic Situation of Russia and Relations with the EU*, PE 219.133, 27 November 1996, p. 4.

53 Clark, Bruce, 'Russia tightens foreign access', *Financial Times*, 30 July 1996.

54 See Chapter 5, pp. 250, 251–2, for the appointment of Vladimir Potanin.

55 Thornhill, John, 'Little demand for second helpings', *Financial Times*, 6 September 1995.

56 Thornhill, John, 'Moscow buys out stake in Zil', *Financial Times*, 15 August 1996.

57 Cited in Ware, Richard, 'Elections in Russia', House of Commons Library, Research Paper 95/128 (London, 1995), p. 28.

58 Frydman, Roman; Murphy, Kenneth and Rapacznski, Andrzej, 'Capitalism with a comrade's face', *Transition* (Prague), 26 January 1996, p. 6.

59 Denton, Nicholas and Freeland, Chrystia, 'Yeltsin to favour Russian banks in telecoms sell-off', *Financial Times*, 19 December 1996.

60 Morvant, Penny, 'Compromise reached on new AIDS legislation', *Transition* (Prague), 26 May 1995, p. 6.

61 Economist Intelligence Unit, *EIU Country Profile 1995–96: The Russian Federation*, p. 23.

62 Russia Centre for Economic Policy, *Russian Economic Trends, Monthly Update, 13 June 1996*, pp. 5, 16.

63 Thornhill, John, 'Russia "must pay taxes to beat poverty" ', *Financial Times*, 15 October 1996.

64 OECD, *OECD Economic Surveys: The Russian Federation, 1995*, p. 124.

65 Economist Intelligence Unit, *EIU Country Profile 1995–96: The Russian Federation*, p. 23.

66 Hearst, David, 'Prices that break Russian hearts', *Guardian*, 25 September 1996; 'Russia's fear-worse factor', *The Economist*, 1 June 1996.

67 Morvant, Penny, 'Alarm over falling life expectancy', *Transition* (Prague), 25 October 1995, pp. 44–5.

68 According to Goskomstat figures (1995) cited in OECD, *OECD Economic Surveys: The Russian Federation, 1995*, pp. 125 and 167.

69 See also Chapter 4, pp. 161–2.

70 Birman, Igor, 'Gloomy prospects for the Russian economy', p. 736.

71 The official subsistence level was, however, calculated at 372,000 roubles in April 1996. Figures from Russia Centre for Economic Policy, *Russian Economic Trends, Monthly Update, 13 June 1996*, p. 32.

72 'Russia's fear-worse factor', *The Economist*, p. 25.

73 Birman, 'Gloomy prospects for the Russian economy', pp. 740, 742.

74 Birman, 'Gloomy prospects for the Russian economy', p. 745.

75 OECD, *OECD Economic Surveys: The Russian Federation, 1995*, pp. 109–10.

76 Russia Centre for Economic Policy, *Russian Economic Trends, Monthly Update, 13 June 1996*, pp. 16–17; see also Thornhill, John, 'Russia's miners strike over late pay', *Financial Times*, 4 December 1996; Anichkina, Miranda, 'Yeltsin "to pay miners" ', *The European*, 5–11 December 1996.

77 This chapter draws heavily on Ware, *Elections in Russia*, pp. 37–41. Figures quoted from Morvant, Penny, 'Corruption hampers war crime in Russia', *Transition* (Prague), 8 March 1996, pp. 23–5.

78 Aslund, Anders, 'Reform vs. "rent-seeking" in Russia's economic transformation', *Transition* (Prague), 26 January 1996, p. 14.

79 Tolstoy, Alexei, *Peter the Great*, Vol. 1, Raduga Publishers (Moscow, 1985), pp. 230–1.

80 According to the typology established by Anders Aslund in 'Reform vs rent-seeking', p. 13.

81 'Moscow's sporting life', Observer, *Financial Times*, 24 May 1996; Tarpischev, Korzhakov and Barsukov voted together on 3 July 1996, as witnessed by the author.

82 Aslund, 'How some Russians got rich'.

83 Burns, Jimmy, 'Italian Mafia linked to Russian criminals', *Financial Times*, 22 May 1996; Patey, Tony, 'Three arrested in Russian mafia crash', *The European*, 19–25 May 1996.

84 Crosnier, Marie-Agnès; Gicquiau, Hervé and Giroux, Alain, 'Russie', in *Le courier des pays de l'Est*, No.408, April 1995, pp. 72–3.

85 'Russia: the crime problem in the Urals and Siberia', *Oxford Analytica*, East Europe Daily Brief, 19 February 1996.

86 Ware, *Elections in Russia*, pp. 37–8.

87 European Union, Moscow Delegation, press release, 23 March 1995.

88 This section draws heavily on Morvant, 'Corruption hampers war crime in Russia', pp. 23–7.

89 Birman, 'Gloomy prospects for the Russian economy', p. 750.

90 See above, p. 129.

CHAPTER 4

The Duma Elections and the Triumph of 'Russia First'

Russia's political landscape was dramatically transformed following the December 1995 Duma elections. The pro-reform 'liberal democratic' parties or blocs performed badly, with only Grigory Yavlinsky's Yabloko surpassing the 5 per cent threshold for party-list seats. Our Home is Russia (NDR), the 'governing' party which was more managerial and professional than democratic, also flopped electorally, reflecting the government's huge unpopularity. Led by Prime Minister Victor Chernomyrdin, NDR's performance augured badly for Yeltsin in the forthcoming presidential elections. On the other hand, the 'red' leftist opposition parties, notably the Communist Party of the Russian Federation (KPRF), made spectacular gains, strengthening the left's position in the state Duma. The 'brown' nationalist vote of Vladimir Zhirinovsky's Liberal Democratic Party (LDPR) remained unexpectedly and ominously resilient. The Duma election results thus suggested that Russia's flirtation with the West's model of liberal democracy was finally over. Instead, the election proved that Western values had been displaced by statist economic policies, a more patriotic-nationalist foreign policy and nostalgia for the past.

The new 'Red Duma' epitomised this shift from the ideals of liberal democracy to the ascendency of Russia First. Those parties or political groups which stood for Western-style democracy and an open market economy were trounced, while protectionist, patriotic-nationalist groupings received the lion's share of the votes cast. Both the nationalists and communists looked backwards, to Russia's days as a 'Great Power', rather than forwards to joining the Western-led family of market economy democracies. The electorate indicated it had lost its faith in the Western model, and switched its support to those advocating Russian-style solutions to the country's ills. Prime Minister Chernomyrdin's 'party of power', Our Home is Russia (NDR), tried to capitalise on this patriotic shift in sentiment by adopting a nationalist slogan for its party name. The party's name 'Our Home is Russia' tried to emphasise the party's nationalist credentials and imply resistance to Western influence. In an effort to reflect the public's Russia First mood, other parties followed suit, including Derzhava (Great Power) and Forward Russia! However, in the case of Our Home is Russia, the party was hampered by its perceived pro-Western orientation and failed economic policies, and suffered at the polls as a result. NDR was also too closely associated with the prime minister and the failures of Yeltsin's administration. In any event, there was little sense of a 'party' structure in Russia, with most political blocs consisting of loose political groups centred around prominent individuals. Only the Russian Communist Party (KPRF) had any national party political organisation along Western lines, most other Russian parties having more in common with political clubs than structured political organisations.

Under the new constitution passed by referendum in December 1993, the Duma itself had relatively little power compared to the president, and a limited capacity to directly influence government policy. The Duma elections therefore did not signify a shift in the balance of power from the executive to the legislative. Yeltsin could come to an accommodation with a left-dominated Duma without having to alter government policy radically. Rather, the importance of the Duma elections lay in the fact that they occurred less than six months before the impending presidential elections, which Boris Yeltsin hoped would give him a second term in office. On the basis of the Duma election results, this looked less than a racing certainty, and had given an unwelcome boost to his main rival, communist leader Gennady Zyuganov. The Duma elections had acted as the Russian equivalent of a 'primary' for the presidential elections by highlighting the predominant electoral issues and reflecting the prevailing political climate in the country. Key political figures made little attempt to dispel the idea that they saw the Duma elections as a dry run for the summer presidential campaign.

Crucially for Yeltsin, the time-lag between the Duma and presidential elections gave the president a chance to re-appraise his policies, personnel and public relations. Paradoxically, although the election of a 'red' Duma and the defeat of his allies was a shock, it proved the catalyst for Yeltsin to galvanise his campaign team and government to ensure his victory the following summer. Complacency in the president's camp evaporated, to be replaced by grim determination as Yeltsin and his advisers geared-up to do everything necessary to win.

Against this background, it was hardly surprising that Yeltsin appeared to make dramatic changes to his policy and personnel following the Duma elections. Much of the change in policy was rhetorical rather than real, but was in tune with the political climate created by the new Duma. By this stage, it was painfully apparent to Yeltsin that he would have to change the public's perception of his administration if he were to stand any chance of reversing his flagging popularity. Shedding the clothes of the avowed democratic reformer, Yeltsin rapidly borrowed those of his successful political opponents, who had advocated a socially responsible economic policy and a more strident and assertive 'Russia First' foreign policy during the Duma campaign. Nationalists and communist leaders were later to claim with some justification that Yeltsin had hijacked the very policies they had propagated during the run-up to the Duma elections in December 1995. The Duma election campaign had shown that there was a broad political consensus on the need for a 'Russia First' foreign policy that cut across party lines, with a particular emphasis on hostility towards NATO enlargement. No future presidential candidate could afford to ignore the strength of the political feeling represented by the 'red–brown' axis, combining economic policy with social security and a more narrowly defined sense of Russian nationalism. In response, Yeltsin recast himself as the 'Good Tsar' who could deliver both the social stability and welfare desired by the electorate, and at the same time reclaim Russia's 'Great Power' status, as demanded by the communists, nationalists and their supporters.

BACKGROUND TO THE 1995 DUMA ELECTIONS: THE NEW CONSTITUTION

The December 1995 Duma elections were held under the terms of the new Russian constitution, adopted by referendum on 12 December 1993, with a vote in favour by a margin of 58 to 42 per cent.[1] The constitution created a very powerful presidency, along the lines of the presidency established by the 1958 constitution of the Fifth French Republic. The constitution was designed to strengthen the executive *vis-à-vis* the legislative, so avoiding a repetition of the constitutional clash in 1992–93. The Congress of People's Deputies (CPD), the paramount Soviet-era legislative body, and its standing body, the Supreme Soviet (parliament), enshrined in the 1978 Soviet constitution, had been particularly obdurate in obstructing Yeltsin's reform programme. President Yeltsin's announcement on 21 September 1993 of his intention to institute direct presidential rule and dissolve the CPD and Supreme Soviet was constitutionally dubious. Pro-parliamentary attacks on the mayor's office and the Ostankino television station led to Yeltsin's orders to storm the White House (the home of the parliament) on 4 October 1993, and to the arrest of Vice-President Alexander Rutskoi and parliamentary Speaker Ruslan Khasbulatov, along with hundreds of others holed-up in the battered parliamentary building.[2]

According to the new Russian constitution, the president is the highest elected official in Russia and head of the executive branch of the Russian government. The president is not only head of state, which was one of the primary responsibilities under the old constitution, but also performs extensive legislative and executive duties. One of the most important state duties of the president is the role of guarantor of the constitution, and of basic human and civil rights for the citizens of the country. The president is also responsible for protecting the sovereignty of the Russian Federation, including its independence and borders. The president outlines priorities for domestic and foreign policies of the state and ensures co-ordination between all government agencies. On foreign policy, the president not only sets foreign policy priorities, but oversees their implementation, and conducts negotiations with leaders of foreign countries and signs international treaties. The president is also commander-in-chief of the armed forces and, as head of state, represents the Russian Federation at home and abroad. In the event of aggression, the president can declare martial law and, in other special circumstances, a state of emergency.

The new constitution empowered the Russian president with a great deal of executive authority. This includes appointing the prime minister in agreement with the State Duma, chairing the meetings of the executive government, and nominating the chairman or proposing the removal of the Central State Bank to the Duma. The president also accepts or rejects ministers' resignations, appoints or dismisses ministers, nominates judges to the Constitutional and Supreme Courts and appoints federal judges. In addition, the president forms and chairs the Security Council, endorses military programmes, forms the administration and appoints and sacks chief commanders of the armed forces. The president's powers of patronage extend to appointing and dismissing Russia's foreign and diplomatic representatives (including ambassadors) after consultation with committees and commissions of the State Duma. Finally, the president is head of the executive administration which is authorised to develop and assist in the implementation of presidential strategies and policies. The president issues decrees and orders which must be carried out throughout the Russian Federation. However, these decrees must not be in contradiction to the constitution or federal laws.[3]

Under the constitution the Federal Assembly, or parliament of the Russian Federation, is the supreme legislative and representative body. The Federal Assembly consists of two chambers (houses), the Federation Council and the State Duma. The Federation Council (Upper House) consists of 178 members. Each of Russia's eighty-nine administrative jurisdictions can send two representatives, one from the executive branch and one from the legislative branch of the local government, to the Council. The State Duma (Lower House) of the Russian parliament consists of 450 representatives who are elected from 225 territorial districts (two representatives from each district). Each deputy (member) represents about 478,000 voters. Members of parliament are elected for a four-year term. The president plays an important part in the activity of the legislative branch of government. The president can call for referendums and new elections to the State Duma, dissolve the Duma, draft legislative initiatives for the Duma, and sign legislation into law and present it to the public. The president has fourteen days to sign any bill sent from the Federation Council. If the president does not sign the bill within this time, the bill returns to the State Duma and Federation Council. The parliament may override the president's veto with a two-thirds majority of both the Federation Council and Duma. If this occurs, the president must either sign the bill into law or face a conflict with the Duma and the Federation Council which could lead to a dissolution of the Parliament.[4]

The new Russian parliament (Federal Assembly) which was elected on 12 December 1993 thus consisted of two chambers, the State Duma (Lower House) and the Federation Council (Upper House). Although the term of the legislature is four years, the first term under the new constitution was set at two years only (hence the Duma elections in both 1993 and 1995). Half the State Duma's 450 members elected in 1993 were elected in one-member electoral constituencies, while the other half were chosen on a proportional basis from a single (federal) list. The Federation Council has 178 representatives, two from each of the eighty-nine subjects of the Russian Federation (republics, krays, oblasts, autonomous oblasts and okrugs, and the cities of St Petersburg and Moscow). The constitution is not clear whether representatives of the Federation Council are to be elected or appointed. An interim procedure introduced for the 1993 election allowed each subject of the Russian Federation to elect two representatives to the Federation Council.

The 1993 general election was the first time that multi-party politics was practised in Russia, and was broadly held to be free and fair, despite complaints about lack of equal access to the media. The election result was a major disappointment to reformist movements like Russia's Choice, Yabloko, and Russian Unity and Accord, which only obtained 30 per cent of the vote. Yegor Gaidar's Russia's Choice party won only 15.5 per cent of the party-list vote, but the many independents elected for single-member seats fortuitously made it the largest group in the Duma, with seventy-three members. However, the real winner of the 1993 election was Vladimir Zhirinovsky's ultra-nationalist Liberal Democratic Party (LDPR), with 22.9 per cent of the party-list vote and sixty-four members.[5] The LDPR relied upon Zhirinovsky's leadership and mercurial personality for its electoral support, and thus performed less well in individual contests in electoral constituencies. Zhirinovsky's vote was seen as a protest vote, both against the failures of the government's reform programme, and as a reaction to the events surrounding the storming of the White House.

ISSUES IN THE 1995 DUMA ELECTION CAMPAIGN

The new Russian constitution of 1993 stipulated that elections to the Duma should be held in December 1995. Article 13 of the Russian constitution of 12 December 1993 recognises political pluralism and a multi-party system in the Russian Federation. However, the procedures for electing members to the State Duma and the Federation Council are laid down in federal law, which has to be agreed between the president and parliament. Before the elections took place, there were fears that

President Yeltsin might postpone the 1995 Duma elections, using disagreements over electoral law as the excuse. These fears were not as groundless as they might at first appear. Yeltsin was admitted to hospital on 26 October 1995, with suspected heart problems. Around the same period, the Central Electoral Commission refused to register a number of parties (including Yabloko), the Duma challenged the electoral law, while at the same time the Supreme Court asked the Constitutional Court to rule on whether the electoral law complied with the constitution. The Electoral Commission also published a list of eighty-seven candidates for the Duma who allegedly had criminal pasts, but included the names of former Soviet dissidents, such as human rights activist Sergei Kovalev, alongside armed robbers. On 15 November, Boris Yeltsin confirmed that the Duma elections would go ahead on 17 December 1995, but speculation increased that they would be postponed. Both the communists and Yabloko had predicted possible postponement as far back as spring 1995, a fear which was repeated nearer the elections by Yabloko leader Grigory Yavlinsky.[6] Yavlinsky believed the postponement of the Duma elections would be a prelude to cancelling the presidential elections due in June 1996. The outcome would be autocratic rule by Tsar Boris and his Imperial Court in the Kremlin. The abandonment of any pretence at Western-style democracy would be Russia First in its most extreme form.

Yeltsin's heath was a continuing cause for concern. In April 1995 Yeltsin's spring holiday was extended due to his high blood pressure, and in July 1995 he was admitted to hospital complaining of acute chest pains. Appointments were cancelled and a planned visit to Norway was postponed following the July health scare. The October 1995 illness appears to have been a recurrence of Yeltsin's cardiac problems, resulting in the president being hospitalised for a month and not returning to his duties in the Kremlin until the end of December. Together with the constitutional disagreements over electoral law, it appeared that the president's ill health had prepared the ground for a postponement of the Duma elections. There was considerable doubt as to whether President Yeltsin wished to postpone the elections, since the new Duma was likely to be even less conciliatory than the previous one. Yet the president's powers are such that he does not have much to fear from a hostile parliament. Yeltsin had signed a decree on 14 July 1995, providing for the Duma election to take place on 17 December, which a number of observers noted was close to the last possible moment for the elections to take place at all.[7]

Electoral laws have a decisive impact on the organisation of an electoral campaign since they lay down the procedures governing the eligibility of political parties. Yeltsin had proposed amending the electoral law by reducing the number of members elected by proportional representation from 225 to 150, so increasing the numbers of members elected by the first-past-the-post method from 225 to 300. Yeltsin argued this would reduce representation for extremist parties, who benefited from proportional representation, and rationalise the number of political parties in Russia, so ensuring greater political stability in the Duma. He also wanted to boost the representation of local elites, who were more favourably inclined towards him than in the past. However, the majority of parliamentary deputies were wary of changing electoral law so close to the elections, and argued that a proportional list system improved party discipline.

A conciliation committee found a compromise on 8 June 1995. As in 1993, 225 members would be elected by proportional representation, with parties needing to obtain 5 per cent of votes cast to be represented. Any party wishing to stand had to collect 200,000 signatures before 22 October 1995. The minimum turn-out required was 25 per cent. None of the lists could have more than twelve candidates from Moscow or St Petersburg or candidates occupying a federal post (such as a minister). In return for these concessions, Yeltsin obtained guarantees regarding the electoral law on the forthcoming presidential elections. Each candidate would need to obtain one million signatures (Yeltsin had wanted two million), with no more than 7 per cent of those signatures being collected in the same region or republic. A 50 per cent turn-out would be required to make the presidential election valid.

Disagreement between the Duma, Federation Council and president also meant that full elections for the Federation Council failed to take place. Members of the Duma advocated that members of the upper chamber be elected directly by regional governments and legislative bodies. Members of the Federation Council would have to be full time, and give up any other offices they held. They would be accountable to the electorate and integrated into the legislative process which had not been the case previously. The president's administration, by contrast, proposed that regional governments and heads of law-making bodies be directly appointed to the Federation Council. The role of the upper chamber would be principally to protect the interests of the local governors, and its legislative role would be limited. The two positions were based on different constitutional models, one giving the Federation

Council the status of a senate, the other a council of governors. The Federation Council between 1993 and 1995 had a status somewhere between the two models, making little use of its right to initiate legislation and take part in joint working parties.

On 19 September 1995 President Yeltsin proposed that regional elections should be held only after the June presidential elections. This obviously suited the president, since he had personally appointed the majority of regional governors, and so he would be guaranteed a supportive Federation Council in the run-up to the crucial presidential elections. Nor did the president want to encourage the development of the Federation Council along the lines of the US Senate, dominated by political parties which would be more difficult for the Kremlin to control. The governors of the sixty-six regions were not keen to put themselves before the electorate, many for the first time. Deadlock with the Duma ensued until, on 17 November 1995, the Duma adopted a new bill on the formation of the Federation Council. According to the bill, the regional governors and the heads of local parliaments would automatically become members of the new Council (the Council's term of office ended on 13 December 1995). Yeltsin allowed gubernatorial races to be held in December 1995 in Primorsk Krai and in eleven other oblasts of the Russian Federation. Most of the regions selected for early elections were chosen because the president was fairly sure his appointees would be re-elected. The bulk of Russia's regions were due to hold gubernatorial elections in December 1996. Yeltsin had postponed these elections three times since 1991, so that he could keep his appointees in place as long as possible. Yeltsin had managed to keep his malleable Federation Council up to and beyond the coming presidential election.[8]

The refusal of the Central Electoral Commission (CEC) to register some political parties, including Yavlinsky's Yabloko and former Vice-President Rutskoi's 'Derzhava' (Great Power), created the first crisis in the 1995 Duma election campaign. President Yeltsin intervened on 31 October 1995 by asking the CEC to explain its decision. Former Prime Minister Yegor Gaidar threatened that Russia's Choice would boycott the election if its fellow liberal party, Yabloko, was not registered. According to the CEC, Yabloko was refused registration because it failed to provide a written declaration from six candidates (out of a total of 206), who had left the party's list. After an action before the Supreme Court, Yabloko, Derzhava and other political parties were allowed to participate in the elections. The general perception was that the Electoral Commission had been somewhat overzealous in attempting to exclude anti-government political blocs from the elections on flimsy pretexts.[9] The events surrounding the registration of parties led Russian politicians to re-open the debate on electoral law. Members of the Duma brought a case before the Constitutional Court to establish whether the electoral law was compatible with the constitution. The Duma called an extraordinary session on 4 November 1995 to discuss the law. The majority of the Duma wanted to curb the powers of the CEC, which took 'arbitrary decisions during the registration process'. Deputies also wanted to abolish the 5 per cent threshold for representation in the Duma.[10]

While awaiting a decision from the Constitutional Court on the electoral law's compliance with the constitution, both President Yeltsin and Prime Minister Chernomyrdin reiterated their intention to go ahead with the elections on 17 December. International pressure against postponement had been rising, and both Yeltsin and Chernomyrdin were aware that postponement would be taken as a sign of political instability by the West.[11] On Monday 20 November, the Constitutional Court declared that it would not re-examine the electoral law, thus confirming that the elections would take place on 17 December. However, the absence of a court judgment was of some concern, because it left open the possibility that the electoral law, and the legitimacy of the Duma, could have been challenged after the elections. Political observers were aware of the precedent set by President Nazarbayev of Kazakhstan, who dissolved the Kazakh parliament after the Constitutional Court declared the elections illegal, due to procedural violations. Sergei Filatov and Georgi Saratov, members of Yeltsin's presidential administration, stated openly that there was a real danger of the electoral law being called into question after the elections. Given the fact that the Constitutional Court was widely believed to be in the president's pocket, there were fears that the administration was keeping its options open, so that it had the possibility of declaring the elections null and void at a later date. If the legislative elections were annulled, this would give the presidential administration the excuse to postpone the presidential elections scheduled for 16 June 1996. Such was the background spirit of mutual distrust and suspicion that accompanied the December 1995 Duma elections.[12]

CAMPAIGN ISSUES: THE ECONOMIC SITUATION AND RUSSIA FIRST TO THE FORE

Surprisingly, Chechnya was not a major issue in the Duma election campaign itself. As the relative importance of Chechnya as an election issue dwindled, the importance of the economic situation grew. Following the Chechen hostage-taking in the southern Russian town of Budennovsk on 18 June 1995, the Duma organised a motion of censure against Victor Chernomyrdin's government. However, the prime minister survived the censure vote on 21 June, as it was not supported by a majority of Duma deputies. Instead of the required 226, only 189 members supported it (109 voted against and 47 abstained). A few hours before the vote President Yeltsin had announced the dismissal of Victor Yerin, minister of the interior, Nickolai Yegorov, security minister, and Yevgeny Kuznetsov, the governor of Stavropol. Kuznetsov was responsible for the region in the Northern Caucasus which included the ill-fated town of Budennovsk, where Chechen rebels took over a thousand Russians hostage in the local hospital, after a bloody firefight. Two assaults on the hospital building by interior ministry troops resulted in the deaths of 150 people but failed to force the rebels out. Chernomyrdin's mediation with the Chechen rebels in Budennovsk (who were later given free passage back to Chechnya) ended the hostage crisis with no further casualties, and boosted the prime minister's standing in the short term. General Grachev, Russian defence minister, kept his post despite a wave of criticism, while General Kulikov, chief of operations in Chechnya and one of the peace negotiators in Grozny, was appointed interior minister. Yeltsin was abandoned by the reformist parties Russia's Choice and Yabloko, as a result of their opposition to the president's handling of the conflict in Chechnya.

Anti-Western and Russia First rhetoric was a feature of the 1995 Duma campaign. Members of the Duma overwhelmingly condemned NATO air strikes against the Bosnian Serbs in former Yugoslavia. NATO had launched the air strikes on 30 August 1995, two days after the Bosnian Serbs shelled Sarajevo market, killing thirty-seven civilians.[13] The crisis over Bosnia escalated in September 1995, as Moscow presented the action as discrimination against the Bosnian Serbs, while other groups (for example the Croats over Krajina) were treated more gently. The Russian foreign ministry went so far as to say the bombing could lead to 'genocide' and exceeded the UN mandate. A statement issued in Moscow stated 'the very survival of the current generation of Bosnian Serbs, who are actually facing genocide, is called into question.'[14] At the heart of the dispute, Moscow felt humiliated that it had not been consulted by NATO before the airstrikes. NATO's apparent indifference to Russia's opinion on the matter, and its disregard for Moscow's desire to be treated as a 'great power', with important interests in the region, were doubly wounding. In Russia First terms, the interests of the Russian Federation were being ignored by the West, while Moscow was being treated as a junior partner in the Balkans. Given the prevailing political and domestic climate in Russia, this sent very disconcerting signals to the Russian public and the political elite. The Kremlin was also worried by the way the United States had effectively squeezed Russia out of any decisive role in the Balkans, as it had been sidelined in the Middle East.[15] From Moscow's point of view, NATO was acting as a transparent vehicle for Washington's increasing ascendency in Europe. US-led military intervention in Bosnia also fuelled Russian fears about growing American domination of the European continent, should NATO enlarge to the east. The airstrikes further played into the hands of Russia's nationalists and communists, who loudly proclaimed their support for the country's historic former Slavic allies, the Serbs. Yeltsin's opponents in the Duma ostentatiously paraded their Russia First credentials, and the president was forced to respond by taking a tougher diplomatic line with the West in defence of the Bosnian Serbs.

An extraordinary Duma session held on 9 September 1995, which witnessed a fist fight between extreme nationalists and liberal reformers (Vladimir Zhirinovsky also grabbing Yevgeniya Tishkovskaya by the hair), called for Foreign Minister Andrei Kozyrev's dismissal, a special session of the UN Security Council, an end to sanctions against Serbia and the suspension of Russia's participation in NATO's Partnership for Peace (PfP). In an indirect allusion to the Russia First strategy, the Russian Communist Party (KPRF) attacked government policy as a betrayal of national interests. Communist leader Gennady Zyuganov called Foreign Minister Andrei Kozyrev 'the minister of national shame' and called for members of the armed forces to be allowed to fight as volunteers for the Serbs. Kozyrev was widely blamed for Russia punching below its weight in international affairs. Leaders in the Duma called for him to be sacked because of 'multiple, serious mistakes that have led to the humiliating failure of Russia's Balkans policy'.[16] Vladimir Zhirinovsky, leader of the ultra-nationalist Liberal Democratic

Party (LDPR), helpfully suggested that Russia should dispatch its Baltic Fleet to the Adriatic to protect the Serbs, while other members of the LDPR advocated supplying anti-aircraft missiles to the Bosnian Serb forces. On behalf of the moderate nationalist bloc, the Congress of Russian Communities (KRO, which was not represented in the Duma), Lebed argued that the Bosnia operation revealed NATO's true nature as a threat to Russian security. To defend itself against potential Western aggression, Lebed contended, Russia should strengthen its 'nuclear shield'. Vladimir Lukin, Yabloko chair of the Duma committee on foreign relations, said Russia was being treated 'like a country bumpkin' by the West.[17]

The rhetoric underlined the ascendency Russia First had attained amongst Moscow's political elite. Russia, the argument ran, should no longer be treated as a junior partner by the West in the Balkans. Its interests and views should be respected by the West, as befitting a 'Great Power'. The howls of rage in the Duma thinly disguised a pervading sense of humiliation at how easily Russia was ignored in the new unipolar world dominated by the United States. Russia First would reverse this trend, and lead to Russia being taken seriously on the world stage. In this world (as envisaged by the Duma), Russia's vital interests would be protected and her word would once again carry real weight in international negotiations.

President Yeltsin, although he largely ignored the Duma's resolution on Bosnia, strongly condemned the air strikes, saying they could lead Russia to reconsider its relationship with NATO, particularly its participation in the PfP programme. He told Spanish Prime Minister Felipe Gonzalez that the air strikes were 'unacceptable'. Yeltsin reiterated his opposition to any expansion of NATO and suggested this could accelerate the formation of a Commonwealth of Independent States (CIS) military bloc. He said, 'Those who insist on an expansion of NATO are making a major political mistake. The flames of war could burst out across the whole of Europe.'[18] On 12 September, Belarussian President Alexander Lukashenko enthusiastically announced his support for the proposed bloc, in contrast to Ukraine's opposition.[19]

The prime victim of these political manoeuvres was Andrei Kozyrev, who was swiftly coming to the end of his career as foreign minister. Reviled by the nationalists and communists in the Duma, who saw him as selling out Russia's interests to the West, and publicly dressed-down by Yeltsin, Kosyrev's days were clearly numbered. Yeltsin openly berated the foreign ministry for its poor record and established a commission to improve its performance.[20] On 19 October, Yeltsin publicly announced he was looking for a successor for Kozyrev, adding that the foreign minister had proved incapable of co-ordinating all Russia's foreign policy interests. 'Dissatisfaction remains. I see no improvement in his work,' the president concluded.[21] Although Yeltsin offered his 44-year old foreign minister a reprieve the next day, it was apparent that Kozyrev did not enjoy the president's confidence. Kozyrev's was a convenient scalp to offer the opposition, so deflecting criticism from the president and signalling a shift in policy away from Kozyrev's overtly pro-Western stance to a Russia First strategy. The foreign minister wisely sought a seat in the Duma as a bolt-hole, and relinquished his office to represent Murmansk following the elections in December. Kozyrev was the first and major victim of Yeltsin's switch to a fullblown Russia First policy . In order to defuse the row over Bosnia, on 27 September 1995, NATO offered Russia a formal agreement, building upon proposals for a 'special relationship' with the Russian Federation, agreed with Kozyrev in the Netherlands in May 1995. The agreement would be separate from the PfP, offering regular dialogue between Russia and NATO.[22]

Another contentious issue between Russia and the West at this time was the Conventional Forces in Europe (CFE) Treaty, signed in November 1990, which Yeltsin felt excessively limited the number of Russian conventional forces which could be stationed on Russia's western flank, particularly the Caucasus. With the war in Chechnya, the Kremlin effectively presented NATO with a *fait accompli*, since it was in violation of the treaty from 17 November 1995. A compromise by NATO, to allow flexibility in troop deployments by reducing the size of the Northern Caucasus military district on the western flank, was welcomed by Moscow. Nevertheless. to show its general displeasure with the West, particularly NATO enlargement, the Duma also stalled on ratifying the START II treaty on the reduction of strategic nuclear forces. Many Duma deputies also felt that if NATO were to enlarge to the east, this would not be the time to scale-down Russia's nuclear capability to defeat a conventional attack.[23]

The Duma elections of December 1995 were thus taking place in an atmosphere of soured relations between Russia and the West. The European Union tried to play its part in improving the political atmosphere in the run-up to the parliamentary elections. Leading a delegation from the Russian Duma and Federation Council to the European Parliament on 25–26 September 1995, Oleg Bogomolov made it clear that Russia did not want to be isolated in the new European architecture. The Russians were especially eager to see the implementation of the Partnership and Co-operation Agreement (PCA) between the EU and Russian Federation. The PCA had been signed by the Heads of State in Corfu in June 1994, but had been put on ice since the conflict in Chechnya. Although mainly a trade agreement, with political co-operation clauses, the PCA was a symbol of acceptance and collaboration between Russia and the West. The PCA was thus important for the pro-Western reformists within the Federal Assembly, who could point to some tangible benefits from co-operating with the West. Membership of the Council of Europe, finally gained in January 1996, was important for the same, symbolic, reasons. In its haste to support the pro-western factions in the Duma, and in an attempt to influence the continuation of a Western-orientated strategy in the Kremlin, the European Parliament ratified the PCA in November 1995, with the blessing of the Council of Ministers and the Commission. Meanwhile, the original cause of the suspension of the ratification process, the war in Chechnya, raged on unabated. The human rights clause of the PCA, calling for respect for democratic and civil rights, was tactically ditched in the interests of broader East–West relations. Sadly, the electorate remained unimpressed, and Russian relations with Europe in their wider sense had no impact whatsoever upon the Duma elections or Yeltsin's shift in policy towards Russia First.[24]

Bosnia and NATO created some froth, but the Duma campaign and election was really about the state of the Russian economy. It is hard for those in the West to appreciate the impact of seeing an ordered, albeit inefficient, economy collapse around you, and with it witness the disappearance of your life's savings as they evaporated under a storm of hyperinflation. Millions of jobs in effect vanished (with many more people remaining under-employed), and millions of people, including professionals, found they no longer had the means to subsist. Most of Russia's population had suffered a decline in their quality of life since the beginning of Yeltsin's term as president. Some 60 per cent of the population, around 88.9 million people, had seen their standard of living drop since 1991, following the introduction of reforms, while only 10 per cent (14.8 million) had benefited. In general, purchasing power by the end of 1995 was half its 1991 level, with 40 per cent of the population (59 million) living below the poverty-line. The gap between rich and poor continued to widen, while salaries decreased in real terms for the majority. Pensioners, miners and teachers began demonstrations throughout the country, to obtain salaries owed over several months. Industrial production carried on falling (the economy shrinking by about 3 per cent in 1995), large amounts of capital left the country and the social infrastructure, particularly the health service, continued to deteriorate.[25] The implosion of the command economy also witnessed a growing crime epidemic, which impacted upon the public's consciousness and the Duma election campaign.

POLITICAL FRAGMENTATION AND RUSSIA FIRST IN THE DUMA ELECTIONS

By the electoral deadline of 16 June 1995, 269 parties, electoral associations and blocs comprising 5,675 candidates had registered to take part in the Duma elections. To be put on the ballot, parties were required to collect 200,000 signatures by 2 October, with no more than 7 per cent of them coming from any one of the eighty-nine subjects of the Federation. Of the 450 seats up for election, 225 would be elected on a federal, proportional basis, subject to parties reaching 5 per cent of the vote. The remaining 225 seats would be directly elected on a simple-majority, constituency vote. Even with the increased threshold, forty-three parties and blocs qualified for registration for the federal-list seats, with more than 2,750 candidates contesting the 225 directly-elected single-mandate seats (making an average of ten to twelve candidates per constituency).[26] The Russian electorate was thus faced with a bewildering choice in what was only the second free election to the Duma since the dissolution of the Soviet Union. This fragmentation of the political scene also constituted a setback for President Yeltsin, who in April 1995 called for the formation of two large political parties. The prime minister, Victor Chernomyrdin founded 'Our Home is Russia' (NDR), a centre-right party based on support from the industrial and financial elites. Ivan Rybkin, the Speaker of the Duma formed a centre-left party bringing together the bosses of small and medium-sized enterprises and state-sector workers. The Kremlin hoped the establishment of a two-party system would stabilise the political scene up to the June presidential elections.

The presidential administration decided to try to create a two-party model, along the lines of the American system, since it was felt that the attempt to create a single government bloc had failed in the past. Sergei Shakrai, leader of the Party of Unity and Accord, convinced Yeltsin and Chernomrydin that a single party would also lack a broad electoral base, and might encourage government opponents to create their own alternative bloc. On 25 April 1995, Chernomrydin and Rybkin formally announced their agreement to form their centre-right and centre-left blocs respectively. The constituent assembly of Chernomyrdin's 'Our Home is Russia' (NDR) was held on 12 May 1995, with more than 300 delegates and 200 guests attending. Chernomyrdin outlined the party's objectives, which were to work for the election of a responsible parliamentary majority and to lay the foundations for a government made up of experienced and professional members. One of the new party's aims was therefore to bring political stability to Russia, essential if economic reforms were to continue.

Prime Minister Chernomyrdin had not been involved with electioneering for two years. As head of the government, he was aware of the need for a stable parliamentary majority to support economic reforms. NDR was based around the personality of the prime minister, who had been encouraged by Yeltsin to enter the political arena. Victor Chernomyrdin was a former member of the Soviet Communist Party (CPSU) from 1961 to 1991, who spent most of his career in the gas industry, becoming deputy minister in 1982 and reaching the rank of minister in 1985 under Mikhail Gorbachev. In 1989, Chernomyrdin set up Gazprom, a company he chaired until 1992, when he replaced Yegor Gaidar as prime minister. Chernomyrdin presented himself to the public as an efficient manager, above party in-fighting and without a definitive ideology. His stature had also improved (over the short term at least), with his cool handling of the Budennovsk hostage crisis in June 1995, and the subsequent abortive censure motion in the Duma. As a former head of Gazprom, Chernomyrdin had the backing of representatives of the Russian industrial complex, including the Union of Oil Producers, the Motor Vehicle Alliance and the Association of Russian Banks.

NDR had considerable backing from regional leaders, who were supportive of Yeltsin and his prime minister. President Shaimiev of Tartarstan, and the mayor of St Petersburg, Anatoly Sobchak, were amongst prominent supporters. Personalities from the arts, such as the film director Nikita Mikhalkov, also offered their support. NDR had branches in eighty of the Russian Federation's eighty-nine territorial units. Nevertheless, in spite of its extensive backing, NDR faced difficulties. Linked to the government, NDR was naturally associated with the poor economic situation and the conflict in Chechnya. Three key government figures, Andrei Kozyrev, Sergei Shakrai and Anatoly

Chubais (responsible for the government's privatisation programme), weakened the bloc by their defections. In particular, Chernomyrdin was attacked for maintaining lucrative financial links with Gazprom. 'Nash Dom Gazprom' ('Our Home is Gazprom') was a common saying through the election campaign, with allegations that Gazprom was bankrolling NDR.

Ivan Rybkin's attempts to form a centre-left bloc, known as Accord, were less promising than Chernomyrdin's endeavours with NDR. Ivan Rybkin, the 49-year-old Speaker of the Duma, was an agricultural specialist from Voronezh and former Communist Party member. Rybkin first came to prominence owing to his opposition to Yeltsin when he was co-chairman of the Supreme Soviet during the crisis in autumn 1993. He became speaker of the Duma with the support of the Agrarian and Communist Parties. Gradually, Rybkin moved nearer to Yeltsin's camp, becoming a member of the Security Council in May 1994. The purpose of the bloc was to provide leadership for the Agrarians and other centre-left parties, such as Women of Russia, the Democratic Party of Russia and the Congress of Russian Communities, and to provide a counter-weight to the communists and ultra-nationalists. However, Rybkin's attempt to form a broad centre-left coalition was a spectacular failure. Mikhail Lapshin, leader of the Agrarian Party, declined to enter into an electoral pact with Rybkin, deciding instead to maintain his party's independence and unity rather than join a bloc too closely associated with the government. Women of Russia, the Federation of Independent Trade Unions and the Industrial Party also decided to steer clear of Rybkin's bloc, so avoiding being tainted by the government's unpopularity. Neither did Rybkin's connections as group chairman of the Agrarian Party help his bloc win the support of the regional elite, given its status as the Communist Party's 'country cousin'. Without NDR's financial resources, Rybkin's bloc was doomed to failure, and Rybkin's association with Yeltsin's brainchild merely weakened his position as speaker.[27]

As was the case with the 1993 Duma elections, in 1995 the reformist camp was represented principally by Yegor Gaidar's Russia's Democratic Choice (DVR) and Grigory Yavlinsky's Yabloko. Both had distanced themselves from Yeltsin's administration, mainly due to the conflict in Chechnya. Personal rivalries between Gaidar and Yavlinsky, dating back to disagreements over economic policy when Yegor Gaidar was prime minister, meant that a formal pact between the two reformist groups was out of the question. Both Yavlinsky and Gaidar were vying for leadership of the democratic, reformist forces which, in Yavlinsky's case, was seen as a stepping-stone to the presidency. It was moreover convenient for Yavlinsky to distance himself from the perceived failures of Gaidar's economic reforms; he accused Gaidar of benefiting a minority and creating a *nomenklatura* democracy.[28] The DVR bloc itself embraced various small liberal groups, including the small Peasant Party led by Yury Chernichenko, a member of the Federation Council, and the Social Democratic Party of Alexander Yakovlev. Russia's Choice faced the defection of a number of its prominent supporters since 1993. Boris Fyodorov, a former minister of finance, left the DVR to join a competing reformist group, Forward Russia! (VR). Other defectors were Anatoly Chubais, Andrei Kozyrev, Ella Pamfilova (former minister for social security), Gennady Burbulis (former state secretary) and the wealthy banker, Oleg Boiko. DVR's overall representation in the Duma declined from ninety-six to fifty-four by 1 July 1995, while the party progressively lost its influence in committees and the parliament generally.[29] With the defections, DVR's leading figure became Sergei Kovalev, parliament's human rights commissioner noted for his opposition to the war in Chechnya. Politically, Russia's Choice was feeling the backlash from the economic reforms ('shock therapy') Yegor Gaidar introduced as prime minister in 1992.

Although Gaidar's Russia's Choice supported the economic policy pursued by Chubais as minister responsible for privatisation, it opposed the government on Chechnya, the militarisation of the country and the abuse of privileges by the ruling elite. The reformist, pro-market Russia's Choice could only expect to do well in urban centres like St Petersburg and Moscow. Appearing on television on 26 November, Gaidar admitted his party had lost some support since 1993, but he predicted it would register a strong showing among the intelligentsia, entrepreneurs, private farmers, young people and residents of large cities. Gaidar contrasted the DVR with most other parties in that it had not adopted a personal stance for or against the president or government, but instead evaluated each policy question on its own merits. As a result, he said, it had supported government policies it believed would promote financial stabilisation or private property rights but had consistently opposed the government over the war in Chechnya. Gaidar's campaign was curiously inept. On 7 December DVR held a rally to attract the youth vote, where Gaidar appeared under a large poster portraying him with his arm around Winnie the Pooh, with the title 'The Iron Winnie the Pooh'. Youngsters received a free package including baseball caps, a Pooh model and a poster of a nude young couple in bed with the slogan '17 December – wake up in a good mood'. Gaidar's speech to the assembled St Petersburg youth was his standard peroration defending his economic record as prime minister.[30]

Yabloko (Yavlinsky–Boldyrev–Lukin) had been formed as a result of an alliance between economist Grigory Yavlinsky, former chief state inspector Yuri Boldyrev and former ambassador to the US Vladimir Lukin, in October 1993. They were joined by the Republican Party, the Russian Christian Democratic Union and the Social Democratic Party of Russia. Yabloko promoted itself as the main alternative to Gaidar's party in the democratic camp. It advocated strong economic ties with the former Soviet republics, rejected voucher privatisation, and criticised monopolies and corruption. The party had close ties with emerging Russian commercial interests, such as the Most Group and Menatep Bank. Yabloko had opposed Yeltsin in the Duma on a selective basis, without taking up extreme positions. It had, for example, supported the censure motion against the government on Chechnya, but opposed attempts to impeach the president. Grigory Yavlinsky was a vocal critic of the government's economic reform programme and its 1995 budget proposals.[31] He claimed to speak for regional interests, portraying Gaidar as a representative of the Moscow elite.

Yavlinsky was, however, one of a band of 'liberal marketeers', who were proponents of a market-orientated economy. Others in this selective band were the likes of Yegor Gaidar, Sergei Shakrai, Konstantin Borovoi and former Moscow mayor Gavriil Popov. Yabloko's electoral programme, released on 5 December, called for reducing Russia's dependence on raw material exports, correcting errors in privatisation, reviving Russia's far east and rebuilding ties with the CIS.[32] Even such an unimpeachable reformist party as Yabloko was aware of the prevailing nostalgic sentiment in Russia. Many of the electorate hankered after the certainties of the old Soviet Union, and regretted the dismemberment of the former Soviet empire and the loss of Russia's 'Great Power' status. Speaking on Russian television on 8 December 1995, Yavlinsky played to this constituency, calling for effective economic union with the former Soviet republics. Saying that the bloc aimed to eliminate poverty from every home in four years, Yavlinsky also referred to Russians living in the 'near abroad'. He said: 'The worst thing is that there is still no answer in respect of our 25 million fellow citizens who now live, as it were, abroad.' Yavlinsky added that while military or political union with the former republics of the Soviet Union would not work: 'If there is an economic union, everything will be possible. There will be opportunities to co-operate peacefully and freely in the economic sphere. Everything will be possible. This is how we will resolve our Crimean problem and all our other problems.'[33]

Yavlinsky was acknowledging the depths of Russian concern not only about the economic situation, but nostalgia for the loss of the Soviet Union. In referring to Russians in the 'near abroad' and the dispute over the Crimea, Yavlinsky was shamelessly playing the nationalist card and climbing on the Russia First bandwagon. Vladimir Lukin had raised the issue of foreign policy in a television broadcast on 29 November. Russia's foreign ministry he said, in the public's view, carries out 'incorrect policies, policies which often and to a great extent humiliate our country's dignity; policies geared to a certain state, policies which all too often say "yes" to that state'. Yabloko, Lukin said, had tried to reverse foreign policy to prevent further humiliation.[34] Again, the theme of putting Russia First was apparent in Yabloko's campaign rhetoric.

Even Chenomyrdin's NDR and Rybkin's bloc had to respond to the anti-Western climate surrounding the Duma campaign. Chernomyrdin's Our Home is Russia stated that 'Russia must make a firm declaration about the threat to its security in the case of NATO expansion'. Among the measures to counter NATO's expansion were 'the strengthening of the armed forces, the changing of their stationing with the advancement to the front lines of defence, including the mechanisms of the collective security of the CIS countries'. NDR sought to counterbalance NATO by creating a dominant role for the OSCE as the main instrument for military and political co-operation in Europe. The CIS would be developed into a military alliance as a counterweight to the North Atlantic Alliance. The *Moscow News* described this programme as 'a combination of moderate xenophobia with great power policy'.[35] NDR's programme reflected the growing political consensus surrounding the strategy of Russia First. Speaker Ivan Rybkin went further, speaking on St Petersburg's Channel 5 TV on 23 November:

In these present difficult times, Russia has two true allies, the navy and the army . . . We must firmly declare the priorities of our foreign policy today, make them known to everyone. The CIS countries are our priority. Twenty-five million compatriots who have little motherlands, the territories, regions and republics of

Russia – these are our priority, and we shall defend their interests with all means at our disposal.'[36]

With both NDR and Rybkin's bloc, there were strong echoes of a Russia First strategy, with both political groups seeking to re-prioritise Russia's vital interests, marking a shift away from the previous paramountcy accorded to relations with the West. In the future, Russia would turn more of its attention to areas of traditional and historical interest, including its 'near abroad', even if this led to clashes with the West. Russia First reflected not just the resurgence of Russian nationalism or even anti-Westernism, but a determination to assert Russia's identity as a Eurasian 'Great Power' in a world which had come to be overwhelmingly dominated by the United States.

If the reformist Yabloko and the pro-government NDR and Rybkin's bloc were developing Russia First rhetoric, this was nothing compared to the communist and nationalist blocs. One of the rising stars of the election campaign was General Alexander Lebed, the nationally-known former commander of the Russian 14th Army in Trans-dniestr. Alexander Lebed retired from the army on 30 May 1995, and on 4 September confirmed that he would stand for the Duma on the Congress of Russian Communities (KRO) list. Lebed had previously turned down various appointments which would have kept him out of the political arena. The Congress of Russian Communities was formed to safeguard the rights of the 25 million Russians living in other parts of the former Soviet Union (the 'near abroad'). Yury Skokov, a former secretary of Yeltsin's Security Council (from April 1992 to May 1993) played a key role in establishing the KRO in April 1995. Skokov had close links with the military-industrial complex, designs on becoming prime minister, and described himself as a neo-marxist. Skokov was needed by Lebed to organise an effective campaign, giving the general a launch-pad for the presidential elections. Lebed was second (after Skokov) on the national party list, and stood for election in a district in Tula.

The KRO stood for a brand of nationalist statism, seeking to win over voters disenchanted with Yeltsin's policies but opposed to extremist parties. Lebed and Skokov hoped to benefit from discontent arising from market reforms and cutbacks in military spending, by advocating a mixture of strong government, state capitalism and positive nationalism, strengthening Russia's armed forces in the process. A proponent of Russia First, the KRO was firmly opposed to

NATO expansion to central Europe. Lebed hoped to win up to 15 per cent of the vote, taking votes from the Communists, Zhirinovsky's Liberal Democrats, Alexander Rutskoi's Derzhava or Forward, Russia![37] Lebed came in for criticism at the KRO's founding congress in April 1995, where some members called him a 'cheap populist' and a 'lover of the effective phrase' because of his penchant for using cryptic aphorisms to express his ideas.[38]

Lebed's views created disquiet in some quarters. In July 1995, after a visit to Perm in Siberia, the local press attacked his ideas, arguing that 'nationalism is always the flag of war' and that 'the thirst for strict order relies on force that cannot exist without blood'.[39] In the election campaign, Lebed concentrated on the country's economic circumstances and tackling soaring crime, on one occasion saying that over the previous year there had been one million more deaths than births, and that only one-third of Russian babies were born healthy. He argued that the possible result would be that 'in eighty years time Russians will become an ethnic minority in their own territory'.[40] In the course of an interview published in October, Lebed outlined his views on foreign policy:

> I am deeply convinced that, before the end of this century, we will see the creation of a new state consisting of Russia, Ukraine, Belarus, and, probably, Kazakhstan. That is what is happening, you know. A double standard continues to exist. All of Europe is uniting, and we are dividing. It is time to put an end to this.[41]

Lebed's KRO was a force for moderation compared to other nationalist groups. Major General Alexander Rutskoi, Hero of the Soviet Union and Russian vice-president from 1991 to 1993, founded Derzhava (Great Power) in 1995. The former vice-president had been one of the organisers of the Communists for Democracy in the Russian Congress of People's Deputies, and an early supporter of Yeltsin. Rutskoi had been declared acting president by the Supreme Soviet, but he was imprisoned for his part in the battle for the White House in October 1993, and released in February 1994 under a Duma amnesty. Elected chairman of the Russian Social Democratic People's Party (RSDNP), his attempt to include the RSDNP in Derzhava caused a split among the Social Democrats led by Vasily Lipitsky (who went on to co-found the Social Democratic Union).[42] Denounced by the Social Democrats for its chauvinist ideas, Derzhava was launched in March

1995 to fight the Duma election and back Rutskoi for the presidency.

Derzhava stood for restoring Russia's imperial borders of 1916 (with the exception of Poland and Finland) and forcing former Soviet republics to reintegrate by cutting off Russian supplies of electricity, oil and gas. Combining nationalism with neo-imperialism, Rutskoi's Derzhava stood on an aggressive Russia First platform. Within Russia, it proposed eliminating all the Federation's ethnic divisions, replacing them with provinces ruled by a unitary state. Derzhava condemned the war in Chechnya, rejected the buying and selling of land and any form of capitalism, in favour of social justice and equality. Rutskoi hoped to gain support from anti-communist patriotic voters who opposed Zyuganov's Communist Party as too orthodox, but failed to take Zhirinovsky's LDPR seriously. Rutskoi blamed the 1917 revolution for the country's woes, and blamed the communists for letting him down in 1993. He further claimed he had been duped into serving as Yeltsin's vice-president, as the president later came to break his election promises. The country's leaders had betrayed Russia, he argued. Derzhava, Rutskoi told television viewers in St Petersburg, would restore order and halt the destruction of the nation. 'Quite frankly, I trust no-one, just like many of you,' he told his audience.[43]

While it was possible to write off Derzhava as of little likely political significance, the same could not be said of Vladimir Zhirinovsky's Liberal Democratic Party of Russia (LDPR). The ultra-nationalist LDPR had topped the poll in 1993 with 23 per cent, and still had fifty-four deputies in the Duma. Holding its founding congress in December 1989, the LDPR programme called for an expansion of Russia's borders, the division of the world into spheres of influence, the creation of a strong executive, a crackdown on crime, the acceptance of some market reforms, the replacement of Russia's ethnically defined districts with purely territorial divisions, and a reduction in the price of alcohol. The LDPR was a vehicle for Vladimir Zhirinovsky, and was dependent upon his personal following. Populist and xenophobic, Zhirinovsky clearly touched on a sense of frustration, despair and nostalgia for Russia's greatness amongst the country's electorate. While Zhirinovsky aired his political views on free television political broadcasts, his paid advertisements sought to entertain television viewers and grab their attention. In one 15-second slot he appeared singing an apolitical song with the popular rock duo Dyuna. Another advert showed him dancing in a disco, while one commercial showed a couple in bed together, discussing who to vote for. Perhaps the most creative television advertisement showed a sexy singer holding Zhirinovsky's picture and singing 'Without you, the world would be so boring,' and video shots of the LDPR leader in swimming trunks.[44]

Zhirinovsky's anti-Western rhetoric almost reached paranoic proportions, with accusations that there was a conspiracy to destroy Russia. On 14 December 1995, he told *Radio Rossii*:

> NATO pilots are using the orthodox Serbs as practice for their military skills . . . There will be another June 22 [the date on which the Germans invaded Russia in 1941], when American troops will land on our air fields. They have already practised in Ukraine. US paratroops landed in Odessa. Novorossisk will be next . . .

He accused the CIA of trying to kill President Yeltsin, as part of 'a general, total war against Russia, which is being fought by the West, the USA, the CIA, Israel, and Mossad and our own fifth column'. Earlier in December, speaking on Moscow radio, Zhirinovsky had accused the CIA of fomenting the war in Chechnya.[45] Zhirinovsky's anti-Western rhetoric was the most extreme version of Russia First put before the Russian electorate.

On the Left, anti-Western rhetoric was almost as marked as amongst the nationalist parties. By far the most important party on the Left was the Communist Party of the Russian Federation (KPRF), led by Gennady Zyuganov. The KPRF returned to the political arena on 30 November 1992, after the Constitutional Court partly overturned Yeltsin's November 1991 decree banning the party. With 500,000 party members in 20,000 regional and district branches spread across the entire country, the KPRF was the largest and best organised party in Russia. In the 1993 Duma election, the party had come third, behind Zhirinovsky's LDPR and Russia's Choice. The party had good access to the print media through its party paper *Pravda Rossii* and its close connections with *Pravda*, *Sovetskaya Rossiya* and up to 120 other publications. The KPRF's third congress, held on 21–22 January 1995, adopted a programme of removing the 'party of national betrayal' from power constitutionally, restoring the Soviet Union by voluntary means, strengthening the country's position on the world stage, pursuing Russia's traditional interests, cracking down on crime, and overcoming the Federation's economic crisis by reversing the government's privatisation policies and returning to state regulation of the economy.

Meeting American businessmen in Moscow in October 1995,

Zyuganov tried to appease his Western critics by promising lower taxes and tariffs, and by saying that the KPRF would not repeat the mistakes of the Communist Party of the Soviet Union (CPSU). Unlike the CPSU, the KPRF would not try to impose a monopoly on truth, power or property, he claimed. However, reminding some observers of his anti-Gorbachev speeches of the 1980s, Zyuganov said the state should control energy, transportation, communications and the military-industrial complex.[46] The KPRF programme was a clear instance of a Russia First strategy, asserting the primacy of Russian state interests in both domestic- and foreign-policy terms. Yet even Zyuganov did not venture as far as the Communists–Workers Russia for the Soviet Union bloc, led by Victor Anpilov and Victor Tyulkin, who advocated a return to Soviet-style socialism, the re-nationalisation all means of production and total state control of foreign trade. Zyuganov had rejected an offer from Anpilov and Tyulkin to form a single communist electoral bloc earlier that year, preferring to cultivate a more moderate image.[47]

Zyuganov repeatedly returned to the theme of Russia First during the 1995 Duma campaign. Writing in *Sovetskaya Rossiya* on 18 November, Zyuganov drew on the lessons of Lenin's approach to the October 1917 revolution, calling for a 'peaceful revolution' to change economic policy and restoring 'the independent international position and true sovereignty of Russia'. Zyuganov said this would involve reviving a union of some former Soviet republics 'on a voluntary basis'.[48] Later the same month, the newspaper *Segodnya* quoted Zyuganov as saying that the reintegration of the former Soviet republics had 'extraordinarily large significance' for his party. The Communist Party leader said he favoured a quick economic union with Ukraine, Belarus and Kazakhstan, and added that Russia could reunite with the other republics as soon as its economy started to improve. Zyuganov only proposed one condition for co-operation with the Caucasus regions of Russia: 'a thousand-year treaty banning secession'.[49]

Other Communist leaders took up the Russia First theme. In St Petersburg, Yury Pavlovich Belov, first secretary of the KPRF's Leningrad region, stated in a television broadcast that NATO was now at the gates of Russia, waiting to dictate to it as it dictated to the Serbs:

> Restoration of the union state, our historic fatherland, is the main goal of the Communist Party of the Russian Federation . . . A wide, popular-patriotic movement, uniting all patriots, from the patriotically-inclined worker to the patriotically-inclined private

entrepreneur, is needed and the path to create the historic fatherland is not easy, above all on a voluntary basis, avoiding the threat
of civil war'.[50]

The Agrarian Party, led by Mikhail Lapshin, was the KPRF's main
ally. With its 250,000 members it was the second largest party in Russia
(in terms of membership), behind only the Communist Party. It had
branches in all of the eighty-nine territorial units of the Russian
Federation. Rejecting an alliance with Rybkin's bloc, the Agrarians
wished to distance themselves from Yeltsin's administration, despite
having two party members in the cabinet (Agriculture Minister
Alexander Nazarchuk and Deputy Prime Minister Alexander
Zaveryukha). Since its founding congress in February 1993, the
Agrarian Party of Russia (APR) was one of the most stable political
parties in post-Soviet Russia. Mikhail Lapshin had been APR's only
chairman, and its programme had been largely unaltered. The second
party congress, held on 29 September 1995, formed the electoral bloc
APR, consisting of Lapshin's party, the Agrarian Union and the trade
union of the agro-industrial complex. The APR opposed market reform
in the agrarian sector, it voted against the sale of land, voucher privatisation of agricultural enterprises and the private ownership of land. In
1993, the APR obtained 10 per cent of the vote nationwide and one-
third of the rural vote, winning thirty-three seats (boosted to fifty by
deputies from single-member rural constituencies). The APR inherited
the rural organisation of the Communist Party of the Soviet Union
(CPSU), as well as the newspaper *Selskaya zhizn*. Often described as
the KPRF 'country cousin', the APR signed a co-operation agreement
with the Communist Party in July 1994. However, on several key issues,
several of the APR's members had supported the government.

During the 1995 Duma campaign, although mainly concerned with
rural issues, the Agrarian Party took up the anti-Western, nationalistic
Russia First theme. Speaking for the APR in an television election
broadcast on 27 November, Alexander Artsibashev complained that
when Yabloko was not allowed to register for the elections, America
threatened to stop deliveries of foodstuffs to Russia. 'They know which
string to pull!', he added. Artsibashev continued:

One has the impression that the reformers have set themselves the
task of halting production in Russia altogether, including
foodstuffs, so that the West can always keep us dangling on a hook.

They need a seller's market. They need a poverty-stricken, mute Russia. In Moscow, and the Moscow Region, even before the law on land has been adopted, foreigners have put so many fences up around their offices and the firms acting for them there that sometimes you can't even find the road to get past them.[51]

In another television broadcast on 28 November, Vasiliy Starodubstev, a leader of the Agrarian Party, said, 'Experts who know their subject very well say today that there have been no reforms. Instead, Western capitalists have given a special order to destroy our great country and its economy. To my great regret, the capitalists have been extremely successful . . .'[52] The anti-Western rhetoric was crude but, judging by the election results, effective.

THE DUMA ELECTION RESULTS:
A VICTORY FOR RUSSIA FIRST

The results of the Duma elections, held on Sunday 17 December, were a devastating blow to Chernomyrdin's 'party of power' (NDR) and a setback to President Yeltsin's re-election hopes. The Duma elections were widely described as a 'dress rehearsal' for the presidential elections to be held the following June. But this dress rehearsal had been little short of an electoral disaster for Chernomyrdin and Yeltsin. The Communists (KPRF) under Gennady Zyuganov almost quadrupled the party's representation in the Duma compared to the 1993 election, rising from forty-five to 157 seats. In percentage terms, the KPRF topped the poll with 23 per cent. Left-wing parties also did well in the single-mandate constituencies, winning eighty-eight out of 225 seats (fifty-eight KPRF and thirty others). Together with their allies on the Left (including some independents), the Communists could muster an overall majority in the Duma. On 16 January 1996, three leftist factions (KPRF, Agrarians and Popular Power) registered in the Duma held a total of 221 seats, five short of a majority in the 450-seat lower house. Whilst Zhirinovsky's LDPR vote had halved since 1993, his ultra-nationalists still received 11 per cent of the vote, much higher than expected by observers. Apart from Zhirinovsky's fifty-one deputies, a further eight nationalists were elected in the first-past-the-post single-mandate seats. However, the pro-government, reformist and centrist parties performed relatively badly, and in some instances, catastrophically. Yegor Gaidar's Russia's

Democratic Choice slumped from seventy-six seats to just nine, winning only 3.8 per cent of the vote. Chernomyrdin's pro-government NDR, despite the massive amount of effort and money committed to the campaign, gained just 10 per cent of the vote and fifty-five seats. Yavlinsky's Yabloko won 6.8 per cent of the vote and forty-five seats, 1 per cent down on its 1993 performance.[53]

Overall, the election results were a triumph for parties espousing 'Russia First' principles. Communists, nationalist parties and their allies won 36.1 million votes, over 52 per cent of the votes cast. Pro-government, reformist and centrist parties won over 26.5 million votes, around 38 per cent of the votes cast, and in percentage terms about the same level as in 1993. Undoubtedly, the big winners of the elections were the KPRF, who saw their vote share increase by 10 per cent, rising from 6.6 million votes in 1993 to 15.4 million in 1995. The turn-out, at 64.4 per cent, with 67 million voters, was higher than in 1993 (54.8), while only four parties crossed the 5 per cent barrier to win a share of the federal list seats: the KPRF, LDPR, Our Home is Russia and Yabloko. It is a fallacy to suggest that the pro-government and reformist blocs were the only parties to suffer disproportionately in terms of the distribution of seats, due to the electoral system. The four pro-government and pro-reform parties which stood in 1993 split into thirteen for the 1995 elections, making it more difficult for any one party to surmount the 5 per cent hurdle. However, looking at the distribution of seats compared to votes gained, there were both winners and losers from the electoral system. While the KPRF was over-represented in the Duma on a strictly proportional basis, so were the NDR and Yabloko.

Small nationalist parties and ultra-Left parties also were under-represented in the Duma, for example Lebed's Congress of Russian Communities obtained 4.3 per cent of the vote and five seats, compared to Yabloko's 7 per cent and forty-five seats. Similarly, the Communists–Working Russia for the Soviet Union obtained just one seat with 4.5 per cent, compared to NDR's fifty-five seats with 10 per cent. Some 60 per cent of votes cast had no impact on the distribution of federal-list seats. As intended by Yeltsin, the main losers of the 5 per cent barrier were the small extremist parties, especially the nationalists. One per cent of the vote cast for Chernomyrdin's NDR elected 5.4 deputies, yet the same percentage vote only elected 2.9 nationalists, or 3.3 reformist deputies. On this basis, NDR was the main beneficiary of the electoral system along with the KPRF.[54]

While the electoral system distorted the detail, this could not detract from the fact that Yeltsin's most vociferous opponents, the communists and nationalists, had achieved over 50 per cent of the votes cast. The only two avowedly pro-government parties, NDR and Ivan Rybkin's bloc, had between them received 11 per cent of the vote. Over 80 per cent of the electorate had voted for parties critical of Yeltsin's government. Worse still, Communist leader Gennady Zyuganov, Yeltsin's main opponent for the forthcoming presidential elections, had received a huge electoral fillip. Yeltsin was faced with a 'Red Duma' and an increasingly assertive 'red–brown' opposition, attacking the president's domestic and foreign policies. The KPRF went on to elect one of their members, Gennady Seleznyev, as speaker of the Duma, and obtained sixteen chairs of committees and commissions. The Duma was rapidly transformed into Zyuganov's presidential campaign headquarters.[55]

A strong north–south divide was apparent in the election results on 17 December. Much of the anti-reform vote was concentrated in provinces south of the 55th parallel, with the KPRF also enjoying strong support in the belt of provinces surrounding Moscow. The Communist Party came first in sixty-two of Russia's eighty-nine territorial units, nearly matching the LDPR's success in 1993, when Zhirinovsky won in sixty-four regions. The KPRF's support was concentrated in the region around Moscow, the central black-earth zone, and parts of the Volga and North Caucasus. The Communists won more than 40 per cent of the vote in Orel, Tambov and several of the ethnic republics of North Caucasus. The KPRF's support in these areas was almost certainly a result of the adverse effect of economic reforms, with rising unemployment, chronic under-employment (with factories operating well below capacity), falling real incomes and wage arrears of several months. The KPRF polled 48 per cent in the Siberian oblast of Kemerovo, the centre of the coal miners' strikes that had challenged the Soviet government in 1989. The KPRF waged a strong campaign in the regions, based on their superior organisation and well-known local candidates. The Communists made little use of commercial television advertisements, concentrating instead on propaganda through their supportive journals and newspapers, and their regional networks. The KPRF was probably the only party which did not rely upon its leader for the bulk of its support. There was one worrying aspect of the KPRF's electoral support, however. More than 60 per cent of KPRF supporters were over 50 years old, while only 30 per cent of Yabloko's voters were over 50.[56]

Zhirinovsky's LDPR won in thirteen of Russia's territorial units

(Subjects), including Vologda Oblast and the Komi republic in northern Russia and the far eastern provinces of Primorsk Krai and Magadan. The LDPR received support from both sides of the 55th parallel, especially from areas in the distant north and far eastern provinces where supplies were very poor and voters felt abandoned by Moscow. Zhirinovsky, the consummate outsider, appealed to these voters' sense of isolation and alienation. The LDPR did better outside urban areas with more than a million voters, and in several autonomous okrugs in Siberia and the far east. Zhirinovsky did particularly badly in Moscow and St Peterburg, and the developed oblasts surrounding them, where the electorate tended to be more prosperous and better educated. Both the KPRF and the LDPR did well amongst less educated voters with low incomes. The Communists and Zhirinovsky's LDPR drew more than half their supporters from families with a monthly income of less than 235,000 roubles ($50) per household member. The LDPR was the party of the most dispossessed, with about 10 per cent of its supporters on a monthly income of less than a paltry 50,000 roubles ($11) per household member. Yabloko and the NDR, however, attracted a higher percentage of better-educated and wealthier voters, mainly in the cities. In excess of 65 per cent of Yabloko's support came from voters with a monthly income of more than $50 per household member. Yabloko's attempts to attract less well off communist voters by attacking the government (rather than the KPRF) and condemning the late payment of pensions and wages fell on stony ground. One Yabloko poster ran the slogan 'We are not fighting communism. We are fighting poverty' with no perceptible effect in communist heartlands.[57]

Examples of how the vote split among social groups could be seen all over Russia. In the Khanty-Mansii Autonomous Okrug in Siberia, NDR won in the oil-producing urban centre of Surgat, reflecting Chernomyrdin's connections with the energy sector. But the LDPR did better in the rural areas, and came top in the region as a whole. Similarly, the city of Murmansk voted for Yavlinsky's reformist Yabloko, while the surrounding area went for Zhirinovsky. While the city of St Petersburg voted for Yabloko, Leningrad region put the KPRF in first place. Yabloko itself only managed to come top in two areas, St Petersburg (16 per cent) and Kamchatka (20 per cent), where a popular local candidate stood for Yavlinsky's party in the far east. Yabloko scored particularly well amongst St Petersburg's intelligentsia and professional classes. Elsewhere, Yabloko was hit by its poor regional organisation. Chernomyrdin's pro-government NDR led in nine regions, including several of the ethnic regions, where local elites could deliver the vote for Moscow. NDR topped the poll in Tartarstan (29 per cent), Kalmykiya (24 per cent) and Tyva (28 per cent). The NDR was credited with 48 per cent support in Chechnya, but with widespread allegations of fraud and local detestation for Moscow this result was discounted by international observers, despite the Central Electoral Commission's insistence that the figures were accurate. More plausibly, NDR won in Moscow (19 per cent), traditionally a bastion of reform, where many of Russia's new entrepreneurs and government employees live. NDR's support in Moscow contrasted with the LDPR's poor showing in the city, where they obtained only 3 per cent of the vote, and displayed the gap between city and provincial voters.[58]

Although generally unpopular outside Moscow, the NDR did gain some support by employing Western election techniques. Voters in Samara received a letter apparently personally signed by the prime minister, which led some pensioners to feel obliged to vote for NDR. However, NDR's other attempts at Western-style campaigning seemed to have less effect, including German supermodel Claudia Schiffer's appearance in the capital, and a rock concert featuring MC Hammer. The impact of television on the campaign was mixed. Zhirinovsky's clowning on paid-time television gained him attention, while he used his free television time to repeat his favourite themes of a Western conspiracy to destroy Russia, and the need to protect ethnic Russians.[59]

State television and radio each allotted one hour of free broadcasts daily, divided equally amongst the forty-three political groups and candidates by lot. Additionally, advertising time could be purchased. Some thirty-five of the forty-three parties purchased advertising on television, which cost between $10,000 and $30,000 per minute on Russian public TV (ORT). According to electoral law, candidates in single-mandate seats were allowed to spend up to 1,000 minimum salaries ($13,000), while the maximum for an electoral association or bloc was 10.9 billion roubles or $2.4 million. The Central Electoral Commission provided 80 million roubles ($16,000) of state funds for registered political parties or blocs. The limits were widely flouted by political parties, especially NDR which had an extensive billboard and advertising campaign. Nevertheless, most blocs and parties had less impact with their advertising than Zhirinovsky (who paid for 171 minutes of television advertising). NDR paid for six hours of television advertising, on top of official coverage of Chernomyrdin's duties as prime minister, but won only 10 per cent of the vote. Ivan Rybkin's bloc, third in the paid for advertising league, with its 'talking cows' advertisements, bought 157 minutes of television, and scored around 1 per cent. The lesson seemed to be that if the audience did not like the message, television advertising was a waste of money.[60]

The 1995 Duma elections included a number of also-rans. Yegor Gaidar's campaign to discredit the communists, combined with his boring broadcasts, failed. Lebed's KRO also performed disappointingly (4.3 per cent and five seats), failing to differentiate itself from the KPRF, and with Lebed damaged by being placed number two to Yury Skokov, a former Yeltsin ally. Military figures generally did badly, with only two of the 118 'official' military candidates being elected. General Rutskoi's Derzhava won 2.5 per cent of the vote, but failed to win a single seat. Single-interest groups like the Women of Russia also saw their support drop, from 8 per cent to 4.6 per cent (from twenty-three seats to three), as they were perceived as self-seeking and pro-government. In the Women of Russia's case, many of the leaders came from the Soviet Union's official women's movement, and consisted of former party apparatchiks. Women of Russia also lost support to the KPRF, which projected itself as the party of social protection and economic moderation, themes previously taken up by the women's movement.[61]

The leftist Agrarian Party saw its vote slip to 3.7 per cent from 8 per cent in 1993, and its seats drop from thirty-three to twenty. Lapshin's Agrarian Party lost supporters at the federal level to the KPRF, which was seen as a more effective opponent of Yeltsin's government. At a local level in predominantly rural areas, the Agrarian Party did better in single-mandate contests, picking up a respectable twenty seats. Former Soviet Prime Minister Nikolai Ryzhkov's leftist Power to the People won nine single-mandate seats and 1.6 per cent of the vote, while the Stalinist Communists–Workers Russia for the Soviet Union also won one seat and a surprising 4.5 per cent of the vote (more than Gaidar's Russia's Choice). There was disappointment for the centre-left, as the Social Democratic Union, led by former Moscow mayor Gavriil Popov, failed to win a single seat and only got 0.13 per cent of the vote. The Social Democrats pro-Western campaign, with billboards and television election broadcasts referring to 'Social Democracy:The Opportunity Russia Missed in 1917' and 'Social Democracy:A Window onto Europe', together with a list of governing Western social-democratic parties, played badly. With 88,642 votes out of an electorate of 107 million, the Social Democrats scraped in below the Beer Lovers' Party, with 428,727. The concept of social democracy simply did not exist in the Russian political constellation, being mainly subsumed in the KPRF. The Social Democrats pro-Western campaign was also totally at odds with the prevailing Russia First climate at the time of the Duma elections.[62]

President Yeltsin's reaction to the 'Red Duma'

President Boris Yeltsin's response to the victory of the Communist Party and the nationalists was to sweep away most of the remaining liberal reformers from the government, changing policy to emphasise 'welfare populism' and a more assertive form of Russian nationalism. Much of the change in policy was rhetorical rather than real, but the pattern was clear. Stealing the clothes of his successful opponents in the Duma, there would be more social concern for the welfare of the Russian people, and a stepping-back from the overtly pro-Western policy of the past. As the 'reformers' were ousted from the Kremlin, the internal balance of power was tilted towards the 'hardliners' gathered around the president. Rather than present himself as the champion of reform and the leader of the democrats, Yeltsin would henceforth reinvent himself as the 'Good Tsar', the personification of Russian nationalism and Russia First.

The results of the Duma election had been bad enough. On top of this, Yeltsin knew that it was not only his government which was unpopular. Opinion polls taken to ascertain the level of support for potential presidential candidates showed that Yeltsin's personal standing with the electorate was dire. In September 1995, before the Duma elections, Yeltsin was running in fourth place on just 7 per cent, behind Alexander Lebed (14 per cent), Grigory Yavlinsky (12 per cent) and Victor Chernomrydin (10 per cent).[63] Yeltsin's popularity rating had fallen to 3.2 per cent in March 1994, and plummeted further after the beginning of the war in Chechnya, reaching 2.9 per cent in January 1995 and 2.7 per cent in March 1995. By the end of 1995, only 2 per cent 'completely supported' the Russian president, 28 per cent were 'in disagreement with some of his actions', and 52 per cent thought he should resign.[64] The parties that did best in the Duma election were those clearly opposed to the president and his policies, the communists and nationalists. For Boris Yeltsin the answer was obvious: the reformers would have to go.

President Yeltsin began his purges by dropping Foreign Minister Andrei Kozyrev and First Deputy Prime Minister Anatoly Chubais. Chubais had overall responsibility for Russia's economic policy, and had been the architect of the country's privatisation programme. Sergei Filatov, the reformist head of administration was also removed, together with a number of other high-ranking officials. According to *The Economist*, Kozyrev and Chubais were 'the two men most closely associated with the only remotely successful policies in Russia for the past few years'.[65] Andrei Kozyrev had been Russia's foreign minister since October 1990, when the Russian Federation was part of the Soviet Union, and was Yeltsin's longest-serving minister. Kozyrev's resignation, when it came on 5 January 1996, was hardly unexpected. The foreign minister's position had been undermined by the changing political climate in the Duma and the country over several years, and he had finally been abandoned by Yeltsin himself.[66] Although a presidential spokesman said that Western countries 'should not regard the resignation of Andrei Kozyrev from the post of foreign minister as any kind of threat or as an indication of change in Russia's foreign policy', this was largely discounted by political observers. It was apparent that Kozyrev's effective sacking was a gesture to communist and nationalist parties which criticised his policies as too pro-Western. The Russian Communist Party was jubilant over the foreign minister's departure. 'All Kozyrev's blunders have been in favour of the West,' said a party spokesman. Western countries were dismayed by the departure of Kozyrev, but not surprised by the exit of the liberal career diplomat. 'Russia's relations with the West have been completely transformed during his time as foreign minister and Kozyrev personally can take a large part of the credit for that,' said one Western diplomat. In future, they added, Russian policy was bound to become more nationalist in style, if not necessarily in substance, to reflect the increasingly anti-Western mood in the country.[67]

The prime minister's claims that neither Kozyrev's nor Chubais's departure was linked to the Duma election results merely confirmed suspicions that they were. Yeltsin timed the departures to have maximum political effect, so ensuring that he would be seen as responding to the criticisms of his opponents and the will of the Russian electorate. Despite the presidential statement that there would be no change in foreign policy, the liberal *Nezavisimaya Gazeta* newspaper felt that it was 'obvious that the course which the new head of the foreign ministry pursues will differ strikingly from that of

Kozyrev'. Western diplomats believed the Kremlin was already intent on pursing a more assertive foreign policy, one source saying: 'The change in Russian foreign policy has already taken place. It was just that Kozyrev was unable to articulate it effectively enough.' Kozyrev had tried to adapt to the tilt in policy, but not far or fast enough to save his political skin. The foreign minister's compensation was a Duma seat in Murmansk, the political equivalent of being sent to Siberia.

President Yeltsin indicated an immediate change in political gear at a press conference held on 19 January, his first major press appearance since his heart trouble the previous October. Appearing at times weak and disorientated, Yeltsin called for a stronger CIS security pact to counter the dominance of the United States and NATO, and lambasted his sacked economics minister. Addressing a summit of the CIS, Yeltsin had tried to win support for a collective security system as a counterweight to the United States and NATO, which he said were 'continuously strengthening their military potential'. Yeltsin had previously expressed opposition to NATO expansion, but the anti-US rhetoric was seen as an attempt to adopt the anti-Western tone and platform of the recently victorious communists and nationalists. Red-faced and blustering, Yeltsin also attacked Chubais, saying: 'The fact is that Our Home is Russia got only 10 per cent of the vote – this is Chubais. If Chubais had been removed earlier, before the elections, it would have been 20 per cent.' Yeltsin told the press conference that Chubais 'sold off our major enterprises for a song. This cannot be forgiven.' Western diplomats noticed the 'total change of attitude'. Yeltsin was adopting a 'Russia First' strategy in both the domestic- and foreign-policy spheres. The real question was: how much of this was rhetoric and what, if anything, would change substantively?[68]

Yeltsin had already given notice that the evolution of a Russia First strategy was to be more than a rhetorical, passing fad. The diplomatic world was startled by Yeltsin's appointment of Yevgeny Primakov as foreign minister on 9 January 1996. Primakov had been head of Russia's external intelligence service (SVR) since it had been hived off from the Soviet KGB in 1991. The Kremlin's chief spymaster, an Arabic speaker and Middle East expert, he had been a candidate member of the Soviet Politburo in the 1980s. The 67-year-old Primakov was renowned for his warm relations with some of the more dubious regimes of the Middle East. Primakov's international profile reached its height during the 1991 Gulf War, when he conducted a round of meetings with President Saddam Hussein of Iraq, aimed at defusing the crisis.

The SVR (Russia's equivalent of Britain's MI6) had complained about the activities of Western spies in Russia, and had given a high priority to re-establishing Russia's sphere of influence in the Commonwealth of Independent States (CIS). Peter Rodman, a former senior US official, took Primakov's appointment as 'a dramatic sign of an anti-Western turn in Russian policy'. Primakov was the archetypal Kremlin survivor, transforming his views as required to meet the needs of the day. A loyal careerist at first, a moderate centrist under Brezhnev, a liberal under Gorbachev, a fierce politician of the conservative wing under Yeltsin, Primakov had shown far more political adaptability than his predecessor, Andrei Kozyrev. Kozyrev's pro-Western school had argued that confrontation with the United States was costly and ultimately futile, and only full-scale partnership with America could guarantee Russia an influential place on the international stage. Kozyrev accepted that this partnership with the United States could lead to the severing of close links with old friends (as had occurred with Cuba).

While Yevgeny Primakov favoured co-operation with the West over issues such as crime and non-proliferation, he had a different philosophy, more in keeping with the ascendency of Russia First. Primakov argued that Russia's security services should aim to 'prevent the creation of a unipolar world', a veiled reference to preventing the United States from consolidating its position as the world's only superpower. He was a relentless critic of NATO's plan to expand towards the east, and insisted that his priority as foreign minister would be to strengthen Russia's status as a 'great power'. On 12 January the newly appointed foreign minister echoed sentiments expressed by Yeltsin the previous October: 'The point is that in spite of the present difficulties, Russia was and remains a great power. Her foreign policy should correspond to that status.'[69]

Primakov said that one of his priorities would be to 'diversify' Russian foreign policy, again, coded language for saying that he would not make Kozyrev's mistake of relying on friendly ties with the West. Foreign Minister Primakov also made it clear that this would mean a shift towards increasing the importance of relations with the 'near abroad', particularly through the CIS. Although Primakov did not go as far as promising to recreate the Soviet Union, he said 'strengthening of integrationist tendencies within the former Soviet Union' would be one of his principal goals. Primakov was signalling a shift in emphasis from an overtly pro-Western foreign policy to one which attached increased importance to developing Russia's influence within the CIS and its 'near abroad'. This did not, of course, mean abandoning good relations with the West. Primakov stated that he hoped his appointment would not make him a *persona non grata* for the US public. However, giving a glimpse of his tough background, Primakov advised Japan, which had asked for the return of the Kurile Islands seized at the end of the Second World War, 'to wait another generation' before raising the issue again.

Speaking on foreign policy in the interval between the two presidential rounds of voting in the summer, Primakov comprehensively laid out his philosophy on relations between Russia and the West. Russia should not isolate itself, he felt, but should regard the CIS as a 'top priority', with diplomacy supporting 'centripetal trends' existing in the post-Soviet space. Primakov favoured integration, but also accepted the sovereignty of CIS members. But he believed that although they shared some common interests, 'Russia and the West are divided by profound differences. These differences are developing negative trends which oppose Russian foreign policy in every area.' This involved dividing the participants of the Cold War into winners and losers, attempting to create a unipolar world (one of his favourite themes) where decisions were taken in just one capital. Russia would simply become a supplier of raw materials to the world economy. To counter these tendencies, Russia would develop links with other nations, such as China. Primakov added, 'we cannot concentrate on one direction no matter how important it is'. It was necessary to develop areas of mutual concern with the West, whilst protecting Russia's interests and minimising the opportunities for confrontation. Primakov had given journalists a blow-by-blow account of Russia First in the foreign-policy sphere.[70] As could be expected, Primakov's appointment was warmly welcomed by Russia's nationalists.[71]

Anatoly Chubais's sacking was just as symbolic as Kozyrev's enforced departure, and even more so to Western economists and markets. Chubais was the last leading market reformer who had been in Yegor Gaidar's radical pro-market government of 1991. He had been relatively successful in seeing through Russia's controversial and rapid mass privatisation programme, and had implemented the stabilisation plan before being removed from office. A trained economist, Chubais attended the Leningrad Institute of Engineering and Economics, where he became an assistant professor. A supporter of Gorbachev's *perestroika*, in 1990 he headed the Committee on Economic Reform at Leningrad City Council. In November 1991, the 36-year-old Chubais was appointed chair of the Russian Federation's Committee on State Property Management. Chubais was the only leading member of that team still in government in December 1995. He introduced Russia's privatisation programme, launched by Gaidar's government in July 1992. Chubais's method of 'voucher' privatisation was highly controversial, with allegations that the programme enriched a privileged few while the vouchers quickly became relatively worthless. Promoted to first deputy-prime minister on 6 November 1994, Chubais was given responsibility for Russia's overall economic policy. By the end of 1994, 75 per cent of Russia's medium-sized and large industrial enterprises had been privatised. About the same percentage of small companies had also become private, with nearly 52 per cent of the gross domestic product produced in the private sector.

In the West, Chubais gained the reputation for being 'Russia's most effective administrator', and his presence in the cabinet appeared a litmus test for Russia's continuing economic reforms and continuing Western financial support. The Russian daily newspaper *Izvestiya* claimed his resignation would be a catastrophe, since 'Russia's international credibility depends on him'. Chubais was credited with making privatisation in Russia irreversible, and being the one market reformer having the ability to 'get things done' in Moscow. Politically, Chubais remained a member of Gaidar's Russia's Choice Party, symbolising his commitment to reform. Seemingly indifferent to personal material gain, a rare contrast with the ubiquitous graft in Russian government, Chubais drove an old Zhiguli and lived in a modest two-room flat.[72]

Prime Minister Chernomyrdin had made a last minute attempt to co-opt the Communist Party's social and economic agenda two days before the 1995 Duma elections. Chernomyrdin (who favours Armani suits) appeared on television to speak about his difficult blue-collar childhood, when his family lived 'from kopek to kopek'. The prime minister was, he said, determined to 'fight poverty'. The shift from fighting inflation to fighting poverty was highlighted after the elections by Alexander Shokhin, a leading NDR politician and former Yeltsin cabinet minister. Shokhin said the Duma election results showed a 'certain shift to the left in Russian society', which required the government to make 'changes in economic policy to take account of the fact that a certain social fatigue has set in, fatigue of the population'.[73] Western economists feared that higher social spending in the run-up to the presidential election could jeopardise the aims of lower inflation and a stable rouble.

In his first post-election appearance, hoping to calm Western financial circles, Chernomyrdin pledged that 'the government intends to continue its economic course' and vowed to bring down inflation and deliver economic growth the following year. But behind the scenes, Russian government officials were stating that the goal of financial stabilisation was to be superseded by social welfare spending and attempts to stimulate economic growth. The pace of privatisation would also be slowed. Previously, financial stabilisation (as demanded by Western financial institutions) was the primary aim of Russian economic policy. However, following the shock of the Duma election results, government economic policy switched emphasis from Western-influenced financial stabilisation and privatisation programmes to social welfare and economic growth. Currying favour with the West by pursuing financial stabilisation at the cost of declining social spending became less important to the Kremlin than the political survival of Yeltsin's administration. Russia First thus came to dominate Moscow's economic policies, as it had already come to influence the direction of Russia's foreign policy. Despite his sacking, Chubais, the government's former standard-bearer for market reforms, insisted that economic reforms would continue. But even Chubais had his doubts, and appealed to Yeltsin not to abandon the path of economic reform: 'I am deeply convinced,' he said, 'that a reversal of economic policy, particularly at this moment, five months before the presidential election, would be a monstrous mistake.'[74]

Yeltsin had two alternatives when it came to economic policy. He could press on regardless of the Duma election results and the obvious unpopularity of the economic reforms, hoping that by June the benefits of a thriving market economy would outweigh the painful memories of the recent past. Alternatively, he could steal the Communist Party's agenda of boosting social spending and propping up inefficient sectors of the economy. Characteristically, Yeltsin placed priority on adopting the latter course while still trying to reassure the West that economic reforms remained on track. For President Yeltsin, the calculation was quite straightforward. Communist leader Gennady Zyuganov was the only serious challenger for the presidency in June 1996. Other presidential contenders, such as Yavlinsky, Zhirinovsky and Lebed, had ruled themselves out of the running by their relatively poor performances in the Duma elections. The threat of a Chernomyrdin challenge had also evaporated with the poor showing of Our Home is Russia. Yeltsin therefore had to act swiftly to neutralise the perceived popularity of the policies of his main challenger: Gennady Zyuganov. On the foreign policy front, this was partly achieved by replacing Kozyrev with Primakov. When it came to economic policy, Yeltsin indicated the shift by sacking the pro-market Chubais. Yeltsin had by these two bold moves indicated his preference for Russia First policies in both the foreign and domestic spheres. The sacking of Chubais at this time was a highly symbolic act by Yeltsin, since the wily Kremlin insider epitomised the government's unpopular Western-orientated economic policies.

Yeltsin's timing in sacking his deputy prime minister, just before the International Monetary Fund was due to confirm a $10.2 billion extended fund facility (which Chubais had been instrumental in securing), was taken as a sign of Yeltsin thumbing his nose at the West for domestic consumption. Chubais was replaced by Vladimir Kadannikov, head of the car-giant Avtovaz . As a representative of the heavily-subsidised state sector, Kadannikov was the perfect antidote to the dynamic reforming Chubais. Although he had preached the message of reform, Kadannikov had run Avtovaz in the traditional Soviet manner, relying on large-scale state subsidies. As Robert Cotrell has remarked, 'the news of Kadannikov's appointment was thus received warmly by reformers and "red-bosses" alike: the former feared someone worse, the latter recognised one of their own'.[75]

Sergei Filatov, another member of the liberal reformist camp who was closely associated with Chubais, was Yeltsin's third major personnel change. Filatov, Yeltsin's chief of staff, was replaced by Nikolai Yegorov, the hawkish nationalities minister sacked by the president to ward off a vote of no confidence in June 1995 over the Budennovsk crisis. Sergei Filatov was in effect demoted to a post in Yeltsin's re-election campaign team. Yeltsin's statement that Filatov's role would cover 'ideological work', was taken to mean that he would be used as a bridge to the liberal reformers such as Gaidar and Yavlinsky, to try to win their support prior to the presidential election. Yegorov was the president's representative to Chechnya from November 1994 to February 1995, during a period of bitter fighting. *Izvestiya* reported that Yegorov's appointment as chief of staff had immediate consequences, as Moscow decided to bombard the Dagestani village of Pervomaiskoe, which contained a band of rebel Chechen hostage-takers led by Salman Raduev.[76] The result was another disaster for the Russian Federation's armed forces as, greatly outnumbered, the Chechens escaped from the village with the Russian hostages who had survived the fusillade. The incident showed that brutality and ignorance were back in vogue in the Kremlin. From Yeltsin's point of view, Yegorov's appointment showed that he had decided to 'get tough' on Chechnya, and that he was distancing himself from his former liberal reformist advisers.

Just in case the message was not clear enough, Yeltsin dropped a group of second-tier ministers. Deputy Prime Minister and reformer Sergei Shakhrai, Minister Without Portfolio Nikolai Travkin and Deputy Prime Minister and State Property Chairman Sergei Belayev all left the government on being elected to the Duma. Yeltsin also sacked Agriculture Minister Alexander Nazarchuk, after his Agrarian Party failed to cross the 5 per cent barrier. Yegor Gaidar and Sergei Kovalev both voluntarily withdrew from the presidential council. As well as sweeping away the reformers at government level, Yeltsin chose to surround himself with several 'hardliners', who were close to him personally and mostly supporters of the war in Chechnya. General Alexander Korzhakov, head of the presidential bodyguard, was given the additional but ill-defined role of 'mobilising people throughout the country'. Korzhakov, who already yielded disproportionate power over policy and in controlling access to the president, was joined by Mikhail Barsukov, a friend and ally. The two men were personally close and related through their children, Barsukov's son being married to Korzhakov's daughter. Barsukov was appointed head of the Federal Security Service (FSB), successor to the KGB.

Oleg Soskovets, known to have close connections with the military-industrial complex (particularly the metals industry), was promoted to deputy prime minister in charge of links with industry, especially the defence sector. A former manager of a metallurgical plant in Kazakhstan, Soskovets was one of the main organisers of NDR's Duma campaign, and was the only first deputy prime minister in the government after Chubais's departure. In effect, Soskovets was appointed head of the presidential campaign headquarters, with day-to-day responsibility for running Yeltsin's campaign. By mid February, there were rumours of Chernomyrdin's impending resignation and replacement by Soskovets.[77]

Others in Yeltsin's presidential campaign team were Victor Ilyushin and Yury Luzhkov. Victor Ilyushin, an old crony from Yeltsin's days as regional Communist Party boss in Yekaterinburg, was appointed chief of the presidential aides. Yury Luzhkov, mayor of Moscow, was roped in to deal with the construction industry and the city of Moscow. The inclusion of Korzhakov and Barsukov in Yeltsin's campaign team was

seen as a worrying sign of how far the president was willing to go to get
re-elected. There was no obvious role for Korzhakov's bodyguards in
the campaign, apart from to intimidate the opposition, and Barsukov's
presence indicated a willingness to gather intelligence and engage in
dirty tricks against the president's opponents. Yeltsin's inner circle
dropped all pretence of trying to balance the pro-reformers and
'hardliners' at the heart of the Kremlin. Yeltsin's closest associates were
either 'hardliners' or career cronies.[78]

Yeltsin's tough approach to the presidential elections was demonstrated in mid February, when, on the very day he formally announced
his intention to stand for the presidency, he sacked the respected head
of independent Russian television, RTR. Oleg Poptsov's sacking was
seen as a move by Yeltsin and his administration to manipulate the
state-owned RTR in the run-up to the presidential elections, ensuring
that the television station ran pro-government stories. RTR had been
particularly critical of Yeltsin's policy in Chechnya. The move against
RTR was preceded by the president barring the NTV television
network from the Kremlin. NTV had aired interviews critical of Boris
Yeltsin and his closest advisers, describing Alexander Korzhakov,
personal friend and closest presidential adviser, as 'a family retainer
who fetches slippers' and Victor Ilyushin as a 'jealous courtier in
constant pursuit of Yeltsin's attention'. Both acts contradicted Yeltsin's
statement on the freedom of the press, and many Russian and Western
journalists felt it was a backward step on the country's road to democracy. It was no coincidence that both actions took place around the time
when Yeltsin announced his candidacy for the presidency, on 16
February in Yekaterinburg. Yeltsin's message to the television media
was transparent. Either he would get their 100 per cent support or he
would put them under immense pressure until they delivered it.
Speaking just before he announced his candidacy in Yekaterinburg, and
showing his new tough image, Yeltsin opposed a quick withdrawal from
Chechnya, and called for Chechen leader Dzhokhar Dudayev to be
shot.[79]

Yeltsin's annual 'State of the Nation' address made on 23 February
1996 set out his stall for the presidential elections, and clearly borrowed
the populist clothes of his opponents in the Duma. Yeltsin's passages
about the 'unjust redistribution of the burdens of reform from the
strong to the weak', led the *Moscow Times* to comment that they might
have come from Gennady Zyuganov. Yeltsin echoed the Communist
leader further by pinning much of the blame for most of the popula-

tion's plight on the Chernomrydin government. He berated
Chernomrydin for 'focusing on financial stabilisation and forgetting
about people living on wages and pensions'. Yeltsin's frequent attacks
on Chernomrydin's government became a campaign tactic that seemed
to bring some success, distancing the president from the blame attached
to the country's parlous economic and social state. Chernomyrdin
became a useful scapegoat and thus, paradoxically, of more use to the
president in office than sacked. In any event, Yeltsin's room for
manoeuvre on the economic front was circumscribed by the need to
maintain the confidence of Western investors and institutions. The day
before his speech, Yeltsin had signed an agreement with the IMF for
the $10.2 billion funding facility, which was contingent upon sound
economic performance assessed monthly by the institution. Any
slippage would have an impact upon investment, capital flight and
nervous capital markets. In any event, even if the government let rip
with the money supply, this would have a limited effect on consumption and living standards in the four months before the election. Yeltsin
knew it was better to promise a better future, and spend money where it
could have an immediate impact.

Yeltsin's 'State of the Nation' speech thus committed the president to
a loosely elaborated 'action plan' that covered the five areas of
economic policy that corresponded with the electorate's principal
concerns.[80] President Yeltsin promised that public sector wages would
be paid on time, savings wiped-out by inflation during 1991–92 would
be compensated, and an insurance system would be set up to protect
savings from outside speculators. Measures would be taken to stimulate
the private sector to prevent unemployment from climbing, and
housing would be made available to those who were homeless. Fulfilling
this wish-list would meet the concerns of the electorate identified during
the Duma elections, and was carefully crafted by Yeltsin's advisers to
defuse the growing discontent with the president's handling of the
economy. The only question which remained was whether the president
could deliver on his promises. To anyone with a basic knowledge of the
Russian economy, the answer was no, but the electorate was realistic
enough to know that if Yeltsin achieved a quarter of his stated aims,
they would be a lot better off.

One of the most pressing issues was the question of unpaid wage
arrears, which led to repeated strikes and stoppages. In a blatant signal
of political support, the director of the International Monetary Fund
(IMF) Michel Camdessus gave his blessing to Yeltsin's promise to pay

off public sector wage arrears by 31 March 1996. Camdessus incredibly claimed there was room in the federal budget to pay off the wage arrears, as long as this was confined to public sector employees. Predictably, the Russian budget later ran over target and the IMF suspended its loan facility in July 1996, after Yeltsin had been safely re-elected president. Of course Yeltsin's promise on paying wage arrears was not completely met, but thereafter spending pledges became an almost daily feature of Yeltsin's election campaign. In putting his re-election above the need for the economic stabilisation demanded by the IMF and the West, Yeltsin was putting his interests and the require-ments of the Russian electorate first. The new concern for the welfare of Russia's citizens and the heightened emphasis on the country's domestic interests were examples of Yeltsin's acceptance of Russia First policies on the economy. With his 'State of the Nation' address, the presidential election campaign had truly begun.

CONCLUSION

President Boris Yeltsin's strategy to establish a malleable Duma, more favourably inclined to his government than the parliament elected in 1993, failed miserably. His abortive attempt to reduce the number of proportionally elected seats made no difference to the outcome of the elections. In fact, Chernomyrdin's pro-government NDR was saved from oblivion by the proportional-list system. Nor did Yeltsin's aim of creating a tame two-party model succeed, as Ivan Rybkin's efforts at establishing a centre-left bloc ended in ignominy. However, the intro-duction of the 5 per cent hurdle, opposed by the Duma, did restrict the influence of small extremist parties in the Lower House, particularly the nationalists. Yeltsin had also been successful in ensuring that the Upper House of parliament, the Federation Council, remained largely unelected and therefore supportive of the president.

The campaign itself highlighted a number of issues, but was dominated by the poor economic situation, and the general feeling of disenchantment amongst the majority of the electorate. Other issues included crime, corruption, the bombing of Bosnian Serbs (early in the campaign) and NATO enlargement. The communists and nationalists combined attacks on economic mismanagement with an appeal to put 'Russia First' in domestic and foreign policy. Politicians from across the political spectrum railed against Russia's diminished status in the world, and its perceived humiliation by the West. Anti-Western rhetoric was endemic, and came from some surprisingly 'moderate' quarters. The honeymoon with the West, brief as it was after Russia's independence in 1991, was finally over. Foreign Minister Andrei Kozyrev was an early and obvious victim of the change in the political atmosphere. In spite of some flaws in the Duma election campaign itself, international observers were satisfied it was broadly a free and fair expression of the Russian peoples' democratic will. The election was marred by the deaths or assassination of five candidates for the Duma, evidence of the violence prevalent in Russian society and probably connected to mafia interests.[81]

For Yeltsin, the results of the Duma election were a wake-up call. The Siberian bear, awakened from its winter hibernation, found itself in a hostile world. Although he had taken no direct part in the Duma elections, Yeltsin knew that the results were a massive vote of no-confidence in his government. His greatest rival for the presidency, Gennady Zyuganov, was ensconced in the 'Red Duma' and provided with an enviable launch-pad for his forthcoming bid to become president. Policies would have to change, heads would have to roll, but if Boris Nicolaevich Yeltsin was certain of one thing, it was that he was determined to win the presidential elections that summer, and secure a second term.

Once awakened, Yeltsin acted swiftly, sacking the members of his government most closely associated with Western-orientated policies: Andrei Kozyrev and Anatoly Chubais. Having cleared-out most of the liberal reformers from the government, Yeltsin started to emphasise the 'welfare populism' and social concern laid out in his address to the nation in February 1996. Stealing the policy clothes of his opponents, Yeltsin also indicated a shift in gear away from the overtly pro-Western policies of the past. Instead, the emphasis was on building the CIS as a counterweight to NATO. Yeltsin's new Russia First approach to foreign policy was epitomised by the appointment of Yevgeny Primakov as foreign minister. As the 'hardliners' eclipsed the 'reformers' in the Kremlin, Yeltsin shed his democratic mantle, reinventing himself as the people's benevolent tsar. By adopting Russia First, ditching the democrats and outflanking the communists and nationalists, Yeltsin was on course to build a winning campaign strategy.

NOTES

1 Rose, Richard and White, Stephen, *Boris Yeltsin's Changing Popular Support*, Studies in Public Policy, Number 261, Centre for the Study of Public Policy, University of Strathclyde (Glasgow, 1996), p. 20.

2 European Parliament, *Background Note on the Political and Economic Situation in Russia*, official document, PE 210.446, 4 November 1994, p.2; Rose and White, *Boris Yeltsin's Changing Popular Support*, p.20; The Economist Intelligence Unit, *EIU Country Profile: Russia*, Economist Group (London, 1996), p. 5.

3 OSCE/Office for Democratic Institutions and Human Rights (ODIHR), *Russian Presidential Election 1996: International Observer, Mission Briefing Book* (Moscow, 1996), pp. 55–63.

4 OSCE/ODIHR, *Russian Presidential Election 1996*, pp. 61–3.

5 European Parliament, *Background Note on the Political and Economic Situation in Russia*, pp. 2–5; Reuters, 'Communist surge in Russia', *New York Times*, 30 December 1995.

6 European Parliament Russian Delegation meeting with Zyuganov and Yavlinsky, at which the author was present, 21 March 1995.

7 European Parliament, *Report on the Observation of the Legislative Elections in Russia of 17 December 1995*, official document for the *ad hoc* delegation for the observation of the elections in Russia, PE 216.096, 18 January 1996, p. 2.

8 European Parliament, *Update on Background Note*, official document for the *ad hoc* delegation for the observation of the elections in Russia, PE 214.879, 30 November 1995, pp. 2–3; Paretskaya, Anna, 'Regional governors could offset "Red Duma" ', *Transition* (Prague), 23 February 1996, pp. 34–5; European Parliament, *Background Note on Preparations for the General Election to be Held in Russia on 17 December 1995*, official document, PE 214.860, Brussels, 9 November 1995; Orttung, Robert, 'Rybkin fails to create a viable left-center bloc', *Transition* (Prague), 25 August 1995, pp. 35–6.

9 Author's discussions with the political blocs, Moscow and St Petersburg, December 1995.

10 European Parliament, *Note on Recent Political Developments in Russia*, official document, PE 215.315, 21 November 1995, pp. 3–4.

11 The European Parliament also made an official approach urging that the elections should go ahead on 17 December 1995.

12 European Parliament, *Update on Background Note*, pp. 2–3.

13 'NATO declares war on the Bosnian Serbs: UN threats finally backed by force', *The Economist*, 2 September 1995.

14 Thornhill, John, 'Kozyrev may be Balkans fall-guy', *Financial Times*, 13 September 1995.

15 The European Union had the same complaint against the United States, but with less justification, after over three years of failed diplomatic and peace-keeping initiatives.

16 Thornhill, John, 'President Yeltsin warns NATO of "flames of war" ', *Financial Times*, 9 September 1995; Thornhill, John, 'Debate on NATO sparks fighting in Russian parliament', *Financial Times*, 11 September, 1995.

17 Freeland, Chrystia and Clark, Bruce, 'Anger in Russian parliament over Bosnia strikes', *Financial Times*, 10 September 1995.

18 Thornhill, 'President Yeltsin warns NATO of "flames of war" '.

19 'Russia: Bosnia anger', *Oxford Analytica*, Daily Brief, 15 September 1995; Solodovnik, Sergei, 'Russia's foreign policy fails in Balkans crisis', *Moscow News*, 22–8 September 1995.

20 Thornhill, 'President Yeltsin warns NATO of "flames of war" '; Thornhill, 'Kozyrev may be Balkans fall-guy'.

21 Thornhill, 'Yeltsin seeks replacement for Kozyrev', *Financial Times*, 20 October 1995.

22 On Kozyrev's background and career, from 1991 to early 1995, see Chapter 2, pp. 36–9; on Kozyrev and NATO, see also Chapter 2, pp. 47–50.

23 On CFE see Chapter 2, pp. 36, 51–2; on START II see also Chapter 2, pp. 51–4; on the attitude of the Duma, author's private meetings with deputies, 1994–96.

24 The author did not vote for ratification of the EU–Russian PCA in the European Parliament.

25 European Parliament, *Background Note on Preparations for the General Election to be Held in Russia on 17 December 1995*, pp. 4–5; European Parliament, *Report on the Observation of the Legislative Elections in Russia*; author's personal observations; *EIU Country Profile: Russia*, p. 42; see also Chapter 3, pp. 128–34, for a fuller treatment of the question of the impact of economic reforms on the Russian population.

26 OSCE, *Report on the Elections to the State Duma in the Russian Federation*, OSCE Parliamentary Assembly (Copenhagen, 1996); European Parliament, *Report on the Observation of the Legislative Elections in Russia*, p. 3; Belin, Laura, 'An array of mini-parties wage futile parliamentary campaigns', *Transition* (Prague), 23 February 1996, p.15.

27 See Rybkin's book, *We Have to Live in Accord* (Moscow, 1994), for Rybkin's political background.

28 Chinayeva, Elena, 'Profile: Grigorii Yavlinskii, "A Brilliant Loser" ', *Transition* (Prague), 1 December 1995, p. 36.

29 Belin, Laura and Orttung, Robert, 'Parties proliferate on eve of elections', *Transition* (Prague), 22 September 1995, pp. 43–4; European Parliament, *Background Note on Preparations for the General Election to be Held in Russia on 17 December 1995*.

30 Open Media Research Institute (OMRI), 'Special report, no.12, 8 December 1995', *OMRI Daily Digest* (Prague), p. 1.

31 Author's meeting with Yavlinsky, Moscow, 21 March 1995.

32 Belin, Laura, 'An array of mini-parties wage futile parliamentary campaigns', *Transition* (Prague), 23 February 1996, p. 18.

33 BBC, *Summary of World Broadcasts*, BBC Monitoring Service, 12 December 1995.

34 BBC, *Summary of World Broadcasts*, BBC Monitoring Service, 29 November 1995.

35 Solodovnik, Sergei, 'Our Home is Russia, but where is the window on Europe?', *Moscow News*, 24–30 November 1995.

36 BBC, *Summary of World Service Broadcasts*, BBC Monitoring Service, 27 November 1995.

37 For a more in depth analysis of Lebed's career and thinking, see Chapter 5, pp .224–9

38 Orttung, Robert, 'Profile: Alexander Lebed: President Yeltsin's most dangerous rival', *Transition* (Prague), 1 December 1995, p. 18.

39 *Permskie novosti*, 26 July 1995, cited in Orttung, 'Profile: Alexander Lebed', p. 18.

40 BBC, *Summary of World Service Broadcasts*, 12 December 1995. Lebed was speaking in an election broadcast on Russian TV channel, 8 December 1995.

41 *Kontinent*, 12–18 October 1995, cited in Orttung, 'Profile: Alexander Lebed', p. 19.

42 The author has met Vasily Lipitsky on several occasions to discuss developments in the Social Democratic movement in 1994–5, including Barcelona in February 1995, Moscow in March 1995, and Brussels in September 1995.

43 BBC, *Summary of World Service Broadcasts*, BBC Monitoring Service, 13 December 1995; Rutskoi on St Petersburg Channel 5 TV on 8 December 1995.

44 BBC, *Summary of World Service Broadcasts*, BBC Monitoring Service, 22 November 1995; LDPR election advert, St Peterburg Channel 5 TV, 15 November; NTV Moscow, 20 November 1995; Belin, Laura, 'Television plays a limited role in Duma elections', *Transition* (Prague), 23 February 1996 pp. 21–2.

45 OMRI, 'Special Report, no.14, 15 December 1995', *OMRI Daily Digest* (Prague, 1995), p. 2; BBC, *Summary of World Service Broadcasts*, SWB, 12 December 1995; Zhirinovsky on Ostankino Radio Mayak, Moscow, 8 December 1995.

46 NTV reporting Zyuganov's speech of 22 October 1995, cited in OMRI, 'Special Report, No. 1, 27 October 1995', *OMRI Daily Digest* (Prague, 1995), pp. 3–4.

47 OMRI, 'Special Report, No. 5, 10 November 1995', *OMRI Daily Digest* (Prague, 1995), pp. 2–3.

48 OMRI, 'Special Report, No. 8, 21 November 1995', *OMRI Daily Digest* (Prague 1995), p.4.

49 *Segodnya*, 29 November 1995, cited in OMRI, 'Special Report, No. 10, 2 December 1995', *OMRI Daily Digest* (Prague, 1995), p. 1.

50 BBC, *Summary of World Service Broadcasts*, BBC Monitoring Service, 23 November 1995; election broadcast on St Petersburg Channel 5 TV, 20 November 1995.

51 BBC, *Summary of World Service Broadcasts*, BBC Monitoring Service, 6 December 1995; APR election broadcast, St Petersburg Channel 5 TV, carried on 27 November 1995.

52 OMRI, 'Special Report, No. 11, 5 December 1995', *OMRI Daily Digest* (Prague, 1995), p. 4.

53 See author's article, 'The end of Yeltsin and the return of communism?', *Labour Focus in Eastern Europe*, Vol. 53, March 1996, pp. 4–8.

54 On the same basis the figure for the KPRF would be seven deputies (OSCE, *Report on the Elections to the State Duma in the Russian Federation*, Annexes 3 and 4); European Parliament, *Note on the Political Situation since the Last Duma Elections*, official document, PE 217.414, 3 April 1996, pp. 2–3; Orttung, Robert, 'Duma elections bolster leftist opposition', *Transition* (Prague), 23 February 1996, pp. 6–11.

55 European Parliament, *Note on the Political Situation since the Last Duma elections*, pp. 2–4.

56 Orttung, Robert and Parrish, Scott, 'Duma votes reflect north–south divide', *Transition* (Prague), 23 February 1996, pp. 12–14; Oates, Sarah, 'Vying for votes on a crowded campaign trail', *Transition* (Prague), 23 February 1996, p. 27.

57 Oates, 'Vying for votes on a crowded campaign trail', pp. 26–9; Belin, 'An array of mini-parties wage futile parliamentary campaigns', p. 18; Yabloko means 'apple' in Russian, and was used as the party's campaign symbol.

58 Orttung and Parrish, 'Duma votes reflect north–south divide', pp. 12–14; author's meeting with OSCE observer team, Moscow 18 June 1996; author's meeting with Nikolai Ryabov, chairman of the Central Electoral Commission, 2 July 1996.

59 See above, pp. 170–1 for Zhirinovsky's use of television.

60 OSCE, *Report on the Elections to the State Duma in the Russian Federation*, pp. 8–9; European Parliament, *Report on the Duma Elections*, p. 4; observing the election in St Petersburg, the author discovered NDR's contract with St Petersburg city for election posters equalled one-tenth of the maximum allowable amount for the entire campaign; Belin, 'Television plays a limited role in Duma elections', pp. 20–3; Belin, 'An array of mini-parties wage futile parliamentary campaigns', pp. 15–17.

61 On Women of Russia, see Belin and Orttung, 'Parties proliferate on eve of elections', pp. 46–7; author's various discussions with deputies of the movement, European Parliament, EU-Russian delegation, 1994–96.

62 OSCE, *Report on the Elections to the State Duma in the Russian Federation*, annexes 3 and 4; Orttung, 'Duma elections bolster leftist opposition', pp. 7–10; on Social Democrats, see author's article on Duma elections, 'The end of Yeltsin and the return of Communism?', in *Labour Focus in Eastern Europe*; OMRI, 'Special Report, No. 5, 10 November 1995'; OMRI, 'Special Report, No. 14, 15 December 1995', *OMRI Daily Digest* (Prague, 1995); Popov, Gavril, Lipitzky, Vasily and Bogomolov, *Declaration by the Social Democrats of the Russian Federation to the Electorate*, contained in Official Document of the Party of European Socialists; author's meetings with Social Democrat leaders Vasily Lipitsky and Oleg Bogomolov, 1995–6, Moscow, Barcelona and Brussels; author's meetings with leaders of St Petersburg Social Democrats, December 1995.

63 Freeland, Chrystia, 'Russia set to spurn Yeltsin and reform, says poll', *Financial Times*, 29 September 1995.

64 Rose and White, *Boris Yeltsin's Changing Popular Support*, pp. 24–5.

65 'Chubais and Kozyrev, sacked for success: assessing Chubais and Kozyrev', *The Economist*, Vol. 338, No. 7949, 20 January 1996.

66 On Kozyrev's background and career, including his progressive turning away from a 'liberal' position see Chapter 2, pp. 36–9. See also chapter 2, pp. 47–50 for Kozyrev's position on NATO.

67 Thornhill, John, 'Moscow's foreign minister resigns', *Financial Times*, 6 January 1996.

68 MacKenzie, Jean, 'Yeltsin calls for NATO alliance', *Moscow Times*, 20 January 1996.

69 See Chapter 2, p. 37 for Yeltsin's comments and pp. 45–54 for a fuller discussion on the question of NATO enlargement.

70 Primakov is quoted by Gankin, Leonid, 'Primakov's campaign speech', *Moscow News*, 27 June–3 July 1996.

71 On Primakov's appointment and Kozyrev's departure, see Clark, Bruce and Thornhill, John, 'Kozyrev introduced Russia to a world it still mistrusts', *Financial Times*, 6 January 1996; Thornhill, 'Moscow's foreign minister'; Clarke, Bruce and Thornhill, John, 'Old foe of the West is new Russian foreign minister', *Financial Times*, 10 January 1996, and Freeland, Chrystia, '"Russia aims to regain great power role," says Primakov', *Financial Times*, 13 January 1996.

72 Chinayeva, Elena, 'Profile: Anatoli Chubais, a Kremlin survivor', in *Transition* (Prague), 1 December 1995, pp. 38–9.

73 Freeland, Chrystia, 'After the dress rehearsal', *Financial Times*, 20 December 1995.

74 Freeland, Chrystia, 'Russian reform on ice: Yeltsin's shift in personnel and policy', *Financial Times*, 20 January 1996.

75 Cotrell, Robert, 'Russia's parliamentary and presidential elections', *Government and Opposition*, Vol. 31, No.2, Spring 1996, p. 171.

76 *Izvestiya*, 20 January 1996.

77 On personnel changes, see: Olshansky, Dmitry, 'New campaign game' and editorial, *Moscow Times*, 16 February 1996; European Parliament, *Note on the Political Situation since the Last Duma Elections*, pp. 2–7; Orttung, 'Duma elections bolster leftist opposition'; Freeland, Chrystia and Thornhill, John, 'President Yeltsin fires three top Kremlin hardliners', and 'Showdown in the Kremlin dark', *Financial Times*, 21 June 1996.

78 Olshansky, 'New campaign game'.

79 Shchedrov, Oleg, 'Yeltsin: Dudayev "should be shot" ', *Moscow Times*, 16 February 1996; Coudenhove, Sophia, 'Yeltsin aide denies "disciplining" NTV', *Moscow Times*, 14 February 1996; Olshansky, 'New campaign game'.

80 Crosnier, Marie-Agnès, 'Bilan économique de la présidence Eltsine, 1991–1996', *Le Courier des pays de l'Est: La Russie de Boris Eltsine*, No. 408, April 1996, p. 9.

81 European Parliament, *Report on the Duma Elections*, p. 5.

CHAPTER 5

'RUSSIA FIRST' IN THE 1996 PRESIDENTIAL ELECTION CAMPAIGN

THE PRESIDENTIAL ELECTION CAMPAIGN PROPER: THE FIRST ROUND

TEN CANDIDATES stood in the first round of the Russian presidential election held on 16 June 1996.[1] From the beginning of the campaign, it was evident that the main struggle would be between Boris Yeltsin and Communist leader Gennady Zyuganov. Of secondary importance would be the performance of Yabloko's Grigory Yavlinsky, the LDPR's Vladimir Zhirinovsky and retired General Alexander Lebed. The other five presidential candidates were no-hopers: Mikhail Gorbachev, desperately unpopular former president of the Soviet Union; Svyatoslav Fyodorov, famous eye-surgeon; Yury Vlasov, former champion weight-lifter; Martin Shakkum, businessman and head of 'Reform Foundation'; and Vladimir Bryntsalov, billionaire pharmaceutical industrialist and self-promoter. This was the second presidential election in the history of the Russian Federation, and the first for a president of a sovereign Russian state, following the collapse of the Soviet Union in 1991. The first presidential election took place on 12 June 1991, before the demise of the Soviet Union, and was won by Boris Yeltsin with 57 per cent of the vote (the president's tenure of office is five years).

To register for the 1996 election, each candidate had to have the backing of an electoral association or initiative group, and collect at least a million signatures in support of their nomination. By all accounts only the Communists relied on the voluntary collection of signatures, the other candidates paying professionals to collect the number required for nomination.[2] Allegations were also made that factory directors sympathetic to Boris Yeltsin threatened workers that they would not be paid unless they signed the president's nomination form.[3] No more than 7 per cent of the signatures were permitted to come from any one republic or region of the Federation. All candidates had to be registered by 16 April, and the Central Electoral Commission (CEC) had to confirm all registrations by 16 May, the official date for the start of the election campaign. The official campaign for the first round ended at midnight on 13 June. At least 50 per cent of the registered voters had to take part in the ballot for the election to be valid. In order to win, a candidate needed to win over 50 per cent of the votes cast. If no candidate achieved this result, a run-off would be held between the two top candidates (similar to the French presidential system). Turnout in the second round also had to comprise at least 50 per cent of registered voters.[4]

THE WEST'S SUPPORT FOR PRESIDENT YELTSIN

Western support for President Boris Yeltsin's re-election bid was hardly subtle. This had already become apparent with the European Union's decision to un-freeze a Partnership and Co-operation Agreement with the Russian Federation (held up by the war in Chechnya), the release of IMF credits and Russia's admission to the 38-nation Council of Europe on 26 January 1996. The latter decision in particular was warmly welcomed by the president's administration, and was used as a propaganda tool to portray how Russia was now accepted as an equal member of the European family of nations. Yeltsin had insisted that a refusal to admit Russia 'would be interpreted as a refusal to support those who are fighting for democratic principles and democratic institutions in Russia'. The Russian president warned European politicians that failure to admit Russia to the assembly would offer tacit support 'to those who seek to resolve the Chechen problem with savage, terrorist methods'.[5] Endorsement by the Council of Europe was depicted as an acknowledgement of the success of Russia's democratic and economic reforms, and the progress it had made under President Yeltsin's benevolent guidance.

In Moscow, President Yeltsin's adviser for international affairs, Dmitri Riourikov, declared that the vote in the Assembly of the Council of Europe was a victory for good sense for Europeans and recognition of the progress achieved in Russia.[6] Yeltsin said in response to Russia's admission that 'Russia is Europe [and] a bridge between Europe and Asia. We must foster stronger links with the international community.' Russia, Sergei Medvedev (the president's press secretary) stated, would bring great social, scientific, historic and cultural potential to the Council of Europe. Medvedev believed that the admission of Russia constituted 'an important step towards the creation of a European democratic space', which showed a desire to 'prevent the emergence of new dividing lines on the continent'.[7] The message from the administration was that Russia was no longer regarded as a backward outcast in Europe, and that its population should be proud of the country's achievements under its reformist government. However, the propaganda coup provided by Council of Europe membership did not imply any change in the direction of the country's Russia First strategy. Membership of the Council of Europe had no impact whatsoever on Russian policy, as the war in Chechnya continued unabated, and the government blithely ignored its commitment to abolish the death penalty. Russia's Council of Europe membership was criticised by some other members' delegations, notably the Estonians and Moldovans, but the West Europeans (with US support) ensured the vote on Russia's membership was carried with ease, by 164 votes to thirty-five.[8]

Russia First was built on nostalgia for the loss of Russia's empire and superpower status. Russian politicans and the public felt humiliated by the loss of status and influence, and the pervading sense that the West no longer took Russia seriously as a 'great power'. For this reason, it was vital that Yeltsin was seen to be recognised by the West as a world leader, and that Russia appeared to regain the status of a 'great power' at international summits and negotiations. The West's support for Yeltsin pandered to these Russian sensibilities, and reinforced the feeling that Russia was regaining its influence in the world. Western leaders' courting of Boris Yeltsin seemed to underline international recognition of Russia's return to the role of a global 'superpower'. In turn, this perception enhanced Yeltsin's credibility with the Russian electorate, and underpinned the Russia First strategy. Indeed, Russia First depended upon the Russian Federation being taken seriously as a 'great power', so that the country had the necessary diplomatic weight to secure its own vital interests. The desire to be accepted and respected by the West, while at the same time remaining suspicious of Western motives, had been a recurrent theme throughout Russian history.

In February 1996, German Chancellor Helmut Kohl visited Moscow just days after Yeltsin announced his candidacy for the presidency. Kohl gave forceful backing to Russia in general, and Yeltsin in particular: 'My position is to give Russia help, so she can help herself,' he said. 'This is a firm rebuff to those who say there is no point in helping Russia any more. That is a stupid, idiotic idea. If we do not help, developments [in Russia] will certainly take a turn for the worse.' Kohl defended his loyalty to Yeltsin, who he said had shown himself to be a 'reliable partner' by 'tactfully' withdrawing Russian troops from Germany. The German chancellor promised, 'I am the kind of person who does not forget such loyalty.' To further assist the president's electoral bid, Kohl said the vexed question of NATO enlargement should only be considered after the US presidential elections in November. He also hinted that he and his European colleagues would work to enable Russia to join the Group of Seven club of Western industrial nations. Kohl's patronising offer to 'help' Russia may have ruffled some Russian feathers, but it did nevertheless underline powerful Western support for Yeltsin's economic and democratic reforms. Kohl's overt support for the president showed that Germany and the West feared any likely alternative to a Yeltsin administration. Apart from offering financial support, Kohl was also offering a degree of political support over Russia's desire to join the G7 and concerns over NATO enlargement. The fact that Kohl cared who won the presidential elections, and was brazenly courting Yeltsin, enhanced the president's standing further. The electorate could reason that if Kohl was also offering Russia money, who were they to argue?

Kohl's visit was timed to take place just a day before the arrival of Michel Camdessus, managing director of the International Monetary Fund (IMF), who was expected to sign a $10 billion loan deal with Russia. The need for financial assistance was growing more desperate. Wage arrears were estimated at around $4.3 billion, and President Yeltsin had pledged they would be paid over the next fortnight.[9]

The IMF duly signed the $10.2 billion (£6.6 billion) three-year loan on 22 February, the day after Chancellor Kohl's visit. The loan was the second highest in the IMF's history, following the bail-out of Mexico the previous year. Michel Camdessus, announcing the deal in Moscow, predicted the Russian economy would grow by between 2.2 and 4 per cent annually over the next two years, and 6 per cent thereafter. In exchange, the Kremlin promised to axe oil and gas export tariffs by July 1996 and stick to a tight fiscal and monetary policy, designed to bring inflation down to 1 per cent a month by the end of the year. The IMF loan came on top of a £3.8 billion loan granted the preceding year by the same institution. Camdessus said that Yeltsin's pledge to pay off wage arrears could be accommodated within the budget, provided this only covered the estimated £467.5 million owed to federal workers.[10] In another overtly political statement, Camdessus warned that if a new Communist administration chose to abandon the president's economic policies, the IMF would not hesitate to withdraw financial aid. The IMF chief also said the programme would not permit 'back-tracking' on privatisation, in an apparent response to Communist Party calls for a partial return to state ownership.[11] However strong the anti-Western rhetoric associated with Russia First, the reality was that Russia needed Western financial support. From the Kremlin's point of view, the stronger the drift towards a Russia First strategy, the stronger the argument for financial support for Yeltsin's administration. The Kremlin could argue that while Yeltsin had to adopt some aspects of Russia First, he was containing more extreme political elements who would develop antagonistic positions towards the West, were he to lose the presidential election. The West was therefore induced to provide financial support to President Yeltsin and his government for fear of someone far worse if he lost in the summer. For the West, the priority was to back Yeltsin and stop Gennady Zyuganov and his allies seizing control of the Kremlin.

Predictably, the Communists bridled at Camdessus's utterances. In May, Anatoly Lukianov, a leading figure in the KPRF and a former member of the Soviet Politburo, said the Communists would 'not tolerate the diktat' of the IMF, if Gennady Zyuganov became president. Lukianov stated that while a Communist government would seek to maintain good relations with the IMF, it would refuse to bow to the Fund's strict economic demands. 'We will not under any circumstances break relations with them [the IMF] but we will also not allow them to so unpardonably command us,' Lukianov added.[12] Lukianov's language was relatively moderate compared to Zyuganov's own past disparagement of the IMF, which had likened its behaviour to that of the Nazi *Gauleiters* who occupied areas of the Soviet Union in the Second World War.[13]

While IMF officials stressed the IMF loan was made 'on the basis of an economic programme, not on political considerations', few observers believed it. The IMF loan was only agreed with backing from the White House and the other G7 governments. American, British and other Western governments continued to insist they supported the democratic process, rather than a specific presidential candidate, with diminishing credibility. Behind the scenes, Western diplomats were more forthright, one admitting, 'To the extent that Yeltsin represents a process we support, a process which we think is in the best interests of the Russian people and of the West, we support him.'[14] Speaking after a meeting with Yeltsin in March, Warren Christopher (US secretary of state) left little doubt that Washington was backing the Russian president in his fight with Gennady Zyuganov. Christopher promised Clinton would persist with his policy of throwing all his weight behind Yeltsin, who represented the best hope for continuing reform in Russia. Christopher said:

I am sure that President Clinton will come here to follow basically the line that he has followed ever since the beginning of his presidency, and that is to support the reforms and support those who are carrying out the reforms. That has brought him into strong support for President Yeltsin on prior occasions.[15]

Christopher's words of support were echoed by Chirac's pro-Yeltsin government in Paris.

The G7 Summit held in April in Moscow on nuclear security issues was a barely disguised attempt to shore-up President Yeltsin's authority in the run-up to the presidential elections. The leaders of the group of seven main industrial countries and Russia decided on a largely prearranged set of proposals on nuclear co-operation, storage and joint measures against theft. Russia was responsible for around 1,200 tonnes of fissile material, kept in 900 poorly protected storage sites, and patrolled by demoralised and underpaid guards. There were fears that terrorist groups or states could steal or illicitly buy the components required to build a nuclear bomb. The United States was spending about $800 million a year to help Russia secure its nuclear facilities and decommission its nuclear weapons.[16] However, there was no doubt the location and timing of the G7 Summit was designed to boost Yeltsin's international standing amongst his demoralised electorate.

At the time, Yeltsin was trailing his main opponent Gennady

Zyuganov in the opinion polls, with the latest survey giving them 29 and 37 cent per respectively. The Russian parliament had just declared a day of mourning in response to the latest military disaster in Chechnya following a rebel attack on a federal motorcade. Barely three weeks after President Yeltsin's unilaterally announced ceasefire in Chechnya, fifty-three soldiers had been killed and fifty-two wounded in the attack. Speaking to a stunned parliament, Defence Minister Pavel Grachev had offered to resign, and said that a total of 122 Russian soldiers had been killed since the ceasefire. President Yeltsin baldly stated that there had been no Russia military operations in Chechnya and that the situation there was 'not bad'. Yeltsin added: 'No military operations have been carried out since March 31' [the date of the cease-fire], although some rebel bands were 'still running around'. In fact, since announcing the ceasefire, scores of Chechen villages had been bombed and surrounded by Russian forces, with the Russians taking heavy losses. Clinton responded by endorsing Yeltsin's position that Chechnya was part of Russia, but called for a peaceful settlement of the conflict. The proposed mediator, Tartarstan's President Mintimer Shaimiyev, declared he would not start talks with separatist leader Dzhokhar Dudayev until the fighting stopped.[17]

G7 leaders avoided open endorsement of President Yeltsin at the one-day summit on 19 April, but came pretty close. President Clinton praised the Yeltsin administration's economic reforms, which he said were bearing fruit after very difficult years. 'Real progress is being made,' Clinton remarked. In contrast, Clinton referred to Gennady Zyuganov in less than fulsome terms: 'I don't think we should be under any illusions that people run for offices on platforms that they intend to implement, and therefore all elections involve choices and have conse-quences.' The relationship between Washington and Moscow would be defined by the poll, he added. In an American presidential election year, a Communist win in Russia would be seen as a set-back for President Bill Clinton's foreign policy. A Zyuganov victory would have given ammunition to Clinton's domestic Republican opponents, with concomitant implications for defence spending and the budget.[18] Gennady Zyuganov could be expected to develop a more aggressively anti-Western version of Russia First, with increased domestic economic protectionism, a foreign policy based on the 'voluntary' re-creation of the Soviet Union, and a commitment to restoring Russian sovereignty over Chechnya.

On meeting Prime Minister John Major for half an hour at a reception in Moscow, Gennady Zyuganov bluntly told the British leader not to meddle in Russian affairs.[19] The Communist Party was clearly incensed that the G7 summit was being used to boost Yeltsin's presidential campaign. Zyuganov had recently published a book of essays entitled 'Over the Horizon', in which he wrote that the West was humiliating Russia by imposing its ideas and culture on the country. The Communist leader told the press that he feared the West wanted to use the summit 'as a way of interfering in Russian internal affairs'. He concluded: 'Some regard the summit as a sign of support by the West for Boris Yeltsin, others as an attempt to pressurize Russia.'[20] Meanwhile, John Major promised Yeltsin another £50 million from Britain's 'know-how fund' to help Russia's transition to capitalism. France's President Jacques Chirac joined the chorus of support by issuing a joint communiqué with Yeltsin saying that Russia was 'an inseparable part of the European security architecture'. The communiqué also endorsed Russia's view that the Organisation for Security and Co-operation in Europe (OSCE) should be the main security structure on the continent. This was seen as part of Russia's attempt to weaken the influence of the US-led NATO alliance in Europe.[21]

Despite the warm glow of the West's support at the G7 summit, Yeltsin felt it necessary not to give ammunition to his political opponents. While backing an international ban on nuclear tests, Yeltsin reserved the right to re-start tests if the treaty broke down, and said Russia would not dismantle its testing installations. In a bow to his Russia First strategy, Yeltsin insisted that Russia would take responsibility for safeguarding its nuclear arsenal and re-affirmed his opposition to the eastward enlargement of NATO. Yeltsin felt that he had clinched a deal of sorts with Clinton on NATO expansion. The Russian president said Clinton had pledged to use his influence to ensure that enlargement was not speeded up. Yeltsin said: 'I think a two-way agreement might be worked out. In our view, it might include a provision that no country may be accepted [for NATO's membership] without Russia's agreement.'[22] The latter statement may have been purely for domestic consumption on Yeltsin's part, but John Major confirmed that 'NATO wants a good and close relationship with Russia. I do not think there is any threatening aspect at all about NATO expansion, nor is there any hurry about it.'[23] If Russia was not stopping NATO enlargement, it was at least slowing it down. President Yeltsin's efforts to get Russia accepted as a full member of the G7 group of industrial nations were less successful. Hopes of upgrading the G7 to a G8 with equal participation by Russia were dashed. Yeltsin sought to bring even greater pressure to bear on the G7 to give him an equal status when the group next met in Lyons on 27–30 June, at the height of the presidential election campaign. In the event, due to Yeltsin's ill-health, Victor Chernomyrdin attended in the president's place. The G7 had still not admitted Russia as its eighth full member, and Chernomyrdin was not invited to take part in the G7's economic discussions, arriving in Lyon later to discuss international terrorism and other global issues.

How much effect all this Western support had on Russia public opinion is difficult to quantify. 'Summits mean as much to ordinary people in Russia as life on the moon,' said Yury Shekhochikin, a liberal parliamentarian. 'Visits by Western leaders do not have the same resonance as they did in the days of Reagan and Thatcher.' Russia's exclusion from membership of the G7 club was treated scornfully by the Communists. Alexei Podberyozkin, deputy chair of the Duma's foreign affairs committee, said: 'Anyway, Russia is already a leading industrial power, so it shouldn't have to ask France or Japan for permission to be one.' Stealing his main opponents' clothes, Yeltsin followed up the G7 summit with a visit to China on 24 April. Zyuganov's electoral programme called for relations with China to be a top Russian priority, and Yeltsin duly obliged by announcing that his forthcoming visit would put in place a 'constructive partnership for the 21st century'.[24] Ironically, Chinese officials made it clear they would prefer Yeltsin to beat Zyuganov in the presidential election. Officials in Beijing said: 'We are more familiar with Boris Yeltsin, and we have good relations. His visit to Beijing went well. Zyuganov is unknown, for us. We don't know what he might do.' Yeltsin was regarded as a good business partner for China, while China provided a vast market for Russian arms and technology. The Chinese rebuff was embarrassing for Zyuganov, since he cited China as an example of a communist country which had modernised its economy and attracted large-scale investment without kowtowing to the West.[25]

Final support from the West came via multinational financial institutions. On 23 May Yeltsin received a visit from James Wolfensohn, president of the World Bank, who praised Russian economic reform and held out the hope for additional loans worth $800 million. At the same time, Christian Noyer, president of the Paris Club of creditor nations, said Russia would be welcome to join the Club. This was largely because Russia itself was owed $100 billion, arising from its former role as political and financial patron of the Third World. In the 1980s, three-quarters of bilateral net disbursements by the Soviet Union went to three countries – Cuba, Mongolia and Vietnam. In April, the Paris Club had agreed to the re-scheduling of $40 billion in Russian government loans, the largest deal done in the Club's forty-year history. Some of the debts owed to Russia dated from after the Soviet period. All the former Soviet republics owed Moscow money, mainly for energy imports. Ukraine paid no energy debt or interest for about two years, running up a bill of $4 billion (subsequently it had kept up payments). The Communists and nationalists made a campaign issue of debts owed to Moscow, calling for a cancellation of credit and aid to foreign countries, including the CIS. Russia also chose this period to make a bid to join the Organisation for Economic Co-operation and Development, the Paris-based economic advisory agency sponsored by the leading industrialised countries.[26]

Leaders of the Commonwealth of Independent States (CIS) joined their Western counterparts in endorsing Boris Yeltsin's presidential bid. On 17 May leaders of eleven former Soviet republics gave public and unanimous support to President Yeltsin in an attempt to boost his election campaign. The CIS leaders voiced concern that a Communist win on 16 June might lead to civil war in Russia or jeopardise their independence. Meeting at a CIS summit in Moscow, the leaders issued a statement backing Yeltsin's efforts to promote a 'democratic society' and prevent a 'return to the past'. Avoiding a 'return to the past' under the Communists was one of Yeltsin's dominant campaign slogans. Some CIS leaders also felt that given the Communists' attitude to economic support, they would do better under Yeltsin than Zyuganov. Others, mindful of the experiences of Russia's hand in the internal conflicts in Moldova, Georgia, Azerbaijan and Armenia, were more cautious, but regarded Yeltsin as the lesser of two evils. Like the West, CIS leaders felt Yeltsin was far from perfect, but he was less imperfect than the alternative, Gennady Zyuganov.[27] Both Western and CIS leaders felt Zyuganov, as a more vocal and ideologically committed proponent of Russia First, represented a greater potential threat to international stability and their national interests. With Zyuganov, there was always the danger that he would evolve an aggressively anti-Western version of Russia First, re-building part of the former Soviet Empire as a counter-weight to NATO, and re-creating a centralised socialist economy. Yeltsin, by contrast, was unlikely to adopt such an extreme strategy, either by inclination or design.

CAMPAIGN ISSUES IN THE FIRST ROUND

The campaign issues which arose in the presidential election had already been catalogued in the Duma contest the previous December. Yeltsin neutralised the opposition by identifying areas of unpopular government policy, and adopted his opponents' strategies to develop a broad political consensus. This was particularly apparent with foreign-policy issues, but also applied to the domestic sphere. The main concerns of the electorate were still the state of the economy, falling living standards (for the majority) and wage arrears, rising crime and the deterioration of the social infrastructure, including health and education. Underlying all this was a profound sense of loss of Russia's great power status, and a feeling that the quality of life for most people had deteriorated since the demise of the Soviet Union. Chechnya became more of an issue as the war dragged on and Russian losses mounted, symbolising weakness at home and fostering criticism from abroad. Opinion polls showed that from November 1995, Chechnya had overtaken wage arrears as the most pressing of voters' concerns. Yeltsin himself repeatedly acknowledged that he would not win the presidential election unless he could achieve peace in Chechnya and the withdrawal of Russian troops. In foreign-policy terms, there were very few differences between the policies of Yeltsin and Zyuganov. The differences had more to do with style and presentation than content. Yeltsin had become increasingly assertive towards the former Soviet republics of the 'near abroad', strongly opposed NATO enlargement and courted Eastern countries like China and Iran, taking a generally more independent line from the West. The only perceptible differences related to the war in Chechnya, attitudes to re-creating the Soviet Union (Yeltsin preferred working through the CIS) and the response to NATO enlargement. Zyuganov was even more sceptical of NATO's Partnership for Peace (PfP) initiative than the president's administration, and opposed a climb-down over Chechnya.[28]

Yeltsin's ability to outmanoeuvre the opposition, particularly Zyuganov, was brilliantly exposed by the president's handling of the Duma's vote on 15 March to revoke the treaty abolishing the Soviet Union. Zyuganov believed the Duma vote would help commit a broad nationalist-patriotic bloc to his presidential bid, and undermine the president's strategy to steal the Communists' clothes as the best guarantor of the reintegration of the former Soviet states. Zyuganov was, however, primarily seeking to consolidate his Communist coalition, the Bloc of Popular Patriotic Forces. Some hardliners, including Victor Anpilov (leader of Working Russia), had declined to back Zyuganov while the KPRF's commitment to restoring the Soviet Union appeared lukewarm. After the Duma vote, Anpilov – together with Stanislav Terekhov of the Officers' Union – declared their formal support for Zyuganov's presidential bid. However, the main effect of Zyuganov's tactical move was to coalesce CIS support for Yeltsin, portray the nationalist-communist opposition as irresponsible and out of touch with reality, and boost Yeltsin's standing as a mature statesman.[29]

In essence, the Duma voted (by 250 to ninety-eight) to declare null and void a resolution adopted by the Supreme Soviet of the Russian Republic (RSFSR) on 12 December 1991, which denounced the treaty establishing the Soviet Union. The Duma also carried a resolution calling for legal force to be given to the referendum of March 1991, which was in favour of maintaining the existence of the Soviet Union and was carried by 252 votes to thirty-three. Strictly speaking, neither resolution actually denounced the Belovezhye Agreement, signed by the leaders of Russia, Ukraine and Belarus on 8 December 1991, which buried the Soviet Union and established the CIS. Nor did either resolution have any legal force whatsoever. Communist deputies who moved the resolutions admitted that it was a political gesture which was not intended to not harm relations with former Soviet republics. Gennady Zyuganov said the vote was the first step in a gradual re-creation of the Soviet Union which would accelerate when he won the presidency. However, it was plain that the CIS (which replaced the Soviet Union) was also a target of the Duma vote. Zyuganov's election programme, which was published in *Sovetskaya Rossiya* on 19 March, stated:

> We advocate the abrogation of the Belovezhskaya Pushcha agreements [setting up the CIS] which have brought so much suffering and sorrow to all the peoples, and caused colossal damage to the [former Soviet] republics' economies and security . . . This does not mean that somebody is going to be forcibly annexed tomorrow, or especially that somebody's sovereignty is going to come under attack . . . We will take all the necessary measures so that fraternal ties are restored, first and foremost between Russia, Ukraine, Belarus and Kazakhstan. This will lay the foundation for the phased restoration of a union state on a voluntary basis.[30]

Boris Yeltsin immediately counter-attacked, calling the vote 'scandalous'.

'Neither Ukraine nor any other former Union republic is going to march into the Soviet Union with a red flag,' he added. The president stated that his own plans for economic integration with the former Soviet states were now speeding up. Yeltsin argued that the resolutions had done great harm to Russia, while the Communists themselves were only interested in 'politicking' in the run-up to the elections.[31] In a prepared statement, Yeltsin declared the resolutions were 'actually intended to create a political and legal impasse in Russia'. He continued:

> The resolutions adopted by the Duma cannot resurrect the Soviet Union; they can only create uncertainty as to the legal status of the Russian Federation . . . Behind a smokescreen of disingenuous theorizing about the further integration of the peoples of the countries of the Commonwealth of Independent States, the Duma's resolutions actually lead in exactly the opposite direction . . .

> – they erect barriers along the road to genuine integration;
> – they revive extremist nationalists in the CIS countries and the Baltic States;
> – they severely undermine the position of our fellow countrymen in those countries.
> Such actions constitute nothing other than a betrayal of Russia's interests.[32]

Yeltsin said he rejected the Duma resolutions as 'politically explosive and illegal unilateral decisions'. He repeated his belief that integration was a 'voluntary matter' and that integration through the CIS would continue. The president instructed Foreign Minister Yevgeny Primakov to inform foreign countries that the Duma resolution did not affect the status of the Russian Federation in international law, its rights or international commitments. Responding to the president's furious reaction, Gennady Zyuganov described Yeltsin's statement as 'hysterical', and repeated his view that any recreation of the Soviet Union must be realised on a peaceful step-by-step basis.[33]

Prime Minister Victor Chernomyrdin disparagingly declared that the 'lawmakers either do not know or do not understand what a considerable amount of work is being done by Russia in the CIS to achieve real, not declaratory, integration of the Commonwealth (CIS)'.[34]

Disapproval from the West and the near abroad was overwhelming. US Secretary of State Warren Christopher denounced the Duma vote as 'highly irresponsible' and pledged continued American support for Ukrainian independence. The response from the CIS and Baltic states was predictably harsh. Eduard Shevardnadze, president of Georgia and former Soviet foreign minister, declared the vote 'stupid', and cancelled a meeting with the Communist speaker of the Duma, Gennady Seleznyev. The Belarussian foreign minister, Ulazdimir Syanko, condemned the Duma for 'discrediting the integration process which is gaining momentum in the CIS and particularly between Russia and Belarus'.[35] President Lukashenko of Belarus, the most pro-Russian CIS leader, even declared he saw Belarus 'only as a sovereign state, but in a union with Russia and all others who wish to join such a union'.[36]

Other leaders queued up to condemn the vote, including President Leonid Kuchma of Ukraine, President Akayev of Kyrgyzstan, President Aliyev of Azerbaijan and President Saidov of Tajikistan. President Ter-Petrosian of Armenia said the resolution was 'an act of provocation directed against the sovereignty of the member-countries of the Commonwealth of Independent States'.[37] Later the Armenian president was reported as saying that reintegration would end, and the CIS cease to exist, the 'day after' an election win by Gennady Zyuganov. The Baltic states of Estonia and Latvia were almost apoplectic over the Duma's actions. An Estonian foreign ministry statement said: 'The Duma's decision demonstrates the incapacity of several deputies to comprehend the development of historical events.'[38] The Latvian foreign minister, Valdis Birkavs, said the resolution showed how strong the tendency was to restore the Soviet Union and return to the past.[39] President Yeltsin's Russia First policy, involving closer integration with the CIS to re-establish Russia's influence in the near abroad, proved far more credible than Zyuganov's alternative strategy of attempting to re-create the Soviet Union. In the process, Zyuganov damaged his own electoral prospects and improved Yeltsin's standing with CIS leaders and the Russian public.

Following the torrent of condemnation, Yeltsin made his master-stroke. On 29 March he signed an integration agreement with three CIS countries. The agreement initially provided for a customs union between the four countries of Russia, Kazakhstan, Belarus and Kyrgyzstan. An inter-state council was established, consisting of the four presidents, their prime ministers and foreign ministers. After a signing ceremony in the Kremlin, President Yeltsin said the 'system of co-operation should resemble co-operation between the countries of the European Community'. He hoped the customs union would lead to a single currency, but said the creation of a single state would only be possible in the distant future with an appropriate legal and constitutional base. Yeltsin announced the hope that all other CIS countries, plus the Baltic states, might be persuaded to join the union. But Yeltsin also said that no country would have to renounce its independence: 'No one with a heart can but regret the end of the Soviet Union,' he declared. 'No one with a head can think of creating an exact copy.' The same day, the Belarussian parliament approved a proposal by President Lukashenko to sign a treaty creating a union between Russia and Belarus the following week.[40]

Outflanked, Yeltsin's presidential opponents tried to strike back. In an unusual joint statement, three presidential hopefuls denounced the four-nation customs union. Grigory Yavlinsky, Svyatoslav Fyodorov and General Alexander Lebed condemned the agreement as a hasty pre-election ploy, embarked upon without proper consultation with the Russian people. 'The political games over the integration of CIS countries are becoming increasingly dangerous,' the statement said.[41] Alex Podberyozkin, a foreign-policy adviser to Gennady Zyuganov, later complained that Yeltsin had co-opted the Communists' agenda on strengthening ties with the CIS countries and defending Russia's 'core national interests'.[42] Yeltsin's manifesto, *Programme of Action for 1996–2000*, outlined the president's foreign-policy priorities. Top of the list was the 'Achievement of the maximum possible integration with the CIS on the basis of free will and mutual benefits.' The second priority was to protect the rights and interests of Russian citizens in the 'near and far abroad'. Other priorities included building relationships with partners in the 'West and East' on the basis of equality, improving relations with Asia (especially China, India and Japan) and the Middle East, the creation of a united and democratic Europe free of dividing lines, expanding new and traditional markets and meeting Russia's commitments in the field of human rights.[43]

The overall result of the clash with the Duma was a triumph for Yeltsin's campaign team. Together with other stratagems, Yeltsin's fight-back on foreign policy helped close the gap in the opinion polls. Before the vote in the Duma, Yeltsin was trailing Zyuganov. A poll taken in late February suggested that Yeltsin was on 11 per cent compared to Zyuganov's 24 per cent. In mid-March, the corresponding figures were 15 and 25 per cent. By the beginning of May, some opinion polls gave Yeltsin a 4 per cent lead over his Communist rival. As Communist Party campaign strategists themselves predicted, Yeltsin narrowed Zyuganov's lead and then overtook him in the run-up to the vital first round.[44] Foreign policy was not the only area where Yeltsin stole Zyuganov's policy clothes. He also managed to achieve much the same effect in the domestic sphere.

For President Yeltsin, adopting a Russia First strategy was an electoral necessity. Yeltsin reacted to the evolving political and economic climate which had given birth to Russia First, and ensured that he put himself in the vanguard of the politicians advocating a Russia First strategy. While he had previously espoused the concept of Russia as a 'great power' , it had been the 1995 Duma election results which had confirmed the ascendency of Russia First as the dominant political school of throught in Russia. It was political opportunism, and the need to respond to changing public and political conceptions, which led President Yeltsin to adopt a more assertive Russia First strategy. In so doing, President Yeltsin wrong-footed his political opponents, constrained the drift to a more aggressive anti-Western attitude, and united the electorate behind a populist programme. The president exploited the drift towards Russia First, devised a credible programme embracing foreign and domestic policy, and used it as a campaign device to ensure his own re-election.

Gennady Zyuganov generally portrayed himself as the presidential candidate who would protect the social welfare system and jobs of those employed in the state sector. President Yeltsin decided to tackle the problems of the economy, especially the issue of wage arrears, by throwing money at the electorate. Yeltsin made no secret of his strategy, telling voters during a campaign visit to Arkhangelsk that he had 'come with deep pockets'. In his attempt to neutralise Zyuganov's domestic appeal, Yeltsin took steps to raise the income of poorer groups, such as pensioners, teachers and large families. He also targeted areas in the far north and far east, which had suffered particular hardship. Despite falling tax revenues, Yeltsin raised spending. On 5 June, President Yeltsin notoriously ordered the Central Bank to transfer 5 trillion roubles ($1 billion) to the federal budget to help the government pay for defence plants, teachers' wages and benefits, and vacation allowances for inhabitants of the far north. Sergei Dubinin, Central Bank governor, said the bank would appeal to the Constitutional Court, as the move to transfer the bank's 1994 profits jeopardised its independence and was illegal. Between April and June, the Central Bank's foreign currency reserves fell by $3.5 billion, which represented the cost of propping up the rouble as the government printed money to fund some of Yeltsin's spending promises.[45] In Russia First terms, Yeltsin was placing populist policies and his desire for re-election above the demands from Western financial institutions for economic probity, 'sound money' and financial constraint.

Some of Yeltsin's spending promises were to take effect immediately, others were not due to come into force until 1997 (if ever). They included: more than 30 trillion roubles to pay state sector wage arrears between 1 January and mid May; 4.5 trillion roubles to compensate pensioners for savings devalued by economic reforms; higher social benefits to single mothers and tax breaks to families with children; $30 million to purchase imported medicines for Chernobyl victims; 3.8 trillion roubles to pay wage arrears and summer holiday allowances for teachers; a hundred scholarships for young scientists; higher pensions for college and university lecturers; 2.8 trillion roubles to pay for defence orders; 142 billion roubles to the Pechora miners to pay wages and benefits; 40 billion roubles for a timber-processing plant in Arkhangelsk; increased support for war veterans; state support for small businesses; low-cost housing and discounts on rail and air tickets for citizens travelling to central Russia from the far east. Travelling across Russia, Yeltsin dispersed spending promises like confetti. Two harvesters and a car promised for a group of Chechen villagers, 3 billion roubles to build a church in Stavropol, and 133 billion roubles for the miners of Vorkuta in the remote north. On one campaign visit Yeltsin reputedly promised £1.3 million in ten yards of a walkabout. And every step of the way the president was signing decrees to give effect to his pledges, sometimes by the side of mine-shafts or tanks. On 6 June, Yeltsin had to sign a decree on enforcing his decrees, which although theoretically valid throughout the Federation, were often ignored in practice in the regions.[46]

Pushing the bill through parliament to transfer the $1 billion from the Central Bank, Yeltsin once again wrong-footed his Communist opponents. The KPRF initially opposed the bill, but rapidly backed down when they realised the political significance of opposing Yeltsin's measure, which promised, amongst other things, payment of wage arrears affecting millions of people. The KPRF had long complained about teachers' poor working conditions and wage arrears. Yeltsin now delivered the means to begin tackling the problem. Zyuganov could only stand on the sidelines and offer muted support.[47] Pursuing ever more populist policies, President Yeltsin pledged to keep vodka prices down, and pitching for the Communist vote, even went so far as to restore the use of the Soviet red flag (minus hammer and sickle) during official ceremonies.[48] Yeltsin adopted a new strategy in three other areas to neutralise his Communist opponent. He pledged to abolish conscription, watered-down his commitment to deregulate the privatisation of land, and launched a fresh peace-initiative to settle the Chechen conflict. Yeltsin had admitted the war in Chechnya was his 'biggest mistake'. The conflict, which his defence minister Pavel Grachev said could be sorted out by two parachute regiments in two hours, had become a serious electoral liability.[49]

The pledge to abolish conscription by the year 2000 was made on 16 May, when Yeltsin signed a decree laying down that by the beginning of the second millennium, 'the armed forces would be made up of voluntary, contracting citizens . . . with conscription abandoned'. The president signed another decree, according to which only volunteers would be sent to battle zones. Both decrees were designed to boost the president's popularity with parents anxious about their sons, most of whom were young conscripts, being sent to Chechnya. Yeltsin's decrees found favour with Alexander Lebed, who had argued for a 'leaner and meaner' Russian army to replace the ill-equipped and ineffectual 1.5 million force. For good measure and to impress liberal reformers, Yeltsin also proposed limiting the death penalty by stages, bringing Russia into line with the recommendations of the Council of Europe.[50] President Yeltsin's second promise was included in his election manifesto, and was a nod in the direction of the Agrarian Party, who were extremely influential in country areas. Yeltsin qualified his support for the free sale of agricultural land, calling for more regulation in the area of agricultural land sales, so preventing the creation of large agricultural monopolies.[51]

In a *coup de grace,* Yeltsin invited Chechen leader Zelimkhan Yandarbayev (who had replaced Dzhokhar Dudayev, killed in April 1996) to the Kremlin to sign a peace deal. Yandarbayev was pictured smiling on Russian television at the signing ceremony held on 27 May. Yeltsin cunningly held the Chechen delegation at the Kremlin for 24 hours while he made a whistle-stop visit to Chechnya, to be filmed telling Russian troops the war was over. Dudayev's widow even said she would vote for Yeltsin, despite widespread stories that the Russians had set Dudayev up by bombing a satellite telephone dish in a field during peace negotiations. The peace accord supposedly halted military activities and promised a prisoner exchange, but ignored the question of Chechnya's status. The Chechens knew that the peace accord would help Yeltsin's re-election, but had calculated that a Zyuganov win might lead to a stepping-up of the war. Most communists and nationalist leaders were opposed to granting sovereignty to Chechnya, and a communist president might have launched an all-out assault on Chechnya, in contradistinction to Yeltsin's shambolic campaign. Yet the peace agreement with Yeltsin might lead to a Russian troop withdrawal and a settlement once the presidential election was out of the way. Following his 'peace agreement' with Yandarbayev, there was no doubt Yeltsin had the forthcoming presidential election in the bag. The Russian people wanted to believe the war was over, even though they still doubted whether the president had truly achieved peace. While many Russians did not support ceding sovereignty in Chechnya, they were also sick of the slaughter, and hoped for a peaceful and honourable settlement of the conflict. By promising peace without ceding sovereignty, the Kremlin could present its Russia First strategy as remaining intact. Russia had not, on the face of it, compromised its territorial integrity. Yeltsin had closed the opinion poll gap with Zyuganov by the end of April; by the end of May he had a seven-point lead. The only question remained whether Yeltsin had done enough to win on the first round.[52]

THE MEDIA CAMPAIGN

President Yeltsin had already laid the groundwork for his media campaign by sacking the head of RTR state television, Oleg Poptsov, in February, and banning the independent television company NTV from the Kremlin. Both moves were seen as attempts to intimidate the media in the run-up to the presidential election.[53] Yeltsin dominated television output, gaining 53 per cent of the coverage for the ten presidential candidates on ORT, RTR and NTV, the three main national television channels. Zyuganov's television coverage in the first round stood at 18 per cent.[54] In late March, Igor Malashenko, the head of the independent television station NTV, joined Yeltsin's campaign team.[55] This was the equivalent of American television mogul Ted Turner joining a US presidential campaign committee or the director general of the BBC joining John Major's re-election committee. On 11 June, Gazprom, the state-controlled gas producer and Russia's largest company (formerly headed by Chernomyrdin), announced its purchase of a 30 per cent stake in NTV. Gazprom strongly supported Yeltsin's re-election bid, and the NTV acquisition six days before the presidential poll was not without significance. Eighteen months before, Vladimir Gusinsky, the head of Most bank who sold the NTV stake to Gazprom, watched his security guards being beaten up by General Alexander Korzhakov's presidential bodyguards. Gusinsky later fled the country for almost a year, fearing arrest or worse. His alliance with Gazprom signified a pact between Chernomyrdin's gas and oil lobby with Moscow Mayor Yury Luzhkov's financial lobby (which included Most bank). The attack on Gusinsky's bodyguards was seen as Korzhakov's warning to the Most media group not to be so critical of the Kremlin, and a message to Luzhkov to dissuade him from thinking about standing for the presidency. The media was incensed by the episode, with the front page of *Izvestiya* demanding 'Who is running the country – Chernomrydin, Yeltsin or General Korzhakov?' Yury Luzhkov subsequently gave Yeltsin full support in the presidential campaign.[56]

Although each candidate was entitled to thirty minutes of free time on each of the state-controlled television channels (RTR, ORT and TV-5), Yeltsin's coverage was overwhelming and sycophantic. As Zyuganov said, 'We wake up with Boris Nicolaevich and go to sleep with Mr Yeltsin.' Candidates were allowed to spend $2.9 million on their campaigns, although this was clearly exceeded by Yeltsin's team, bearing in mind television and poster advertising costs. In Moscow and St Petersburg, Yeltsin's posters were on every street corner. One flaw in electoral law allowed for sympathisers or supporters to pay directly for advertising or campaign material, and such spending did not pass through candidates' electoral accounts.[57] Democratic models may have been imported from the West, but they were not fully grafted onto the Russian body politic. Russia's traditional autocratic response to political discourse held sway, and the Russian public took it for granted that this would be the case.

The 'independent' national print media also heavily backed President Yeltsin, with only the traditional left or nationalist press supporting Zyuganov. *Rossiiskaya Gazeta, Rossiiskiye vesti, Izvestiya* and the high-circulation *Moskovsky Komsomolets* and *Argumenty i Fakty* were overtly pro-Yeltsin. *Segodnya* was generally critical of Zyuganov and positive towards Yeltsin, while *Nezavisimaya Gazeta* gave Zyuganov minimal coverage. Newspapers supporting Zyuganov included *Pravda* (soon to be shut), the anti-semitic *Zavtra, Sovietskaya Rossiya* and numerous communist journals. Unlike Yeltsin's campaign tours, Zyuganov's visits to the regions were rarely covered in the national media. Zyuganov did, however, do better in the regional media, where each territory of the Federation had its own television channel, and where the regional press were more sympathetic or objective. The Communist candidate did better than most of the other candidates, like Grigory Yavlinsky, for example, who disappeared from the television screens. Yavlinsky, voting on 16 June, told reporters that the campaign was run on similar lines to the Brezhnev era, due to the Kremlin's domination of the airwaves. Unfortunately for Zyuganov, most of the national coverage he did receive was blatantly negative or deceptive.[58]

Two leading liberal newspapers circulated scare stories reportedly based on the Communist Party's programme. *Komsomolskaya Pravda* reported that within three months of the presidential election, Russians holding US dollars would have to exchange them for 10 per cent of their value. It also said Zyuganov would impose limits on foreign travel and confiscate private property. *Moskovsky Komsomolets*, the Moscow daily, stated Zyuganov intended appointing hardliners to his cabinet, included Stalinist Victor Anpilov and General Albert Makashov. Later, *Komsomolskaya Pravda* admitted they made up the manifesto story. Zyuganov also found himself the butt of the 'God Forbid!' freesheet, mysteriously funded and delivered free to millions of homes. 'God Forbid!' cost an estimated $10 million alone to distribute, in excess of Yeltsin's entire legal campaign budget.[59] Virulently anti-communist, the paper pictured Zyuganov as a surgeon holding scalpels like a hammer and sickle. At the same time, Russian national television showed endless documentaries of the gulag and Stalin's era, and stressed the electorate should fear bringing back the 'Red Terror'. The media lost its objectivity, which had started to flourish in the critical coverage of the war in Chechnya and disapproval of the government's performance. Tsarist or Soviet-style pro-Yeltsin propaganda became the order of the day.[60] Russia's traditionally autocratic political values had once again come to the fore.

Zyuganov and the other candidates, including Yavlinsky, Gorbachev and Bryntsalov, complained about the biased media coverage, to little effect.[61] Western journalists lamented the blow to the country's nascent democracy, while Russian journalists were unrepentant. 'Yeltsin is a bastard,' said one Russian political commentator. 'I hate the guy but I'll vote for him, because I know where I am with him. We can go back to attacking this regime after he gets in again. I know what the communists are like. We'll all lose our jobs if they get in.' Sergei Chugayev, political reporter at *Izvestiya* took a similar line 'We are more opposed to the Communists than we are in favour of the president. I will not write anything right now to hurt him. We leave that for after the elections.' One journalist, Alexander Minkin, of *Ponedelnik* was told by his editor: 'Write what you want, only do not touch Yeltsin.' Minkin replied: 'Breathe what you want, except for air.'[62]

In May, the FSB, successor to the KGB, decided to play the anti-Western electoral card by threatening to expel nine British diplomats, following the arrest of a British agent in Moscow. Highlighted by the media, the move momentarily soured Russo-British relations, but was opposed by the Russian foreign ministry, who condemned 'over-emotional reactions and hasty decisions'. Mikhail Barsukov, nationalistic head of the FSB and friend of Alexander Korzhakov, saw the action as a way of gaining nationalist support for Yeltsin, by showing that the president strongly defended Russian interests against the West. After back-room negotiations involving British Ambassador Sir Andrew Wood, the matter was quietly defused.[63] More ominously, the media was used to float the idea of postponing the presidential elections altogether. On 27 April, thirteen senior businessmen and bankers signed a letter in *Nezavisimaya Gazeta* calling for a political compromise which would prevent civil war and conflict in Russia between the 'Reds and Whites'. By implication it implied a postponement of the elections. The leader of these thirteen, Boris Berezovsky (president of the Logovaz group), was closely allied to Lieutenant-General Alexander Korzhakov.[64]

Korzhakov himself deliberately spoke to the Western press about postponing the presidential elections. The former KGB officer and Yeltsin's drinking 'banya buddy' of a number of years standing, Korzhakov's role as head of the presidential bodyguard placed him closer to the president than anyone else. Increasingly, Korzhakov was also meddling in state policy, becoming the Rasputin of modern Russian politics. Mikhail Barsukov, FSB boss, was a Korzhakov friend and protégé. So when the president's confidant talked of postponing the elections, the West became nervous. Alexander Korzhakov told the *Observer* newspaper:

A lot of influential people are in favour of postponing the elections, and I'm in favour of it too, because we need stability. If we have the elections, there is no way of avoiding a fight. If Yeltsin wins, the radical opposition will claim the results were falsified and there will be unrest. If Zyuganov wins, even if he wants to take a centrist line, the same people won't let him.

Later the same day, Korzhakov again urged postponement, telling Interfax: 'Society is split. Even families are split, some for Yeltsin, others for Zyuganov. Such a division of souls is dangerous.' At this stage of the campaign, Yeltsin was still trailing Zyuganov by 6 per cent. Nevertheless, Yeltsin slapped down Korzhakov, repeated that the election would go ahead and told Western leaders he would win comfortably. Yeltsin realised that a postponement of the elections would be a diplomatic disaster in terms of Russia's relations with the West, and could lead to a massive fall in Western financial support and investment.[65]

Yeltsin's media persona underwent a remarkable transformation during the course of the campaign. From a trailing underdog with drink and health problems, Yeltsin re-invented himself as a vigorous, energetic campaigner, at one and the same time the 'Good Tsar' and Russian *muzhik*. Visiting twenty-four cities in less than four months, Yeltsin even appeared dancing at a youth rock and roll concert.[66] The Russian electorate was enthralled and entertained, especially when Yeltsin's performance was contrasted with Zyuganov's dour appearance. Yeltsin frankly admitted he and his government had made mistakes, but with a straight face announced that he was the only person who could put things to rights. 'I have made mistakes,' he wrote in his manifesto, 'but I know better than anyone how to correct them.'[67] No other candidate could hope to match Yeltsin's charisma, or his bare-faced cheek.

On 23 March he overhauled his campaign team, taking personal control of the campaign. Apart from Chernomyrdin, the team included Deputy Prime Minister Yury Yarov, former chief of staff Sergei Filatov, Victor Ilyushin, Korzhakov, Barsukov, Nikolai Yegorov and Igor Malashenko of NTV. Also involved were Moscow mayor Yury Luzhkov, Anatoly Chubais (sacked in January), and Yeltsin's 37-year-old daughter Tatyana. Soskovets stayed on the president's campaign team but was removed as its head after Yeltsin became increasingly dissatisfied with his performance and replaced him by Sergei Filatov. Filatov's official title was head of the All-Russian Movement of National Support for Boris Yeltsin.[68] A mixture of liberal reformers and hardliners, all of the revamped campaign team were personally trusted by Yeltsin.[69]

THE CANDIDATES AND THE FIRST ROUND RESULTS

By polling day there were ten of the original eleven candidates on the ballot paper, as Aman Tuleyev, a hardline communist and governor of a mining region in Siberia, withdrew in favour of Gennady Zyuganov. The election result of 16 June was actually a big disappointment for Boris Yeltsin. The president had hoped to win a majority on the first round, and had worked hard on his regional governors to deliver victory in the provinces (threatening them with the sack if they failed).[70] The turn-out had been the first indication that Yeltsin would have to fight a second round, with 72 million voters participating out of a total electorate of 105 million. The 68.5 per cent turn-out, although respectable, was not as great as Yeltsin's advisers had hoped, given their assumption that a high turn-out would maximise the reformist or anti-communist vote. The president's campaign team took it for granted that the Communist Party's organisation, and the commitment of its supporters, would deliver the maximum vote for Zyuganov. In the event, Yeltsin scored 35.28 per cent (26.6 million votes), leading the poll just ahead of second-placed Gennady Zyuganov on 32.03 per cent (24.2 million). The gap between Yeltsin and Zyuganov was a lot smaller than indicated by Russia's unreliable opinion polls. Alexander Lebed surprised most observers by coming a strong third with 14.52 per cent (10.9 million), and Gorbachev surprised nobody by coming seventh with a predicted 0.51 per cent of the vote (386,000). The first round of the presidential elections confirmed what had already become apparent with the Duma elections the previous December. Russia First was the dominant school of thought across the political spectrum, with pro-reform presidential candidates faring badly. Those candidates who stood on Russia First platforms performed relatively well, while those who were perceived as pro-Western or pro-reformist generally did badly. The one overtly liberal reformist candidate, Grigory Yavlinsky, only obtained 7.34 per cent of the vote (5.5 million), coming fourth behind more assertive Russia First candidates. Yeltsin, Zyuganov and Lebed, with their strong Russia First platforms, dominated the poll. Vladimir Bryntsalov, Yury Vlasov, Martin Shakkum and Svyatoslav Fyodorov shared Gorbachev's fate of receiving less than 1 per cent of the vote.[71]

Yeltsin's popular vote had fallen by a quarter compared to 1991, when he won the first round of the presidential elections with 57 per cent. The incumbent president's support fell in eighty-six out of the eighty-nine territories of the Russian Federation. Nevertheless, Yeltsin clearly won in St Petersburg and Moscow, obtaining an overall majority of votes cast in the capital. The president also obtained 60 per cent of the vote in his regional powerbase of Sverdlovsk in Siberia, did well in much of the western part of Russia, and in central Russia where the energy workers backed him in areas like Tyuman, Perm and Sakha (oil prices were rising). Yeltsin also led in the far east, with Lebed coming a strong second. Zyuganov performed well in the agricultural southwest and the 'Red Belt' of southern Russia, although not as well as in the Duma elections. Lebed performed well in the far east (squeezing Zhirinovsky's vote), Yaroslavl, Ivanovo, Tula (where he had been based in the army), and in the military areas of Murmansk and Arkhangelsk. Yavlinsky scraped in second in St Petersburg with 15 per cent, well behind Yeltsin and just ahead of Zyuganov. Yavlinsky, however, made little impression elsewhere, and even came in fourth behind Lebed in Moscow. Zhirinovsky found that he was squeezed on all sides, by Yeltsin, Lebed and Zyuganov. In particular, Zhirinovsky's powerbase in the far east had been destroyed by the more moderate Russia First stances taken by both Yeltsin and Lebed. Zhirinovsky's best showing was still in the far east in Primorsk and Chita, although his overall share of 5.70 per cent (4.3 million) put him in an insignificant fifth place.[72]

The five presidential candidates who received less than 1 per cent of the vote had no real impact on the campaign. Olympic weight-lifter Yury Vlasov and businessman Martin Shakkum were all but invisible during the campaign, although the latter had prepared several presidential decrees for the first day of his presidency. Vladimir Bryntsalov, 49-year-old billionaire owner of Fereyn (the Russian pharmaceutical giant) and Duma deputy had entered the presidential campaign to boost his profile, rather than with any serious political purpose. Famous for exposing his wife's bottom on prime-time television, Bryntsalov was the epitome of Russia's 'new rich': garrulous, confident and heavily protected by armed bodyguards. Bryntsalov's association with the Russian Socialist Party was not a true reflection of his political orientation, if it can be said he had one. Bryntsalov's wife, Natasha, twenty years his junior, complemented his campaign with boasts of her $18,000 monthly allowance, and the size of her husband's 'organ'. The well-known and respected eye surgeon Professor Svyatoslav Fyodorov, aged 68, was a more serious candidate, who advocated and practised profit-sharing and co-operative style capitalism. Unfortunately,

Fyodorov also overestimated his own political clout, and unwisely testified to his admiration for Adolf Hitler.[73]

Mikhail Gorbachev was the most famous of the no-hope candidates. Widely blamed for the dismemberment of the Soviet Union and the chaotic introduction of *perestroika* and economic reforms, Gorbachev was trailing significantly in the polls from the start. As if this were not bad enough, he was also regarded as a pro-Western former leader who had betrayed the country by selling out Russia's interests to the West. Asked why he was bothering to stand when it looked like he would be humiliated, Gorbachev said it was because 'neither Yeltsin nor Zyuganov was fit to be president'. Gorbachev also felt his own participation would make it less likely that the elections would be cancelled.[74] Besides, Gorbachev plainly detested both men. Yeltsin had undermined and helped remove him, while Zyuganov was a former second-rank apparatchik whom he would have disdained to talk to in the old days. The former Soviet president was upset by the way Russia's media had ignored him, and once during the campaign claimed someone tried to assassinate him when he was punched in the face on a 'meet the people' tour. Addressing a crowd in Krasnogvardeysk, Gorbachev had rhetorically asked the audience, 'Should we give power back to the communists?' 'Yes, the communists. It was better then,' the crowd enthusiastically replied, clapping. This was never going to be Gorbachev's come-back campaign.[75]

Grigory Yavlinsky, the articulate 44-year-old English-speaking economist with strong Harvard connections, ran a poor campaign and was completely outwitted by Yeltsin. Disregarded by the pro-Yeltsin media, Yavlinsky's reputation as a liberal reformer made him the favourite candidate for many in the West. Yet despite his liberal credentials, which should have enabled him to challenge Yeltsin as the main democratic opponent to Zyuganov, Yavlinsky was completely outflanked by the president. When Yeltsin invited Yavlinsky into the Kremlin for two hours of talks in early May, he unwisely accepted, no doubt in the hope that he would be offered the premiership in the president's post-election government. Instead, Yeltsin ignored Yavlinsky's demands for an end to the war in Chechnya, economic policy changes, and the sacking of four ministers (including Chernomrydin and Grachev), and publicly portrayed the liberal economist as a supplicant for office. Yavlinsky's campaign never recovered from the blow to his standing as an independent candidate.

Reportedly assisted by Tim Bell, Margaret Thatcher's PR guru,

Yeltsin had underlined his position as the only candidate who could stop Zyuganov. Like it or not, democrats like Yegor Gaidar reluctantly admitted they would back Yeltsin to stop the Communists winning. Feeling ridiculous and outmanoeuvred, Yavlinsky railed against the president, urging the electorate to vote against 'stupidity' and calling Yeltsin's presidency 'the bloodiest autocratic regime' since Stalin. Trying to present himself as the leader of the non-communist democratic opposition to Yeltsin, he said: 'If Boris Yeltsin wins the elections, the oligarchic, monopolistic, criminal and corrupt regime will grow stronger in Russia.' Already viewed by many as a pushy young man with an oversized ego, the display of spleen merely weakened his campaign further. One of the strongest charges that can be laid against Yavlinsky is that he lacks real political intuition, fatal in a politician seeking high office. Yavlinsky also had the disadvantage of facing anti-semitism from some quarters in Russian society. His Jewish background did not endear him to the country's numerous anti-semites, especially prevalent in rural Russia.[76]

The biggest winner of the first round was retired Lieutenant General Alexander Lebed, described by his devoted troops in the 14th Army as having 'the physique of Arnold Schwarzenegger and the brain of Albert Einstein'. In a variation of a George Bernard Shaw joke, some commentators have unkindly suggested the comparison should be reversed. Lebed's constituency tended to be the less educated and well-off voters who had previously voted for Zhirinovsky, but he also took votes off the Communists, beating Zyuganov in Murmansk and Arkhangelsk. He won a large share of the military vote, and even won votes from some sections of the middle class who were sick and tired of rising crime and corruption. For some of the electorate, who did not wish to support Yeltsin on the first round, a Lebed vote signified disenchantment with the president's regime without letting Zyuganov into the Kremlin. Many of these voters switched to Yeltsin in the second round, but their dissatisfaction with Yeltsin's administration had been registered. Forty-six-year-old Lebed, also known as Sasha, appeared the personification of the honest, Russian soldier: tall, blue-eyed and straight-talking. A self-declared teetotaller, Lebed stated that someone in Russia had to remain sober. Attractive to women voters (Lebed means Swan in Russian) despite his broken nose, some even admitted voting for him because he looked so smart in his uniform, and had a sexy, deep, gravelly voice.[77] As a Kremlin outsider, Lebed had the political advantage of not being tainted with the corruption of the old *nomenklatura*.

Lebed summed this feeling up: 'All of today's democrats are yesterday's communists, and high ranking ones at that. This is more true of Yeltsin than anyone else.'[78]

Lieutenant General Alexander Ivanovich Lebed was born on 20 April 1950, in Novocherkassk in the Rostov region, and was from a working-class background. In 1937 his father was late for work twice and sent to a labour camp for two years. General Lebed rose swiftly through the ranks, serving as the commander of a battalion in Afghanistan in 1981–82, where he was decorated with the Red Star. He took part in operations to quell unrest in the Caucasus in 1988–89, both in Georgia and Baku in Azerbaijan, where he helped put down an independence movement with loss of civilian life. A general by the age of 38, Lebed commanded an airborne division in the city of Tula in 1988–91, which he later represented in the Duma. After being ordered into Moscow by General Grachev, head of airborne forces, Lebed repelled an attack on Yeltsin's White House in 1991. He later claimed he would have carried out a direct order to take the parliament's headquarters.

In June 1992, Lebed assumed command of the 14th Army in Moldova, as fighting escalated between the Moldovans and the ethnic Russians in the so-called Dniester Moldovan Republic. It was at this time that Lebed attained national fame by protecting the ethnic Russians, enforcing a ceasefire, and attacking his military and political superiors for incompetence. Famously describing Yeltsin as a 'minus', Lebed also ripped into Defence Minister Grachev for alleged corruption and ineptitude for failing to reform the army. On more than one occasion, Lebed referred to Grachev as a 'prostitute'. Grachev, Lebed's former commander in Afghanistan, had become known as 'Pasha Mercedes' for allegedly enriching himself and fellow generals in the Russian withdrawal from Eastern Europe (particularly Germany). His denunciations grew in intensity following Russia's entanglement in the Chechen conflict and the disastrous assault on Grozny. The two-star General Lebed once offered to bring peace to Chechnya if he were given a regiment 'made up of the sons and grandsons of state Duma deputies and cabinet ministers'.[79]

A thorn in the side of Grachev, Lebed resisted attempts to remove him from the army, but resigned on 30 May 1995 to run for a seat in the Duma. The women of Tiraspol in Moldova, beside themselves with grief at his departure, lay down on the runway in a vain attempt to prevent their hero's departure. However, Lebed's election to the Duma in December 1995, as number two on the Congress of Russian

Communities (KRO) list, was not his first foray into politics. In September 1990, at the congress of the Russian (RSFSR) Communist Party he was elected a member of the party's Central Committee on the leftist-radical Movement of Communist Initiative ticket. Three years later, he was elected deputy of the Supreme Soviet of the Dniester Moldavian Republic for Tiraspol, obtaining 87.5 per cent of the poll. Lebed resigned his seat in mid-October 1993, in protest at the Dniester government's refusal to sack ministers who had sent soldiers to defend the White House against Yeltsin's tanks.'[80]

General Alexander Lebed has caused a degree of disquiet with his political views. In 1994, he voiced approval of General Pinochet's success in Chile, arguing that Pinochet was able to revive Chile by 'putting the army in the first place.' The dictator had managed to turn round the economy while killing 'fewer than 3,000 people'.[81] 'His so-called bloody regime lifted Chile from the ruins, forced everybody to work, revived the economy, restored a feeling of ownership among the people, then legally turned power over to a civilian government,' Lebed said.[82] Lebed later preferred to praise General Charles de Gaulle, who although a strong leader, had better democratic credentials. His commitment to democracy has also been brought into question by numerous other articles and statements. In an article published in *Nezavisimaya gazeta,* Lebed rejected democracy as harmful for Russia. The same piece called for the creation of a coalition of 'left, left-centrist, and patriotic forces', presumably with Lebed as leader.[83] In October 1995, Lebed came out with the following *bons mots*:

> Democracy is a good word. But in order for it to become a reality in Russia, a colossal amount of work is required. It is still early to speak about it. We will achieve it in two or three generations. I won't live to see that time, and you won't either.[84]

The monarchy, a single-party system and a parliamentary republic had all failed. In his view only a presidential system of government remained: 'A tsar, a general secretary, and a president are all the same – a form of authoritarian government.' This was the way it should be, he argued. After the first round, Lebed upset the West by describing the Mormons as 'mould and scum', using the term 'Jew' in a pejorative sense, and calling for tougher visa requirements for foreign businessmen, who came to Russia to 'steal'.[85] Lebed told Russians, 'We are the most intelligent country in the world: 74 per cent of the world's inventions have their origins in Russia.'[86] In July 1995, one Russian opinion poll gave Lebed 38 per cent, against only 8 per cent for Yeltsin in a possible run-off with the president.[87] However, by September 1995 Lebed had slipped to 14 per cent, and was still falling.[88] The electorate were starting to have their doubts about whether Lebed was ready to be president. The question of political maturity has continued to dog Lebed.

After his less than triumphant result with the KRO in the December Duma campaign, Lebed had almost been written off for the presidential elections. Lebed ran on a platform called 'An Ideology of Common Sense', which emphasised economic liberalisation, combating crime and corruption, protecting Russians living in the near abroad, and military reform. It also advocated the creation of a Union of Slavic Republics (the reincarnation of the Soviet Union).[89] Lebed further called for Russia to take 'appropriate countermeasures' if Russians living outside the Russian Federation were mistreated.[90]

Retired General Alexander Lebed came across to the electorate as a moderate nationalist, and a protector of the motherland, minus the unstable adventurism of Zhirinovsky. Zhirinovsky's book *Last Push to the South* said Russian soldiers would bathe their feet in the Indian Ocean. Asked whether he would serve under a President Zhirinovsky, Lebed said: 'No, I don't want to wash my feet in the Indian Ocean.'[91] Lebed repeatedly stressed that Russia had had enough of wars, whether in Afghanistan, Chechnya, or elsewhere. On Chechnya, he argued that the rebellious republic should be allowed to leave the Russian Federation if its people voted to do so in a referendum.[92] When it came to NATO enlargement, Lebed modified the outright opposition which he had displayed in the Duma election campaign. Although he thought expansion unwise, he felt that it was up to the West if it wanted to waste money on enlargement to the east:

> Personally, I am calm about this issue. Maybe others want to be more propagandistic, but I think that Russia simply cannot be aggressive any more. We have exhausted our appetite for wars. We do not want to fight any more . . . Russia is not planning to fight anyone. Truly this is so. And so this mighty fist is being developed to do battle with the air.[93]

Notwithstanding, Lebed had a plainly Russia First outlook when it came to foreign policy, saying:

I am deeply convinced that, before the end of this century, we will see the creation of a new state consisting of Russia, Ukraine, Belarus, and, probably, Kazakhstan. That is what is happening, you know. A double standard continues to exist. All of Europe is uniting, and we are dividing. It is time to put an end to this.[94]

Lebed adopted an uneasy *laissez-faire*, free-market attitude to the economy, based on low taxes and stringent tax collection. These ideas had been borrowed from Sergei Glazev, leader of the Democratic Party of Russia, and Lebed confessed he was no economic expert: 'I freely admit I'm no economist. My job is to restore order and instil conditions in which a normal market economy can operate. So I'll pave the way, and then I will locate intelligent economists to work out the details of economic policy.'[95] However, Lebed's real Russia First instincts were displayed in his 'foreign thieves' outburst, when he called for tighter visa restrictions to keep 'thieves' out of the country. On 27 July 1996, Lebed had said: 'Everyone comes to Russia to steal. I'm against this. Russia's wealth is for Russia.' His comments came after Russian authorities refused entry to Boris Jordan, one of the best-known foreign investors in Russia, giving no explanation for their decision. Suspicions were raised that this was because Jordan had upset influential business rivals in Russia. Alexander Lebed believed law and order had to precede economic reform. He said on this subject:

> If we free honest entrepreneurs and bankers from the criminals' dictates, our goods will be less expensive. Businessmen and bankers won't have to share their profits with the mafia; they'll be able to create more jobs and pay higher wages. If there is a bureau-crat, minister or governor who wants to side with the criminals, let him also do time with the criminals.[96]

Lebed railed against the 'bandits' who ruled the country, arguing that Yeltsin and Zyuganov were part of the old communist *nomenklatura*. 'We could clamp down on criminals if our top authorities obeyed their own laws. But no one believes that our authorities and criminals aren't one and the same.'[97]

As an individual politician, Alexander Lebed epitomised Russia First. A patriotic and upright former general, his nationalist credentials were unquestionable. His occasional outbursts against foreigners (including religious groups and businessmen) merely underlined his ideological hostility to 'Western' influences, especially the Western-inspired democratic model. The only concession to Western ideas was a hazy commitment to economic liberalisation, which in any event could be seen as in Russia's national interests. Lebed's nationalism was reinforced by his attitude towards re-integrating the CIS and his aggressive stance on defending Russians in the near abroad. For many Russians, Lebed symbolised what Russia First was about: a strong, powerful, incorruptible and independent Russia. Under Lebed, Russia would be respected in the world, while it clamped down on corruption and illegality at home. Lebed did not inititiate, lead, follow or exploit Russia First. He simply instinctively believed in it, and came to personsify Russia First in the minds of the Russian electorate. The secret of Lebed's success was that he was more personally identified with Russia First than any other single Russian politician, including Boris Yeltsin.

Yeltsin's presidential team realised Lebed was a great asset to their campaign. By opening up access to the pro-Yeltsin media, the president's team ensured that Lebed was the only opponent of the president to receive extensive television and newspaper coverage in the last days of the campaign. Yeltsin's campaign managers also gave Lebed $20 million to fund an extensive advertising campaign in the media in the crucial few days before the first round vote.[98] In what was almost certainly a pre-election agreement with Lebed, the general's profile was given a substantial boost, at the expense of rivals Zyuganov and Zhirinovsky. Yeltsin publicly announced he had identified the candidate who would be the next president after himself (an oblique reference to Lebed), a view shared by the fatalistic General Lebed. On 16 June Lebed had told television viewers that he was destined to rule Russia.[99] Lebed's creaming-off of the nationalist vote gave Yeltsin his narrow win over Zyuganovin the first round, and destroyed Zhirinovsky's campaign. The ultra-nationalist LDPR leader, who had once attended a meeting in the Duma on a motorbike (not as stupid as he acts, Zhirinovsky speaks four languages and graduated from the prestigious Institute of Asia and Africa, and the law faculty of Moscow State University), was finally well and truly beaten.[100] Alexander Lebed, Mr Russia First, was the newly appointed kingmaker. Rejecting overtures from Zyuganov's camp, Lebed was appointed secretary of the national Security Council by President Yeltsin on Tuesday 18 June, two days after the first round.

Gennady Zyuganov's presidential campaign was in fact a relative success compared to his party's efforts in the Duma elections in

December 1995. By building a broad coalition of the Left (his popular-patriotic forces), Zyuganov had received backing from two hundred public organisations, and ensured he was the only candidate of the Left to represent the communists with some nationalist support. Nevertheless, Zyuganov was still presented as the Communist Party's candidate by Yeltsin and his other presidential adversaries. Zyuganov actually increased both the share (22–32 per cent) and the number of votes (15–24 million) obtained by the Communist Party compared to the December poll, and even broadly scored better than all the leftist parties combined (they had received 32 per cent and 22 million votes). Even so, Zyuganov's campaign cannot be said to have been a triumph. He had failed to make a breakthrough, and it was clear that his vote was approaching a ceiling. With an ageing supporters' profile, the Communists' vote could only decline in the middle to long term. Adding up the votes of the other presidential candidates, whose supporters were likely to switch to Yeltsin, it was already clear that Zyuganov had lost the second round. Zyuganov had campaigned vigorously in the regions, but as the pre-election period progressed, he was increasingly overshadowed and outwitted by the president.

Gennady Andreyevich Zyuganov, aged 51, was born in the village of Mymrino, in a farming area in Russia's Black Earth region, 250 miles south of Moscow. His parents, neither of whom joined the Communist Party, were schoolteachers. Zyuganov himself went on to study mathematics at the Pedagogical Institute in the regional capital of Orel, where he led the students' union and the local Komsomol Communist youth organisation. Climbing the regional party apparatus in Orel, he became CPSU party secretary of Orel city and then head of department in the region. In 1983, he was invited to Moscow to work for the Soviet Communist Party's (CPSU) Central Committee, where he rose to become deputy head of the ideology department. At the first congress of the KPRF in June 1990, he was elected secretary and member of the Politburo of the party's Central Committee. Elected to the Duma in 1993, he became leader of the party's faction in the parliament from January 1994. In 1995, Zyuganov was awarded a doctorate in philosophy at Moscow State University. Though he had a respectable career, Zyuganov never reached the first rank of the party's apparatus. Zyuganov's political break came with the demise of the Soviet Union. As most members of the *nomenklatura* jumped ship for better jobs in the private sector or switched political allegiance, Zyuganov and others grimly remained loyal to the Communist Party (CPSU), even when it was banned under Yeltsin in the early 1990s. Many former apparatchiks either missed the opportunities others grabbed, or ideologically found themselves unable to abandon long-held beliefs. Zyuganov was probably one of the latter. His writings, although turgid, are full of the historical struggle between 'Westernisers' and xenophobic Slavic purists. Adrian Karatnycky said of Zyuganov's books: 'He has a deep historical view of Russia's mission as the opposition to the dissolute West. He's a big believer in the decline of the West and the emergence of a new civilization.' Zyuganov believes in a reborn Russia, prosperous, powerful and pure.[101]

Zyuganov's foreign policy has been well documented, and its Russia First themes were successfully adopted by President Yeltsin. On Chechnya, Zyuganov was almost as hawkish as Yeltsin, calling for a peace conference, but warning that Russia's 'territorial integrity' was at stake. Chechen rebels who did not accept the results of the peace conference would, in his words, be dealt with 'harshly'.[102] On domestic policy, Zyuganov was heavily criticised because he tried to appear all things to all people. Speaking to Western listeners, for example to a business audience in Davos in Switzerland, he would appear a mixed-economy 'social democrat'. At the World Economic Forum in Davos in February, Zyuganov promised lower taxation, stable conditions for foreign investment and guaranteed rights for private ownership. He also said the KPRF was more of social-democratic party.[103] Addressing an audience in Siberia, he would resemble a Soviet-style xenophobe. It is difficult to penetrate Zyuganov's political mask, but the answer to Zyuganov's true beliefs probably lies somewhere between the two. He is, like everyone else, a product of his upbringing and experiences. He bears the burden of Russia's endemic racial bigotry (especially anti-semitism) and was trained in the rigid Communist Party apparatchik school. Zyuganov knew he had to change with the times, but it was hard for him, and harder still for the 500,000 ageing party members whom he led. Zyuganov had to keep the party with him, and this dictated his receptiveness to new ideas (such as 'social democracy'). There were, however, some tangible differences of style to his old CPSU days. Zyuganov scrapped the party's opposition to Russian Orthodoxy, and he proudly paraded his endorsements from the Orthodox Church. Attending a rally in Novosibirsk in Siberia under a huge banner reading 'The Orthodox Church for Zyuganov', two icons were held over his head. In his standard campaign speech, Zyuganov revealed he had been endorsed by Father Vladimir, the spiritual leader of the nationalist Cossack movement. Yet again, Yeltsin had gone one better, receiving the approbation of the Patriarch, Aleksy II.[104]

Zyuganov's standard campaign pitch included criticising President Yeltsin for destroying the Soviet Union, ruining Russian industry and the country's scientific base, causing the Chechen war and failing to deal with rising crime and corruption. According to Zyuganov, the contest was not one between 'democracy' and 'communism', but rather: 'the choice is very simple: either you are for Russia and the Russians, or you are against them'. This was Russia First in its most crude and simplistic form. Calling the president *Mister* Yeltsin (a foreign form of address), Zyuganov implied he was a Western agent, out to destroy the interests of the country.[105] Zyuganov's favourite joke on the stump was 'I drink considerably less than Mr Yeltsin, but a little more than Mr Gorbachev.' Gorbachev had introduced a highly unpopular anti-alcohol campaign during the years of *perestroika*. Another preferred line was to regale his audiences with miserable and morbid statistics. 'Do you know what is the biggest queue in Russia today?' he would ask. 'It is the queue for the cemetery.' Zyuganov would point to the 1 million Russians who died the previous year, falling life expectancy and rising infant mortality.[106] Warming to his subject, he said:

> If you took all the investors who have been swindled since Yeltsin came to office, they would form a queue from Moscow to Lake Baikal. If you lined up the hungry people in our country, the queue would stretch from Moscow to the Urals. And if you took the unemployed, the queue would reach the Volga at least.[107]

Russia had taken hundreds of years to build an empire and was shrinking to the borders it had in the fifteenth century. 'Our territory,' he boomed, 'is reduced to the one we had three to four hundred years ago. Our living standards are now the level of the 1950s. The level of the banditry is what we had at the end of the civil war.'[108] President Yeltsin was 'a Western agent . . . who has betrayed the interests of his country'.[109] He referred to meeting foreign bankers and the lessons he learned from recent trips to the far east. Why is it, he asked rhetorically, that in four years of reform Russia attracted just $5 billion (£3.3 billion) of foreign investment, while Hungary attracted $30 billion and China $100 billion.[110]

Zyuganov also showed a reformist side when he told an audience in Voronezh that the old Communist Party was not blameless:

> We really have only ourselves to blame. We weren't doing the necessary reforms. We maintained command administrative distance which suited wartime conditions but was completely obsolete for today's needs. The party tried to conserve its monopoly of ownership of power and truth, but it ended up by not only destroying itself but our country.[111]

When speaking to students at Novgorod University in March, he again presented his reformist face, saying he would increase support for industry, science and education, reform the tax code and attract greater foreign investment.[112] But Zyuganov patently failed to win over the young in significant numbers, either in Novgorod or elsewhere in Russia. Nor was this due solely to the lack of any great personal charisma. Dull as his speeches could be, Zyuganov was a genial, personable figure of some charm. But try as he might, Zyuganov seemed to be offering the remedies of the past for the ills of the present.

To understand Zyuganov's real political soul, one has to look at his writings, his manifesto and his much-maligned economic programme. Significantly, Zyuganov mentioned the word 'communism' only once in his election manifesto, while the term 'fatherland' was used on no fewer than nineteen occasions.[113] In the early 1990s, Zyuganov used to visit the home of Alexander Prokhanov, editor of the ultra-nationalist and anti-semitic *Zavtra* newspaper. At Prokhanov's home, Zyuganov used to have political discussions with politicians, generals and intellectuals of the far Right and Left, forming imaginary cabinets. Zyuganov became a member of *Zavtra's* editorial board.[114] In a sense, Zyuganov is more a nationalist than a communist. Zyuganov became even closer to ultra-nationalists when, after August 1991, he became chairman of the co-ordinating council of the People's Patriotic Front of Russia, and leader of the National Salvation front (a group including Bolsheviks, neo-fascists and a general of the KGB). At meetings two flags were displayed, the red Soviet banner and the black, yellow and gold of the tsarist era.[115]

Zyuganov's political thinking is to be found in two books, *Beyond the Horizon* and *Russia and the World.* Zyuganov lamented the early passing of Stalin, and repeatedly stated in speeches that Stalin had 'only' killed about half a million people 'and most of those were party members'. Stalin, he wrote, 'understood the urgent necessity of harmonising new realities with a centuries-long Russian tradition.' If Stalin had only lived a few more years, he would have 'restored Russia and saved it from the

234 · RUSSIA FIRST

cosmopolitans'. Zyuganov is referring to the Jews. In *I Believe in Russia*
he stated that there had been much to fear from Jewish influence since
the nineteenth century. 'The ideology, culture and world outlook of the
Western world became more and more influenced by the Jews scattered
around the world. Jewish influence grew not by the day, but by the
hour.' The Jewish diaspora came to control the financial life of the
continent, he argued. The West was trying to create a liberal-democ-
ratic heaven on earth. The planet, he believed, would come to be ruled
over by a 'united world government', supported by representatives of
the Trilateral Commission and the American Council of Foreign
Relations. International institutions like the UN, IMF and World Bank
had gone out of their way to undermine Russia. Zyuganov wished
Russia had taken the advice of the Chinese (a model he admires) to not
take *glasnost* too far under Gorbachev. His works reek of slightly
paranoic, anti-Western rhetoric. Zyuganov told an American
businessman he would not adopt 'social democracy' as a label, simply
because 'communist' was a good trademark in Russia. In reality,
Zyuganov was some way from being what would pass for a social
democrat in the West.[116]

Attacked for being unrealistic, Zyuganov's economic policies were
different from the centrally-planned economic models of the Soviet era.
According to one commentator, they more resembled the Alternative
Economic Strategy advocated by the British Labour Party in the early
1980s. In fact, they were a domestic version of Russia First, and part of
an economic package of measures designed to restore Russia's
economy. Zyuganov had pledged on the campaign trail that 5 million
Russians were involved in small businesses and to get rid of them would
cause a civil war. Therefore he felt: 'We have to keep all forms of
ownership. I am in favour of every family keeping its own plot of
land.'[117] Calling for a mixed economy, the programme also outlined a
more active role for the state, particularly in the oil and gas sectors.
Russia should not become a 'raw material appendage for the West', and
subsidies and protective measures would be used to help domestic
industries. Energy and transport prices should be subsidised. Taxes
should be lowered and monetary discipline relaxed. Import duties and
taxes would be raised, and capital flight blocked. There would be
increased spending on social welfare, pensions, education and science.
Russia would not incur further foreign debt.[118] In its tone and content,
Zyuganov's economic policy was pure Russia First. None of this,
however, helped Zyuganov's campaign. Zyuganov was still portrayed

by the media as a throw-back to the old Soviet Communist Party and the excesses of Stalinism. Lebed, by contrast, had the advantage of epitomising Russia First, whilst not having to carry the ideological and electoral burden of a career in the Communist Party. Yeltsin's presidential team borrowed the useful parts of Zyuganov's programme and ditched the rest. After the votes had been counted on 16 June, attention switched to the Kremlin and the wheeling and dealing of those political forces who really mattered. Yeltsin needed Lebed's backing to ensure victory in the second round. With the support of 'Mr Russia First' himself, Yeltsin's victory over Zyuganov was guaranteed. [119]

APPOINTMENTS AND SACKINGS BEFORE THE SECOND ROUND

The run-up to the second round was dominated by the appointment of Alexander Lebed as secretary of the Security Council, and the sacking of the 'hardliners' surrounding Boris Yeltsin. The secretary of the Security Council oversaw internal security, defence and the FSB (the former KGB). General Lebed immediately made a bid for greater powers, saying he expected Yeltsin to extend his remit to areas such as Russia's 'financial independence', capital flight and the plight of millions of people defrauded by bogus investment funds.[120] Lebed's statement was an early challenge to the authority of Prime Minister Chernomyrdin, who was responsible for running the economy. The Kremlin in-fighting had already begun.

The first head to roll was that of General Pavel Grachev, the unpopular minister of defence. Grachev's demise had been predicted many times before and the only remarkable fact about his departure was that it had been delayed for so long. Yeltsin had kept Grachev in post for two reasons. First, General Grachev had been instrumental in ensuring Yeltsin received army backing during the attempted coup of August 1991, the president's finest hour when he had defended Russian democracy atop a tank outside the White House. Grachev had organised the defence of the White House, and thenceforth became one of Yeltsin's 'inner circle', and a personal friend. Second, it was politically expedient for Yeltsin to retain Grachev while at the same time publicly castigating him for the Chechen disaster, conveniently shifting the blame away from himself. General Grachev had been one of the instigators of the conflict, assuring Yeltsin that the rebels would be rapidly crushed. He later claimed Russia's young conscripts were dying with 'smiles on their faces' in Chechnya. Grachev had also been tainted by allegations of corruption, and under suspicion following the death of a journalist (via a bomb in a briefcase) who had been investigating the charges. The defence minister had laughed off the death, saying the journalist had probably been 'playing with explosives'.[121] The president would choose the most politically opportune moment to sack Grachev, so obtaining the maximum credit for his removal.

With the appointment of Alexander Lebed on 18 June, Grachev's time had come. Lebed had repeatedly attacked Grachev, and the defence minister's sacking would seal Yeltsin's alliance with the new security chief, while showing the public a new broom had entered the president's administration. Yeltsin said : 'This is not simply an appointment. This is a unification of two politicians. All those who voted for Alexander Ivanovich [Lebed] have given an order to the president to fulfil the good things they have seen in the programme of Alexander Ivanovich.' The 'clean-up' operation advocated by Lebed could be seen to be in hand. Sacked the same day Lebed was appointed (technically the defence minister 'resigned'), Grachev took himself off to his country dacha, where defence sources were quoted as saying he had been 'drinking vodka ever since'. Yeltsin reportedly drove out to Grachev's dacha to find the general in an alcohol-induced depression. Grachev's pistol had been confiscated, following fears he might commit suicide. According to the defence sources, Yeltsin promised his friend he would 'sort something out' after the elections. Mikhail Kolesnikov, head of the general staff, was appointed acting defence minister.

Yeltsin followed-up Grachev's removal by sacking seven generals in the defence ministry, who were all closely allied to Grachev. This can be seen as part of the Yeltsin–Lebed pact. In return, Lebed predicted that 'no less than 80 per cent' of the 11 million people who voted for him would vote for President Yeltsin. The seven generals included Grachev's chief of staff, Valery Lapshov; Colonel General Dmitry Kharchenko, head of the general staff department and a relative of Grachev's; and Lieutenant General Vladimir Shulikov, former deputy commander-in-chief of the notoriously corrupt Western Group of Armies (Russian forces formerly based in Europe). Also sacked were the deputy head of the general staff (Colonel General Anatoly Victor Barynkin), and the head of the defence ministry's ideology department (Lieutenant General Sergei Zdorikov).[122]

The removal of Alexander Korzhakov, Mikhail Barsukov and Oleg

Soskovets was not pre-planned by Yeltsin. His hand was forced by an extraordinary move by the three men to precipitate a crisis and postpone the second round. On the night of Wednesday 19 June, members of General Korzhakov's presidential security guard seized two of President Yeltsin's campaign aides outside the White House (government headquarters). The two men were Arkady Yevstafyev, a former Chubais aide and television executive, and Sergei Lisovsky, a rock club manager and millionaire pop impresario. Lisovsky had been particularly involved in arranging rock concerts to garner the youth vote. Both men were carrying a box allegedly containing $500,000 (£320,000) in cash. The two men claimed the money was from a legal source and was to pay for the pop concerts put on by Yeltsin's campaign team.[123] While Yevstafyev and Lisovsky were questioned at gunpoint for eleven hours, NTV alerted Chubais, who contacted Lebed. Late that night, Russian television news reported that the arrest of the two aides had been the work of Korzhakov and Barsukov, and had been an attempt to thwart democracy and prevent the second round taking place. General Lebed conducted a live television news conference at 4 a.m. on Thursday morning, giving the plotters a stern warning. 'Attempts are being made to wreck the second round,' he said, 'Any mutiny will be crushed, and crushed with extreme severity. Those who would plunge the country into the depths of bloody chaos do not deserve pity.'[124]

Yevstafyev and Lisovsky said Korzhakov's men had tried to obtain compromising information about Chernomyrdin and Chubais, using the alleged illegal government funding of Yeltsin's campaign as a pretext. 'They kept saying that the president would win anyway, but that it would be thanks to true patriots, and not to people who had greased their way into his favour,' Yevstafyev told reporters. Anatoly Chubais felt the detention was a ham-fisted attempt to remove Chernomyrdin and the reformers from office, so providing the plotters with an excuse to postpone the second round and mount a coup. The Russian media reported that the three men had hoped to convince Yeltsin to replace Chernomyrdin with Soskovets, and cancel the second round of elections. Conspiracy theorists calculated that Soskovets then might seek to replace Yeltsin, which would be possible if Yeltsin became physically incapacitated.[125] The issue of illegal election funding itself was a real one. Apart from the $500,000 removed from the White House, experts estimated that Yeltsin had spent as much as $10 million on the 'vote or you lose' campaign before the first round, and nearly

$15 million on hidden advertisements in the local press (compared to a legal spending ceiling of just under $3 million).[126]

However, the significance of the White House arrests was that they led to the removal of Yeltsin's 'inner circle'. On the morning of Thursday 20 June, President Yeltsin held a meeting with Korzhakov and Chubais. Looking tired and drawn, Yeltsin then went on Russian television to announce the sacking of Korzhakov, Barsukov and Soskovets. It had clearly been a difficult decision for Yeltsin to sack his three friends, particularly Korzhakov and Barsukov, with whom he liked to relax in the sauna over vodka and gherkins. Yeltsin said he sacked the three to get 'fresh faces into his team', but he also displayed anger over the stupidity of the three plotters. He told the media: 'What, is the president supposed to be working for Korzhakov?' The president went on: 'I was never under Korzhakov's thumb. Can't you understand the fact that he lacks it up here? I don't want to be precise what he lacks, but it's the main thing.' Referring to the three sacked men, Yeltsin said: 'They have taken too much and given too little.'

The president had been indulgent towards the three men for a long time. However, the trio had plainly over-reached their authority and potentially undermined the president politically. It was the first time in eleven years of friendship that Yeltsin felt personally let down by Korzhakov. By saying they had taken too much and given too little, Yeltsin meant the trio had benefited from the perks of office (and more besides) but left him to shoulder the burden of his re-election campaign almost single-handed. Nevertheless, Yeltsin turned the situation to his own political advantage. Sacking Korzhakov, Barsukov and Soskovets gave the president the opportunity to show that he was 'cleaning-up' the Kremlin in response to the strong anti-corruption law and order campaign, led by Alexander Lebed. The three men were notoriously unpopular outside the Kremlin's inner sanctum. The sackings also reinforced the Yeltsin–Lebed pact, giving General Lebed all the political scalps he could wish for. The reformers, led by Anatoly Chubais, were jubilant that the 'hardliners' or 'war party' had been so decisively defeated in the Kremlin power struggle. But Yeltsin now became personally isolated, as he removed the very people on whom he had (unwisely) come to rely. Zyuganov's attempt to make political capital from the crisis failed miserably. The president had sacrificed his friends, but in the process had guaranteed his victory in the second round.

Korzhakov had feared that Yeltsin could lose the presidential election. This had been given more credence by the defeat of the reformist mayor of St Petersburg, Anatoly Sobchak, in May. Russia had also been threatened with political instability, as bombs exploded in Moscow, one killing four people and injuring twelve on the underground on 12 June.[127] Some commentators saw the bombs as the work of those wanting to call off the elections, others saw them as acts of terrorism by Chechen separatists. However, on balance, what Korzhakov and his colleagues feared most was the arrival in the Kremlin of Alexander Lebed, and the threat this posed to their political survival. The White House incident was the trio's attempt to fight back, while they still could. Of course the plot badly backfired, playing into the hands of Lebed and Chubais.

The sacking of Alexander Korzhakov was highly symbolic. He had come to be regarded as a latter-day Rasputin, with far greater influence on the president than his post would indicate. General Alexander Korzhakov was born in 1950, and joined the KGB twenty years later, where he eventually met Boris Yeltsin. In 1985, when Korzhakov was a major in the KGB's Ninth Directorate (responsible for guarding government officials), he was assigned to protect Yeltsin, who had just been brought to Moscow as CPSU secretary of the Central Committee. Korzhakov followed Yeltsin to his new post of first secretary of the Moscow city party. When Gorbachev sacked Yeltsin from the Politburo in 1987, the two men kept in touch, and Korzhakov offered to continue protecting his boss without pay. Yeltsin recalled in his memoirs how, when he was elected to the People's Congress in 1989, Korzhakov would drive him around in his own car, a Niva. Yeltsin wrote: 'On our days off, I sometimes visited him in his quaint little native village outside Moscow. There wasn't enough room for us all in his small cottage, so we set up a tent outside, and went fishing and swimming in the river.' Once Korzhakov tore off a car door with his bare hands to rescue Yeltsin from a car accident. Korzhakov set up a security service when Yeltsin became chairman of the Russian parliament in 1990, and another when he was elected president the following year. During the August 1991 coup, Korzhakov was at Yeltsin's side, guarding him and preparing possible escape routes if it became necessary to use them. Later, in the autumn of 1993, Korzhakov and his side-kick Barsukov personally led the crack Alpha battalion into the White House, to capture the seat of the rebellious Duma. By March 1995, Sergei Filatov, Yeltsin's chief of staff (later removed), complained about the growing power of Korzhakov's *apparat*, which included its own research centre and up to 20,000 staff. Filatov claimed some Kremlin staff held conversations by scribbling on pieces of paper to circumvent being bugged.[128]

At 46, Korzhakov was a government minister in charge of presidential security, a key member of the Security Council, involved in Russian arms exports, and the commander of 40,000 troops based outside Moscow at the call of the president. In May Korzhakov's status had been officially confirmed when Yeltsin issued a decree making him the president's first assistant with the rank of minister. Korzhakov also participated in a lucrative tax-free alcohol concession run by the National Sports Fund, headed by Shamil Tarpischev, Yeltsin's tennis coach. Increasingly, Korzhakov came to meddle in affairs of state, ranging from advocating a military solution to the Chechen crisis to publicly arguing for a postponement of the presidential elections. On 30 November 1994, Korzhakov wrote to Prime Minister Chernomrydin, advising him to reassess Russia's agreements with the World Bank over oil exports. Korzhakov believed they were not in the best interests of Russia, writing: 'Concluding these agreements will increase the dependence on foreign capital . . . and consequently reduce the competitiveness of potential Russian exports . . . This is absolutely impermissible.' He said a commission of inquiry should be set up under his ally, Oleg Soskovets. Two days later, Korzhakov's men attacked Most bank's bodyguards, a practical demonstration of the security chief's political and physical muscle.

President Yeltsin's relationship with Korzhakov over the years had been extremely close. Korzhakov gave Yeltsin his papers in the morning, opened his car doors, and stayed up with him when he could not sleep. Korzhakov would often join Yeltsin's family for lunch over the weekend at the president's country dacha. Korzhakov was at Yeltsin's bedside when he was ill in the summer and autumn of 1995, controlling access to the president, and reputedly even refusing to hand over the black box containing the nuclear attack codes to Chernomyrdin when requested. Yeltsin had literally put his life in Korzhakov's hands, and his bodyguard was there with him at all the defining moments of his political life. It was rumoured that Yeltsin 'over-slept' at Shannon airport, missing a meeting with the Irish prime minister on the tarmac, after a drinking bout with his buddy, Korzhakov, who was always ready with his hip-flask of vodka. Yeltsin recalled in 1994: 'To this day, Korzhakov never leaves my side, and we even sit up at nights during trips together. He is a very decent, intelligent, strong and courageous person. While outwardly he seems very simple, behind the simplicity is a sharp mind and an excellent and clear head.' While Yeltsin retracted his views on Korzhakov's intelligence, it is clear he felt a great deal of loyalty and affection towards his friend and bodyguard. It was not an easy decision for Yeltsin to sack Korzhakov, after all they had gone through together. But in the end, Yeltsin could and would not allow his shadow to walk on his own.[129]

The White House incident gave an insight into the presidential style of government that had evolved under Boris Yeltsin. Yeltsin had developed an imperial style harking back to the days of the tsarist court. Gorbachev, Fyodorov and Zyuganov complained that Yeltsin was acting like a modern day tsar, complete with his own 'inner circle' of courtiers.[130] Korzhakov's rise was an example of how, like Alexander Menshikov under Peter the Great, a *muzhik* (a down to earth, strong fellow) could come from nowhere to reach the pinnacle of power and influence beside his tsar. In this world, power was not dependent on office or ability, but rather proximity to the tsar. The tsar, like Yeltsin, would surround himself with people he could trust and relax with, and upon whom he would shower his considerable favours. Other modern courtiers would include men like Victor Ilyushin, the president's closest remaining adviser, who had followed his leader from his relatively humble beginnings as party boss in Yekaterinburg.

Nor were these comparisons with Russia's tsarist past wholly fanciful. Yeltsin's Russia had re-introduced the two-headed eagle as its symbol of statehood (replacing the hammer and sickle), while the presidential guards wore early twentieth-century tsarist uniforms, costing £600 a time.[131] Even at Yeltsin's inauguration ceremony as president on 9 August 1996, the tsarist symbolism was overpowering. The tsarist emblem of the two-headed Russian eagle was borne aloft on the presidential standard, while music from Glinka's *A Life for the Tsar* accompanied the proceedings. Strengthening links with Russia's imperial, orthodox past, the head of the Russian Orthodox church was on hand to bless the re-elected tsar-president. Zhirinovsky remarked after the ceremony: 'We have just sworn in a very good tsar.'[132]

Ruling with the increasing use of tsarist decrees or *ukasy*, Yeltsin had also re-established the imperial system of gubernatorial rule in the provinces, albeit with the reluctant introduction of an elective system. The result of all this, in Duma Speaker Gennady Seleznyev's memorable phrase was to create 'a democratic dictatorship'.[133] However, surprisingly, both Yeltsin and Zyuganov shared an admiration for Peter the Great, the former as a role model, the latter as an example of a great reformer. Zyuganov (who labelled Yeltsin the 'tsar-president'), demonstrated the contradictions of modern Russia by displaying both a bust of Lenin and a picture of Peter the Great in his private office in the Duma.[134] In Yeltsin's own mind, he had already become the 'Good Tsar', dispensing favours on his campaign tours of the provinces. Yavlinsky, however, was less impressed, and attacked the president's courtiers: 'Don't speak to me any more about the good tsar and the bad boyars [aristocrats]. Boris Yeltsin himself invited them to work with him and he is responsible for what they do.'[135] The image of the 'Good Tsar' cultivated by Boris Yeltsin complimented the Kremlin's Russia First strategy. A powerful, latter-day tsar evoked Russia's 'great power' past, and eschewed accusations that the country was slavishly emulating Western democratic or economic models. Russia was clearly adopting its own political and economic models, based on its historical traditions and experiences.

Although the vote had been largely a fair exercise in democracy, Russia was still some way from having a Western-style democratic system. In looking to the past to justify his authority, Yeltsin effortlessly reverted to the Russian traditions of the tsarist period. It was as if the communist interregnum had been a historical abberation, with occasional bows to the ageing communist electorate (hence the use of the Red Flag at some official ceremonies). Yeltsin's administration pointed backwards to a period of authoritarianism, rather than forwards to a wholly democratic future. After all, in the history and psychology of the Russian people, authoritarianism, however they might complain about it, was a more familiar system than Western-style democracy. Zyuganov too, understood the nostalgia for Russia's pre-Soviet past, and repeatedly referred to the frontiers of the former Russian Empire. While many of the trappings of tsardom were a matter of personal style, the fact that Russians accepted Yeltsin's projection of himself as a modern tsar should worry those who believe Russia is on the verge of becoming a Western-style democracy. Meanwhile, back at the Kremlin, while one group of courtiers had been ejected, others were taking their place. The new and immediate struggle would be between the courtiers surrounding 'Prince' Lebed (supported by 'Count' Luzhkov), and those defending 'Prince' Chernomyrdin, with 'Count' Chubais and the reformist aristocrats bobbing from side to side. Yeltsin looked on, like an ageing and gradually failing King Lear.[136]

President Yeltsin was still game enough to attempt to play his tradi-

tional court tactics of divide and rule. Before the first round, Yeltsin
had held out the possibility of a series of pacts, deals and even the
formation of a national coalition government. Yeltsin had floated the
idea of a broadly-based government of national unity in May.[137]
Yavlinsky was still waiting by the telephone for the president's call after
the first round of voting. After the 16 June vote, Yeltsin appealed to
'honest communists' to vote for him, saying Russia should not be
divided between reds and whites. Hinting at the idea of forming a coalition on 27 June, Yeltsin said he was 'ready for a dialogue and co-operation with everyone whose main priority is the fate of Russia'.[138] The
week before, Zyuganov had suggested forming a coalition government,
naming fourteen candidates to form the government (including non-
communists), and hinted that he would be willing to serve under
Yeltsin as prime minister.[139] However, Zyuganov's suggestion was seen
as an act of political desperation, while Yeltsin's call was cleverly timed
to cream-off communist support before the second round vote. In
reality, Yeltsin had no intention of doing a deal with Zyuganov, but
hoped to pick off some of the Communist's leader's more moderate
supporters. Zyuganov's advances to Lebed before and after his
appointment as secretary of the Security Council had been firmly
rebuffed.[140] Pictured in the Kremlin by Russian television on the day of
his appointment, Lebed said he had chosen a new idea, and rejected an
old one.

Yeltsin's campaign team sought to narrow the odds further by
switching polling day from the traditional Sunday to Wednesday 3 July.
This was achieved through the mechanism of declaring 3 July a national
holiday (via a presidential decree) and obtaining the support of the
malleable Central Electoral Commission, led by the pro-Yeltsin Nikolai
Ryabov. The idea was that Yeltsin's supporters were more wealthy than
the average communist voter, and might be away at their weekend
dachas and not bother to vote in the second round. Apathy, and a poor
turn-out by Yeltsin supporters was the one factor which could have
deprived Yeltsin of victory.[141] On election day itself, Moscow mayor
Yury Luzhkov, who had been re-elected mayor on 16 June with over 90
per cent of the vote, appealed on local radio for Muscovites to stay in
the city and vote. Luzhkov's role in the campaign (apart from mobilising financial backing) had always been to ensure the Muscovites
backed Yeltsin.[142]

Yeltsin had also received personal endorsement from presidential
candidate Svyatoslav Fyodorov, while Yavlinsky and Zhirinovsky both

said they could not support Zyuganov. Yavlinsky went further, telling his electorate to participate actively in the second round, and warning that a vote against both candidates could mean indirect support for Zyuganov.[143] In any event, Yeltsin was guaranteed support from the majority of Yavlinsky's voters, who would vote for the president to keep Zyuganov out. General Lebed's endorsement was more problematic. There was no guarantee that Lebed's voters would all troop out to support the president. Yeltsin had already made efforts with his personnel changes to woo Lebed's vote, and the general's appointment was also likely to appease Lebed's electoral constituency. A vote for Yeltsin would be a vote to keep Lebed in the Kremlin. In a further effort to attract Lebed's 11 million voters, in a campaign trip to the Baltic enclave of Kaliningrad, Yeltsin echoed Lebed's call for 'freedom and order'. The president promised he would defend the rights of Russian speaking minorities in the Baltic states. Yeltsin said: 'guaranteeing the basic rights and freedoms of our compatriots is a priority for me'. Russia First had once again raised its head in the race for the presidency.[144]

Just in case anyone thought Lebed had gone soft after his appointment to the Kremlin, he made his infamous speech describing Mormons as 'scum and mould'. General Lebed said they were a threat to the country's security, imported specifically to weaken Russian moral fibre and destroy the state. He promised his supporters to get back the money they had lost by pyramid selling, return Cossacks to their land, work for economic union with Ukraine and Belarus, expel foreign sects, and promote Russian artists and culture. For good measure he said that Ukrainians, Russians and Belarussians were 'one people', who would eventually be brought back into a 'mutual embrace'.[145] Lebed referred to himself as a 'semi-democrat', and told the host of Russian public television's *Rush Hour* that he would fight crime by 'shooting [people] but reasonably, with minimum waste for the police and other power-wielding structures'. The reservist general then announced that he wanted to increase his power over security issues, and favoured restoring the vice presidency to institutionalise his status as Yeltsin's right-hand man.[146] Lebed's outbursts had already been publicly slapped-down by Chernomyrdin, who had dismissed the retired general's claims to have put down a coup by generals linked to Grachev as 'nonsense' and told him to tone down his remarks in future.[147]

Lebed was concerned by the fact that his new office did not in itself guarantee him a say over security policy. The Security Council, although important, was essentially a consultative body which prepared decisions for the president. Lebed's authority was thus dependent upon his political standing, and usefulness to the president. He was thus dispensable unless he could carve out a role for himself, a move bound to be resisted by other Kremlin insiders. As in-fighting in the Kremlin intensified, Lebed's supporters were given the unmistakable impression that their man was determined to shake up the president's government. Now the only cloud on the horizon was Yeltsin's deteriorating health. Yeltsin cancelled his planned attendance at the G7 summit in Lyon at the end of June, and sent Chernomyrdin in his stead. Despite his campaign team's skilful attempt to give tactical reasons for Yeltsin's non-appearance at Lyon, it was obvious his health had once again taken a turn for the worse.[148]

THE SECOND ROUND RESULTS AND THE NEW GOVERNMENT

The election campaign between the first and second rounds had focused on the appointment of Alexander Lebed and the sacking of Yeltsin's former 'inner circle'. The rest of the campaign between the two rounds was largely a non-event. Yeltsin disappeared from public view after last being seen in the Kremlin on Wednesday 26 June, drinking copious toasts of vodka with a group of army cadets.[149] Yeltsin cancelled a planned campaign trip to Tula on Thursday 27 June, and failed to appear at a Friday meeting with farmers at the Kremlin. Zyuganov stayed in Moscow, and his campaign stalled as it appeared the Communists ran out of money and confidence. In effect, Zyuganov and his campaign manager Kuptsov decided they had no chance of winning, and settled into a mood of dejection and defeatism.[150] The Russian media ignored Yeltsin's absence from the political scene, and the Russian electorate was generally unaware of the president's latest ill health. Election aides claimed Yeltsin had a 'sore throat' and needed a few days rest after the strenuous campaign.[151] A bizarre pantomime was conducted by Yeltsin's campaign team, as the election proceeded in the absence of the main political figure (unthinkable in the West). Russian television maintained a flow of stories on Yeltsin's statements, but used archive film of the president. A special diet of anti-communist propaganda was broadcast, showing starving children, executions, ration cards and the gulag. The accompanying message said: 'The

Communists didn't even bother to change their name. They won't change their methods.'

On Monday 1 July, two days before the poll, a frail Yeltsin was recorded on Russian television news, telling the electorate to reject the Communist challenge by Zyuganov, and go out and vote. In a two minute address, Yeltsin, speaking in a slow and deliberate voice, told the Russian people there was only 'one road to a normal life'. The president continued that in the first round of the elections 'the majority of you voted for a free and normal life, and also said firmly that the time had come to wed freedom and order, to care for the people. I accepted your will as a direct mandate for action.' Zyuganov tried to make the president's health an issue, but was ignored by the Russian media. 'Today they are suggesting we vote for a living corpse,' Zyuganov said somewhat indelicately.[152] On election day itself, Yeltsin failed to turn up at his usual polling station in the exclusive Western Moscow suburb of Krylatskoye. His press office had transported four bus-loads of the international media to witness the historic event, as they had done for the first round. However, despite the promise that Yeltsin would come and vote at 9 a.m., then 10 a.m., it later transpired that he had already voted at a sanatorium near his country dacha 15 kilometres away, in Barvikha. Yeltsin and his wife had applied for a transfer vote the day before, which enabled the president to vote where he chose. The calculation was that if the president was well enough he would vote at Osennyaya Street, Krylatskoye. In the event, Yeltsin was so unwell that he voted at Barvikha, with only his private camera crew representing the hundreds of inquisitive media. At Osennyaya Street, Chernomyrdin assured those present that Yeltsin was in good form and working. The prime minister said he would be meeting the president that afternoon.[153]

On 3 July, Russia elected a president many observers speculated could already be dead. Nevertheless, on paper Yeltsin performed well in his run-off against Zyuganov. The turn-out, at 68.89 per cent, was only marginally down on the first round (69.81 per cent), an achievement in itself for Yeltsin's campaign team. The final poll showed Yeltsin with 53.83 per cent, against 40.30 per cent for Zyuganov, with a relatively high 4.83 per cent voting against both candidates. In terms of actual votes, this gave Yeltsin 40,203,948 and Zyuganov 30,102,288, with 3,604,462 voting against both candidates. Yeltsin's vote had jumped from 26.6 million to 40.2 million between the two rounds of voting. The vote was a respectable one for Zyuganov, and, although he failed to achieve a breakthrough, he could point to a substantial increase in his vote compared to the first round, where he scored 32 per cent and 24.2 million votes. With 30.1 million votes, Zyuganov had doubled the number of votes the KPRF had received in the Duma elections the previous December. However, with an ageing electorate, the Communist vote had peaked, and Zyuganov had lost the last chance for the KPRF to regain power in its current form.

Across the country, the results were much the same, with Yeltsin picking up votes from the other candidates and Zyuganov's vote being squeezed in many areas. Zyuganov still obtained a majority in cities and territories like Adygeya, Chuvashiya, Voronezh, Kursk, Tambov and his native Orel (where he received his highest vote of 63 per cent). Elsewhere, Yeltsin increased his vote, receiving over 70 per cent of the poll in Moscow and St Petersburg, picking up votes in the 'Red Belt' of the south (almost doubling his vote in 'red' Volgograd) and the far east (such as Primorsk and Irkutsk). Yeltsin obviously benefited greatly from the switch in votes from Lebed to himself.[154]

The Communists complained that an additional 1 million voters had been added to the electoral register since the Duma elections, giving scope for extensive fraud.[155] On the whole, this did not occur on a significant scale, although there was concern in some areas about the use of 'transfer votes' which enabled voters to vote outside their own districts. The day before the poll, Ryabov, head of the Central Electoral Commission, introduced a new rule whereby voters could simply present themselves and ask for a transfer vote, with no control over 'double-voting'. There were signs that thousands of 'extra' voters were bused into some areas of Moscow and the provinces, but the scale of such fraud was not enough to invalidate the poll. Despite earlier fears of widespread vote-rigging, international observers generally declared the elections free and fair, with some criticism of the 'unbalanced' media coverage.[156]

The election result was hailed as a sign that Russia had made progress at underpinning economic and democratic reform. Yeltsin's victory was welcomed by President Clinton, Chancellor Kohl and other Western leaders, with the European Union also joining in the chorus of praise for the conduct of the elections. The EU's Irish presidency called the result 'a historic milestone in the consolidation of democracy in Russia and a considerable achievement for the Russian people'. Warm congratulations flooded in from China, which was relieved that Zyuganov had been defeated. The Communist leader himself conceded defeat and said he accepted the outcome of the elections. The focus of attention now shifted even more to Yeltsin's health, the battle for the succession in the Kremlin, and the formation of the president's new government.[157]

In a nationally televised address on 10 July, a halting Boris Yeltsin called for 'serious corrections' to economic reform to revive industrial production and improve living standards. Renominating Chernomrydin as prime minister, Yeltsin said the elections had highlighted 'his own drawbacks and the government's mistakes'. It was now essential to give industry a 'second wind', to provide people with work and increase the prosperity of every Russian family. Alexander Lebed would be given wide powers to enforce law and order. Yeltsin promised: 'The struggle against corruption in all echelons of power will be the most important direction of my work.'[158] However, the most enduring image was of a sickly president, trying to keep a grip on the reigns of power.

Boris Yeltsin's health continued to cause feverish speculation, which was not dampened by the president's appearance at his inauguration ceremony on 9 August. The inauguration took place against the background of renewed fighting in Chechnya. Looking stiff and heavily made-up, Yeltsin appeared to have difficulty with the presidential oath and failed to make the expected acceptance speech. The ceremony was pared to a bare 17 minutes. A presidential aide, Grigory Saratov, said of Yeltsin: 'He's an elderly man. There is nothing you can do about it,' but added Yeltsin was 'in wonderful intellectual and psychological shape'. Yet according to Marshall Goldman of the Harvard Research Centre, Yeltsin himself said he was prone to depression. Goldman continued: 'He's got a bad liver, he's got circulatory problems, he's got a bad heart.' Goldman believed that alcoholism had also taken its toll.[159]

With the formalities out of the way, Yeltsin could now move on to form his new government. Many of the people appointed were familiar faces. Victor Chernomyrdin was confirmed prime minister by the Duma on the day after the inauguration, on 10 August.[160] Because of his ties to gas monopoly Gazprom, Chernomyrdin was often accused of self-enrichment at Russia's expense. In the run-up to the Duma elections the previous year, former Deputy Prime Minister Boris Fyodorov had charged Chernomyrdin with receiving 1 per cent of Gazprom's stock when it was privatised, making him a dollar billionaire. Former secretary of the Security Council (and Lebed ally) Yury Skokov called the prime minister 'the chief mafioso in the country'.

During his address to the Duma, Chernomyrdin vigorously rebutted the accusations, telling deputies that 'all claims that I am one of the richest men in Russia are absolutely groundless', and denied that he had any properties or savings abroad. He also offered to produce a formal declaration of his income. Chernomyrdin was reconfirmed prime minister with ease.

Originally a compromise candidate for the premiership, when the Russian Congress of Peoples' Deputies refused to approve Yegor Gaidar, Chernomrydin kept on most of Gaidar's ministers and continued his predecessor's strict financial policies. His re-appointment signalled economic stability, and comforted Western financial institutions. Loyal to Yeltsin and an opponent of the former 'war party' in the Kremlin over Chechnya, Chernomyrdin was seen as a competent manager with no obvious replacement on the immediate horizon. His weaknesses were a lack of charisma, the political failure of his party in the Duma elections, and his association with Russia's economic decline.[161]

Yeltsin had already replaced the 'hard-liner' Nikolai Yegorov with Anatoly Chubais as his chief of staff on 15 July. The return of the former privatisation architect was hailed as a victory for the liberal reformers. However, Chubais's appointment reflected his consummate skill as a Kremlin insider, and one who had proved himself extremely loyal and useful to the president during the election campaign.[162] Chubais's skill as an administrator and Kremlin fixer was of more importance to Yeltsin than his political orientation. In his dual role as head of the presidential administration and chief presidential aide, Chubais would play a vital role as Yeltsin's gatekeeper, helping to set the political agenda and planning policy implementation. Chubais had responsibility for all Yeltsin's advisers, Yegorov's staff and the presidential security service (previously Korzhakov's domain). The president's administration employed more than a thousand staff, helping to develop policy and supervising most areas of government policy. With Yeltsin in poor health, Chubais's potential ability to control access to the president would give him enormous power. Yeltsin's chief of staff was also in charge of preparing all documents for the president's signature, and in some cases decrees were signed by Chubais and endorsed with a rubber stamp bearing the president's inscription.[163] Chubais's appointment was also seen as strengthening Chernomyrdin's position in the Kremlin. Although Chubais and Chernomyrdin had had their differences in the past, the two were seen as probable allies in the struggle to limit Lebed's growing influence, and to counter a Lebed–Luzhkov axis.[164]

The new government appointed by Yeltsin and announced by Chernomyrdin was broadly similar to its predecessor. The prime minister announced the appointment of the 59-year-old former presidential aide Victor Ilyushin, and 35-year-old Oneximbank president Vladimir Potanin as first deputy prime ministers in the new cabinet. Potanin took charge of the economy, while Ilyushin was responsible for social policy. Ilyushin had worked as a Yeltsin aide since his boss's days as regional party chief in Sverdlovsk (since renamed Yekaterinburg) in the early 1980s. Born into a worker's family in Nizhny Tagil in the Ural mountains, he graduated in electrical engineering in 1974 from the same college where Yeltsin studied. After working in a iron and steel mill, he began a career in the Communist Party in Sverdlovsk, where he met Yeltsin. Since that time, Ilyushin had stuck close to his boss. A former Komsomol (Communist Youth) official, Ilyushin served as Yeltsin's gatekeeper for more than a decade. He became head of Yeltsin's secretariat (and later senior aide) when Yeltsin became chairman of the Russian Supreme Soviet in 1990. Ilyushin worked out Yeltsin's monthly schedule, divided into 15-minute slots. Only Korzhakov had better control of access to the president. Ilyushin arranged the president's trips, always accompanying him, and gave him his official papers in the morning and last thing at night. During the presidential campaign, Ilyushin was one of the three key players, the others being Chernomyrdin and Chubais. Ilyushin's sideways move to a first deputy premiership was a response to Chubais's appointment as Yeltsin's chief of staff. Chubais's new role would eclipse Ilyushin's status within the president's administration. However, by becoming first deputy prime minister, Ilyushin had positioned himself to become a possible future prime minister, if Chernomyrdin was sacked or became president, either temporarily because of Yeltsin's ill-health, or in his own right if he was elected to the post. Either way, Ilyushin had ensured he remained a player in the Kremlin's internal power games.[165]

Another Kremlin insider, Alexander Livshits, was appointed one of seven deputy prime ministers, responsible for finance. Livshits replaced Vladimir Panskov, whom Chernomrydin had criticised the previous month for failing to implement Yeltsin's decrees. Livshits, aged 50 and chief presidential economic aide, had been appointed head of a strengthened finance ministry, and given the task of raising more tax revenue and closing the widening budget deficit. He had been appointed chief economic aide in 1994, and appeared regularly on Russian television to tell workers that their wages were on the way. Livshits had studied mathematics and economics at the Moscow Economics Institute and wrote his thesis on President Reagan's economic policies. A professor and author of a text book on the basics of the market economy, Livshits was regarded as a pro-reform intellectual with no real administrative experience. But as an indication of the Russia First influence on domestic policy, he believed Russia should move away from the tough anti-inflation policies of the early years of reform. He said: 'We have done enough worrying about percentages of inflation, now we have to start worrying about growth.'[166] Vladimir Kadannikov, who had replaced Chubais the previous January as first deputy prime minister responsible for monetary and finance policy, was also sacked. Oleg Lobov was demoted from his post of first deputy prime minister to the more junior rank of deputy prime minister. Interior Minister Anatoly Kulikov, Foreign Minister Yevgeny Primakov and Economics Minister Yevgeny Yasin all remained in post. Overall, Chernomrydin cut the number of federal departments from eighty-nine to sixty-six.[167]

Alexei Bolshakov, aged 56, was appointed as the most senior of the three first deputy prime ministers. An engineer from the western city of Pskov, Bolshakov would deputise for Prime Minister Victor Chernomyrdin. He took responsibility for industry, construction, transport and communications and the use of mineral resources. Said to be an ally of Chubais, Bolshakov was previously responsible for coordinating relations with the other members of the Commonwealth of Independent States. A practitioner of Russia First, Bolshakov went to Iran in 1995 to assure the country that Russia would honour its agreement to build the controversial nuclear reactor opposed by the United States. Bolshakov had acquired a less than complimentary reputation by antagonising some of the CIS members.[168]

The two most significant changes were the appointment of Vladimir Potanin, and Colonel General Igor Rodionov as defence minister (appointed by Yeltsin on 17 July). Vladimir Potanin, aged 35, was the youngest of the three deputy first prime ministers. Chairman of Oneximbank, he built the bank up to be the fourth largest institution in Russia, with assets of $3.4 billion. Potanin was the exception in the new government, which largely consisted of male middle-aged *apparatchiks*, who had made their careers in the Soviet era, but had backed Yeltsin at the right time. After studying international economics at the Moscow

State Institute for International Relations, the training school for future diplomats, he then worked for seven years at the foreign trade ministry. But after the Soviet Union collapsed, Potanin saw the main chance and, exploiting contacts in the old Soviet trade bank, Vneshhtorgbank, he helped found Oneximbank in 1993. Potanin would be responsible for setting macroeconomic policy and Russia's stabilisation programme.

On the face of it, Potanin was a dynamic young banker with proven financial and administrative skills. He was the epitome of the market-orientated Russian businessman, committed to developing Russia's role in the global economy. However, there was another side to Potanin's appointment. He was also one of a group of bankers who had backed Yeltsin financially during the presidential election campaign. Extremely well connected to the Kremlin, Potanin had been instrumental in designing the controversial shares-for-loans privatisation scheme in 1995, under which the government transferred packets of shares in top industrial companies to a handful of Russian banks, in return for loans. Through this means, Oneximbank acquired a 38 per cent stake in Norilsk Nickel, the world's largest nickel producer. It also obtained 51 per cent of Sidanco, which had huge oil reserves in Russia's far east. The week before Potanin's appointment, Yeltsin signed a presidential decree giving tax breaks and other privileges to Norilsk Nickel worth up to $1 billion. The decree had all the signs of being a big presidential pay-off to loyal friends. Potanin's appointment can thus be seen as a reward for a loyal ally, and a clever Kremlin operator. Although Potanin said he would relinquish his position as chairman of Oneximbank, concerns remained that his appointment reflected the development of a uniquely Russian form of incestuous state capitalism. The new Russian businessman tended to put himself, and Russia's commercial interests, above the niceties and regulations of a Western-style market economy. It was capitalism, Russia First style.[169]

The appointment of Colonel Igor Rodionov (aged 59) as defence minister was in response to Lebed's public lobbying and Yeltsin's desire to balance his team between the Chubais–Chernomyrdin faction, and the weaker Lebed–Luzhkov ticket. Rodionov's appointment was essential to keep Lebed on side, and to prove that the president was listening to his national security adviser. The appointment also underlined Yeltsin's commitment to a Russia First strategy, which ensured that Rodionov stayed in post even after Lebed was later sacked. General Rodionov was head of the army general's military academy, where he was respected by senior officers. In the mid-1980s, Rodionov had commanded the 40th Army in Afghanistan. In 1988, General Rodionov became commander of the Trans-Caucasian Military District. He became known by some as the 'Butcher of Tbilisi' after troops under his command killed nineteen peaceful demonstrators in the Georgian capital in April 1989. A Soviet parliamentary commission in 1989 blamed Rodionov and two other generals for instigating the massacre. The general's supporters say he was told to break up the demonstration by the Communist Party, and was only obeying orders. Later that year he was appointed commander of the Voroshilov Military Academy of the General Staff. Lebed and Rodionov met when the two served together in Georgia in the 1980s. During the Duma elections, Rodionov openly backed Lebed's Congress of Russian Communities (KRO), and took part in the founding congress of Lebed's Honour and Motherland movement the previous autumn (which organised Lebed's presidential campaign). Lebed lobbied publicly for Rodionov's appointment, and his aides said the president had appointed the general defence minister at his security adviser's request. Lebed said, on the day Rodionov was appointed: 'The president has acted very wisely and all Russia will gain from this appointment.' Rodionov's appointment was generally welcomed in the Duma, with some reservations from the liberal democrats, who remembered the events in Tbilisi.[170]

With his memories of Afghanistan, General Rodionov believed Russia should avoid foreign conflicts and concentrate on its domestic problems. He said in one interview: 'I do not now see an external threat to Russia. The biggest threat is from within Russia. Russia must be saved from itself because it could break apart like the Soviet Union.' In his first interview as defence minister, he told ITAR-TASS that his first task would be to 'deal with hot spots' where our people are being killed, such as Chechnya, Tajikistan and Bosnia. Then he would turn to military reform, making the armed forces leaner and more combat-ready. Introducing Rodionov to Russia's military top brass at the Barvikha spa on 18 July, Yeltsin told his generals to transform the army into an all-volunteer force by the year 2000, as he had promised by issuing a presidential decree to that effect in May. Rodionov's appointment hardly strengthened the liberal faction in the Kremlin, but it did provide Lebed with a valuable ally in the government. It also reinforced the Russia First tendency in Yeltsin's administration, without taking an anti-Western path.[171]

The new government hand-picked by Boris Yeltsin did not indicate either a change in direction or style. The one sop to the president's opponents was the appointment of the Communist Aman Tuleev as head of the CIS Affairs Ministry. Tuleev had withdrawn from the presidential race in favour of Zyuganov, and there were suggestions his appointment was to ensure he did not defeat the incumbent governor of Kemerovo in the forthcoming election.[172] Yeltsin, although ailing, was still playing his divide and rule tactics against his own appointees in the Kremlin. He sought to strengthen Chernomyrdin with the appointment of Chubais, but nevertheless improved Lebed's hand by bringing in Rodionov. Most of the appointments were rewards for long-serving and loyal apparatchiks. For Yeltsin, loyalty and personal service were always more important than ability. Potanin's appointment signalled a limited infusion of new blood, and a payment of old debts.

Lebed soon found himself under increasing pressure to deliver in a hostile environment. The president, mindful of giving too much power to his security chief, gave him the well-nigh impossible tasks of clearing up crime and corruption, and bringing peace with honour to Chechnya. When it looked as if Lebed was delivering peace in Chechnya at the end of August 1996, agreeing a ceasefire and troop withdrawal with the Chechens (putting the question of Chechnya's status on hold for five years), the support from Yeltsin and Chernomyrdin was tepid at most. All three men realised that the real battle was not over Chechnya, but over the succession. Under the constitution, Chernomyrdin would take over as acting president for three months, if the president was permanently incapacitated. The problem was there was no mechanism for deciding when the president was incapable of ruling. For Chernomyrdin, it was crucial to limit Lebed's popularity and successes, until he could build up a position whereby he could inherit Yeltsin's crown. Lebed was eventually sacked on 17 October 1996 because he represented a threat to the power of the Kremlin's insiders, including Chernomyrdin, Chubais, Interior Minister General Kulikov and President Yeltsin himself. Lebed had in any event already served the Kremlin's purpose by ensuring Yeltsin's victory in the second round of the presidential elections. Increasingly thereafter, Lebed became superfluous to requirements and a mere irritant who had to be neutralised. In the shadows lurked Yury Luzhkov and a bevy of ambitious courtiers.

Meanwhile, the Russia First strategy, dictated by the Duma and presidential elections, continued unabated. Any presidential hopeful could not ignore the political reality represented by the ascendency of Russia First. While the media resumed its criticism of the government, Russia asserted its Russia First policy. During negotiations in Vienna on 10 July on the global export of weapons and sensitive dual-use technology, the Russian Federation refused to bow to Western pressure to disclose information about arms sales. The discussions, to replace the cold war Co-ordinating Committee on Export Controls (Cocom), became bogged down when the Russians refused to compromise. 'We expected the West not to treat Russia as a country which represents a threat,' said one Russian diplomat. Instead, the Russians suggested notifying arms exports after they had been delivered, which was unacceptable to the West. Russia was set to export £4.5 billion's worth of arms in 1996. On the domestic front, Russia First was also apparent in the new commitment to prioritise social protection, rather than low inflation. Although Alexander Livshits promised the government would not abandon its stabilisation programme and would keep inflation to below 2 per cent, he also promised to redistribute spending to ensure that delayed pensions were paid. In short, in Livshits's phrase, 'the rich should help the elderly'.[173] A day later, on 10 July, Yeltsin had pledged to keep the factories open and stimulate production, even at the cost of higher inflation.[174]

Yeltsin had won the presidential election campaign, but with a huge amount of effort. The Russian people had expressed their democratic will, but the conditions of the campaign hardly compared with a 'normal' election in the West. Yeltsin had shown himself the best political operator in Russia, despite his bouts of ill health. He had manipulated and dominated the media, and skilfully outmanoeuvred all his political opponents. A vast amount of money had been spent on getting Boris Yeltsin re-elected. At the end of it all, one group of courtiers had been replaced by another. Democracy in Russia was still at an early stage of development. But what was certain was that those who expected Russia to evolve along Western lines in terms of its democratic and economic system were to be cruelly disappointed. The election of Boris Yeltsin was not a triumph for Western-style democracy with a concomitant market system. It was a victory for Russia First, which had now come to dominate Russia's political agenda. Russia was evolving its own brand of democracy and market economy: a Russian hybrid version. As a result, Russia had not followed Western or Eastern models, but had begun to evolve its own Eurasian identity.

NOTES

1 An eleventh candidate, Aman Tuleev, dropped out days before the poll in favour of Gennady Zyuganov.

2 The KPRF was the first to reach the million target, see Orttung, Robert, 'Voters face a red and white choice', *Transition* (Prague), 31 May 1996, p. 7.

3 Author's meeting with Valentin Kuptsov, Strasbourg, 25 April 1996.

4 OSCE/Office for Democratic Institutions and Human Rights (ODIHR), *Russian Presidential Election 1996: International Observer, Mission Briefing Book (Moscow, 1996)*, see 'Federal Law on the Election of President of the Russian Federation,' pp. 106–22.

5 Freeland, Chrystia, 'Yeltsin raises the stakes for Council of Europe', *Financial Times*, 24 January 1996.

6 'Council of Europe: Green light from the Parliamentary Assembly for Russia's accession: the final decision to be taken by the Committee of Ministers in ten days', *Agence Europe*, No.6654, 27 January 1996, pp. 5–6.

7 Council of Europe, *Actualités Russes*, No. 1161, 2 February 1996, p. 3.

8 *Agence Europe*, No.6652, 25 January 1996, 'Council of Europe: Green light from the Parliamentary Assembly for Russia's accession - The final decision to be taken by the Committee of Ministers in ten days', *Agence Europe*, pp. 5–6.; On Germany's attitude to Russia, Council of Europe, etc. see Boyes, Roger, 'Germany's wooing of uneasy Russia unsettles nerves in Central Europe', *The Times*, 7 February 1996.

9 Freeland, Chrystia, 'Kohl rewards Yeltsin's loyalty', *Financial Times*, 21 February 1996; for Germany's relations with Russia, see Boyes, 'Germany's wooing of uneasy Russia unsettles nerves in Central Europe'.

10 See also Chapter 4, pp. 187, 190 on the IMF loan.

11 Freeland, Chrystia and Corzine, Robert, 'IMF's Dollars 10.2bn loan to Russia boosts Yeltsin', *Financial Times*, 23 February, 1996.

12 Freeland, Chrystia and Thornhill, John, 'Russian Communist rejection of IMF "diktat" may endanger loan', *Financial Times*, 22 May 1996.

13 Thornhill, John, 'Communists boost Kremlin campaign', *Financial Times*, 5 March 1996.

14 Walker, Martin, 'West gives Yeltsin a boost', *Guardian*, 27 February 1996; supported by the author's discussions with senior diplomats in Washington, Brussels and Moscow.

15 Beeston, Richard, 'Yeltsin wins open support from US', *The Times*, 23 March 1996.

16 See Schulz, Martin, MEP, *Report on the Communication from the Commission to the Council and the European Parliament on the Illicit Traffic in Radioactive Substances and Nuclear Materials*, European Parliament, PE.214.162/DEF, 2 February 1996.

17 Hearst, David, 'Chechenia mars Russian summit of world leaders', *Guardian*, 19 April 1996; and Hearst, David, 'War? What war? asks Yeltsin', *Guardian*, 22 April 1996.

18 On this point, see 'Russia: Zyuganov Economics', *Oxford Analytica*, 5 June 1996.

19 McSmith, Andy, 'Major's mask of neutrality slips as Russia's Communist frontrunner delivers rebuff', *Guardian*, 20 April 1996.

20 Copley, Joy, 'Cool reception for Major', *Daily Telegraph*, 20 April 1996.

21 Clark, Bruce and Freeland, Chrystia, 'Yeltsin backs worldwide ban on nuclear testing', *Financial Times*, 20 April 1996.

22 Hearst, David, 'War? What war? asks Yeltsin'.

23 Copley, Joy, 'Cool reception for Major'.

24 Clark, Bruce, 'Yeltsin looks to Asia as G7 keeps him out of the club', *Financial Times*, 23 April 1996.

25 Crawshaw, Steve and Reeves, Phil, 'China feels "comfortable" with win for Yeltsin', *Independent*, 13 June 1996.

26 Bowley, Graham, 'Russia is "welcome to join" Paris Club', *Financial Times*, 23 May 1996; Kaminski, Matthew, 'Russia seeks to call in old debts', *Financial Times*, 24 May 1996; author's meeting with political groups in the Duma, Strasbourg and Moscow, 1996.

27 Kaminski, Matthew, 'CIS leaders try to bolster Yeltsin's poll prospects', *Financial Times*, 18–19 May 1996; author's meeting with the CIS parliamentary delegation, Brussels 1996; see also Chapter 2 on the CIS in general and pp. 58–60 for the institutional development of the CIS.

28 'Russia: Zyuganov Economics', *Oxford Analytica*, 5 June 1996; author's meetings with Yeltsin's chief of staff, Sergei Filatov, June 1996 (where author was given a copy of Yeltsin's election programme, 1996–2000); author's meetings with Valentin Kuptsov (Strasbourg and Moscow, 1996) and Gennady Zyuganov (Moscow, June and July 1996); author's observation of the presidential election campaign in Russia, June–July 1996.

29 European Parliament, *Documents on the Resolution Adopted by the State Duma Declaring Null and Void the 1991 Treaty Revoking the Soviet Union*, Official document, Delegation with relations with Russia, PE 217.412, 1 April 1996, Brussels, p. 27.

30 *Sovetskaya Rossiya*, 19 March 1996; European Parliament, *Documents on the Resolution Adopted by the State Duma Declaring Null and Void the 1991 Treaty Revoking the Soviet Union*, pp. 2–3; Meek, James, 'Duma "resurrects" the Soviet Union', *Guardian*, 16 March 1996; De Waal, Thomas, 'Russian MPs vote in favour of reviving the Soviet Union', *The Times*, 16 March 1996.

31 Meek, 'Duma "resurrects" the Soviet Union'; De Waal, 'Russian MPs vote in favour of reviving the Soviet Union'.

32 Statement by President Yeltsin cited in European Parliament, *Documents on the Resolution Adopted by the State Duma Declaring Null and Void the 1991 Treaty Revoking the Soviet Union*, p. 4.

33 European Parliament, *Documents on the Resolution Adopted by the State Duma Declaring Null and Void the 1991 Treaty Revoking the Soviet Union*, pp.4–5. Zyuganov admitted this would not include the Baltic states, who were vehemently opposed to any form of integration with Russia. Author's meeting, June 1996.

34 *ITAR-TASS*, 16 March 1996.

35 Kaminski, Matthew and Thornhill, John, 'US denounces vote by pro-Soviet Duma', *Financial Times*, 20 March 1996.

36 *ITAR-TASS*, 16 March 1996.

37 *ITAR-TASS*, 16 March 1996.
38 Kaminski, 'CIS leaders try to bolster Yeltsin's poll prospects'; Kaminski and Thornhill, 'US denounces vote by pro-Soviet Duma'.
39 *ITAR-TASS*, 16 March 1996.
40 De Waal, Thomas, 'Yeltsin invokes Soviet era with economic union', *The Times*, 30 March 1996; see also section on the quadrilateral treaty and bi-lateral treaty with Belarus, Chapter 2, pp. 60–2 and p. 83.
41 De Waal, 'Yeltsin invokes Soviet era with economic union'.
42 Kaminski, 'CIS leaders try to bolster Yeltsin's poll prospects'.
43 Yeltsin, Boris, *Russia: Citizen, Family, Society, State. Programme of Action for 1996–2000* (Moscow, 1996), pp. 113–14.
44 European Parliament, *Documents on the Resolution Adopted by the State Duma Declaring Null and Void the 1991 Treaty Revoking the Soviet Union*, p. 27; Kaminski, 'CIS leaders try to bolster Yeltsin's poll prospects'; author's meeting with Valentin Kuptsov, Strasbourg, 1996.
45 Morvant, Penny, 'Yeltsin seeks to buy voters' allegiance', *Analytical Brief*, OMRI, 14 June 1996, Vol. 1, No. 172; 'President Yeltsin out in front', *The Economist*, 15 June 1996, p. 25; Thornhill, John, 'Central Bank attacks Yeltsin "violation" ', *Financial Times*, 11 June 1996.
46 Morvant Penny, 'Yeltsin seeks to buy voters' allegiance'; Hearst, David, 'Yeltsin the winner on Victory Day', *Guardian*, 10 May 1996; Hearst, David, 'Will the wad win it for Boris?', *Guardian*, 9 June 1996.
47 Thornhill, John, 'Yeltsin given the cash to meet poll pledges', *Financial Times*, 6 June 1996.
48 *ITAR-TASS*, 15 April 1996; Meek, James, 'The vodka scourge crippling Russia', *Guardian*, 24 February 1996.
49 Anichkina, Miranda, 'Yeltsin turns up trump card', and 'Yeltsin rekindles old flame', *The European*, 30 May–5 June 1996, (London, 1996).
50 Clark, Bruce and Freeland, Chrystia, 'Yeltsin pledges to end conscription by 2000', *Financial Times*, 17 May 1996. On the state of the Russian army see, Institute for Strategic Studies, *The Military Balance: Russia, 1995–96*, Brassey's (London, 1996), pp. 103–20.
51 Yeltsin, *Russia: Citizen, Family, Society, State. Programme of Action for 1996–2000*, p. 63.
52 Reeves, Phil and Womack, Helen, 'Chechen deal lifts Yeltsin's poll hopes', *Independent*, 25 May 1996; Worcester, Robert, 'Pollsters see Zyuganov falling at second hurdle', *The Times*, 25 May 1996; Hearst, David, 'Grachev gaffe fuels fears of vote rigging', *Guardian*, 6 June 1996. On Dudayev's death, see European Press Agency, 'Cloud over Chechnya: Who killed Dudayev', *Inside Russia and the FSU*, Vol. 4, No.5, May 1996, p. 6.
53 See above, Chapter 4, p. 189, on Yeltsin's crackdown on the media.
54 European Institute for the Media, *Preliminary Report, 'Media and the Russian Presidential Elections'*, 4 July 1996, p. 4.
55 'Campaign: no place for FSB chief', Editorial, *Moscow Times*, 26 March 1996.
56 Freeland, Chrystia, 'Gazprom buys 30% of TV channel', *Financial Times*, 11 June 1996; Scott, Carey, 'The Great Purge', *Sunday Times*, 23 June 1996; author's private source.
57 European Institute for the Media, *Preliminary Report, 'Media and the Russian*

Presidential Elections', pp. 1–8; author's meeting with Zyuganov and his campaign manager, Valentin Kuptsov, June 1996; author's personal observations on the campaign in Moscow and St Petersburg.

58 European Institute for the Media, *Preliminary Report, 'Media and the Russian Presidential Elections'*, pp. 3–8; Tacis Democracy Programme, *Media and Democracy in Russia on the Eve of Presidential Elections*, 24 April 1996, pp. 1–29; Philps, Alan, 'Yeltsin hope of quick win dented by low turn-out', *Daily Telegraph*, 17 June 1996; Thornhill, John, 'No space for impartiality', *Financial Times*, 1 July 1996; author's monitoring of the Russian media, 1996; OSCE/Office for Democratic Institutions and Human Rights (ODIHR), *Russian Presidential Election 1996: International Observer, Mission Briefing Book*, pp. 18–20.

59 OMRI, 'Special Report, Russian presidential election, No.11, 27 June 1996', *OMRI Daily Digest* (Prague, 1996).

60 Thoenes, Sander and Thornhill, John, 'Media place glasnost on ice', *Financial Times*, 14 June 1996; as shown to the author during a meeting with Zyuganov and Kutpsov, Moscow, June 1996; author's observations on Russian television coverage.

61 Author's meetings with Zyuganov, Gorbachev and Bryntsalov, June 1996; Thornhill, John, 'Zyuganov hits at treatment by Russian media', *Financial Times*, 10 April 1996.

62 Scott, Carey, 'Red alert as Yeltsin gets the media's vote', *Sunday Times*, 19 May 1996; Thoenes and Thornhill, 'Media place glasnost on ice'; Thornhill, John, 'No space for impartiality', *Financial Times*, 1 July 1996; author's meetings with the Western and Russian press corps in Moscow, June–July 1996.

63 Hearst, David and Norton-Taylor, Richard, 'Open season puts cat amongst the pigeons', *Guardian*, 7 May 1996; Thoenes, Sander and Thornhill, John, 'KGB's heirs burst out of the shadows', *Financial Times*, 8 May 1996; Eyal, Jonathan, 'Why we still play the spying game', *Observer*, 12 May 1996; Scott, Carey, 'Spy capers in a cold election climate', *Sunday Times*, 12 May 1996; author's meetings with Western diplomats in Moscow, 1996.

64 *Nezavisimaya Gazeta*, 27 April 1996; Clark, Victoria, 'Ex-KGB man plots to cheat voters', *Observer*, 19 May 1996; author's conversations with Western diplomats, 1996.

65 OMRI, 'Special Report, Russian presidential election, No.2, 10 May 1996', *OMRI Daily Digest* (Prague, 1996), p. 4; Clark, Victoria, 'Yeltsin's man still his master's voice', *Observer*, 5 May 1996; Hearst, David, 'Fears grow that nervous Yeltsin may delay ballot', *Guardian*, 6 May 1996; author's discussions with senior diplomats in Moscow, 1996.

66 Reeves, Phil, 'Yeltsin rallies youth vote with rock and roll', *Independent*, 6 June 1996.

67 Yeltsin, *Russia: Citizen, Family, Society, State. Programme of Action for 1996–2000*, p. 3.

68 OMRI, 'Special Report, Russian Presidential Election, No.11, 27 June 1996'.

69 *Moscow Times*, 26 March 1996; OMRI, 'Special Report, Russian Presidential Election, No.2, 10 May 1996', p. 2; Nikitinsky, Leonid, 'Sackings: the big kiss off', *Moscow News*, 27 June–3 July 1996. See above, Chapter 4, pp. 188–9, for

the initial composition of the campaign team.

70 Polikarpov, Dmitry, 'Yeltsin predicts victory in the first round', *Moscow Tribune*, 11 June 1996.

71 Figures from official results announced by the Central Election Commission on 20 June 1996.

72 Election results taken from figures from official results announced by the Central Election Commission on 20 June 1996; EU Election Unit, EU Delegation, Moscow, 20 June 1996; Orttung, Robert, 'Looking towards the second round of the Russian elections: the wooing of Lebed gets underway', *Analytical Brief*, OMRI, Vol.1, No.175, 17 June 1996 (Prague, 1996); see also Freeland, Chrystia, 'And so to Lebed', *Financial Times*, 18 June 1996; Hearst, David and Meek, James, 'Boris Yeltsin's fateful power-play', *Guardian*, 15 June 1996; Hearst, David, 'Voters fly the nationalist flag', *Guardian*, 18 June 1996; Anichkina, Miranda, 'Bad losers spell rout for democracy', *The European*, 13–19 June 1996.

73 Author's meetings with Fyodorov, Bryntsalov and Shakkum, June 1996; see also (on Bryntsalov) Hughes, Candice, 'Poll '96: the comic relief', *Moscow Tribune*, 11 June 1996; (on Fyodorov) De Waal, Thomas, 'Russian millionaire takes his cue from Ross Perot', *The Times*, 6 February 1996; Clark, Victoria, 'Cheating can save Russia's democrats', *Observer*, 9 June 1996.

74 Author's meeting with Mikhail Gorbachev, Moscow, 14 June 1996.

75 On Gorbachev's campaign, see Freeland, Chrystia, 'Voters ready to crucify Gorbachev the martyr', *Financial Times*, 18–19 May 1996; De Waal, Thomas, 'Gorbachev aims to inject ideas into anti-Yeltsin battle', *The Times*, 2 March 1996; Reeves, Phil, 'Lukewarm applause for a man out of time', *Independent*, 7 June 1996; Scott, Carey, 'Gorbachev leaves new Russia cold', *Sunday Times*, 24 March 1996; author's meeting with Mikhail Gorbachev, 14 June 1996.

76 Telen, Lyudmila, 'The field after the battle', *Moscow Times*, 20–26 June 1996; Reuters, 'Helping hand from Yavlinski', *Guardian*, 10 May 1996; Reeves, Phil, 'Yeltsin "is bloodiest autocrat since Stalin"', *Independent*, 7 June 1996; Thornhill, John, 'Yavlinski urges vote against "stupidity" ', *Financial Times*, 7 June 1996; author's meeting with Yavlinsky, March 1995. For a profile of Yavlinsky, see Chinayeva, Elena, 'A Brilliant Loser', in *Transition* (Prague), 1 December 1995, pp. 35–37.

77 Author's conversations with voters at the polling stations, 16 June 1996, Moscow region.

78 Quoted in Thornhill, John, 'Yavlinski could yet play leading role', *Financial Times*, 18 June 1996; Lebed actually made this comment in spring 1996.

79 Orttung, Robert, 'Profile: Alexander Lebed: Yeltsin's most dangerous rival', *Transition* (Prague), 1 December 1995; Anichkina, Miranda, 'Kingmaker in the Kremlin', *The European*, 20–26 June; official biographies of the presidential candidates, supplied by the Russian Mission to the EU, Brussels, 29 May 1996; Scott, 'The Great Purge'.

80 'General gets a slice of power' (editorial) *Moscow News*, 20–26 June 1996.

81 *Izvestiya*, 20 July 1994, cited in Orttung, 'Profile: Alexander Lebed'.

82 Steele, Jonathan, 'Pinochet admirer picked by "shock economists" ', *Observer*, 23 June 1996.

83 Quoted in *Nezavisimaya gazeta*, 5 October 1995, cited in Orttung, 'Profile:

Alexander Lebed'.

84 Cited in Orttung, 'Profile: Alexander Lebed.

85 Agence Presse, 'Lebed accuses foreign "thieves" ', *Financial Times*, 28 June 1996; see also 'The Financial Times interview: Alexander Lebed', *Financial Times*, 25 July 1996.

86 Carey Scott, 'Voters blame vodka as "sick" Yeltsin lies low', *Sunday Times*, 30 June 1996.

87 Cited in Orttung, 'Profile: Alexander Lebed, p. 17.

88 Freeland, Chrystia, 'Public opinion opposes Yeltsin and his reforms', *Financial Times*, 29 September 1995.

89 Parrish, 'Russia: what Lebed's policies could mean for the outside world', *Analytical Brief*, Vol. 1, No. 176, 17 June 1996, OMRI (Prague, 1996).

90 Parrish, 'Russia: what Lebed's policies could mean for the outside world'.

91 Hearst, 'Voters fly the nationalist flag'.

92 This was a position he changed on joining the government; see, for example, 'The Financial Times interview: Alexander Lebed'.

93 'The Financial Times interview: Alexander Lebed'; this was repeated in numerous television interviews after the first round.

94 *Kontinent*, 12–18 October 1995 cited in Orttung, 'Profile: Alexander Lebed', p. 19.

95 Anichkina, 'Kingmaker in the Kremlin'.

96 Anichkina, 'Kingmaker in the Kremlin'.

97 Freeland, 'And so to Lebed'; Anichkina, 'Kingmaker in the Kremlin'.

98 Scott, 'The Great Purge'.

99 Meek, James, 'Crown Prince of order with a made-to-measure image', *Guardian*, 18 June 1996; Freeland, 'And so to Lebed'; Anichkina, 'Kingmaker in the Kremlin'.

100 Official biographies of the presidential candidates, supplied by the Russian Mission to the EU, Brussels, 29 May 1996; these events occurred during a meeting between Zhirinovsky and the European Parliament's delegation for relations with Russia, April 1996.

101 Quoted in Carney, James, 'A Communist to his roots', *Time Magazine*, 27 May 1996, p. 32; see also official biography supplied by Russia's Mission to the EU, 29 May 1996; author's meetings with Zyuganov, March 1995, June and July 1996; BBC, *Guide to the Russian Presidential Elections*, BBC Monitoring Service, June 1996.

102 Zyuganov on *Ekho Moskvy* radio, 24 May 1996.

103 BBC, 'Russia: Yeltsin, Zyuganov top presidential poll; Zyuganov comments on his DAVOS statements', *Summary of World Service Broadcasts*, BBC Monitoring Service, 8 February 1996; BBC, 'Russia; Chubais attacks Zyuganov's statements at World Economic Forum' and 'Russia: Zyuganov rejects Chubais criticism at World Economic Forum', *Summary of World Service Broadcasts*, BBC Monitoring Service, 9 February, 1996.

104 Freeland, Chrystia, 'Zyuganov seeks election boost from the "red and passionate" ', *Financial Times*, 6 June 1996.

105 Freeland, Chrystia, 'Zyuganov seeks election boost from the "red and passionate" '.

106 Hearst, David, 'Zyuganov woos with tales of woe', *Guardian*, 11 April 1996.

107 Freeland, Chrystia, 'Mr Nice Guy, leader of "the nation's losers" ', *Financial Times*, 13 June 1996.

108 Hearst, David, 'Russia: red flags fly for Zyuganov', *Guardian*, 2 May 1996.

109 Freeland, 'Mr Nice Guy, leader of "the nation's losers" '.

110 Thornhill, John, 'Zyuganov hits the tracks to hear the voter's woes', *Financial Times*, 29 April 1996.

111 Hearst, 'Zyuganov woos with tales of woe'.

112 Thornhill, 'Zyuganov hits the tracks to hear the voter's woes'.

113 'Russian elections' (editorial), *Irish Times*, 27 May 1996.

114 Carney, James, 'A Communist to his roots', p. 31.

115 Remnick, David, 'Heir of Stalin sells Russia a terrible dream', *Sunday Times*, 12 May 1996.

116 'Gennadii Zyuganov in his own words', excerpts published in *Transition* (Prague), 31 May 1996, pp. 16–17; Remnick, 'Heir of Stalin sells Russia a terrible dream'.

117 Hearst, 'Zyuganov woos with tales of woe'.

118 Russia: Zyuganov economics', *Oxford Analytica*, 5 June 1996; Thornhill, John, 'Zyuganov leaves voters guessing over true instincts', *Financial Times*, 10 June 1996.

119 On why Zyuganov lost, see Golovenko, Alexander, 'Reasons Zyuganov lost are many', *St Petersburg Times*, 12 July 1996.

120 Hearst and Meek, 'Kingmaker throws in his lot with "corrupt" Yeltsin', *Guardian*, 19 June 1996.

121 Scott, 'The Great Purge'.

122 Hearst and Meek, 'Kingmaker throws in his lot with "corrupt" Yeltsin'; Hearst, David, 'Hard men sacked in Kremlin purge', *Guardian*, 26 June 1996; Scott, 'The Great Purge'; Scott, 'Voters blame vodka as "sick" Yeltsin lies low'; Nikitinsky, 'Sackings: the big kiss off'; author's private information.

123 Hearst, 'Hard men sacked in Kremlin purge'; Freeland, Chrystia and Thornhill, John, 'Showdown in the Kremlin dark', *Financial Times*, 21 June 1996; Clark, Victoria, 'Russia's bloodless revolutionary', *Observer*, 23 June 1996; Parish, Scott, 'Yeltsin in surprise move sacks security chiefs', *Analytical Brief*, Vol. 1, No. 188, 20 June 1996, OMRI, (Prague, 1996); OMRI, 'Special Report, Russian presidential election, No.10, 21 June 1996', *OMRI Daily Digest* (Prague, 1996).

124 Scott, 'The Great Purge'.

125 Parish, 'Yeltsin in surprise move sacks security chiefs'; Nikitinsky, 'Sackings: the big kiss off'.

126 OMRI, 'Special Report, Russian Presidential Election, No.11, 27 June 1996'; Hearst, 'Hard men sacked in Kremlin purge'.

127 Thornhill, John, 'St Petersburg sends poll alert to Yeltsin', *Financial Times*, 21 May 1996; Reeves, Phil, 'World's most important poll racked by violence', *Independent*, 13 June 1996.

128 Hearst, 'Hard men sacked in Kremlin purge'.

129 For a profile of Korzhakov, see Hearst, 'Hard men sacked in Kremlin purge'; Freeland and Thornhill, 'Showdown in the Kremlin dark'; Scott, 'The Great Purge'; Nikitinsky, 'Sackings: the big kiss off'; author's meeting with General Alexander Korzhakov, on 3 July 1996, who was voting with General Mikhail

Barsukov and Shamil Tarpischev (at the same Moscow polling station); author's meetings with Moscow politicians, Kremlin staffers, Western and Russian diplomats, 1996.

130 Author's meetings with Mikhail Gorbachev, Svyatoslav Fyodorov and Gennady Zyuganov, June 1996.

131 Meek, James, 'Army elite KGB blue in imperial makeover', *Guardian*, 15 March 1996.

132 Thornhill, John, 'Joyless inauguration of Russia's sickly tsar' and 'Yeltsin ceremony marred by fresh health worries', *Financial Times*, 10–11 August 1996.

133 Author's meeting with Speaker Gennady Seleznyev, Strasbourg, 25 April 1996.

134 Author's meeting with Zyuganov and Kuptsov, 2 July 1996; Thornhill, John, 'Yeltsin's bear has two faces', *Financial Times*, 12 June 1996.

135 Hearst and Meek, 'Boris Yeltsin's fateful power-play'.

136 Additional source on the struggles within the Kremlin: author's information gleaned from Kremlin insiders, members of the Duma and senior Western diplomats based in Moscow, 1995–96.

137 Thornhill, John, 'Yeltsin ponders broad coalition', *Financial Times*, 16 May 1996; 'Yeltsin may shuffle pack to woo voters' (agency report), *Guardian*, 20 May 1996.

138 Hearst, David, 'Yeltsin hints at coalition with Communists', *Guardian*, 28 June 1996.

139 Freeland, Chrystia, 'Zyuganov may seek deal with Yeltsin', *Financial Times*, 20 June 1996; Reeves, Phil, 'Russia's Communists seek coalition deal', *Independent*, 20 June 1996; Hearst, David, 'Zyuganov urges crisis pact', *Guardian*, 25 June 1996.

140 Hearst and Meek, 'Kingmaker throws in his lot with "corrupt" Yeltsin'; Hearst, 'Zyuganov urges crisis pact'.

141 Author's meeting with Nicolai Ryabov, 2 July 1996; author's meeting with Sergei Filatov, Hotel President, June 1996. Ryabov was appointed Russian ambassador to Prague after the presidential election, for services rendered.

142 Thornhill, John, 'Russian voters doubt market view of easy Yeltsin victory', *Financial Times*, 25 June 1996.

143 Hearst, David, 'Election boost for Yeltsin', *Guardian*, 20 June 1996; Ostapchuk, Anna, 'The "democratic alternative": end of story?', *Moscow News*, 27 June–3 July 1996.

144 Thornhill, John, 'Yavlinski party refuses to endorse Yeltsin', *Financial Times*, 24 June 1996.

145 Hearst, 'Yeltsin hints at coalition with Communists'.

146 Parish, Scott, 'How will Lebed impact Russian security policy?', *Analytical Brief* (Prague), Vol. 1, No. 182, 18 June 1996, OMRI; Orttung, Robert, 'Yeltsin's health causes uncertainty on election day', *Analytical Brief* (Prague) Vol. 1, No. 213, 3 July 1996, OMRI.

147 Freeland, 'Zyuganov may seek deal with Yeltsin'.

148 Scott, 'Voters blame vodka as "sick" Yeltsin lies low'; author's private information.

149 Scott, 'Voters blame vodka as "sick" Yeltsin lies low'; author's private information.

150 Author's meeting with Kuptsov and Zyuganov, 2 July 1996.

151 Orttung, 'Yeltsin's health causes uncertainty on election day'.

152 Scott, 'Voters blame vodka as "sick" Yeltsin lies low'; Thornhill, John, 'Frail Yeltsin in TV votes plea', *Financial Times*, 2 July 1996.

153 The author was present at the polling station in Osennyaya Street, Krylatskoye, on 3 July 1996, and met Prime Minister Victor Chernomyrdin there.

154 Election results breakdown provided by the EU delegation in Moscow, 30 July 1996; see also Orttung, Robert, 'Yeltsin wins convincing victory in presidential elections', *Analytical Brief* (Prague), Vol. 1, No. 214, 4 July 1996, OMRI; Rutland, Peter, 'Russia prepares for the second round of the presidential election', *Analytical Brief* (Prague) Vol. 1, No. 202, 28 June 1996, OMRI.

155 OMRI, 'Special Report, Russian Presidential Election, No.10, 21 June 1996'.

156 European Parliament, *Observers' Provisional Statement*, Press Release, Moscow 17 June 1996 and 4 July 1996; OSCE, *Final Statement of the OSCE/ODIHR Observer Mission, Second Round of Voting*, International Observer Mission, Russian Presidential Election, 5 July 1996; author's own observations in Moscow region, 4 July 1996.

157 'Russia: Boris Yeltsin re-elected president – The European Parliament pleased', *Agence Europe*, No.6764, 5 July 1996; 'EU/Russia: declaration by EU presidency on elections', *Agence Europe*, No.6765, 6 July 1996; 'EU/Russia: speaking to members of the Duma, Mr Van Den Broek raises Russia's prospects following the presidential elections and the delay in ratifying the Partnership Agreement', *Agence Europe*, No.6766, 8/9 July 1996; OMRI, 'Special Report, Russian Presidential Election, No.14, 5 July 1996', *OMRI Daily Digest* (Prague, 1996); Boyes, Roger, 'Gleeful Kohl welcomes survival of an old friend in the Kremlin', *The Times*, 5 July 1996.

158 Thornhill, John, 'Yeltsin looks to bring new faces into government', *Financial Times*, 11 July 1996.

159 Babakian, Genine, 'Yeltsin is wild card in inauguration plans', *USA Today*, 9 August 1996; Thornhill, 'Joyless inauguration of Russia's sickly tsar'.

160 Orttung, Robert, 'Duma approves Chernomyrdin as prime minister', *Analytical Brief* (Prague), Vol. 1, No. 273, 12 August 1996, OMRI.

161 Orttung, 'Duma approves Chernomyrdin as prime minister'; on Chernomyrdin, see above, Chapter 4; on career, see especially p. 163.

162 Orttung, Robert, 'Liberals triumphant as Yeltsin appoints Chubais as chief of staff', *Analytical Brief* (Prague), Vol. 1, No. 228, 16 July 1996, OMRI.

163 Author's private information; OMRI, 'Russia', *Daily Digest*, Vol. 2, No. 162, 21 August 1996; Freeland, Chrystia and Lloyd, John, 'Yeltsin can only work for 15 minutes a day', *Financial Times*, 23 September 1996.

164 Orttung, 'Liberals triumphant as Yeltsin appoints Chubais as chief of staff'.

165 Stewart, Gwendolyn, 'Viktor Ilyushin: a sideways move for the consummate apparatchik', *Analytical Brief* (Prague), Vol. 1, No. 284, 15 August 1996, OMRI; Thornhill, John, 'Yeltsin names economic team', *Financial Times*, 16 August 1996.

166 Thornhill, 'Yeltsin names economic team'.

167 Orttung, 'Duma approves Chernomyrdin as prime minister'.

168 Liesman, Steve, 'Yeltsin firmly favours reform in selecting his new cabinet', *Wall Street Journal Europe*, 16–17 August 1996; Thornhill, John, 'Yeltsin names new government', *Financial Times*, 16 August 1996.

169 Liesman, 'Yeltsin firmly favours reform in selecting his new cabinet'; Thornhill, 'Yeltsin names new government'; Thornhill, John, 'Unbuttoned capitalist: man in the news: Vladimir Potanin', *Financial Times*, 17–18 August 1996.

170 Belin, Laura, 'Yeltsin picks Lebed's choice to lead defense ministry', *Analytical Brief* (Prague), Vol. 1, No. 231, 18 July 1996, OMRI.

171 Belin, 'Yeltsin picks Lebed's choice to lead defense ministry'; Freeland, Chrystia and Thornhill, John , 'Yeltsin appoints tough general to defence job', *Financial Times*, 18 July 1996.

172 OMRI, 'Aman Tuleev profile', *Daily Digest* (Prague), Vol. 2, No. 164, 23 August 1996.

173 Thornhill, John, 'Russia to step up reforms of social welfare', *Financial Times*, 10 July 1996.

174 Black, Ian, 'Russia endangers arms pact', *Guardian*, 11 July 1996; Hearst, David, 'Yeltsin's economic programme veers towards the Communists', *Guardian,* 11 July 1996.

CONCLUSION

THE presidential election of July 1996 entrenched Russia First in the polity of the Russian Federation. Russia First has become the dominant political idea in Russia, after the end of the Yeltsin administration's early flirtation with full-blooded Westernisation. Historically, Russia's love affair with the West began under Peter the Great, but attempts at Westernisation have come in fits and starts. The perceived failure of Yegor Gaidar's Western-style economic reforms discredited Westernisation and those who advocated it. 'Shock therapy' caused more pain than gain for the majority of the Russian population. The political reaction and the changing attitudes amongst the electorate created the conditions in which Russia First could flourish. By the Duma elections of December 1995, Russia First had taken root, resulting in the sacking of the last leading reformers from Yeltsin's government.

President Yeltsin's adoption of a Russia First strategy was partly a political gambit to win power in the summer presidential elections of 1996. But it was also the recognition of the appeal of Russia First policies in both the domestic and foreign policy spheres. Yeltsin had previously espoused Russia First policies as far back as 1992, when Russia's foreign interests started to clash with those of the West. Such policies had been advocated by Yeltsin's opponents in the Duma elections of December 1995, and the president freely adopted the communists' and nationalists' programmes to win the presidential election.

Russia First applied to both foreign and domestic policies. In foreign-policy terms, Russia First meant re-asserting Russia's role on the world stage, and defending the country's interests against a sometimes hostile West. This applied, for example, with Russia's promotion of arms exports, which were a way of boosting domestic production (supporting the military-industrial complex) and profits, and rebuilding Russian influence abroad. Inevitably, Russia's interests diverged from those of the West, both in terms of competing for arms exports and in developing new (or re-creating old) spheres of influence. NATO expansion is another example of the apparent incompatibility of the security interests of the West and Russia. Russia's answer is an attempt to slow down NATO enlargement, impose conditions on eastern expansion and formulate a 'special relationship' with the North Atlantic alliance. NATO, for its part, has seen the necessity to assuage Russia's legitimate security concerns. However, Russia First is also partly about re-establishing Russia as a 'great power', and it remains to be seen whether the country will be able to re-create a world role for itself. The political momentum behind Russian foreign-policy assertiveness was given added impetus by Russia First. Hence Russia's tentative moves towards cultivating links with China, the Far East, the Middle East and the 'near abroad' were stimulated by the rejection of Westernisation. Yevgeny Primakov personified the shift in foreign policy away from an exclusively close relationship with the West.

On the domestic front, Russia First was popular since it emphasised retaining control of the Russian economy for the supposed benefit of the population. This applied not only to a renewed emphasis on growth and social provision, rather than controlling inflation and the budget deficit (whatever the official line), but also to ownership and control of Russian enterprises. Western investors found themselves excluded from some of the most lucrative and profitable sectors of the economy, while well-connected Russians made huge personal fortunes. Whether Russia First is effective in terms of economic development is open to debate, but there is no doubt there is an increasing tendency for Russians to pursue their own economic interests, even at the cost of discouraging overseas investment. The influence of the mafia, and the general lack of legal redress, makes the Russian economy a high risk investment for foreigners.

Having won the presidential election, the signals from President Yeltsin were deliberately mixed. There were relatively few new faces in the government, with the return of some old ones. The appointment of the reformer Chubais as chief of staff was counterbalanced by the presence of Alexander Lebed and General Rodionov as defence minister. With Lebed ('Mr Russia First') appointed to the government, there seemed little chance that there would be an early return to the policy of 'Westernisation'. Even when General Lebed was sacked in October 1996, Rodionov stayed on as defence minister, ensuring the continuity of the Russia First policy. Lebed's sacking did not imply a shift away from Russia First. Rather, Alexander Lebed was sacked because he too clearly personified Russia First, and the strong appeal this combination represented to the electorate. Lebed was thus a victim of the success of the Russia First strategy and his own political immaturity. Lasting barely four months as Yeltsin's security chief, Lebed displayed an inability to win allies in the Kremlin. Lebed reacted calmly to his dismissal, saying he had expected it: 'The question was only when. I was the black sheep.'[1] From Boris Yeltsin's point of view, Lebed had already served his purpose by guaranteeing victory in the second round of the presidential elections. Even more problematic, Lebed posed a political threat to the Kremlin's leading insiders, including Chubais, Chernomyrdin, Kulikov and Yeltsin himself. Lebed had made it clear he intended to become Russia's president.[2] Victor Chernomyrdin and Yury Luzhkov both harboured ambitions to inherit Yeltsin's crown, which would be impossible if Lebed retained his opinion poll lead as the most likely presidential successor. Both needed time to build up their position so that they could defeat the former paratroop general. Chernomyrdin lacked charisma and was blamed for the country's poor economic performance, while Luzhkov's power base was restricted to Moscow. Given Lebed's growing popularity in the country (but not the Duma) after the Chechen ceasefire, it was essential from the insiders' point of view to neutralise him as a political force and nullify his high media profile. Yeltsin's excuse for sacking Lebed included allegations that he was not a team player (probably true) and rumoured threats of a coup attempt (almost certainly false). Certainly, there was relief in the Kremlin when Lebed was finally given his marching orders on 17 October.

General Lebed was replaced as secretary of the Security Council by Ivan Rybkin, former speaker of the Duma and Yeltsin loyalist. Rybkin's efforts to establish a centre-left party in the run-up to the 1995 Duma elections had led to his political star waning. Rybkin was seen as a safe (and dull) pair of hands to succeed Lebed. Boris Berezovsky, who ran the Logovaz car and media empire, was appointed deputy of the Security Council as a reward for supporting Yeltsin's camp in the presidential elections.[3] Again, what was noticeable in these appointments was the emphasis placed on loyalty, rather than any attempt to bring new faces into the administration. This had also been displayed with Anatoly Chubais's appointment as head of Yeltsin's administration, after previously being sacked as privatisation chief in January 1996. Chubais was appointed chief of staff because of his loyalty and his abilities as an administrator and Kremlin fixer. His reformist credentials were almost irrelevant.

Anatoly Chubais was undoubtedly strengthened by the departure of Lebed, and the appointment of a centrist figure like Rybkin. However, Chubais had another ace up his sleeve in the person of Tatyana Dyachenko, Yeltsin's daughter. Tatyana Dyachenko had been part of Yeltsin's re-election team, and had supported Chubais over the sacking of Korzhakov, Barsukov and Soskovets on 20 June 1996. The two had developed a close relationship, which further enhanced Chubais's role as chief gatekeeper to the president.[4] Chubais acted as chief adviser, prepared official documents for signing (and was accused of rubber stamping them) and led the president's administrative personnel. Lebed even accused Chubais of preparing a 'regency', which gained some credence during Yeltsin's long absences from work following his heart attack in the summer. The impression remained that Chubais and Prime Minister Chernomyrdin were running the country while Yeltsin became increasingly frail.

Yeltsin, Chernomyrdin and the ruling establishment received a shock from the Duma elections, and only just managed to seize victory from the jaws of defeat in the presidential elections. No politician in Russia can afford to ignore the political forces which have made Russia First ascendent in the country today. Turning to the West, and being seen as ignoring Russia's vital foreign and domestic interests, would be fatal to any aspiring presidential candidate.

But history has undoubtedly moved on since the days of *perestroika* and the Soviet system. The relatively high turn-out in the presidential election (68 per cent) indicates that the Russian people relish their opportunity to vote. The system may not be perfect, and may resemble tsarism more than a modern democracy, but it is a democracy of sorts. Today, the Russian people can elect their tsar. Business and cultural exchanges, together with foreign travel and tourism have opened the country up as never before. There is undoubtedly better understanding between East and West. Russia is anxious to be accepted as a member of the world community, joining the Council of Europe and seeking to join the G7, the World Trade Organisation and the Paris Club of creditor nations. The Russian Federation is keen to become fully integrated into the world economy. How else can Russians prosper?

At the same time, Russia is determined to follow its own path, and pursue its own interests. There will be conflicts with the West, but no serious politician East or West contemplates global war. The level of confrontation between Russia and the West experienced during the Soviet era is dead and buried. Economically and militarily, Russia is no longer a superpower. Russia First also means that the West's attempts to patronise Russia and make it in its own image will fail. Russia is not Europe or America, it is Eurasia. However, as it hankers after its old status as a 'great power', the West can expect further disagreements, as tragically seen over Chechnya and as petulantly expressed in the case of Bosnia. In Chechnya, Russia, following up on Lebed's initiative in August 1996, did agree to a troop withdrawal, ceasefire and a five-year moratorium on settling Chechnya's territorial and constitutional status. It is apparent that the Chechens want nothing less than full independence from the Russian Federation. Presidential elections in Chechnya in January 1997 returned Aslan Maskhadov (a former Soviet colonel and Chechen chief of staff) as the republic's president. Maskhadov had negotiated the Chechen ceasefire and troop withdrawal with the Russians. The settlement over Chechnya remained deeply unpopular amongst Communist and nationalist deputies in the Duma, who believed Russia's territorial integrity has been compromised.[5]

President Yeltsin's health remained a factor complicating Russian domestic and foreign policy, and begged the question of just who was directing Russian policy in Moscow . In the absence of a strong president, the answer appeared to be a core group of Kremlin insiders, led by Chubais and Chernomyrdin. Yeltsin's quintuple heart by-pass operation on 5 November 1996 and speculation on the state of his health intensified the battle for the succession in the Kremlin.[6] In the wings stand figures like Alexander Korzhakov, Yeltsin's erstwhile bodyguard, offering the dubious benefit of his patronage to General Lebed.

Whatever the result of Russia's next presidential election, one thing is certain. Russia First, which played a dominant role in the Duma elections of 1995 and the presidential election of 1996 is here to stay. For the foreseeable future, Russia First is a political fact of life in the Russian Federation. Any presidential candidate will need to adopt a Russia First strategy to win the next election, as Russia continues to evolve its Eurasian identity into the next millennium.

NOTES

1 On Lebed's sacking see Hearst, David and Meek, James, 'Russia plunges into crisis', *Guardian*, 18 October 1996; Freeland, Chrystia, 'Yeltsin sacks "disruptive" Lebed', *Financial Times*, 18 October 1996.

2 See, for example, Thornhill, John, 'Lebed stands ready for Russia's call', *Financial Times*, 16 January 1997.

3 Thornhill, John, 'Russia's Jewish émigrés seek to invest in their homeland', *Financial Times*, February 1 1997.

4 Scott, Carey, 'Yeltsin daughter heads for Kremlin', *Sunday Times*, 22 December 1996; author's private information.

5 The author held the following meetings in late 1996 with both political groups in the Duma and members of the separatist Chechen government: 13 November 1996, European Parliament, Strasbourg, meeting with Chechen Foreign Minister Rouslan Tchimaev and Vice-Premier Noukhaev (Boris Pankin, former Soviet foreign minister under Mikhail Gorbachev, was also present at this meeting); European Parliament's inter-parliamentary delegation for relations with the Russian Federation, Strasbourg, 11–12 December 1996. For media coverage on the situation in Chechnya between August 1996 and January 1997 see Thornhill, John, 'Lebed lifts hopes of a Chechnya ceasefire', *Financial Times*, 13 August 1996; Thornhill, John, 'Chechnya truce agreed to allow civilian evacuation', *Financial Times*, 14 August 1996; Thornhill, John, 'Thousands flee in Grozny ceasefire', *Financial Times*, 15 August 1996; Freeland, Chrystia, 'Truce in Chechnya, war in Kremlin', *Financial Times*, 28 August 1996; Hearst, David, 'Loyal Chechen fumes at Lebed', *Guardian*, 28 August 1996; Freeland, Chrystia, 'Outsider's ignorance pays off for Lebed', *Financial Times*, 31 August–1 September 1996; Reeves, Phil, 'Yeltsin's war of nerves tries his peace emissary', *Independent*, 29 August 1996; Freeland, Chrystia, 'Lebed pushes Chechen agreement', *Financial Times*, 4 September 1996; Freeland, Chrystia, 'Yeltsin lands new blow on Lebed', *Financial Times*, 5 September 1996; Hearst, David, 'Wily Yeltsin turns tables on Lebed', *Guardian*, 4 October 1996; Meek, James, 'Lebed loses Chechenia too', *Guardian*, 19 October 1996; Freeland, Chrystia, 'Chechnya fears over Lebed', *Financial Times*, 19–20 October 1996; Thornhill, John, 'Russians say all troops out of Chechnya', *Financial Times*, 6 January 1997; Hearst, David, 'Guerrilla mastermind wins poll in Chechenia', *Guardian*, 29 January 1997.

6 On Yeltsin's hesitant recovery from heart surgery, see Hearst, David, 'Yeltsin makes shaky start', *Guardian*, 24 December 1996.

INDEX

DATE DUE

GAYLORD			PRINTED IN U.S.A.